GRAPHICS PROGRAMS FOR THE IBM PC®

GRAPHICS PROGRAMS FOR THE IBM PC®

BY ROBERT J. TRAISTER

To Debbie and Rich.

FIRST EDITION
SECOND PRINTING

Printed in the United States of America

Library of Congress Cataloging in Publication Data

Traister, Robert J.
Graphics programs for the IBM PC®.

Includes index.
1. Computer graphics. 2. IBM Personal Computer
Programming. I. Title.
T385.T73 1983 001.55 82-19385
ISBN 0-8306-0156-2
ISBN 0-8306-1556-3 (pbk.)

Contents

Introduction

Today's microcomputer allows even the casual hobbyist to tackle many difficult problems that are impossible (if not highly impractical) for the unaided human. The recreational aspects of microcomputing also exist in abundance, and those who are not careful might even learn something. When the IBM Personal Computer was first introduced, it changed the personal computer market to such an extent that today's trends in sales of all microcomputers would probably have been considered completely fictional a few years ago.

The IBM Personal Computer introduced a 16-bit microprocessor or, more accurately, a processor with 16-bit architecture that still maintains 8-bit compatibility. The market is now moving toward the day when all microcomputers will contain true 16-bit microprocessors and even 32- and 64-bit chips are being considered.

Every make of microcomputer offers some graphics capability. Unfortunately, many lack the necessary features to produce what could be described as professional on-screen graphic images. Some companies that sell several different types of computers may offer one with high-level text mode capabilities and another designed specifically for graphics and very little else. The IBM Personal Computer, however, combines these two modes of operation . . . and does so most efficiently. The IBM Personal Computer rivals even the best text mode machines, as well as those designed for color graphics only. To many persons, the IBM Personal Computer is the best all-around machine presently offered on today's market.

When it comes to graphics, however, many otherwise successful programmers tend to be a bit leery. After all, graphics programming uses different statements and commands than text mode operations. "And besides, graphics operation is just a toy to amuse youngsters." Nothing could be further from the truth. For the most part, graphics programming on the IBM Personal Computer uses most of the same statements and commands as text mode programming. However, a few special commands will allow you to quickly, accurately, and efficiently draw and color a myriad of on-screen objects. You can even animate these objects. It takes only a few hours to get the hang of graphics programming, and believe me, you will be amazed at the simplicity with which highly complex figures can be produced. You will notice the number of lines in your programs shrinking when compared to those for text mode operation. The IBM graphics language is very powerful, so it's not necessary to program every little point on the screen on a point-by-point basis. If you want to draw a circle, you use the circle statement. A line is drawn with the line statement. You can even fill in various objects with a multitude of different colors by simply painting them onto the screen. You guessed it! This is done with the paint statement.

This book is far more than a collection of previously written programs presented on a "here they are; do what you want with them" basis. Each element of graphics programming is thoroughly explained, and short sample programs are used to clarify these explanations. You will then see listings of program lines and also printouts of what should appear on the screen. The programs are then taken apart, often on a line-by-line basis, to explain the purpose of each one. With the information provided here, you can produce a graph of your company's earnings or your yearly consumption of energy, and even a pictorial display of our solar system. You can reproduce highly complex line drawings and write programs that will display random patterns that are determined by the computer.

And you can do all of this, plus much more, by using programs that are a fraction of the size of those required to perform simple operations in text mode. I am certain you will be amazed at the simplicity of programming graphics on the IBM Personal Computer. You will be even more amazed at what can quickly be written and displayed on your color monitor.

Warning: graphics programming can be habit-forming. As habits go, however, this is one that is beneficial and will aid you in future programming efforts (text or graphics) on the IBM Personal Computer.

Special thanks to Frederick Computer Products in Frederick, Maryland, for supplying me with not only an IBM Personal Computer system, but also with a wealth of personal documentation to go along with it. Also thanks to Amdek for supplying me with the color monitor and to Jack Strick & Associates for programs and information.

The IBM Personal Computer

On August 12, 1981, IBM Corporation, the recognized leader in large computers, announced its smallest, lowest-priced computer system, the IBM Personal Computer. While IBM had been studying the personal computer market for some time, the program that produced the IBM Personal Computer had begun only thirteen months prior to the August 12th announcement date.

As far as popularity of this machine is concerned, even IBM was surprised. Sales of the IBM Personal Computer greatly exceeded even the most optimistic expectations of IBM marketing personnel, and this machine is rapidly coming to the forefront in overall microcomputer sales. Why? There are many reasons, with the name of IBM Corporation figuring prominently in the picture. It would be fair to say the IBM's name has stimulated immediate interest among all personal computer owners and potential owners. Of course, this can be a mixed blessing. When most people think of computers, they think of IBM, and vice versa. Therefore, any computer that bears the IBM Corporation emblem is automatically expected to be outstanding. Following long-established traditions, IBM has come through with a product that is deserving of their name.

Probably the most talked-about feature of the IBM Personal Computer is its 16-bit microprocessor. Most other personal computers are still built around the 8-bit microprocessor. The IBM Personal Computer uses the Intel 8088 Microprocessor, which is really an 8-bit microprocessor with 16-bit architecture. This means processing is done on the 16-bit level, but input/output is handled at 8 bits. At this stage in microcomputer development, this type of microprocessor is ideal. The 8-bit input/output bus allows for two-way communication on the 8-bit level, but processing is handled at 16 bits. This gives the IBM Personal Computer the power of a 16-bit machine with compatibility with the more common 8-bit interfaces.

HARDWARE OVERVIEW

The basic IBM Personal Computer is shown in Fig. 1-1 and consists of the system unit, an 83-key adjustable keyboard, and the IBM monochrome display monitor. The following section provides separate discussions of each of the block components of the entire system. This will be useful to readers who have not yet purchased an IBM Personal Computer, as well as to those who have, since there is a good possibility that they have not purchased every option available.

System Unit

The system unit, shown in Fig. 1-2, is the heart of the IBM Personal Computer. It contains all processing circuitry and will internally accommodate up to two 5¼″ disk drives. The

Fig. 1-1. The IBM Personal Computer system, in its basic form, includes the system unit, keyboard, and monitor. (Courtesy IBM Corp.)

Fig. 1-2. The IBM Personal Computer system unit.

interior of the unit contains five system expansion slots, shown in Fig. 1-3, which will allow for the insertion of memory cards and various adapters for the printer, monochrome display monitor, color/graphics monitor, asynchronous communications adapter, and game controls. The system board is mounted at the bottom of the system unit enclosure and contains the microprocessor and all pertinent circuitry. In basic form, 16K of read/write memory (RAM) for user programs is contained on this board in five memory chips. There are three additional rows of memory sockets that will allow for on-board expansion to 64K. The system expansion slots must be used for any additional memory expansion, which is handled by memory boards containing up to 64K each. Using the slots, storage capability may be increased to a maximum of 256K of RAM.

The IBM Personal Computer contains a very powerful read-only memory (ROM). This gives the system versatile on-board capability. Whereas most personal computers may contain less than 6K or ROM, the IBM Personal Computer contains 40K. For this reason, the computer exhibits many of the traits of a minicomputer rather than a microcomputer. Included in the 40K of ROM is an enhanced version of the popular Microsoft BASIC-80 Interpreter.

Fig. 1-3. Five system expansion slots are located inside the system unit.

The system unit also includes a jack for the attachment of a user-speaker, which can produce tones. The keyboard is also plugged directly into the system unit.

For video output, the user has a choice of connecting, with the proper adapters, a high-quality IBM monochrome display, a color or black and white monitor, or, through a customer-supplied RF modulator attachment, a color or black and white TV set. Computer-generated video output may vary from a simple 40 × 25 character alphabetic display, to an 80 character-per-line text presentation, to a high-resolution graphic image. The printer is also connected to the system unit through an adapter.

When turned on, the system unit automatically runs a power-on self-test to verify system readiness. If the validation is successfully completed, the BASIC ROM Interpreter (cassette level) is made ready and identified on the display screen. The user may now enter a program from the keyboard or load it from a cassette recorder. If a failure is found, an identifying number will appear on the screen.

If a disk drive is installed, the system unit automatically loads from the disk in drive A. This is typically the disk operating system (DOS) or an application program. The DOS may in turn invoke the Disk or Advanced levels of BASIC, followed by the manual or automatic execution of one or more BASIC programs.

Highlights of the system unit include:

1. Intel 8088 Microprocessor.
2. 4.77 MHz clock speed.
3. Up to 256K random access memory.
4. 250ns memory access time.
5. 410ns cycle time.
6. Parity checking.
7. 63.5 watt power supply; cooling fan.
8. Approximate dimensions: 16″ depth, 20″ length, 6″ height.
9. Approximate weight: 21 lbs (without diskette drive).
10. Powered by a standard 110-volt, 60-Hz source.

Highlights of the enhanced version of the Microsoft BASIC-80 Interpreter (cassette level) found in the ROM of each system unit include:

1. Select 40 or 80 character display lines.
2. Full screen editor for easy program creation and modification.
3. Up to 16 foreground and 8 backgound colors (with appropriate monitor adapter).
4. Automatic line numbering.

5. 40-character variable names (all characters significant)
6. Multiple statements per program line.
7. 250 characters per program line.
8. Comments on program lines.
9. Up to 17-digit numeric precision.
10. Supports sequential cassette files.
11. Error trapping.
12. Addressable workspace up to 60K.
13. Integer/real/string variables.
14. Single and double precision floating point numbers.

Keyboard

The keyboard, which is shown in Fig. 1-4, is attached to the system unit with a six-foot coiled cable, permitting adaptation to a variety of work environments. The 83-key keyboard, with an adjustable typing angle, offers commonly-used data and work processing functions in a design that combines the familiar typewriter and calculator pad layouts. All non-control keys are repeating. Ten program-supported function keys (a total of 40 possible functions using keyboard shift keys) are standard. Special symbols, such as those used to draw lines, may be accessed with a combination of keys. Other keys, like those used to print the current screen contents, correct a typing error, or *scroll* a long document, are clearly labeled. Access to all 256 characters (ASCII and special) is provided by the use of the ALT key.

Fig. 1-4. The IBM Personal computer keyboard.

The approximate dimensions of the keyboard are: 8″ depth, 20″ length, and 2.5″ height. The approximate weight is six pounds.

IBM Monochrome Display

The IBM monochrome display, shown in Fig. 1-5, is a high-resolution device with an 11½″ diagonal, antiglare, green phosphor screen and brightness and contrast controls. The screen area provides for 25 rows of 80 characters each. Characters are 7 × 9 dots in a 9 × 14 box. Both upper and lower case letters can be displayed. The character attributes provide underlining, blinking, high intensity, reverse image, and nondisplay functions. In addition to the normal alphanumeric characters, a large number of special characters are provided. A set of line graphic characters is supported for simple display drawings.

The IBM monochrome display is supplied with signal and power cables. The signal cable is plugged into the IBM monochrome display and printer adapter, which is inserted into the second system expansion slot on the left as viewed from the front of the system unit. The power cable is plugged into the system unit. The approximate dimensions of the display unit are 14″ depth, 15″ width and 11″ height. The weight is approximately 17 pounds.

Fig. 1-5. The IBM monochrome display.

The monochrome monitor is one of the best on the microcomputer market. Unfortunately, it does not possess high-resolution graphics capabilities. Any serious graphics work will require a color/graphics monitor and a matching adapter card, although the IBM monochrome monitor may be used for limited graphics work. This involves calling up ASCII characters to be printed on the screen within the program. Using this method of programming, bar graphs may be easily drawn, along with squares, rectangles, and other geometric designs. It takes a little more programming, however, when compared to doing graphics on those units equipped with color/graphics adapter cards and appropriate monitors.

IBM Monochrome Display and Printer Adapter

The IBM monochrome display and printer adapter is a plug-in card that provides for the attachment of both the IBM monochrome display and the IBM 80 CPS matrix printer. The adapter provides cable connectors for attachment of the printer and the display at the rear of the system unit. The card, which is shown in Fig. 1-6, should be plugged into the second system expansion slot on the left, as viewed from the front of the system unit. Although, the monochrome display adapter also contains printer adapter circuitry, you can buy a separate printer adapter if you intend to use a monitor other than the IBM monochrome display. The combination monochrome display/printer adapter card costs approximately $300, whereas the discrete printer adapter card is only $150.

Color/Graphics Monitor Adapter

The color/graphics monitor adapter, shown in Fig. 1-7, provides for the attachment of a television frequency display to the IBM Personal Computer. Either a *direct-drive RGB* (red-green-blue) signal or a *composite* video signal can be selected. The display can be a monitor, or, through a customer-supplied radio frequency modulator, a standard TV set. Several companies manufacture modulators that will directly interface with the IBM Personal Computer. IBM does not offer this device. Either a color or black and white monitor or TV can be attached.

Sixteen foreground and eight background colors are supported in text (character) mode. This attachment also provides support for four-color medium resolution graphics (320 dots horizontal, 200 dots vertical), and black and white high-resolution graphics (640 dots horizontal, 200 vertical). 256 characters are available in text mode, 128 in medium- or high-resolution graphics. The adapter provides 16K of built-in memory to store multiple display screen contents and supports a customer supplied light pen. The adapter should be plugged into the second system expansion

Fig. 1-6. The IBM monochrome display and printer adapter board.

Fig. 1-7. The color/graphics monitor adapter board.

slot on the left as viewed from the front of the system unit.

When you used a color/graphics monitor and the IBM Advanced BASIC language (BASICA) you can easily draw circles, rectangles, and lines. With these features, the IBM Personal Computer is a very powerful graphics display generator.

IBM 80 CPS Matrix Printer

The IBM printer, shown in Fig. 1-8, is an 80 character-per-second bidirectional matrix printer, which uses pin-feed, continuous form (4-inch to 10-inch width) multipart paper. Under program control, 40, 66, 80, or 132 character lines can be selected. Both horizontal and vertical tabs are supported. Twelve type styles are available.

Several features of the printer make it especially easy to use. When first turned on, it runs a self test even if it is not connected to the system unit. This is shown in Fig. 1-9. A bell sounds when it is out of paper. Paper is simple to load and adjust. The ribbon cartridge can be changed quickly, and the print head is a low-cost item that can be replaced by the user. The printer responds to a variety of commands that control page spacing, select the desired character style, and skip to a specified row or column.

The printer, which uses a signal from a 12-volt, 60 Hz source, requires a signal cable for connection to either the IBM monochrome display and printer adapter or the IBM printer adapter. A six-foot signal cable described below may be purchased from IBM. The printer comes with a six-foot-power cable and is powered from a separate 115-Vac source. The approximate printer dimensions are 16″ wide, 15″ deep, and 4.5″ high. It weighs approximately 13 pounds.

Printer Adapter

The printer adapter, shown in Fig. 1-10, provides for attachment of the IBM 80 CPS matrix printer. This option is used when the color/graphics monitor adapter is selected instead of the IBM monochrome display and printer adapter.

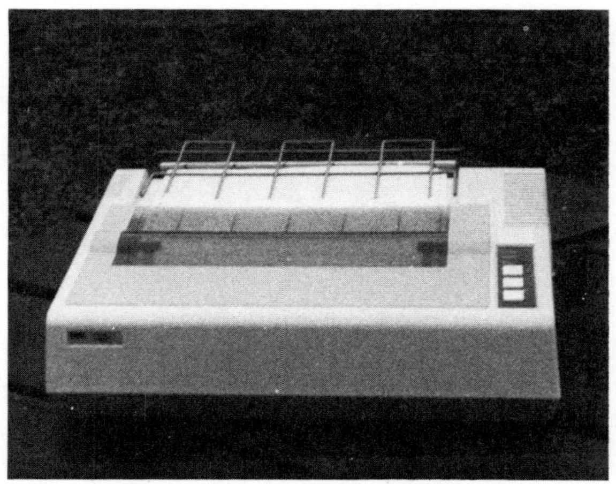

Fig. 1-8. The IBM 80 CPS matrix printer.

```
 !"#$%&'()*+,-./0123456789:;<=>?@ABCDEFGHIJKLMNOPQRSTUVWXYZ[\]^_`abcdefghijklmn
!"#$%&'()*+,-./0123456789:;<=>?@ABCDEFGHIJKLMNOPQRSTUVWXYZ[\]^_`abcdefghijklmno
"#$%&'()*+,-./0123456789:;<=>?@ABCDEFGHIJKLMNOPQRSTUVWXYZ[\]^_`abcdefghijklmnop
#$%&'()*+,-./0123456789:;<=>?@ABCDEFGHIJKLMNOPQRSTUVWXYZ[\]^_`abcdefghijklmnopq
$%&'()*+,-./0123456789:;<=>?@ABCDEFGHIJKLMNOPQRSTUVWXYZ[\]^_`abcdefghijklmnopqr
%&'()*+,-./0123456789:;<=>?@ABCDEFGHIJKLMNOPQRSTUVWXYZ[\]^_`abcdefghijklmnopqrs
&'()*+,-./0123456789:;<=>?@ABCDEFGHIJKLMNOPQRSTUVWXYZ[\]^_`abcdefghijklmnopqrst
'()*+,-./0123456789:;<=>?@ABCDEFGHIJKLMNOPQRSTUVWXYZ[\]^_`abcdefghijklmnopqrstu
()*+,-./0123456789:;<=>?@ABCDEFGHIJKLMNOPQRSTUVWXYZ[\]^_`abcdefghijklmnopqrstuv
)*+,-./0123456789:;<=>?@ABCDEFGHIJKLMNOPQRSTUVWXYZ[\]^_`abcdefghijklmnopqrstuvw
*+,-./0123456789:;<=>?@ABCDEFGHIJKLMNOPQRSTUVWXYZ[\]^_`abcdefghijklmnopqrstuvwx
+,-./0123456789:;<=>?@ABCDEFGHIJKLMNOPQRSTUVWXYZ[\]^_`abcdefghijklmnopqrstuvwxy
,-./0123456789:;<=>?@ABCDEFGHIJKLMNOPQRSTUVWXYZ[\]^_`abcdefghijklmnopqrstuvwxyz
-./0123456789:;<=>?@ABCDEFGHIJKLMNOPQRSTUVWXYZ[\]^_`abcdefghijklmnopqrstuvwxyz{
./0123456789:;<=>?@ABCDEFGHIJKLMNOPQRSTUVWXYZ[\]^_`abcdefghijklmnopqrstuvwxyz{|
/0123456789:;<=>?@ABCDEFGHIJKLMNOPQRSTUVWXYZ[\]^_`abcdefghijklmnopqrstuvwxyz{|}
0123456789:;<=>?@ABCDEFGHIJKLMNOPQRSTUVWXYZ[\]^_`abcdefghijklmnopqrstuvwxyz{|}~
123456789:;<=>?@ABCDEFGHIJKLMNOPQRSTUVWXYZ[\]^_`abcdefghijklmnopqrstuvwxyz{|}
```

Fig. 1-9. The printer self test pattern.

Printer Cable

The printer cable shown in Fig. 1-1 is a signal cable used to connect the IBM 80 CPS matrix printer to either the IBM monochrome display and printer adapter or the printer adapter. A printer stand is also available that supports the IBM 80 CPS matrix printer and holds fanfold paper.

Fig. 1-10. The discrete printer adapter board.

Memory Expansion Kits

The 16K memory expansion kit allows up to 64K of memory to be plugged into the system board. This memory is available in 16K increments and must be used to provide the first 64K of memory.

The 32K memory expansion unit is used to increase the memory beyond the 64K on the system board. One or more of these units may be installed. Each unit provides an additional 32K of memory. The system board must first contain 64K of memory before these units can be used. Each unit requires a system expansion slot.

The 64K memory expansion unit, shown in Fig. 1-12, is used to increase the memory beyond the 64K on the system board. One or more of these units may be installed. Each provides an additional 64K of memory. The system board must first contain 64K of memory before these units can be used. Each unit requires a system expansion slot.

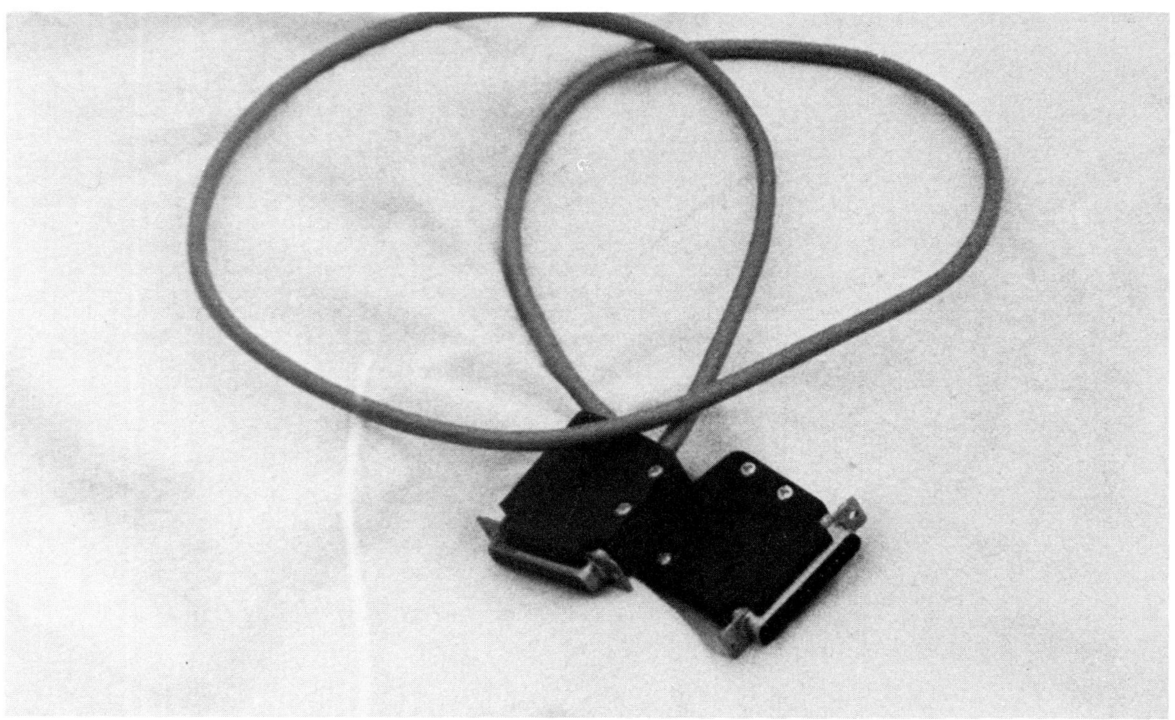

Fig. 1-11. The signal cable is used to connect the printer to the system unit.

5¼″ Disk Drive Adapter and Disk Drive

The 5¼″ disk drive adapter, shown in Fig. 1-13, allows up to two 5¼″ 160K disk drives to be installed inside the system unit. These user-installable drives allow the IBM Personal Computer to read, write, and store data on 5¼″ disks. Storage capacity is approximately 160K per disk. The disk drive has the following characteristics: 48 tracks/inch, 40 tracks/disk, 300 revolutions/minute, 8 ms track-to-track access time, and 20,480 bytes/second transfer rate. IBM also offers an optional disk drive which will store up to 340K. Figure 1-14 shows a 5¼ inch disk of the type used with the IBM Personal Computer.

Most persons will order the IBM Personal Computer with the disk drive adapter and at least one disk drive. My unit contains two drives, which I have found to be most convenient, owing to the larger number of programs that must be stored and run when writing books on programming. The disks are used with the IBM disk operating system (DOS) program.

Asynchronous Communications Adapter

The asynchronous communications adapter, shown in Fig. 1-15, provides the IBM Personal Computer user with a channel to data processing or input/output devices outside of

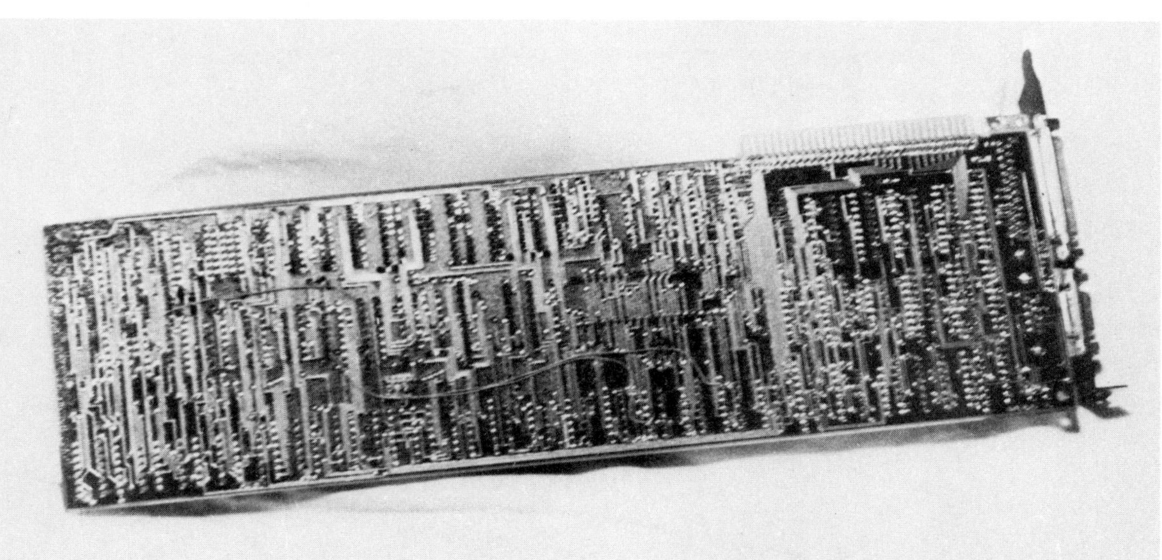

Fig. 1-12. The 64KB memory expansion board.

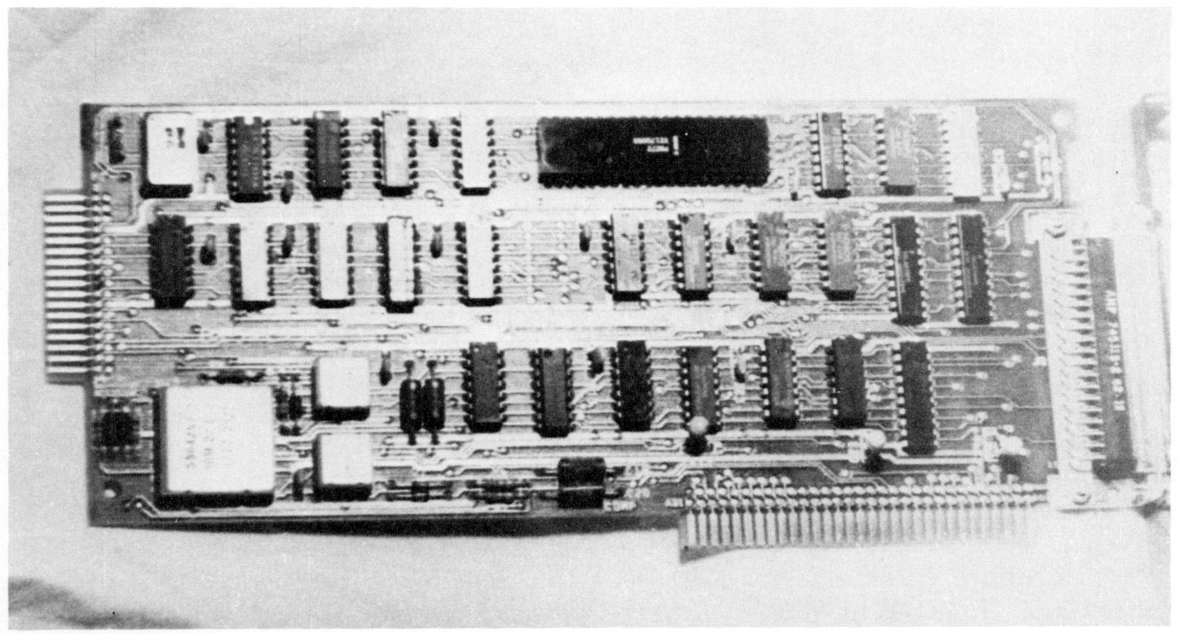

Fig. 1-13. The IBM 5¼″ disk drive adapter.

Fig. 1-14. A 5¼″ disk.

the immediate system. These can be connected by telephone using a plug-in modem, or directly by cable when the device is nearby. This allows the IBM Personal Computer to contact other IBM Personal Computers, large host computers, paper tape readers, laboratory instruments, speech synthesizers, or other machines providing the popular RS-232C asynchronous interface. The adapter is flexible enough to match most of the computers and related products available in the microcomputer marketplace. A user's program allows for the selection of from 50 to 9600 bits per second; 5, 6, 7, or 8-bit character format, as well as the type of parity and the number of stop bits to reflect the attached device. When communication has been established, this same program performs the read/write function and allows for interrupts to permit the program to perform data processing tasks, such as calculating, disk reading or writing, or printing, and to resume communications when a signal appears on the line.

The asynchronous communications adapter has been verified to communicate with an IBM Series/1 with feature #1610, 2901/2092 attachment card using a sample program provided on the IBM Personal Computer DOS

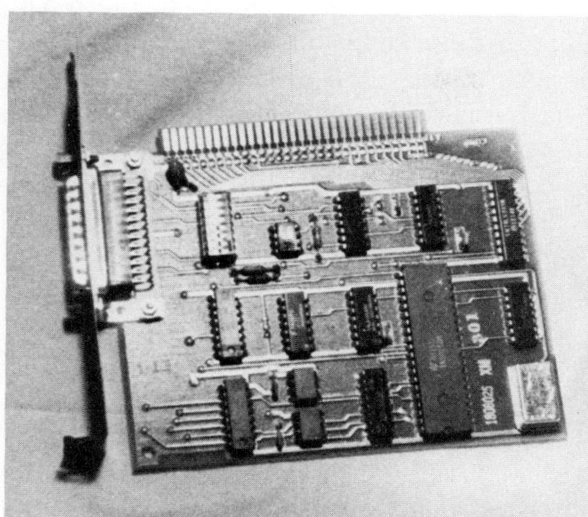

Fig. 1-15. The IBM asynchronous communications adapter board.

disk, and an application program running on Realtime Programming System 5 and Event Driven Executive Version.

The asynchronous communications adapter provides an EIA RS-232C interface. One 25-pin "D" shell, male-type connector is provided to attach various peripheral devices. In addition, a current-loop interface is located in the same connector. A jumper block is provided to select manually either the voltage or the current loop interface.

BASIC language application programs supporting communications will require a disk-based, 32K (minimum) system, IBM DOS, and the BASIC language extensions that include communications support.

Game Control Adapter

The game control adapter supports either two customer-supplied joysticks for video game interaction, allowing the user to move an object on the screen in any direction; or up to four customer-supplied game paddles for simple horizontal or vertical movement.

The IBM Personal Computer is an extremely versatile machine which is available with many different options to form systems that will perform a myriad of functions. This book addresses the high-level graphics capability of the IBM Personal Computer, which in my opinion, is its most exciting mode of operation. To perform true graphics operations, you will need the IBM Personal Computer, along with the color/graphics board, a minimum of 64K memory, a disk drive and adapter, and of course, IBM DOS. Additionally, you will need a color monitor, which can be a color television receiver providing you have a modulator or one of the composite or direct-drive video monitors. These are discussed in detail in a later chapter. You will undoubtedly also want to have the IBM printer and printer adapter, although these are not mandatory. If you have recently purchased an IBM Personal Computer, you're undoubtably still discovering the many exciting features it offers. The information contained in this book is designed to help you take advantage of the high-level graphics functions built into this personal computer.

WARRANTY AND MAINTENANCE

When considering any piece of electronic equipment, especially a complex machine such as the IBM Personal Computer, a major factor is the warranty and maintenance program that has been established by the manufacturer. IBM has long been known for their excellent maintenance programs on everything they sell, and the IBM Personal Computer is certainly no exception. This machine has a warranty period of three months, and service may be obtained by delivering the malfunctioning machine element (system unit, keyboard) to an IBM Product/Service Center, an IBM Customer Service Division (CSD) designated service location, or an authorized IBM Personal Computer dealer. Warranty service is also available by mailing the malfunctioning unit to the IBM National Support Center in Greencastle, Indiana. Proof of purchase from IBM or an authorized IBM Personal Computer dealer is required to obtain warranty service.

Warranty service by IBM includes the repair of the system unit and the replacement of the monochrome display, the matrix printer, and the keyboard. The replacement unit will be a similarly configured unit in good working order. The malfunctioning unit becomes the property of IBM.

Customers desiring warranty service from IBM must call the toll-free number for the National Support Center and provide information, including the results of the problem determination Diagnostic Aid program, machine serial number and location, and whether the malfunctioning unit will be carried to a service location or mailed to the National Support Center.

Units taken to a service location will be picked up by the customer. For units mailed to the National Support Center, the customer must pay shipping charges to the center and insure or assume risk of loss or damage in transit. IBM will pay these charges for return shipment to the customer's location. It is IBM's objective to repair the customer's system unit in one or two days. If the repair is performed at the National Support Center, shipping time should be added to the repair time. If the malfunctioning unit is the monochrome display, the matrix printer, or keyboard, it is IBM's objective to have a replacement unit available at a service location within 24 hours of notification to IBM. If the customer ships the malfunctioning unit to the National Support Center, it is IBM's objective to ship a replacement unit within 24 hours of receipt.

If a customer requests warranty service on a unit IBM would ordinarily elect to replace rather than repair, the customer may choose to have the unit repaired at the National Support Center instead of exchanged at an additional charge. It is IBM's objective to repair the malfunctioning unit in one or two days. Shipping time should be added to the repair time.

Maintenance service is offered by IBM and is available under the terms and conditions of the IBM Personal Computer Service Agreement, Warranty Extension Option, and Annual Option. The Warranty Extension Option is available only if selected prior to or during the warranty period. The agreement commencement date is concurrent with the start of warranty and continues for twelve months. At the end of the twelve months, the service agreement will be renewed automatically under the Annual Option, which is discussed later in this section. Written notice of any applicable price changes are provided prior to renewal. Customers not wishing to renew must withdraw their machines from the agreement.

The Warranty Extension Option provides for IBM-arranged pickup of the malfunctioning unit and replacement with a similarly configured unit in good working order at a location designated by the customer. Pickup and delivery is available if the unit is located within a designated service area, normally within a 3-mile radius of a service location. Service continues to be available by carry-in to a service location or mail-in to the National Support Center.

The Annual Option may be selected during the warranty period, and if accepted by IBM, the commencement date will be the day after the end of warranty. If this agreement is selected after the end of the warranty period, IBM must inspect the machine at the National Support Center. There is a charge for this inspection. If repairs are required to qualify for this agreement, IBM will provide an estimate and upon customer authorization, the work will be performed. The customer will be billed at the time and material rates in effect at that time.

The service provided by the Annual Option is the same as that provided by the Warranty Extension Option. The term of this option is twelve months, and it is automatically renewed annually. Written notice of any applicable price changes will be provided prior to renewal. Customers not wishing to renew must remove their machine from the agreement.

Under both the Annual Option and the Warranty Extension Option, the customer may choose to have a unit repaired rather than replaced at the National Support Center. In that case, it is IBM's objective to repair the malfunctioning unit in one or two days. Shipping time is added to the repair time.

The following customer responsibilities apply during warranty and under the Service Agreements:

1. Identifying the malfunctioning unit through problems determination using the Diagnostic Aid program.

2. Notifying IBM, through the National Support Center's toll-free number, of the malfunctioning unit and providing all required information, including results of the Diagnostic Aid program, machine serial number, and location.

3. Preparing the malfunctioning unit for shipping in the original or equivalent container. IBM will provide shipping containers for purchase by the customer.

4. Removing all non-IBM devices or features prior to delivery to IBM.

5. Accepting, unpacking, and checking the replacement (or repaired) units.

The National Support Center will be accessible via a toll-free number to receive notification of hardware problems and to assist the customer in isolating a problem to a specific unit. The Center will obtain certain customer information, provide advice on equipment disposition related to the customer's agreement, assist in isolation of the malfunctioning unit, and coordinate pickup and delivery when required.

Agreements are not transferrable in the event of the loss or sale of a unit. Time and materials service is only available via mail-in to the National Support Center in Greencastle, Indiana. Labor, parts, service, and all transportation costs are billable to the customer.

In addition to the Diagnostic Aid program, the customer may purchase Advanced Service Aids, which will enable him to trace a problem to an under-the-cover field-replaceable unit (FRU). Personnel using the diagnostic package must have completed the service training requirement for the IBM Personal Computer. If the customer has the technical ability to follow the written service procedures, the customer will be able to perform many of the necessary repairs.

The IBM Personal Computer is a customer setup machine. The allowance for setup is one day. Detailed setup instructions are included with each machine. The customer is responsible for unpacking the system components, attaching them correctly and running the diagnostic program. Customers using DOS disk and any software that requires the use of disk are responsible for producing backup copies of the original disk, when copying is permitted, and according to the terms and conditions of the IBM Program License Agreement.

The IBM Personal Computer is subject to the controls of its environment. Customer management is responsible for the selection, implementation, and adequacy of these controls.

TECHNICAL ASSISTANCE

A newly-formed Personal Computer Assistance Center will provide telephone assistance to customers installing IBM-marketed software for the IBM Personal Computer for a period of three months after the data of installation of a system. If it appears that a problem is related to a code defect in the software, the center will document the problem and submit it to the Information Systems Division (ISD). Additional details on the Personal Computer Assistance Center are available at the time of first-customer shipment.

When I received my IBM Personal Computer, it had not been out for very long, and since I was writing a book on this machine, I found it necessary to obtain a great deal more information about its minute functionings, more than might be required by the average user. I found the IBM technical assistance team to be extremely helpful and ready to give input whenever a question arose. Many of the IBM technicians have purchased their own IBM Personal Computers for home use and were more than willing to check out certain ideas I came up with on their machines and on their own time. I got the distinct feeling that IBM personnel were quite excited about the machine and from much more than a sales point of view. One of IBM's strong points lies in backing up what they sell with documentation, assistance, and immediate service. It can be safely said that even IBM does not realize the full operational potential of this still-new computer as yet, and as more and more persons purchase and use this device, new applications and procedures are being discovered almost daily.

SOFTWARE

The IBM Personal Computer is still a brand-new machine, so software, especially from a hobbyist's standpoint, will not be found in the same profusion as for other types of personal computers. However, there are many ready-to-run programs available from IBM, and more and more companies are offering software that is directly compatible with this machine. The purpose of this book is to help fill the software gap. In the text mode, you will find that many of the programs designed to be input by keyboard to other types of microcomputers will run with few modifications on the IBM Personal Computer. Graphics programs, however, may require a bit of redoing in order to get them to run properly on the IBM machine. The next chapter provides an overview of IBM Personal Computer BASIC, noting some of the differences between it and other dialects of this language. The experienced microcomptuer hobbyist should have no lasting difficulties, even when converting programs for graphics operation, but a thorough reading of IBM's BASIC manual will be required, along with a great deal of trial and error at the onset. Quite frankly, I found graphics programming to be somewhat difficult at first, mainly due to the fact that I was accustomed to other machines and their own dialects of BASIC. After a short while, however, graphics programming in IBM BASIC seemed to make good sense, and indeed, can be done more quickly than in the other language I have worked with.

Due to the limited graphics capability of the IBM monochrome display, I found graphics programming for this monitor to be a real challenge. When switching to the color/graphics monitor adapter and full graphics ability, one could easily become firmly entrenched in IBM graphics alone. The Advanced BASIC language (BASICA) offers many shortcuts to graphics programming, and for this reason, I highly recommend the purchase of the IBM Disk Operating System (DOS) program, which contains Advanced BASIC.

The disk operating system is valuable debugging aid and offers easy editing procedures. For example, you can input a program for another machine into IBM BASIC and then switch to DOS and make near-instantaneous changes throughout the program in order to make it compatible with IBM BASIC. Take, for instance, the set statement, which is common to many dialects of BASIC. IBM has no such statement and substitutes PSET or PRESET in its place. If a program contains the set statement, it will not run on the IBM machine. However, once the program is input via the keyboard, you can switch to DOS and issue a single command to change all set statements to PSET or PRESET. This will be accomplished electronically and within the blink of an eye, possibly saving hours of rewrite time. This is but one of the many features of this very powerful operating system. The debug feature (which is separate from the EDLIN feature just described) allows for debugging at the machine level. DOS also offers batch processing and many other capabilities not common in other microcomputers.

Through its release of the IBM Personal Computer, IBM Corporation has given the microcomputer field a truly revolutionary machine that will do many things not normally associated with micrcomputers. The IBM Personal Computer seems to offer more of everything and is a fast machine due to the 16-bit internal architecture of the Intel 8088 Microprocessor. If you have not already done so, you will quickly discover the ease of operation this machine has to offer, along with its highly sophisticated processing capabilities. The programs presented in a later chapter have been written to take advantage of as many of these features as possible and will certainly serve as a useful education in programming the IBM Personal Computer.

IBM BASIC

IBM Personal Computer BASIC is a powerful and versatile language, which is not too different from other BASIC dialects. There are differences, however, and many programs written in BASIC for other machines cannot be run directly. In these instances, some modifications will be required. This is nothing unusual, as dialect modifications are often required for different machines. Fortunately, the BASIC language is quite easy to master and dialect modifications come with equal ease.

The IBM Personal Computer offers three versions of the BASIC interpreter. These are Cassette, Disk, and Advanced BASIC (BASICA). IBM points out that the three versions are upward compatible, meaning that Disk BASIC does everything Cassette BASIC does, and a little more. Likewise, Advanced BASIC does everything Disk BASIC does and offers some additional features.

I have found Disk BASIC to be highly useful. The disk operating system disk also contains Advanced BASIC, which is mandatory for many graphics applications. All programs in this book are run using IBM DOS, although those readers having Cassette BASIC will have no problem using many of the simpler programs.

The nucleus of BASIC is the Cassette version, which is built into the IBM Personal Computer in 32K of read-only storage. You can use Cassette BASIC on an IBM Personal Computer with any amount of RAM. In Cassette BASIC, the only storage device is a cassette tape recorder.

In all forms of BASIC, you will find an extended character set consisting of 256 different characters. If you have the color/graphics monitor adapter, you can draw points, lines, and even entire pictures. The screen is all points addressable in either medium- or high-resolution.

IBM Disk BASIC is a part of IBM DOS, which comes on a 5¼″ disk. You load Disk BASIC into memory using the disk drive. This requires a disk-based machine with at least 32K of random access storage. Disk BASIC has all of the features of Cassette BASIC, but also offers input/output of disk in addition to cassette. An internal clock keeps track of the date and time, and an asynchronous communications (RS-232C) support, in combination with the IBM communications adapter, allows you to communicate with other IBM computers. Disk BASIC also offers support for two additional printers.

The most extensive form of BASIC available for the IBM Personal Computer is called Advanced BASIC (BASICA). This language does everything that Cassette and Disk BASIC do, plus a lot more. Advanced BASIC requires a disk-based machine with at least 48K of random access storage; and like Disk BASIC, is found on the IBM DOS. Special features found only in Advanced BASIC include event trapping, advanced graphics, and advanced music support. The additional graphics statements include circle, draw, get, paint, and put. These operations make it easier to create complex graphics with the computer and a color/graphics monitor adapter. From a musical standpoint, the play statement allows easy usage of the built-in speaker to create musical tones.

BASIC STATEMENTS

This next chapter section can be thought of as an overview of the IBM Personal Computer BASIC language. You will find that many of the statements are similar to or exactly like the statements in other BASIC dialects. Others will be completely different, however.

ABS. This function returns the absolute value of an expression. The absolute value is always positive or zero. For example, the command ABS (5*(–7)) will return the number 35. This is the absolute value, which is always zero or a positive number.

ASC. This function returns the ASCII code for the first character that follows it. Let's assume that A$ = "RADAR". The command PRINT ASC (A$) will return the number 82, which is the ASCII value of the letter R.

ATN. This is a mathematical function that returns the arctangent of the value which follows it. For example, ATN (3) will return the arctangent of 3, which is 1.249046.

AUTO. Auto is a highly useful command which speeds along programming by allowing you to avoid having to type in a number for each program line. This is a command which is not part of an actual program but is input prior to programming in order to generate the automatic numbering sequence. When the auto command is input, the enter button is pressed, a 10 will automatically be printed. You then type in the program line, and when you hit enter again, a 20 appears in the next line position, and so forth. When doing intensive programming, it is often necessary to refer to the previous line number in order to obtain the correct number for the next line. The auto command does this for you automatically. The auto command may also be incorporated after programming has started. For example, if you had entered lines numbered from 10 through 110 and input AUTO 120,10, the line number generator would automatically display line number 120 and advance in increments of 10 from that point on. Of course, many programmers insert lines in steps of 5, 15, or whatever. The auto command can do this as well. Inputting AUTO 5, 5 will cause the first line number to be a 5 and succeeding lines to be numbered in increments of 5. Without these additional numbers, the default is line number 10 and increments of 10. When the additional numbers are inserted, the one immediately following the command will be the next line number. The one following the comma will set the incremental steps.

BEEP. The beep statement causes the computer to output an 800-hertz tone to the internal speaker. The tone lasts for approximately one-quarter second and is used as an audible prompt.

BLOAD. The BLOAD command causes a memory image file to be loaded into memory. When a BLOAD command is executed, the file is loaded into memory, starting at a specified location. This command is immediately followed by the string expression for the file and then by an offset number that specifies the address at which loading is to start. The BLOAD statement is usually preceded by a DEF SEG statement which defines the current segment of storage.

BSAVE. This command saves portions of the computer's memory on a specified device. If the device name is omitted, the machine defaults to the first drive (cassette or disk). When using a dual-disk system, this statement is quite handy in choosing which drive is to receive the input information.

CALL. The call statement is a method of interfacing machine-language programs with BASIC. It calls a machine language subroutine. This statement is followed by the name of a numeric variable whose value indicates the starting memory address.

CDBL. CDBL is a function that converts the numeric expression following it to a double-precision number.

CHAIN. The chain statement transfers control of the machine to another program and passes along the variables from the current program to the one which is to be in control. This allows the operator to easily insert variables input into one program into a new one and greatly reduces overall run time.

CHR$. This function is the opposite of the ASC function previously discussed. It is used to convert an ASCII code into its character equivalent. For example, CHR$(82) will return the letter R. The CHR$ function is used for many purposes, including the writing of limited graphics statements using the IBM monochrome monitor and adapter board. For example, CHR$(219) causes a solid square to be printed on the screen. This image is not available by pressing a single key.

CINT. The CINT function is used to convert a numeric expression to an integer. For example, CINT(37.92) would result in 38. The numeric expression is converted to an integer by rounding its fractional portion.

CLEAR. The clear command frees all memory used for data without erasing the program that is currently in memory. It sets all numeric values to zero and all string variables to null.

CLOSE. The close statement is used to end all input/output to a device or file. This statement may be followed by designators that determine which files or devices are to be closed, but when used alone, close causes all open devices and files to be closed.

CLS. The CLS statement clears the screen. If the screen is in graphics mode, the entire screen buffer is cleared to the background color. The CLS statement is used within a program to erase all printed information which appears on the screen at this point.

COM. The COM statement is used in conjunction with a communications adapter and enables or disables trapping of communications activity. The statement COM(n) ON enables the communications adapter. The same statement followed by OFF disables it. Here, no trapping takes place and no communications activity is remembered. The COM statement followed by STOP disables the adapter. However, any communications activity that does take place is remembered. The variable that immediately follows COM is the number of the communications adapter, of which there may be a maximum of two.

COMMON. The common statement passes variables to a chained program. This statement is used in nonjunction with the chain statement.

CONT. This command stands for continue and is used to resume the running of a program after a break. This avoids the necessity of rerunning an entire program when it has become necessary to stop it during execution.

COS. The COS function causes the computer to return the trigonometric cosine of a number. For example, COS(3.14) will return a −1, which is the cosine of pi radians.

CSNG. This function is similar to CDBL, but converts a numeric expression to a single precision number.

CSRLIN. CSRLIN is a command that causes the screen to print the vertical coordinate of the screen cursor. This allows the operator to obtain the coordinates of the exact position of a point on the screen. This information may later by used within a program to print a character at the same location.

CVI,CVS,CVD. These functions convert string variable types to numeric variable types. These functions are avaiable only in Disk and Advanced BASIC. Using these functions, the actual bytes of data are not changed, but the way BASIC interprets those bytes is.

DATA. The data statement stores numeric end string constants within a program. These constants are accessed by a read statement within the same program.

DATE$. DATE$ is a variable and a statement and is used to set or retrieve the date. The year must be in the range of 1980 to 2099. As an example, if DATE$ = "8/29/83", the printout will be 08-29-1983.

DEF FN. This statement defines and names a function that will be used in a program. The statement is followed immediately by the name of the function and then by an argument or formula that defines the function.

DEF SEG. This statement defines the current segment of storage and is followed by an address that is a numeric expression in the range of 0 to 65,535.

DELETE. The delete command erases program lines. For example, DELETE 30 would erase program line 30. Using this command, you can erase whole sections of programs. DELETE 30-200 would erase all program lines between and including 30 and 200.

DIM. This statement is short for dimension and specifies the maximum values for array variable subscripts and allocate appropriate storage. This is a command which is common to all dialects of BASIC.

EDIT. The edit command is used to display a particular program line for editing purposes. The cursor is then moved to the faulty part of the line, where new information may be input. EDIT 40 recalls line 40 for editing purposes.

END. The end statement is used within a computer program to stop program execution. It closes all files and returns the machine to the command level.

ERASE. The erase statement is followed by the name of a specific array and erases it from storage.

FILES. The files command causes the names of all files residing on a disk to be displayed on the screen. This command is available only in IBM DOS.

FOR AND NEXT. This statement does not differ from other dialects of BASIC and is used to perform a series of instructions within a loop a number of times. The FOR statement is followed by a variable and then by two numeric expressions, one being the initial value and the other, the final value. For example, the program line FOR X = 1 TO 10 would set the starting value of X at 1 and the final value at 10. A next statement must follow in order to allow the loop to be repeated the set number of times.

GOSUB AND RETURN. These are common statements within any dialect of BASIC. They allow for branching to a subroutine and returning from it. GOSUB 130 causes a branch to line 130 during program execution. At some point past line 130, a return statement is required. This latter statement causes BASIC to branch back to the program line immediately following the one containing the GOSUB statement.

GOTO. GOTO is similar to GOSUB, but the branch is unconditional. Using the previous example, a line which reads GOTO 130 will create a branch to line 130, where execution will continue to the end of the program. There is no return statement.

HEX$. This function returns a string representing the hexadecimal value of a numeric expression input in decimal form. This expression must range in value from −32,768 to 65,535. For example, HEX$(32) will return the number 20, which is the hexadecimal equivalent of 32 decimal.

IF. As is the case in other dialects, the IF statement decides the route of programming flow based upon the results of an expression. This statement is often preceded by an input statement. The IF statement may be followed by a then and an else statement, or by GOTO and else. For example, take the line IF A$ = "YES" THEN 250 ELSE 300. This means that if A$, which has been input earlier, is equal to the expression "YES", then the program flow is routed to line 250. If A$ does not equal "YES", program flow is routed to line 300. The then statement could be replaced in this example by a GOTO. The else statement may or may not be used. If must always be followed by a then or GOTO statement.

INKEY$. This is a function that is common to most BASIC dialects and is used to read a character from the keyboard. For example, the line X$ = INKEY$: IF A$ – "" THEN 40 causes the program to stop at this line and then branch to line 40 when any key is pressed.

INPUT. The input statement is used

within a program and stops execution until information is received from the keyboard. INPUT is followed by a phrase in quotes in many cases. This phrase serves as a screen prompt. For example, INPUT "YES OR NO"B$ asks the operator to input a yes or no answer. This line will most likely be followed by one containing an if-then statement, which would act upon the input from the keyboard. Input may be used without an if-then statement as well, such as INPUT "PRESS ENTER TO CONTINUE",B$. The program stops at this line, but then continues when the enter key is pressed. B$ is used here only as an example and any unused string variable will suffice.

INPUT#. This statement reads data from a file or sequential device and assigns them to program variables. The expression is followed by the number used to identify the file when it was initially opened for input and by a variable that has an item in the file assigned to it.

INPUT$. This is a function that returns a string of a specified number of characters read from the keyboard or from a file.

KEY. The key statement controls the ten *soft* keys, which are located on the left-hand side of the IBM Personal Computer keyboard. It also turns the screen printout of the key designations on and off. KEY ON causes a printout at the bottom of the screen listing keys F1 through F10, along with their string expressions. The latter are abbreviated specifications of what each key does. KEY OFF removes this display. KEY LIST causes a separate printout of key functions to be displayed. KEYn,X$ is used to change key functions. For example, KEY 1, LIST would cause KEY 1 to print the word LIST on the screen. When this latter expression is followed by appropriate ASCII coding, the soft keys take on command functions and will automatically input and run a short command.

KILL. This command deletes a file from disk. If a file is named PGM, the command KILL"PGM.BAS" will erase the file from disk.

LEFT$. This function causes the screen to return (print) the leftmost characters of a string expression. Let's assume that A$ = "MY NAME IS RON". If the next line reads B$ = LEFT$(A$,2):PRINT B$, then the screen display will print out MY. This is the leftmost portion of A$, composed of the first two characters. If we inserted the line B$ = LEFT$(A$,5), then the first five characters would be output to the screen.

LEN. The LEN function returns the number of characters in a string. As an example, A$ = "FRONT ROYAL, VA": PRINT LEN(A$) would cause 15, which is the total number of characters within the string, to be displayed. Notice that the spaces have also been counted, as they are part of the string expression.

LET. The let statement, as in most dialects of BASIC, assigns the value of an expression to a variable. For example, LET A = 10 means that the variable A will be equal to the number 10. However, in IBM BASIC, the let statement is optional. The previous example could be replaced simply by A = 10. Since the expression is optional, there is no real reason to use it, as this will slow programming slightly.

LINE INPUT. The line input statement reads an entire line of as many as 256 characters from the keyboard and places it into a string variable, ignoring all delimiters. This statement may be followed by a prompt and the name of the string variable to which the line will be assigned. In Disk BASIC, line input may be immediately followed by a semicolon to allow the cursor to remain on the same line as the prompt.

LIST. The list command, when used by itself, will display all lines of a program currently in memory. You may also follow the expression with a line number, such as LIST 200. Line 200 will then be displayed on the screen. If you input LIST 100-200, then lines 100 through 200 will be displayed.

LLIST. This command is identical to the previous one, except all lines specified are output to the printer.

LOAD. The load command retrieves a program from a specified memory device and reads it into current memory. This command is followed by a quotation mark and the name of the file. For example, LOAD"PGM loads the file named PGM into current memory.

LOCATE. The locate statement positions the cursor on the screen at the point specified. This statement is followed by the screen position. For example, LOCATE 10,30 positions the cursor at row 10 and column 30. This statement may then be followed by a print statement to allow information to be printed starting at the 10,30 position on the screen. The locate and print statements must be separated by a colon if included in the same program line. When used jointly, the locate and print statements take the place of PRINT @ statements, which are common to other dialects of BASIC. There is no PRINT@ statement in IBM BASIC.

LOG. The log function returns the natural logarithm of a numeric expression. For example, PRINT LOG(56) would cause the screen to print out the natural logarithm of 56. You may also use variables and arithmetic expressions with the log function. PRINT LOG(36/6) would return the natural logarithm of 36 divided by 6, or 6.

LPRINT. LPRINT is identical to the print statement, but it sends the information to the line printer. (See print).

LPRINT USING: LPRINT USING is similar to LPRINT, but causes the printer to format the printing in the manner you specify. (See PRINT USING.)

MERGE. The MERGE command merges the lines from an ASCII program file into the program that is currently in memory. This allows one part of a program to be stored on diskette or cassette while another portion of the program is being worked out in RAM. When this latter portion is completed, the two may be merged.

MID$. The MID$ function returns the requested part of a given string to the display. This function is followed by the name of the string, the start character position, and the number of characters to be printed. As an example, PRINT MID$(A$,4,7) would cause the portion of A$ starting with the fourth character and containing seven characters to be displayed.

MOTOR. The motor statement is used to turn the cassette recorder on and off. MOTOR 1 turns the machine on, while MOTOR 0 turns it off. If the motor statement is used by itself, whenever it's encountered in a program, the state of the motor (on or off) will automatically be reversed.

NAME. The name command is used to

change the name of a disk file. Assume that a program has been stored on disk under the name "RED". The command NAME "RED.BAS" AS "BROWN.BAS" renames the file "BROWN". In each case, the .BAS designation is necessary, as all programs stored on disk from BASIC are automatically given this designation within the filename.

NEW. The new command is often used prior to beginning a program. The command deletes the program that is currently in memory and clears all variables. If this command is not used before beginning a new program, and another program is already in current memory, the lines of the program you're working on will automatically take the place of the lines bearing the same numbers in the older program.

OCT$. This function returns a string to the screen which is equal to the octal value of a decimal numeric expression. For example, PRINT OCT$(24) will result in the screen displaying the number 30, which is the octal equivalent of decimal 24.

ON. The on statement is used in conjunction with a GOSUB and return or GOTO statement to branch to one or more line numbers, depending upon the value of the expression. The on statement may also be used in conjunction with the key statement to branch to another line number when the soft keys are used.

PLAY. The play statement is used in Advanced BASIC only, and when coupled with a string expression, outputs tones to the internal speaker. The play statement is used to program computer music and is followed by string expressions composed of the letters A through G, which specify musical notes. There are many other string expression elements which set the octave, note length, pauses and music style.

PRINT. The print statement is used to display data on the screen. It may be followed by a phrase in quotation marks. Here, it will reprint all characters within the quotes. This statement may also be followed by a numeric or screen variable. For example, take the program line A = 1000:PRINT A. The number 1000 will then be printed on the screen. As another example, the line A$ = "ONE THOUSAND":PRINT A$ will cause the expression ONE THOUSAND to be printed.

PRINT USING. The print using statement is used to display strings or numbers using a specific format.

PSET. PSET, along with PRESET, are statements that are used to draw a point at a specified position on the display screen. This is used in graphics mode only and requires the IBM color/graphics monitor adapter. PRESET is almost identical to PSET, but if no color parameter is specified, the background color (0) is automatically selected. If a color designator is used, the two statements are identical. PSET is followed by the X,Y screen coordinates. These coordinates will be followed by the desired color number, which must be in the range of 0 to 3. These expressions replace the set statements common to other dialects of BASIC. IBM BASIC contains no set statement.

RANDOMIZE. The randomize statement causes the program to stop in order to allow an integer expression to be input via the keyboard. This reseeds the random number generator, allowing numbers that are to be randomized (See RND) to be altered each time. The integer expression must be between −32,768 and +32,767. Each time the program is run, the program will stop and a prompt will be displayed on the screen, telling you to input a random number seed. You may also input a fixed number with the randomize statement. This number will be automatically input to the random number generator each time the program is run, and there will be no pause.

READ. The read statement is common to most dialects of BASIC and reads value from a data statement, assigning it to a variable.

REM. The REM, or remark, statement is a portion of a program that is not executed but is included to explain the functioning of the program. These remarks, which follow REM statements, are not displayed or acted upon during the program run, but are there to indicate a program function and are seen within the line listing.

RENUM. The RENUM command is used to renumber all program lines. When used by itself, it automatically numbers the lines in a sequence of 10. For example:

```
    10  A = 5
    15  B – 10
    18  PRINT A + B
RENUM
    10  A = 5
    20  B = 10
    30  PRINT A + B
```

The original program is numbered 10, 15, 18. When this program is complete, the RENUM command is entered, and the new program listing will be sequentially numbered from 10 to 30. When you write a program, you must allow adequate number spacing for the insertion of new program lines. Sometimes, however, reworking a program causes all number spaces to be filled. When this occurs, you simply enter the RENUM command and then list the newly numbered program lines. You now have renumbering in increments of 10 and thus, more spaces between lines to add new program lines. The RENUM command also changes all line number references following GOTO, GOSUB, then and else statements, so it is not necessary to go back through and make these corrections within the program lines to obtain the desired branching. An executable program will be just as executable after the RENUM command has been input.

The RENUM command may also be followed by numeric expressions that set the value of the first line number, the line in the current program where renumbering is to begin, and the increment to be used in the new program line sequence. This command is extremely valuable for producing easy to understand programs.

RESET. In IBM BASIC, the reset command closes all files contained in disk storage and clears the system buffer. If all files are already contained on disk, the reset command is the same as close.

RIGHT$. The RIGHT$ function returns the rightmost characters of a string expression. This is the reciprocal of the LEFT$ function. (See LEFT$)

RND. The RND function returns a random number between 0 and 1. The same sequence of random numbers is generated each time the program is run unless the random number generator is reseeded. (See randomize)

SAVE. The save command is used to save a program in a file on cassette or disk. The command SAVE"PGM" will cause the program to be filed and listed under the name PGM. If you are using cassette BASIC, the program is automatically filed on cassette tape. When using Disk BASIC, the program is automatically filed on the default disk drive (drive A). When used as shown, PGM will be saved in a compressed binary format rather than in ASCII. This conserves storage space. You may also save the program in ASCII by using SAVE"PGM",A.

SIN. The SIN function calculates the trigonometric sine of a number. For example, PRINT SIN(20) returns the sine of 20 in a single precision number.

SOUND. The sound statement causes a tone to be generated through the internal speaker. The SOUND statement is followed by a numeric expression in the range of 37 to 32,767 that corresponds to the frequency of the tone. This may be followed by another numeric expression which determines the duration of the tone.

SQR. The SQR function returns the square root of a numeric expression. For example, PRINT SQR(9) will return the number 3, the square root of 9.

STOP. The stop statement ends program execution and returns the machine to the command level.

SWAP. The swap statement exchanges the values of two variables or array elements. For example:

```
10  A$ = "TWO":B$ = "FOR"
20  PRINT A$,B$
```

The screen printout from this program will be TWO FOR. Using the SWAP statement brings about a different printout, as is evidenced by:

```
10  A$ = "TWO":B$ = "FOR"
20  SWAP A$,B$
```

The screen printout will now be FOR TWO. The two expressions have been exchanged.

SYSTEM. The system command exits BASIC and returns to DOS.

TAB. The tab function advances the cursor to the column designated. For example, PRINT "HELLO" TAB (30) "THERE" will cause the screen to display HELLO at the left-hand side of the screen and THERE at column 30 on the same line.

TIME$. The TIME$ statement (or variable) sets or retrieves the current time. This is very similar to the DATE$ statement.

WAIT. The wait statement suspends the execution of a program while monitoring the status of a machine input port. The program execution is halted until the specified port develops a prearranged bit pattern.

WHILE. The while statement is used in conjunction with a WEND statement to execute statements within a loop as long as a certain condition is true. If a statement is true, the loop is executed until the WEND statement is encountered. This returns execution to the original while statement, and if the expression is still true, the process is repeated.

WIDTH. The width statement is used to set the width of any line in number of characters. If no width statement is used, the default is automatically 80 characters. This is the high-resolution mode. WIDTH 40 sets the display to output lines with a maximum of 40 characters, which is the medium resolution-mode.

WRITE. The write statement is very similar to the print statement, and both are used to output data onto the screen. However, the write statement inserts commas between the items.

This discussion has certainly not included all commands and statements used in IBM BASIC. It is meant to serve as an overview and illustrates the similarities and differences between it and other dialects of BASIC. If you are accustomed to programming another form of BASIC, I think you will find the transition to the IBM Personal Computer version to be quite easy. As a matter of fact, this form of BASIC is more versatile than some other dialects and will allow you to do many things with greater speed using the specialized commands. Certainly, if you are familiar with another form of BASIC, you can start programming right away and should experience little difficulty. However, the time-saving features of this language should be learned to allow you to program faster and more efficiently.

Chapter 3
IBM Personal Computer Graphics

The IBM Personal Computer has excellent, high-resolution graphics and color/graphics capabilities. For color/graphics, it is necessary to purchase and install the optional color/graphics monitor adapter, which fits into one of the system expansion slots inside the system unit. This is a long option card and should be fitted into one of the two slots that are equipped with a front panel guide. About the only disappointment I experienced with the IBM Personal Computer was the fact that the monochrome monitor supplied by IBM is not capable of displaying high-resolution graphics. This limitation lies within the monitor itself, which is designed to present monochrome displays only and cannot operate in the high-resolution graphics mode.

SELECTING AND USING A GRAPHICS MONITOR

In order to obtain high-resolution graphics capability with the IBM Personal Computer system, you will need to obtain a graphics monitor in addition to the color/graphics card. There are several ways to go in choosing a monitor. Probably the least expensive involves using your present black and white or color television receiver. Naturally, the color receiver is to be preferred, since it will allow you to use the many color functions available with this system. Alternately, you may wish to purchase a direct-drive color monitor such as the Amdek Color 2, which is directly compatible with the IBM machine. A direct-drive color monitor will offer superior performance when compared to that of a color television receiver, but since the latter is usually already on hand, the purchase of a color monitor of the direct-drive variety involves a significant expense.

When using a color television as a color/graphics monitor, it will also be necessary to purchase a video modulator that will connect to the composite video output terminal of the color/graphics board. The signal at this output contains all video information, but this has not been output in a form that can go directly to the antenna terminals of the television receiver. To make the composite signal usable, it is necessary to generate a radio frequency signal that can be received by the television set and is modulated with the video information from the composite video jack. This is the purpose of the RF modulator, which can be purchased for about $60. You will see video modulators advertised for as low as $8.00 or $9.00, but some of these may not offer a stable enough signal to yield good results in the high-resolution color/graphics mode of operation. More on this later.

When using a direct-drive color monitor, the 9-pin "D" shell connector must be accessed. This is provided at the rear of the unit and is a part of the color/graphics board. This connector outputs the colors red, green, and blue found on pins 3, 4, and 5, respectively. Pins 6, 8, and 9 form the output terminals for intensity, horizontal drive, and vertical drive, respectively. It will be necessary to obtain the appropriate cable to access the type of direct-drive monitor used. IBM does not offer its own color monitor, so it will be necessary to purchase one from another source. In making a selection, be sure to ask if the monitor in question is compatible with the IBM Personal Computer. Most manufacturers will be able to supply you with the proper connecting cable.

If you elect to use a color television receiver, there is a special output section located on the circuit board that must be accessed. Actually, there are two composite video outputs. One is on the back of the color/graphics board, which is accessed at the rear of the system unit using a photo jack, and the other is a four-pin Berg strip, which is mounted on the side of the color/graphics board. The latter uses only three of the four available (pins 1, 3, and 4). The composite video information is contained on pin 3, pin 4 is circuit ground, and pin 1 provides a positive 12 Vdc output to power the modulator. Some modulators (most, in fact) do not contain their own internal power supplies and will be dependent upon the 12-volt source on the color/graphics card to provide this power. In these instances, it will be necessary for you to obtain a modulator that is equipped with a matching plug to access the four-pin Berg connector. It will be necessary to remove the cover from the system unit and install the modulator plug assembly at the board. A round knockout, which will allow you to route the cable to the modulator, is provided on the rear panel. There is also an additional six-pin Berg strip on the color/graphics board. This is used for the connection of a light pen and is mentioned here to avoid confusion. The six-pin strip is not used for normal graphics work.

Some companies do offer video modulators that contain their own power supplies and do not depend upon the 12-volt potential at pin 1 of the Berg strip. In these instances, the modulator is simply connected to the composite video terminal at the back of the color/graphics board without having to remove the system unit's cover. Using either type of modulator, the output from this device is sent directly to the antenna terminals of your color television receiver. Most video modulators provide dual outputs or a single output that can be switched between channels 3 and 4. If you select channel 3, the computer's video output may be seen by turning your channel select knob to this channel.

When the color/graphics monitor adapter card has been installed in the system unit, there are two basic modes of operation: alphanumeric and graphics. Each of these modes provides further options in both color and black and white. In the alphanumeric mode, each display character position is defined by two bytes in a regenerative buffer that is part of the display adapter. Both color and black and white display adapters use a two-byte character/attribute format. When a color television is used along with an appropriate modulator, the color/graphics adapter will allow for the display of up to 25 rows consisting of 40 characters each, with a maximum of 256 characters. The IBM color/graphics adapter board features an 8 × 8 character box which outputs 7 × 7 double-dotted characters. It also contains 2,000 bytes of read/write memory. Using a direct-drive color monitor, however, there is the capability of displaying 25 rows of 80 characters each. This is established by a read/write memory totaling 4,000 bytes.

Using the IBM Personal Computer and optional color/graphics monitor adapter card, there are three color/graphics modes of operation. High-resolution contains 200 vertical points and 640 horizontal points and outputs in black and white only. Medium-resolution outputs 200 vertical points, 320 horizontal points, and four discrete colors. The low-resolution mode provides 100 vertical points, 160 horizontal points, and a maximum of sixteen colors, which includes black and white. The low-resolution graphics mode requires an 8,000-byte read/write memory, while medium-resolution and high-resolution graphics modes require 16,000 bytes, all contained on the adapter card. Low-resolution color/graphics are not supported in read-only memory.

PREPARING FOR COLOR/GRAPHICS

Assuming that the color/graphics board has already been installed in the IBM Personal Computer's system unit, you have three choices as to how you may proceed. Before going on to the various monitoring arrangements, be sure that you have set the system board DIP switch 1 to reflect your monitor option. If you're using a high-resolution graphics monitor, then switch 5 should be on and 6 should be off. If you're using a medium-resolution television or monitor (40 × 25), then reverse the previous switch positions. When using both the IBM monochrome display and a separate color/graphics monitor, both switches should be in the off position. Be especially careful when making your switch settings, particularly when the IBM monochrome display is to be used in conjunction with a separate color monitor. If switches 5 and 6 are not in the off position for this mode, you can blow a fuse inside the IBM monochrome display. This is a difficult unit to get into and may require the services of an authorized repair center to prevent the voiding of your warranty.

If you have a direct-drive color monitor, all you need is a mating "D" plug to attach to the connector at the rear of the system unit. If you have a standard video monitor that accepts composite video signals or a modulator with its own power supply, use the phono jack directly above the nine-pin connector. If you are using a conventional modulator that doesn't contain its own power source, it will be necessary to remove the system unit cover to gain access to the color/graphics monitor adapter board and its four-pin Berg connector, as mentioned previously.

When running color/graphics on my IBM Personal Computer, I use my Amdek 2 direct-drive color monitor, which does an excellent job. This monitor is discussed elsewhere in this book. Before receiving this monitor, however, I purchased an inexpensive modulator and used my color television receiver with considerable success. Since many readers may elect to use their existing color television receivers, a description of the modulator installation and hookup to the television receiver is in order.

Modulator Installation

I was able to purchase a modulator that is manufactured by M & R Enterprises in Santa Clara, California. This is called the Sup'R'Mod V. Mine cost about $65 and was directly compatible with the IBM Personal Computer. I suspect the compatibility here is attributed to the fact that the input cable is terminated in a four-pin Berg plug, which is actually a part of an adapter that fits a five-pin DIN connector, for which the input plug was originally designed. In other words, you go from a five-pin male DIN connector to a five-pin female receptacle and then into the four-pin Berg plug that mates with the connector on the color/graphics adapter board. A few inches from the Berg plug, there is a toroid core, around which the four wires are wrapped approximately seven times. This forms an interference trap that prevents many of the electronic functionings of the computer from interfering with television reception, both at your monitor screen and at nearby sets. A check with IBM in Boca Ration, Florida assured me that this particular modulator was indeed compatible with their computer, as are many other types. All RF modulators are pretty much alike, although the inexpensive units often do not provide dependably stable output. I popped the lid on my modulator, which is shown in Fig. 3-1, and discovered it to contain a very neat arrangement. Its performance with various television receivers was excellent. However, you should always use a receiver which has automatic fine tuning. I experienced a distortion problem when using a black and white television that was very inexpensive and did not offer the AFT feature. The fact that I got poor performance here may not be directly attributable to the modulator itself, but rather to the television's lack of ability to handle the computer output.

Those of you with television repair experience might be able to do away with the

```
10 KEY OFF:CLS
20 WIDTH 80:DEF SEG=0:A=PEEK(&H410): POKE &H410, (A AND &HCF) OR &H20
30 WIDTH 40: SCREEN 1: SCREEN 0: LOCATE ,,1,6,7
40 KEY ON
```

Fig. 3-1. The Sup'R'Mod V modulator will interface with the IBM Personal Computer color/graphics board.

modulator completely by simply tapping into the first video amplifier stage in any receiver after bypassing the IF amplifiers and tuner. The IBM Personal Computer produces an output from its color/graphics monitor adapter board of approximately 1.5 volts peak-to-peak. This is more than adequate to drive the first video amplifier stage in most television receivers and more than adequate for most RF modulators. (Mine would automatically cut off if the video output exceeded 1.5 volts. This never happened, so it can be assumed that the output level in the computer is slightly less. I measured 1.2 volts from mine.)

I did not elect to access the internal video amplifier in my monitor because, for research purposes, it was necessary to test different types of television receivers. The labor required to access the video amplifier in each would certainly have not been worth the effort, especially when a video modulator can be obtained so easily. Since most persons will go the video modulator route, modulators make a more appropriate discussion for this book.

My video modulator had a selectable VHF output, preset to channel 3 or 4. Some will allow selection of other VHF channels, while others have outputs in the UHF frequency band. Connection was fairly simple. It was necessary to loosen the two rear enclosure screws on the system unit, slide the cover forward, and then locate the four-pin Berg connector on the adapter board. If you have other boards installed around the graphics board, you will not have much room to make the plug connection. Note: The four-pin Berg connector on the adapter board has the second pin clipped away. Only three pins are used for modulator connection. Pin 1 supplies the positive 12 Vdc, pin 2 is not used, pin 3 is the composite video connector, and pin 4 serves as video and dc ground. Before connecting any modulator, you must establish which leads on the modulator plug are designed to accept the various outputs. Don't go by the pin numbers on the modulator itself. For example, the plug on my modulator labeled pin 1 is for ground connection, whereas pin 1 on the Berg connector on the adapter is positive 12 Vdc. This modulator plug, however, was compatible with the IBM Personal Computer by simply reversing it (the plug will fit either way). By connecting pin 1 on the plug to pin 4 on the adapter board, the ground requirement had been met. This automatically brought the other plug connections in line. Pin 4 on the modulator plug accepted 12 Vdc, while pin 2 was the composite video terminal. If you modify other modulators to fit this board, you must determine what inputs are needed and then make suitable connections.

I had a bit of a problem fitting the toroidal adapter inside the system unit case in such a manner that it did not keep the cover from being fitted back in place. The color/graphics monitor adapter board is a long one and should be fitted in either the third or fourth system expansion slot from the right. The board will fit in the remaining three slots, but slots 3 and 4 contain special card guides on the inside of the front panel to better secure the card mechanically.

With the adapter board in the third slot from the right, I simply ran the short length of cable around the rear of the boards in slots 4 and 5 and allowed the toroid to hang down near the keyboard input plug inside the system unit. This brought the adapter plug, which is designed to mate with the DIN connector, very close to the circular knockout in the system unit rear panel. Removing the knockout allowed me to insert the adapter plug through the rear of the unit, where the modulator may be connected or disconnected as desired.

My modulator contained a 4-inch length of 300-ohm cable fitted with connectors for direct attachment to the VHF terminals of the receiver. The modulator unit then hangs in place, but is fitted with two adhesive foam pads to allow it to be attached to the rear of the receiver in a few seconds. My modulator contained a panel-mounted slide switch that allows selection of drive from the computer or from a separately connected television antenna cable, which is accessed by a terminal strip on the side of the unit.

With everything in place, my color television receiver was tuned to channel 4, making sure the modulator channel select switch was also in this position. I activated the computer while watching the television screen. It became apparent immediately that the modulator was getting power, as the television screen was completely blanked (picture goes completely black or gray; no static lines). After the power-on test was completed by the computer, the flashing cursor appeared and a screen display was seen. It was necessary to adjust the fine tuning a bit, along with the contrast and brightness controls for best reproduction. To this day, I have not experienced any interference on my television monitor, nor received complaints from surrounding television owners.

When using a television receiver for monitoring purposes, you may select either medium-resolution or high-resolution screen displays. By the time I got around to the graphics portion of my research, I had become used to viewing the high-resolution display of the IBM monochrome monitor. This is a truly excellent monitor and tends to spoil one. The results obtained in text mode using a television receiver as the monitor were disappointing by comparison. The low-resolution-mode is easiest to read on the screen, but you effectively have half as much space as you do when using the IBM monochrome display. You can switch to an equivalent high-resolution display by inputting WIDTH 80 at the keyboard or with the SCREEN 2 command. Now, you have a full high-resolution display equivalent to the IBM monochrome monitor . . . but only as far as screen space is concerned. When operating in the text mode, I found the high-resolution display print to be extremely hard to read. In graphics mode, it was excellent, but I would not want to work for any length of time in the text mode while in high-resolution. For this reason, most text mode operations using a separate monitor were done in medium-resolution. If you elect not to purchase the IBM monochrome display and want to do some serious text mode operations using another type of monitor, I would recommend going with a high-resolution direct-drive type for most satisfactory results. Of course, after a period of time, you might become accustomed to reading the extremely narrow, close-fitting characters which are displayed on a standard television screen in high-resolution, but this can be a real strain on your eyes. I know because I tried it with over ten different television receivers, none of which performed anywhere near as well as the IBM monochrome display.

For those readers who elect to use their present television receivers with appropriate modulators, you will be pleased to know that all receivers with the automatic fine tuning features did an excellent job during my tests. As a first test, I loaded DOS into my machine and entered Advanced BASIC to run some sample programs. The DOS disk contains about seven color/graphics programs, which include a race car game, pie chart, an example of art, and several others that produce highly colorful displays. These will also run on a black and white television receiver, but of course, you won't see the alluring colors.

Switching Between the Text Mode and the Color/Graphics Mode

I do have a criticism of the color/graphics mode of operation, but it has nothing to do with the machine. When I received my computer from IBM, I also received their Guide to Operations manual, along with a technical manual, and another entitled IBM BASIC. None of these manuals explained how to go from text mode using IBM monochrome display and its appropriate adapter card to the color/graphics mode using the color/graphics card. I originally thought that possibly, both monitors could be operated simultaneously when the appropriate switches were thrown on the system board. I called the IBM Technical department in Boca Raton, Florida and went through an entire checkpoint procedure with them in hopes of getting my color/graphics going. It was only after several hours that the technician and I discovered the fact that it is necessary to run a program to switch between the two modes of operation. Naturally, the technician was aware that this was necessary, but nowhere in any of the IBM manuals was this step mentioned. I was given the program by telephone and was able to switch back and forth readily. IBM has corrected this oversight in their new manuals, but specifically asked that I include the program in each of my books about their machine for the benefit of those who may not have the newer manuals and have not yet decided to switch to the color/graphics mode.

When using the disk operating system and both the color/graphics and monochrome adapter board, the system unit will automatically default to the IBM monochrome display. To switch to the color/graphics monitor, use the program shown in Fig. 3-2. When this is run, the IBM monochrome display will be deactivated and output is automatically fed to the television modulator.

To go back to the monochrome display

```
10 DEF SEG=0
20 POKE &H410, (PEEK(&H410) AND &HCF) OR &H10
30 SCREEN 1,0,0,0
40 SCREEN 0
50 WIDTH 40
60 KEY OFF
70 LOCATE ,,1,6,7
```

Fig. 3-2. This program switches the computer output to the color/graphics monitor.

```
10 DEF SEG=0
20 POKE &H410, (PEEK(&H410) OR &H30)
30 SCREEN 0
40 WIDTH 80
50 LOCATE ,,1,12,13
```

Fig. 3-3. The program switches the monitor output to the monochrome display.

again, another program is required. This is shown in Fig. 3-3. Both monitors will not work simultaneously. To switch between monitors easily, it will put both programs on the same disk. This is done by getting into DOS and then going to BASIC. Enter NEW and then type in the first program. When finished, type SAVE" (name of program). This will automatically save the program on the disk. Do the same for the next program, giving it a different name, of course. I called my program that switches to the graphics monitor "CGA" for color/graphics adapter. The other program was named "MONO" for monochrome.

Once you have input your programs and committed them to the disk, all that is necessary to switch back and forth is to enter Disk BASIC, type LOAD"(name of program), and then press the enter key. The program you selected will be read from the DOS disk. Then type RUN and press the enter key again. The monitor which is controlled by the program you have selected will automatically be activated. To switch to the other monitor, run the other program using the same input technique. You can eliminate the separate load/run functions by typing LOAD "(program name)",R. When you press the enter key, the program will automatically be loaded and run without further keyboard input.

Using these programs, I found the switch from one adapter to the other to be quite convenient and fast. I prefer to use the monochrome display for all entries in text mode and the color/graphics display for graphics work only, although the latter monitor may be used for text mode as well. Unfortunately, there is not enough space available on the system unit top to properly mount both the IBM monochrome display and a television receiver. The top of the monochrome display is slightly slanted, and since this unit has a plastic cover, I do not recommend setting anything on top of it. It will most likely be necessary for you to provide space on your operating table for the television monitor or install a small wall-mounted shelf in close proximity to the system unit and monochrome display. During some of my operations, I used a large screen console color television receiver. The screen was so large that the set could be operated from across the room and still be viewed quite easily from my operating position. The size of the color/graphics screen will determine just how close to the rest of the system it must be placed. Typical color monitors used for computer work will most likely be fairly small with screens of from six to about thirteen inches in width.

TEXT MODE GRAPHICS

Now that the hardware for true graphics operation have been discussed in detail, lets revert to the basic machine which is not equipped with the color/graphics board. Assume that a machine contains only the monochrome display adapter and the display itself. Here, it is not possible to perform complicated graphics operations, but using ASCII characters, you can do some minimal graphics work and produce on-screen charts, limited pictures, and even some moving graphics. Indeed, some of the programs presented in a later chapter will use text mode graphics quite effectively.

In the text mode, the statements used for high-resolution graphics which include circle, color, draw, get, line, paint, preset, pset, put and screen, will not work. This lack tremendously limits the individual who is interested in serious graphics applications, but innovative programming can be used to overcome these limitations. For example, in the graphics mode the line statement, immediately followed by the coordinates of the beginning and the end of the line, can be used to draw a line or even a box. Additions may be made to color the line, to draw a box around these same coordinates, and even to fill in the box with a specific color. In the text mode, however, you can also draw lines and boxes by using some of the many ASCII characters available in this system.

In IBM Personal Computer BASIC, the CHR$ function converts an ASCII code to its equivalent character. The program line PRINT CHR$ (223) will draw a small, filled rectangle on the screen. When you string several of these together, they form a fat line. This would be done using for and next statements. For example, the following program will draw a line in text mode across the middle of the IBM monochrome display screen:

```
10  FOR X = 1 TO 70
20  LOCATE 12,X
30  PRINT CHR$(223)
40  NEXT X
```

This program causes the display to print a total of 70 small rectangles from positions 12,1 to 12,70. Line 12 is at the approximate center of the screen. Since there are 80 possible columns on the screen, the line will extend to within ten places of the right-hand screen edge. A step statement could follow the for statement to cause a dotted line to be printed. STEP 2, for instance, would cause ASCII characters to be printed in every other column, with a space in between. Of course, in true graphics mode, this program could be shortened to:

```
10  LINE(12,1) - (12,70)
```

This would bring about the same results, and because it is only necessary to use a single program line, less memory is used. Using the graphics line statement, we could also color the line or even create a rectangular box over the same coordinates. We could even shorten the last program by simply inputting:

```
10  LINE - (12,70)
```

This assumes that the cursor is already at line 12, column 1. This program causes a line to be drawn from the last point referenced to the point specified (12,70).

Fortunately, we can combine ASCII characters in several ways to produce different graphics results in text mode. For example, in the first program that drew the line, we could change line 30 to:

```
30  PRINT CHR$(223) + CHR$(223)
```

This would effectively double the width of the line, since the two ASCII characters would be printed on top of each other. You could fatten the line even more by adding more plus signs and CHR$ functions.

Vertical lines may also be drawn in text mode by using a similar program that also includes for and next statements. ASCII character 221 is the vertical equivalent of ASCII character 223. The program might look like this:

```
10  FOR X = 1 TO 24
20  LOCATE X,40
30  PRINT CHR$(221)
40  NEXT X
```

This program would cause a vertical series of ASCII characters to appear at the center of the screen, starting at the top and ending near the bottom. This graphics work was done in exactly the same manner as for the horizontal line, except that the variable X defines the vertical portion of the screen at which the ASCII character is to be printed. This is handled in line 20, with the locate statement. Here, the line or horizontal coordinate is the variable, and the vertical coordinate (40) is fixed. We can also increase the width of the vertical line by adding a plus sign and another CHR$ function at line 30. This same program, however, could be replaced with a single program line using the line statement in true graphics mode.

Now, it should be understood how to draw a horizontal and a vertical line using text mode programming. These simple programs may be enough to do some very limited work, but by combining them, we got even better text mode graphics capability. Take the following program, for instance:

```
10  FOR X = 1 TO 70
20  LOCATE 12,X
30  PRINT CHR$(223)
40  NEXT X
50  FOR X = 1 TO 24
60  LOCATE X,40
70  PRINT CHR$(221)
80  NEXT X
```

This will cause a horizontal line to be drawn at the center of the monochrome display screen, followed by a vertical line cutting it evenly. This forms a crude cross. Now, if you want to draw a box in text mode graphics, you would simply adjust the starting and ending coordinates for each line and proceed from there. The following program is a good example:

```
 10  FOR A = 10 TO 20
 20  LOCATE 10,A
 30  PRINT CHR$(223)
 40  LOCATE 20,A
 50  PRINT CHR$(223)
 60  NEXT A
 70  FOR B = 10 TO 20
 80  LOCATE B,10
 90  PRINT CHR$(221)
100  LOCATE B,20
```

```
110  PRINT CHR$(221)
120  NEXT B
```

Each of the two program segments used to draw vertical or horizontal lines on the screen contains an extra locate and print statement when compared with the previous program. I could have used separate for-next statements to draw each of the four lines required to draw a box, but the program shown is far simpler and uses less memory. Lines 10 through 60 cause two horizontal lines to be drawn. The first one is located at vertical position 10. The next is at vertical position 20. The positions of the horizontal lines are determined by a vertical scale numbered from 1 to 25, which can be thought of as extending down the left side of the screen. The position of the vertical lines are determined by a horizontal scale numbered from 1 to 80 (width 80), which may be thought of as lying across the top portion of the screen. This is shown in Fig. 3-4. I think this will help to clear up coordinate determination, since it's sometimes hard to remember that the vertical scale controls horizontal positioning, and vice versa.

The first line is determined by program lines 20 and 30. The cursor is located at horizontal position 10, and the first ASCII character is printed at coordinates 10,10. Line 40 determines the position for the start of the second horizontal line, where the first ASCII character will be presented at coordinates 20,10. With each repetition of the loop, two more ASCII characters are printed across the

Fig. 3-4. In high-resolution text mode, the monitor screen consists of a format of 25 lines high by 80 columns wide.

screen, one at each position, so that you end up with two parallel lines running horizontally. When the loop is completed (x goes from 10 to 20) the program advances to line 70, where the vertical lines are drawn. These are handled in the same manner as the horizontal lines, but using different positions and ASCII characters. The start of the first vertical line will be at 10,10, because 10 is the initial value assigned to the variable B. This is the same position as the beginning of the first horizontal line. At line 100, the position of the second vertical line is established by the locate statement, which causes the ASCII character to be printed at 10,20. These are the same as the coordinates of the last character in the first horizontal line. As this loop repeats itself, the ends of the two horizontal lines are connected with vertical lines and you end up with a box or a square on the screen.

Naturally, rectangles could also be drawn by simply making the horizontal lines longer than the vertical lines, or vice versa. It would be necessary to change the for-next values and to alter the coordinates of either the vertical or horizontal lines, depending upon which set is to be longer. This particular program prints the box at the left side of the screen, but the box could be easily moved by changing the for-next and locate statements to read:

```
10  FOR A = 60 TO 70
20  LOCATE 60,A
```

and so on for both sets of lines.

By combining the text programs used for drawing single lines and boxes, you can draw a robot-like face on the screen. Unfortunately, in text mode, we are pretty much stuck with straight lines and 90 degree angles, so it's quite difficult to obtain any smooth curves or circles.

Crude circles composed of blocks separated by spaces can be made on the screen by choosing many different coordinates and printing ASCII characters in these locations. These circles are certainly not made from linear curves, but they can be useful in some applications. To expect more than this is asking for too much in text mode graphics programming.

I have found that text mode graphics are quite useful for drawing simple block figures and can produce bar charts which look just as good as the bar charts drawn in graphics mode, if you're not interested in color. Several programs in this book will allow you to input information to make highly accurate horizontal and vertical bar charts using text mode programming. Of course, it's easier to operate in the graphics mode, because fewer program lines are required to achieve a certain figure or graph. This reduces the use of memory and also speeds up total programming time, because less lines are input at the keyboard.

COLOR/GRAPHICS

Excellent high-resolution graphics capabilities are available on the IBM Personal Computer in almost any configuration, provided that you have the color/graphics adapter board and a suitable monitor. I highly recommend the IBM Disk Operating System (DOS) for all modes of operation, however. This operating system will also allow you to enter Advanced BASIC (BASICA), which includes additional graphic statements. These are: circle, put, paint, get, and draw. These statements are useful tools in high-powered graphics programming.

Taking the special graphics statements alphabetically, we will begin with circle. This statement is used to draw a complete circle, an ellipse, or a portion of a circle on the screen. This statement is available in Advanced BASIC only and, of course, is limited to graphics programming and not to text mode. The circle statement is followed by two coordinates, such as CIRCLE (100,60). The coordinates specify the center of the circle and may be given in absolute or relative form. The center coordinates are followed by another value which specifies the radius of the circle. This is enough to draw the circle, but you may also follow this value with a number that specifies the color of the circle. This can range from 0 to 3. Start and end angles are also included. These are angles in radians and can range from $-2 \times \text{pi}$ to $2 \times \text{pi}$. These start and end statements determine where the drawing of the circle will begin and where it will end. If the start or end angle is negative, the circle will be connected to the center point with a line. This can be used to generate pie charts easily. The circle statement will be discussed in a later chapter in more detail, showing how it is actually used in a program.

Next comes the color statement, which has some uses in text mode, where it can vary the intensity of the display, cause characters to blink, or underline them. In graphics mode, however, it is used to set a background color and a foreground of any three colors. These colors may be chosen by inserting the correct number following other graphics statements. An example of this is given in our discussion on the circle statement.

The background color can be thought of as the color of the screen prior to the writing of any information on it. You have a choice of fifteen different background colors or black. The color is designated by a numeric expression from 0 through 15 that follows the color statement. Figure 3-5 lists the background colors and their corresponding number designations. The foreground color is called the palette. At any one time, you can choose any or all of three different colors for the palette. The color selection will depend upon the background color used. If the background number is even, you may select the palette colors green, red, and brown. These are selected by inputting 1, 2, or 3, respectively. This number will follow the background color number and is

0	Black
1	Blue
2	Green
3	Cyan
4	Red
5	Magenta
6	Brown
7	White
8	Gray
9	Light Blue
10	Light Green
11	Light Cyan
12	Light Red
13	Light Magenta
14	Yellow
15	White (High-Intensity)

Fig. 3-5. Number designations for various screen background colors using the color/graphics capability of the IBM Personal Computer.

separated from it by a comma. On the other hand, if the background number is odd, the three palette numbers will specify cyan, magenta, and white. The color selected for the background may be the same as any of the palette colors, but if this is so, you will not be able to read any of the printed information, since it will blend with the background.

The draw statement is available only in Advanced BASIC, and it is one of the most useful statements the IBM Personal Computer has to offer the serious graphics programmer. This statement allows you to draw an object. Movement commands, listed in Fig. 3-6, follow the draw statement and are contained in quotations. They do not depend upon specified screen coordinates after the first action is completed. These eight movement commands are quite easy to use. When each follows the draw statement, a different function is accomplished. Each command is followed by a numerical expression which is given in points. It will be necessary to know whether you're operating in high-, low-, or medium-resolution graphics in order to specify the correct number of points in each direction.

Let's return to a programming problem that was discussed earlier in this chapter, that of drawing a box on the screen. This required a relatively large number of program lines while operating in text mode, but in the graphics mode, we can accomplish the same thing with the following lines:

```
10  DRAW "U = 30;R = 30;D = 30;L =
    30;"
```

This single program line will draw a box on the screen. We can substitute an assigned variable as well, as is evidenced by the following program:

```
10  X = 30
20  DRAW "U=X;R=X;D=X;L=X;"
```

You can increase or decrease the area of the box by simply changing the value of X. Using the draw statement, it is extremely easy to produce squares, rectangles, triangles and many other figures on the screen. This can be done using a minimum of program lines and in a very short period of time.

The next graphics command is the get statement. This statement is used in other dialects of BASIC, but in almost every instance, it applies to the text mode of operation. In the graphics mode, the get statement is used to read points from an area of the screen. When combined with the put statement, it serves as the major means of producing on-screen motion. The get statement is followed by the coordinates of an image. It actually reads the colors of the points within a specified rectangular area on the screen into a particular array that is named following the coordinate portions of the statement. The array is used to hold the

D	n	Move down
E	n	Move diagonally up and right
F	n	Move diagonally down and right
G	n	Move diagonally down and left
H	n	Move diagonally up and left
L	n	Move left
R	n	Move right
U	n	Move up

Fig. 3-6. Draw statement commands.

image, so that it may be recalled at any time, and is specified numerically.

The put statement in IBM graphics operation writes colored points onto a specified area of the screen and is followed by the numerical coordinates of the top left corner of the image, by the array designation, and by an action. The action may be AND, OR, PRESET, PSET, or XOR. The AND action is used when you want to transfer an image which already exists under another transferred image. This would probably be brought about by a previous OR action in the statement, which is used to superimpose one image over another. PSET simply stores the data from the array onto the screen and PRESET does the same thing, except a negative image (when compared to the original) is produced. The XOR action is the default and is used specifically for on-screen animation. This action causes the points on the screen to be inverted. When an image is placed against a complex background twice using the put statement, the background is restored to use a put statement which specifies an image already on the screen to avoid leaving a hole. Otherwise, each time an image is moved, the position it filled will be seen against the screen background. When the put statement is used twice, the hole which the original image occupied is simply filled in.

I realize this sounds quite complicated, so to simplify things, we can say you place an object on the screen using PUT with XOR. You will then determine the new position you wish this object to fill and put the object on the screen a second time at the old location. This removes the original image. Then, your next put statement specifying the new coordinates will redraw the same image in the new location. This makes the object seem to move across the screen without leaving any "wake".

Let's assume you want to cause a circle to move around the screen. Using the put statement with XOR, the circle is drawn at one location. We'll call this location A. Your desire now is to move the circle to another point on the screen, location B. The first put statement (with XOR) uses the coordinates of point A. The next put statement also specifies point A. The third put statement specifies point B. The sequence continues with BB, CC, DD, etc., to specify movement to other screen points.

The next graphics command is the line statement, which may be used to draw a line or a box on the screen. As discussed earlier in this chapter the line statement is followed by the coordinates of the points where the line is to begin and end. These coordinates may be followed by a color designator (0 to 3). This may be followed with "B" which will cause a box to be drawn at the same coordinates. This may be replaced with "BF", which also draws a box or rectangle and then fills it in with the selected color. This statement is very useful in programs which involve the drawing of bar graphs.

The paint statement is available in Advanced BASIC only and fills in an area on the screen with a selected palette color. The statement is followed by the coordinates of any point within the area to be filled. These coordinates may be given numerically or in relative form. This statement is used in program lines which follow line, draw, and circle statements to fill in these areas, giving them a solid appearance.

The PSET and PRESET statements are both used to draw a point at a specified position on the display screen. The two are almost identical, and both may be followed by color designations. However, the PRESET statement may be used without a designator. When used in this manner, a black background is automatically selected. If both terms are used with color designator, the two are identical. These statements are used to draw lines and curves using a series of dots. The dots are so closely spaced that when the write is completed, they resemble a continuous line. The PSET/PRESET statement is often used in a for-next loop to speed up the programming process. Each statement is followed by the coordinates of the point and the appropriate color designator.

The screen statement may be used in either text or graphics mode, although it is almost useless in the former. This statement sets up the screen conditions that will be used by the next series of statements. The screen statement is followed by the specification of a mode. 0 specifies text mode, 1, medium-resolution graphics, and 2, high-resolution graphics. This may be followed by a specification that determines whether or not color will be used in the next series of lines.

In this chapter, I have tried to concentrate on those portions of IBM BASIC which relate specifically to graphics programming. As one becomes more familiar with a particular machine, it is quite easy to mix text and graphics programming to enhance the latter mode of operation. Some programs may be classified as graphics only, but many will incorporate a large amount of graphics with a fair amount of text. For example, when designing programs to display graphs and charts, it is usually necessary to provide graph labels in text mode. From a practical standpoint, there is little difference in text and graphics programming, at least from the experienced programmer's point of view. By this, I mean that it is not necessary to switch one's thinking completely when alternating between the two modes of operation. We all know that a print statement in IBM BASIC will cause the following text line in quotation marks to be displayed on the screen. By the same token, a line statement followed by the appropriate designators and coordinates will cause a line or box to appear on the screen. When you practice both text and graphics programming, there is usually no differentiation between the two modes when actually writing the individual program lines.

Of course, there are differences, but these are soon committed to memory (the human kind), and automatic reactions to certain programming problems are the result. The term computer language is quite appropriate, because it is a true language, one which programmers often begin to think in. I can still recall my early days of programming and the realization, after awhile, that at times, I was beginning to view the everyday world in terms of computer programming. For instance, I might see a leaf fall from a tree and mentally convert this occurrence into computer language. This would involve the graphic drawing of a tree and the placement of the leaf using various put and get statements. During intensive periods of programming which might span several weeks or even a month at eight to twelve hours a day, I find that I seem to be losing touch with the normal world. There is probably nothing so aggravating to a noncomputerist as trying to converse intelligently with someone who is thinking in a completely different language. I do not advocate this intensity for everyone, and it's always a good idea to get away from the machine completely for a few days to regain your perspective.

Many persons who have programmed almost exclusively in text mode are a bit hesitant or even frightened of graphics programming. This is due to the human tendency to fear what we do not understand. It's easy to get into the habit of programming the same old way, because this is the only way that is currently understood. Be assured that there is nothing highly exotic about graphics programming when compared with programming in the text mode. Since most persons start with the text mode, a good foundation has already been laid, and you are aware, to a large extent, of how the machine thinks. Mastering graphics programming does not involve the learning of a whole new language, but rather the addition of some new programming techniques, which may be thought of as modifications of text mode programming.

The graphics programming information presented in this chapter can be the start of a learning process, and the programs found elsewhere in this book will give you the practical experience necessary. In my opinion, the best training aid for programmers is a working program that can be input via the keyboard. It is not necessary to understand why this program works the way it does at first. Once the program has been input and debugged, you may then change certain coordinates, program lines, or subroutines just to see what your modifications yield in the on-screen display. You can see what happens when the coordinates of a circle statement are changed, for instance. You can try different combinations of specifications to yield semicircles, three-quarter circles, and even elongated ellipses. Put and get statements are also useful for "hit or miss" program learning. Coordinates may be changed to cause a moving object to alter its path. Once a basic program is set up, even a few modifications can bring about a completely different result. When you learn how to make the changes you want, most of this information can be remembered for use in future programs.

The only way to become comfortable with graphics programming is to jump in with both feet. You may wish to concentrate on one graphics statement per programming day. For instance, you might take the draw statement and put it through every pace imaginable. Be sure to have a notebook on hand so that you may record your findings for future reference. After a bit of practice, you will be referring less and less to this source, as the needed information is committed to human memory. This is not to say that you will reach a point where you will never be stuck. The great attraction offered by computer programming lies in the human tendency to push for more and more. Once you become accomplished in one type of graphics programming, you will want to move on to other statements and more complex programs. Computer programming is an ongoing education that simply never ends. There are as many potential programs as there are human ideas.

Color Monitors

The previous chapter discussed setting up your IBM Personal Computer for color/graphics work using a color television receiver in conjunction with the IBM color/graphics adapter board. It is quite convenient to be able to use a color television receiver, since nearly every home has one. This, of course, requires that a video modulator be connected to the composite video output of the color/graphics adapter board. The modulator outputs a frequency that is within the television tuner's range, and from here on out, the receiver treats the signal as it would any other broadcast station. The color and synchronization information are extracted from the carrier, and the result is a display on the picture tube. Most of the earlier microcomputers used this method of monitoring, and many of them included built-in modulators, so no external devices were necessary. Today, most modern microcomputers can feed a color television receiver, although they usually require an outboard modulator.

While there are many advantages to using a color television receiver as a monitor, most of these address cost only. After all, the receiver is already there and does not require modification, since most modulators connect directly to the antenna terminals and contain a switch, which will allow near-instantaneous connection to a television antenna or cable system when the TV is to be used for its original purpose. However, from a performance standpoint, the television receiver falls far short of optimum. Resolution is a problem when the computer display is to be in high-resolution text mode. Most of the time, it is extremely difficult to read text on a television receiver when the display is in the 80 × 25 character text mode. In medium-resolution (320 × 200 points), it is much easier to read text, and, of course, you have the color capability here. The receiver does all right in reproducing colors from the computer feed, but the colors are often not razor-sharp, and there is a fair amount of bleedover when different colors are displayed in close proximity.

For persons who are serious about color/graphics work using the IBM Personal Computer, the only acceptable monitor is one that is designed specifically for connection to a microcomputer. These fall into two categories: composite and direct-drive.

The composite monitor is very much like your television receiver with the tuner removed. The IBM Personal Computer and its color/graphics adapter board offer a composite video output, which is accessed by means of a four-pin Berg strip on the card proper or by a phono receptacle on the back of the card. Put simply, a composite video signal is one which contains all information (colors, synchronization, etc.) on one channel. When using a modulator, this composite video output is superimposed on the VHF carrier. The television receiver then removes the carrier and separates the three colors (red, green, and blue) and the synchronization signals by means of filter networks. Each of these components is then fed to a separate channel within the receiver. Using a composite computer monitor, it is not necessary to use a modulator, as this stage has been eliminated. The computer signal feeds the filter network directly. It is still necessary for the monitor to break this composite signal into each of its four components before passing them along to the remaining portions of the circuitry.

Let's consider the problem then. When using a television receiver and modulator, the output to the screen will be only as good as the modulator itself and the television receiver's ability to break down the composite signal. This means that there is an inevitable loss, because a certain amount of distortion will be created by the modulator, the television tuner, and the filter networks. Some persons will argue with my use of the word distortion here, but I think the term suffices and is far simpler than trying to explain nonlinear transfers and other aspects that are more suited to theoretical discussions and that the programmer really has little control over.

With all of this in mind, you have to take a very close look at the television receiver itself. If the set is not in perfect adjustment, screen production problems will be more apparent when using the computer than when receiving an off-the-air television broadcast. Television stations themselves differ in quality of broadcast signal, so we're all accustomed to these variations. For example, you may notice that the color from one channel seems to be far better than that from another. These differences may have little to do with the distance each station lies from your reception point. Most of the time, they are brought on by the differences in quality of the processing and transmitting equipment at the station.

If you took a nationwide survey, you would probably find that better than 90 percent of the color television receivers that have been in use for more than a year are out of adjustment. Again, this may not be apparent when viewing a standard picture, it is but when displaying computer information.

While a television receiver is very much like a composite video monitor, or for that matter, even a direct-drive type, it is a much more complex piece of equipment. It includes most of the components of the video monitors, plus a number of other circuit blocks that are used to demodulate the broadcast signals. In other words, there are more circuits to fall out of adjustment. By using a composite video monitor, the VHF or UHF demodulation circuitry is gone, but of course, a filter network is still required to break the composite video output from the computer down into its various stages for feed to other channels.

The modulator itself is often a major source of erroneous screen output when a television receiver is used as a monitor. The Federal Communications Commission sets quality limits on the signals that television stations transmit. For example, the carrier frequency must be within a very limited range of deviation from the assigned frequency. To accomplish this, commercial stations use equipment which costs in the tens of thousands, or even hundreds of thousands of dollars. The modulator that clamps to the back of your television receiver is taking the place of the commercial broadcast transmitter, and it's not going to be quite so good. Of course, there are good modulators and there are those that are not so good. As pointed out in an earlier chapter, I have used the Sup'R 'Mod V modulator, which is often recommended for the IBM Personal Computer. This is a high-quality modulator, costs about $65, and is quite good as far as modulators go. I have also tested less expensive modulators, some of them costing as little as $15. While there are some exceptions, most of these do not provide the frequency stability necessary for serious computer graphics work. I have found that higher-priced equipment is not always best, but in many cases it is, so if you go the modulator route, be prepared to spend $50 to $100.

Composite video monitors are much more efficient than a television receiver and a modulator. They are not terribly expensive, costing from about $150 to over $250. If you subtract the price of the modulator, which is not required, the price seems to be even more reasonable although in contrast to using your own television and spending a maximum of $100 for a modulator, it is an added expense. A good modulator connected to a recently-aligned color television receiver will do almost as well as many composite video monitors.

Again, if you're really serious about computer graphics, the only route to go is that of the direct-drive video monitor. Unlike the monitors already discussed, this type accepts video information in four or more channels. These monitors are often referred to as RGB types, with the letters standing for the colors red, blue, and green. These are the three basic colors, which are combined to give you many other colors. The RGB monitor supplies each of these colors by means of a separate channel. There are also other channels for synchronization. The RGB monitor does not break down a composite video signal, as these are already supplied in separate channels by the computer. Of course, there are no VHF or UHF demodulation stages, so another source of problems has been eliminated. There is no external modulator, so you don't have to worry about frequency stability. The display provided by direct-drive video monitors is far superior to anything that can be had on a television receiver or composite video monitor. The drawback.....RGB monitors are expensive.

Or at least they seem to be at first glance. But let's consider a few other facts before passing judgment. First, the standard IBM Personal Computer configuration consists of the system unit, keyboard, monochrome display and monochrome display/printer adapter board. The IBM monochrome display is absolutely mandatory, if you intend to do all of your color/graphics work with a modulator and television receiver. As was previously mentioned, high-resolution text mode operation is extremely difficult using the television receiver. Most persons switch back to the monochrome display for this type of work. The monochrome display, however, cannot be used for any serious graphics work, color or otherwise.

Now, if you're using the color television receiver for graphics work, you will also have to purchase the IBM color/graphics adapter board and a modulator. The board will cost about $300, and let's assume the modulator costs about $60. This is in addition to the IBM monochrome display/printer adapter card, which will cost about $335, and the monochrome display itself, which sells for $345. Let's add up these figures, and we come up with:

IBM monochrome display	$345
IBM monochrome display/ printer adapter	$335
Color/graphics monitor adapter	$300
Modulator	$ 60
TOTAL:	$1040

Naturally, this assumes that you already have a good television receiver.

This is quite a hefty cost for adapter cards and a monitor that you cannot use for color/graphics work but is mandatory for text mode operation. Now, let's consider the price of a direct-drive color monitor. You can pay anywhere from $500 to over $1000 for such a device, but figure about $700, especially if you're able to purchase it through one of the discount outlets. Add to this the previous amount, and we're over $1700 for complete monitoring capabilities.

However, the picture brightens considerably when you consider the fact that a direct-drive color monitor should serve about as well as the IBM monochrome display for high-resolution (width 80) text mode operation. This eliminates $345! Actually, it eliminates more than that. It also gets rid of the need for the monochrome display/printer adapter board, which sells for $335. Of course, you will still need to use your printer, so this must be replaced with the parallel printer card, which costs only $150. Let's look at these figures:

Direct-drive color monitor	$700
Color/graphics monitor adapter	$300
Parallel printer adapter card	$150
TOTAL:	$1150

When compared with the other figure, it can be seen that for an extra $110, you can have complete color/graphics capability, excellent high-resolution text mode monitoring, and full use of the printer. This is all you need. I'm certainly not saying that it's never necessary or desirable to have the IBM monochrome display and its adapter card. Many persons purchase the IBM Personal Computer for serious text mode work, with color/graphics as an afterthought. In many instances, the color/graphics card will not even be purchased, because text mode work will be handled exclusively. It would not be financially wise to go to the extra expense involved in color/graphics work if it's only to be a plaything. However, if you're going to go to the expense of purchasing the color/graphics card, you will certainly want to consider going with the RGB monitor instead of the IBM monochrome display. In talking with several computer outlets, I have found that many machines are ordered with the color/graphics adapter board only. I would imagine many people are trying to save money here by using a color television receiver as their monitor, and if most of your operations are in medium-resolution, this will do fine. I would imagine, though, that most of these computer buyers will be operating under visual landings whenever they attempt high-resolution text mode operations.

The IBM color/graphics adapter board offers a D-connector output to drive RGB monitors. This is in addition to (and separate from) the composite video output discussed earlier. Here, you have a channel for the colors red, blue, and green and the synchronization. These are the same outputs that are combined for the composite output. With the direct output, however, your RGB monitor does not have to go through the process of extrapolating the various types of information and outputting them to separate channels. For example, the red color channel is connected to the direct-drive red color output terminal at the D connector. The same is true for all the other channels.

When you first view a color display on a good RGB monitor, you will be quite impressed, especially if all your previous monitor experience has involved a color television receiver and modulator. The color images do not waver; they do not bleed over; and they are razor-sharp. The color differences are far more clearly defined than they are on the best color television receivers. When you switch to the high-resolution text mode, each letter or symbol is perfectly defined and quite easy to read, although even the best RGB monitor will probably not rival the monochrome monitor when in text mode operation—but many are almost as good. This is a slight tradeoff, but all you should be concerned with in text mode operation is the ability to quickly and easily read the text display. I think you will find that most RGB color monitors satisfy these requirements completely.

When I first purchased my IBM Personal Computer, the system was fully equipped with everything except an RGB monitor. IBM does not manufacture its own RGB monitor, but does offer several models from other manufacturers. I purchased a modulator; connected it to my console color television receiver, and was quite pleased with the results. However, as my interest in color/graphics work increased, I found that I was not totally satisfied with my color display. I wanted something more.

I contacted Amdek Corporation and inquired about their monitors. There are many fine monitors on today's market, but Amdek is considered by many to be the leader. Indeed, they make several RGB color monitors, a composite video monitor, and even a high-resolution, amber text-mode monitor, all of which are completely compatible with the IBM Personal Computer and do not required special adapter boards. The latter text mode monitor uses an amber foreground instead of green or white, which is standard. The amber foreground is supposed to provide much better readability. The RGB and composite monitors connect to the color/graphics adapter board, while the amber monitor connects to the IBM monochrome display adapter.

Amdek generously agreed to supply their Amdek Color II Monitor for my use in writing this book. Shown in Fig. 4-1, this direct-drive RGB monitor contains a 13-inch picture tube with electrostatic focus, and features self-conversion. I was also supplied with an Amdek cable, one end of which plugs into the back of the color/graphics adapter board and the other into the rear of the monitor itself.

Upon uncrating the Amdek monitor, I was immediately struck by the size of the device. Unlike many computer monitors, this one is quite large. Its weight told me the device had some substance. While I have not taken the monitor apart, I would imagine that it has a power supply which is quite substantial (owing to the weight) and should operate at moderate temperatures, even for long durations. The Amdek monitor looks very much like any 13-inch color television receiver. Its case is styled in much the same manner, but it's not nearly as heavy due to the lack of demodulation cir-

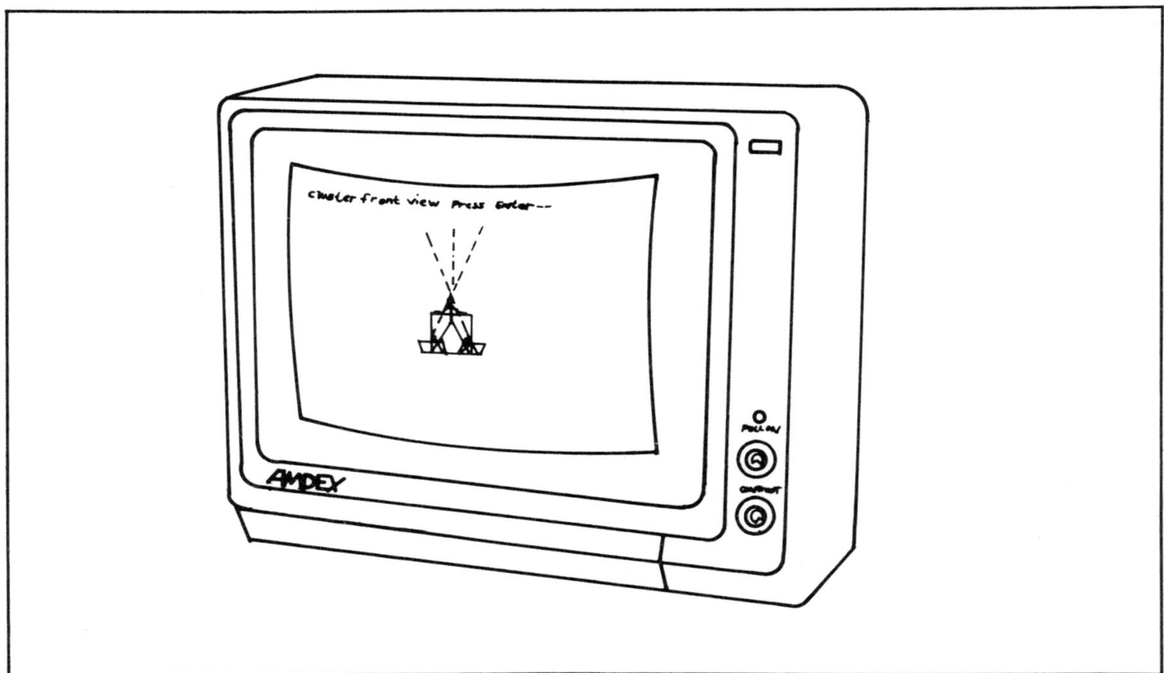

Fig. 4-1. The Amdek Color II RGB monitor.

cuitry. There are only two controls visible on the front panel. One is an on/off switch; the other controls screen contrast. At the bottom of the monitor, there is a snapaway horizontal panel, which, when removed, allows access to the vertical hold and brightness controls. The Amdek monitor's power cord must access a standard wall outlet.

It took me all of three minutes to connect the monitor to my computer and plug it in to the wall. I turned the computer on and keyed up DOS BASIC. I then ran the access program to activate the color/graphics monitor adapter and switched on the Amdek monitor. I loaded the modern art program, which will be discussed in a later chapter, and was delighted to see the nicely-defined color variations, which I'd never been able to witness on the television receiver. The IBM Personal Computer is capable of outputting sixteen different colors, but some of these are simply different shades of the same color. On the television receiver, it was difficult to differentiate between a medium red and a pink, but using the Amdek color monitor, the two colors were clearly defined and easily distinguishable. In many ways, the display on the Amdek monitor looked completely different from the display offered by the television receiver. I was not plagued by any jumpiness on the part of the objects on the screen, nor by any sudden loss of color as often happened with my television receiver. This problem was partially due to the relatively high intensity of television signals from broadcast stations coming in on my cable system. The Amdek monitor is completely removed from broadcast station interference because it doesn't operate in the UHF or VHF spectrum.

Of course, I expected a lot from this excellent RGB monitor and was certainly not disappointed, at least when it came to color/graphics presentation. I then switched to high-resolution text mode and held my breath. You will remember that this mode of operation is the one which comes across the worst on the television receiver. Again, I was delighted. The text mode display was crisp, and each character was extremely well-defined. No, it was not the same as the IBM monochrome display, because the Amdek monitor dosen't use a green or white foreground against a green background. While the Amdek text mode display is different, it is equally as sharp, no one will have any difficulty in running text mode programs on the Amdek Color II Monitor.

Unlike some color monitors, the Amdek Color II offers excellent brightness and contrast. This is due to the fact that the electrostatic deflection is controlled by a 26 kilovolt potential, which is quite high. This means that each line, no matter how thin, is clearly defined, and there is no overtrace or bleed. If a lower potential was used at the electrostatic deflection coil, undoubtedly, the display would not be as good. Incidentally, if you're a do-it-yourselfer and want to go into the Amdek monitor (or for that matter, any monitor) just to see what's there, take my advice and don't. This is especially true if you're accustomed to working on low-voltage solid-state circuits. Coming in contact with a 26 kilovolt supply probably won't kill you (due to the low current supplied), but it can literally throw you for a loop, causing you to break bones and tear tissue along the way. There are really no owner-serviceable parts within the cabinet anyway, so if you develop a problem, you'd better call Amdek or take it to one of their service centers.

If, like me, you've been accustomed to a television receiver pulled into service as a color/graphics monitor, you will undoubtedly run every program you've ever written just to see how it looks on the Amdek monitor. When I'm testing a product, I like to nitpick and not only tell about everything that is good, but everything that is not so good as well. In this case, however, I really can find no fault at all with the Amdek monitor. Being as petty as possible, I could complain about the length of the interface cable (about four feet), which is a little short for my liking. I have made the same complaint about power cords and interface cables attached to nearly every other device I've come in contact with, but my situation is probably a bit different from that of the average consumer. I often find it necessary to test and evaluate many different types of devices, seemingly at the same time. My computer table and workbench become filled quite quickly, and I often find it necessary to locate a new addition to my computer repertoire quite a distance from the system unit. Here, long cables are a godsend. Most persons who buy the Amdek color monitor will undoubtedly set it atop the system unit. Unfortunately, my IBM monochrome display was already occupying this space, so I had to set it to one side to make room for the Amdek monitor. The power cord and interface cable which exits the IBM monochrome display is even shorter than those on the Amdek monitor, so I was in a bit of a quandry until I could get other cables made up. Those persons who have both the IBM monochrome display and the Amdek monitor will probably elect to let one or the other set atop the system unit and place the remaining one to the left or right. Both monitors have adequate power and interface cables to easily handle such an arrangement.

I looked diligently at the color display provided by the Amdek monitor, hoping to find something I could criticize, but I completely struck out. The monitor is every bit as good as Amdek says it is (and possibly a bit better) and should be able to meet every monitoring need imaginable, whether in text or graphics mode. Admittedly, I haven't personally tested other popular makes of color RGB monitors, but I feel fairly safe in saying that it's going to be quite difficult to provide a better display than that provided by the Amdek monitor supplied to me.

The Amdek Color II is billed as an advanced high-resolution color monitor which features RGB, TTL input, and a display which is 560 lines in width and 260 lines in height for a crisp, 80 × 24 character display and exceptionally sharp color/graphics. I have seen these monitors at various prices in advertisements in many computer magazines. Depending on where you shop, you'll end up paying between $700 and $800, so shop around to get the best buy possible. These monitors are certainly not limited to the IBM Personal Computer, and Amdek can supply interface boards for compatibility with other computers where needed.

Of course, microcomputers are not inexpensive, nor is the equipment used for monitoring, printing, and the like. The prices are actually miniscule in comparison with what they would have been years ago, but still, buying a computer usually requires a bit of financial planning and often worry. Undoubtedly, there will be readers who would like to save as much money as possible on a functional IBM Personal Computer system. These persons have probably considered going the route of an IBM Personal Computer with a color/graphics board, parallel printed board, a single disk drive, and of course, the disk drive adapter. Their intentions are to use a modulator and television receiver as their sole video monitoring source. Can you get away with this? The answer is a qualified yes. Your programming time, however, may be slowed a bit. On most television receivers, it's simply impossible to insert readable program lines in the high-resolution text mode. You can, however, insert your program lines in a 40 character width format (medium-resolution) and then run them in high-resolution mode by inserting a "WIDTH 80" program line at the beginning of the run. This will allow you to draw text mode graphics in high-resolution, while inserting the program lines with the screen in the easy-to-read low-resolution mode. Of course, if you're running text programs, it will be necessary to use medium-resolution most of the time. This limits you severely in screen width, and while the information is all there, it looks quite congested. I guess whether you can get away with it or not depends on how finicky you are about your video display.

Even in medium-resolution, you will have difficulty reading program lines when operating in a graphics format. You will find yourself constantly pressing the F10 soft key, which keys up the medium-resolution text mode, when displaying these lines. Different background and foreground colors can interfere severely with your ability to read these lines. You must be able to clearly see the program information in order to execute a proper debugging routine. Actually, the line display in medium-resolution text mode when viewed on a television receiver is quite similar to the displays provided by the screens of many other types of personal computers. The display is certainly decipherable, but it's not very clear when compared to the IBM monochrome display or a good color/graphics monitor.

If you're interested in graphics work but also in a lot of text mode programming, I would suggest that you try out as many different combinations as possible. Some will find that they can operate very efficiently using the television receiver as the sole monitor, while others may require the IBM monochrome display and/or a good RGB monitor. At the midway point are those who don't want to go to the added expense of the monochrome display and adapter board, but need more quality than is offered by a television receiver/modulator combination. These persons may do very well with an inexpensive composite video monitor, which is also midway up the scale regarding text/graphics tradeoffs. Composite monitors do better in high-resolution text mode and medium-resolution graphics mode than television receivers. However, the composite monitor is not as readable as the IBM monochrome display in text mode, nor as accurate in color/graphics mode as an RGB monitor.

There you have it. There are at least three completely different combinations which you can choose from. As I stated earlier, I have the monochrome display and an RGB monitor, but my work with microcomputers involves far more than personal enjoyment (and besides, the increased cost can be written off as a business expense). As impressed as I am with good RGB monitors, I still rely quite heavily on the

IBM monochrome display and would not willingly part with it. However, if I had to go with one of the combinations above, I would certainly elect to purchase a good RGB monitor, a separate parallel printer adapter, and of course, the color/graphics board. This would provide excellent text and graphics programming capabilities with possibly only a shade of a tradeoff in text mode. As you can tell, I am quite enthused about the excellent readability of the IBM monochrome display, although I understand that the newer amber displays which connect directly to the monochrome/printer adapter card are supposed to be even better. Everyone reaches a point, however, when it's time to say "enough!" There are so many new products being offered every month for computers that anyone would become bankrupt quickly by picking up everything. This is especially true of the IBM Personal Computer, which is continuing to make a strong impact on the microcomputer market. Each month, more and more companies are offering "newer and better" software and hardware for this machine. The best thing to do is sit back and take a long look at the market over a six-month period and see which products seem to come to the front. The computer magazines review most of the notables in their issues, and you can write the companies for more information. As you become more knowledgeable about what's out there and as your information portfolio builds, you will probably see some trends starting to surface and be able to make an intelligent decision based upon the movement of consumers within the microcomputer market. I realize that it's difficult at times, especially when some exotic new product suddenly surfaces with a momentous splash. Many of these go on to become market standards, but many others quickly fall by the wayside. Before buying any new product, it's always a good rule to check on the company that sells it. You might check their past performance, see how long they've been in business, and even check the quality of their ads in the computer magazines. Be wary of a product which splashes with full-page ads for several months and then seems to disappear completely. This may be a sign of a marketing failure or a product that has not been thoroughly debugged. This is not meant to indicate that one should stay away from the smaller and newer companies. It just makes good sense to do a little checking to make certain you are dealing with a solvent and reputable company before spending your hard-earned money. You are generally safe in dealing with the well-established companies, although most of these have produced a lemon or two in their time. Nothing can take the place of a hands-on demonstration, and a trip to your local computer store can probably provide you with just his. Personnel at these stores are probably more familiar with what the market has to offer than you are, and most will be glad to offer advice when asked to do so. Asking their advice is a good idea, even if you've already decided on the hardware and software you'd like to buy. I recently learned of one computer manufacturer that sells a disk drive for their machine at a price of over $600. This company does not make the disk drive. They purchase it from another company. You can buy the same disk drive from its manufacturer for about $345 retail. It's information such as this that will allow you to purchase the best system for the least amount of money, and a local computer store that sells a larger number of different brands is in an excellent position to help you. In talking with Art Sherman of Frederick Computer Products in Frederick, Maryland, a supplier of IBM Personal Computers as well as many other makes, he told me that his business is successful because of repeat customers. The repeat business is generated by trying to get the best deal for the customer, not by loading them down with a machine they don't need or don't even want simply because it makes the company more money. In the long run, any computer business which operates on the premise that every sale is a one-shot deal has a good chance of quickly going under. A store that sells many different brands of computers has nothing to lose by telling you the advantages and disadvantages of each. It is safe to say that 100 percent of all microcomputer customers must buy additional software, and most will buy at least one additional peripheral whose cost is a significant percentage of the cost of the original system. No reputable business that intends to be around for any length of time is going to ignore this potential for future sales

At Frederick Computer Products, I was able to see nearly every product in operation, and the personnel there really knew how to put this equipment through its paces. Certainly, there is a good chance that you may not have a local computer store. I sympathize with you, because I'm in the same situation. However, I found the two-hour drive to Frederick Computer Products has saved me thousands of dollars. If you have to drive five hours to visit a store in person, then by all means do so before adding to your IBM Personal Computer system. You will be dollars ahead, and these dollars can either be saved or converted to more equipment that you thought you couldn't afford in the first place.

MODIFICATIONS

This next discussion is aimed especially at those readers who have a fair amount of electronics experience, particularly in the television repair field. As you have probably already garnered from the previous information in this chapter, the various types of color monitors (composite and direct-drive) are basically standard television receivers with a lot of circuits pulled out. It is possible to modify a television receiver in order to convert it to a decent color monitor for connection to your computer. Naturally, the quality of the receiver itself will play a part in how good the converted monitor actually is, but it has been my experience that a lot of the expense tied up in color receivers can be attributed to the sensitivity of the tuner, automatic gain and frequency control circuits, etc. These, of course, address the reception of the VHF or UHF signals, boosting them to a level that is usable by the television circuitry.

Even inexpensive color television receivers can be modified to make highly acceptable color/graphics monitors, since you're not really concerned with the front end, which demodulates the RF transmissions. The automatic frequency control circuits can also be discarded, along with many other circuit blocks. When I say discarded, I don't necessarily mean this in the literal sense. It is not necessary to physically remove these circuits from the chassis. All you have to do is disconnect and bypass them in order to get to the heart of the circuit portion that does the on-screen write.

I have modified television receivers so that they become equivalent to composite video monitors. This is simply a matter of bypassing the tuner/demodulation circuits. The output from a standard television signal is composite video. The output from the color/graphics board of the IBM Personal Computer is also composite video, which is usually fed to a modulator. This places the video information on a television carrier and feeds it to the tuner. What we're really doing is modulating a TV carrier signal and the receiver then demodulates it. The output from the tuner, then, is the same as the input to the modulator. By bypassing the tuner, we avoid the necessity of using a modulator at all.

In a standard color television receiver, the composite video output from the tuner is fed to the first intermediate frequency (IF) amplifier. There are usually at least two of these (and sometimes three) to boost the low-level composite video signal. The composite video output from the color/graphics board is comparatively high, and you may not need all of these amplification stages. In some cases, you may wish to "swamp" the composite video output from the computer with a resistive pad, but you may be able to forego building such a pad by simply sending the input to the second or even the third IF amplifier. You may run into some compatibility problems, but with a little knowledge of electronics and some hit-or-miss experimentation, you can probably work the problem out. When the tuner/detector circuits in the television receiver are bypassed, you have the equivalent of a composite video monitor. Power is usually removed from the tuner by clipping the leads from the power supply. The connection between the output of the tuner and the input to the first IF amp is also removed. This renders the tuner useless, which is what is desired. In other words, you won't be able to switch channels any longer, and the video information from the color/graphics board is fed directly to the circuit sections that perform the on-screen write. It should be possible to install one or more switches to allow a television receiver to be used both for its original purpose and as a composite video monitor.

When making such connections between the color/graphics board and the television receiver, always check the voltage. You want to make certain that you don't accidentally access a high potential contact that can damage the color/graphics board. A blocking capacitor for dc in the line from the color/graphics board will prevent such mishaps from occurring.

Following the last IF stage in a television receiver, the color demodulators are encountered. There are three of these circuits, each of which pulls a portion of video information from the composite signal. The information extracted by these demodulators is the red, green, and blue colors that have been discussed previously. These signals are then fed to the color guns in the television picture tube.

Of course, the best color reproduction will be obtained with a direct-drive or RGB color monitor. This means bypassing the three color demodulator circuits and driving the guns directly with the RGB output of the color/graphics board. This is similar to the first process, only access is obtained directly at the input channel to the color gun. The IBM Technical Reference manual explains the pin connections at the direct-drive output of the color/graphics board. The red channel would be connected to the red gun input, and the same is done for the other direct-drive outputs. Again, a switching arrangement could probably be devised to allow for standard television operation, as well as for direct-drive input if you desire.

I have not attempted this modification, but I would imagine that it would not be very complicated even for a seasoned television repair technician. Again, you may have to decrease the drive level from the color/graphics adapter through a padding network. On the other hand, this may not be necessary at all. Each modification will be dependent on the television receiver circuitry and the drive levels it is designed to accept.

Now, those readers who might wish to make such a modification will probably be thinking that instead of using a small 13-inch screen, which is commonplace in the RGB monitor field, why not use one of the 25-inch console color televisions for a much larger display? This has its good points, but also a few drawbacks. When it comes to picture tube size, bigger is not always better. A television picture is made up of a series of horizontal lines (420 in the United States). These race across the screen at a rate of thirty screens per second to form the picture. If the picture tube is physically small, these lines are physically closer together. If it is large, they are more spread out. When you view a large-screen television from a foot or so away, the picture doesn't seem to be clear. This is because you're unconsciously noticing the distance between the horizontal elements that make up the picture. When you back off a ways, however, the relative size of the screen shrinks in direct proportion to the distance, and you don't see the on-screen display in as much detail. By backing away, you have reduced your perception of the space between lines.

The issue here is one of resolution. Good resolution packs the scan more closely, and therefore, the image appears to be sharper. When the scans are spaced out more, resolution is diminished. Think of it as looking at a black and white picture in a newspaper. It looks fine from a few feet away, but if you bring it right up to your nose, you can see the little points that are combined to form the picture. In this latter mode, resolution has been reduced.

With this in mind, you probably won't want a large 25-inch screen for color monitoring purposes, unless you intend to place the monitor five feet or more away from your programming position. If you intend to set the monitor directly atop the computer's system unit, the 13-inch display is all you need. From a close viewing position, you will not get the color definition you want with a large-screen television. It's quite possible that one of the smaller 10-inch screens will work just as well or even better. Recently, some miniature color televisions have come on the market. I don't recommend these for conversion to color monitors for several reasons. First, the screens, which are usually 7 inches diagonally or less, are too small to display easily readable text. They do provide extremely good resolution when the program is actually run, but they are difficult to use while you're actually writing the program. The second reason for avoiding converting such small units addresses the circuits physically. The tiny boards are crammed into the small case, and it's quite difficult to gain access to them. In a larger television, the circuits are more spread out, and it's easier to make and break connections without doing any accidental damage. Of course, if you're really looking for a miniature color monitor, any of these would probably do the job for you, and you simply can't find better resolution than these provide. Of course, your viewing distance will probably have to be limited to a foot or less.

There are RGB color monitors available commercially that are built on a block-by-block basis. This means that you can add circuits when they are needed. The basic monitor is a direct-drive RGB type, but you can also add a plug-in module which contains IF amplifiers and color demodulators. This converts the unit to a composite video monitor. You can also buy tuner blocks that will allow the monitor to be used as a television receiver. These are quite expensive and are probably not useful to most computer hobbyists.

Persons often ask me about using giant-screen projection television receivers as color/graphics monitors. Generally, these are unacceptable. First, if you've paid $2000 or $3000 for your giant-screen receiver, you probably won't want to void your warranty by making modifications. While these receivers are ideal entertainment devices in large rooms where ten or more people may make up the audience, I feel that most residences do not provide adequate viewing distance to take advantage of them. From a moderate distance, the resolution is extremely poor, and the picture is certainly not bright. Before you attempt any modifications to a giant-screen system, it might be best to connect a modulator to the antenna terminals and use the composite video output from the color/graphics board as a drive source. I think you will see exactly what I mean by low-resolution and a generally dull picture. The lack of brightness tends to blend the colors together. Additionally, you must remember that the medium-resolution mode of operation on the IBM Personal Computer is made up of only 320 lines compared with the standard of 420 or more for television transmission. This is true whether you use a modulator or convert a television receiver for direct-drive or composite video monitoring purposes. This is one of the reasons for the poor performance of television receivers and modulators when used to monitor the high-resolution graphics mode, which is composed of 640 lines. Here, it's necessary to cram the 640 lines output from the color/graphics board into a display consisting of only 420 lines. This compression distorts the information often making it unreadable.

A major problem in the conversion of television receivers to make good video monitors has not been touched on to this point. This involves the quality of the receiver to be converted. Most conversions involve older television receivers. Many of these are tube types, probably out of adjustment, and their picture tubes have often gone soft. In a direct-drive conversion, all you're really concerned with is the picture tube, power supplies, and synchronization detection circuits. If the picture tube is marginal, your best result will be marginal. Few people will want to spend $400 or so on a new television receiver and then convert it for monitoring purposes only. True, this is about half the price of a good RGB monitor, but chances are your conversion results will not offer quite as high quality color reproduction as will a stock RGB device. You're taking a chance here, and there are several tradeoffs.

Of course, you might consider purchasing a new picture tube for an older set if the rest of the needed circuits seem to be in good working order. This might mean an expenditure of $100 or so, and here, the price is more acceptable.

This discussion on television receiver conversion is admittedly a bit vague, especially when you consider the fact that a different procedure will be required for each different make and model of color television receiver. Remember also that I have not actually made an RGB conversion, and while I know that it is possible, for many persons it may not be the practical way to go.

As mentioned before, the conversion I did involved making the equivalent of a composite video monitor, and this was handled by removing power from the tuner and accessing the first IF amplifier channel with the composite video output line from the color/graphics board. This works surprisingly well, although it was necessary to swamp the composite video output from the standard 1.5-volt peak-to-peak value to slightly less than .5 volt. The conversion was done under emergency conditions when my modulator had failed and I absolutely had to have a color monitor to meet a deadline. The set was later reconverted to its original status when my RGB monitor arrived.

If you like to tinker and have an old color or black and white television receiver, you might take it apart and experiment a bit. If you arrive at a successful conversion, you may then want to try your talents at converting a good color receiver to switchable television/RGB monitor operation. The old television set can serve as an exercise in learning, without fear of doing any costly damage. Protect your color/graphics board channel, however, with a blocking capacitor to avoid popping any of the components by an accidental high-potential charge.

Chapter 5

Text Mode Graphics Programs

Throughout this book, I have mentioned text mode graphics as opposed to high-resolution graphics or color/graphics. The IBM Personal Computer with the monochrome display is capable of producing only text mode graphics. I call this type of graphics text mode graphics because the same statements and commands used to produce them are also used to produce on-screen text. We can generate many of the same displays that are produced in the high-resolution graphics mode in text mode graphics. However, in most cases, many more program lines will be needed in text mode graphics than when using the specialized commands in Advanced BASIC and in the high-resolution mode of operation.

In text mode graphics programming, we rely heavily on for-next and locate statements. The latter are used to identify a certain set of coordinates on the screen and often, the values produced by the for-next loops are inserted into the coordinate designations following the locate statements.

Certainly, it is possible to produce animation when operating in text mode, but this is a fairly slow process when compared with high-resolution graphics. More lines are required to draw the text mode graphic figures, and still more are needed to specify the full range of screen positions or coordinates it will assume throughout a program run. To put it simply, the computer has to work harder or think harder when producing and animating text mode graphics than when doing the same things in the high-resolution mode. When I refer to text mode animation as a slow process, I'm not referring directly to the speed of the animated graphic figures in traveling, let's say, from the left side of the screen to the right. The term slow more accurately describes the process by which the figure is drawn, erased and then drawn again. Due to the persistence of the IBM monochrome display (the afterglow which remains after a graphic figure has been erased), you will still see the fading figure that has been erased prior its being printed at its next position. A trace, which consists of the screen glow at the positions where it was previously presented, is left behind the moving object.

Now, when it is necessary to move two objects simultaneously on the screen, the process is slowed even more. Actually, it's not possible to move two objects simultaneously, but we can simulate that appearance by programming in a special way. Let's assume that we want to write a road race type of program where two vehicles travel from left to right across the screen. The program would be set up so that vehicle A is drawn first and then erased. This is immediately followed by the drawing and erasure of vehicle B. As soon as the second vehicle's image has been erased, the computer will draw vehicle A again, but at a different position. This vehicle is then erased and vehicle B is drawn again at an advanced position. This process continues back and forth until the race is over. It is usually necessary to include time delay sequences between the drawing and erasure process by using for-next statements. When the completed program is run, you can see, upon close inspection, that only one vehicle is drawn at a time. From a moderate distance, however, this effect is not as obvious, and there is the appearance of simultaneous object motion. Of course, the problem with the screen traces is doubled, but by adjusting character intensity with the screen control knob, this can be reduced to a minimum.

When text mode graphics is used for printing bar graphs and other such displays, the appearance is more in line with high-resolution graphics displays. Here, no animation is involved, and from a visual standpoint, text mode graph programs (not graphics, but graph) are very pleasing to the eye and contain just as much information as an identical program written for high-resolution graphics mode. Again, however, the number of program lines that must be input in the text mode will be much greater than the number required for the same effect using high-resolution graphics programming.

All of the programs in this chapter are written in the text mode. This means that a minimum IBM Personal Computer configuration consisting of the system unit, keyboard, monochrome display, monochrome display adapter, preferably a cassette recorder, and possibly a printer will suffice. It is not necessary to have the color/graphics adapter board and a graphics monitor or television receiver. You may be amazed at just what can be accomplished by using a few programming tricks to produce some very pleasing graphics statements such as color, pset, preset, line, draw, paint, put, get, and others will not run at all or, in some cases, will not have any noticeable effect on the display. Should one of these statements be used while in text mode, an "Illegal Function Call" prompt will be displayed on the screen.

A previous chapter provided a great deal of discussion on text mode graphics programming, so if you're unclear as to what it's all about, I would suggest rereading this portion of the book before going further. You may elect, however, to input one of the programs in this chapter and then use it in conjunction with the discussion on text mode graphics to gain a clearer understanding of just what is taking place.

Each program included in this chapter is accompanied by an explanation of how it works. This is often handled on a line-by-line basis confined to certain program blocks. I feel this is more appropriate than simply including a program listing by itself. If you know the functioning of each program block, it is far easier to write your own original programs using the same methods and referring to the program listing as a guide. The explanations also make program modification far simpler. You will find that few programs in any book do exactly what you want them to. There is such a broad range of personal needs and desires that the program writer must strive for the best compromise. Undoubtedly, you will find many of the programs in this book to your liking, but eventually, you will probably want to make modifications to suit your own needs. Through such modifications and experimentation, your ability to quickly and successfully program the computer to do what you want it to will increase, and your knowledge of graphics programming in general will reach a higher plateau.

Figure 5-1 shows a simple program that

```
10 CLS
20 KEY OFF
30 INPUT"TYPE A";A
40 INPUT"TYPE B";B
50 INPUT"TYPE C";C
60 INPUT"TYPE D";D
70 INPUT"PRINT E";E
80 INPUT"TYPE F";F
90 CLS
100 FOR A=1 TO A:LOCATE 5,A:PRINT CHR$(219)
110 NEXT A
120 FOR B=1 TO B:LOCATE 8,B:PRINT CHR$(219)
130 NEXT B
140 FOR C=1 TO C:LOCATE 11,C:PRINT CHR$(219)
150 NEXT C
160 FOR D=1 TO D:LOCATE 14,D:PRINT CHR$(219)
170 NEXT D
180 FOR E=1 TO E:LOCATE 17,E:PRINT CHR$(219)
190 NEXT E
200 FOR F=1 TO F:LOCATE 20,F:PRINT CHR$(219)
210 NEXT F
```

Fig. 5-1. Horizontal bar graph program in text mode.

will generate a horizontal bar graph consisting of up to six bars emanating from the left side of the screen and traveling toward the right. This program is more for discussion purposes than for practical use, although it may be run on the IBM Personal Computer to chart relative values.

The values are input in lines 30 through 80. I have assigned the top bar the name "A" and proceeded downward on the screen to the last bar, "F". The values that are input must be integers between 1 and 80 because they serve to indicate the horizontal screen positions. Therefore, no value may be input which is greater than 80, or an illegal function call will result. As an example of how this program displays information, assume that you input 20 for the value of A. Line 100 will insert this value into the for-next loop, which may be stated as: A = 1 TO 20 in this case. The second statement in the line positions the cursor at the coordinates of 5,A, which are 5,1: 5,2; and so forth up to 5,20. The print statement on line 100 causes solid ASCII block characters to be written into each of the positions specified by the advancing coordinates. After the loop cycles through 20, the program continues with line 120, where the process is completed for the next bar in the graph. Notice in the locate statement of line 120 that the starting position for the second bar is three spaces further down the screen than for the first.

The result of inputting 20 for the value of A in line 30 is a solid bar between coordinates 5,1 and 5,20 on the monitor screen. A value of 30 would extend the line ten more places horizontally. If you do not want a bar at any particular position, simply press the enter key when the screen prompts you to type in a value. In the for-next statements, the variables will then be automatically assigned a value of 0 and no ASCII block characters will be printed. Figure 5-2 shows the screen display.

This is a very basic program and does not generate axes lines. Also, many graphs use keyed-in values from 0 to 100, while this one uses from 1 to 80. To form a practical, working program to display information on the screen, this sample program could be slightly modified to allow for the input of values from 0 to 100 by simply multiplying these values by a fraction, 4/5, which will yield a maximum of 80 when a maximum of 100 is input. What we're doing here is increasing the maximum value that can be input while still keeping the maximum display value at 80. A graph displays the relative size or value, so as long as all the values input to our modified program are multiplied by the same fraction, the bar lengths will be proportional.

Looking at the original program again, it should be clear that each ASCII block character is printed beside an identical character that was printed in the previous cycle of the loop. Using ASCII character 219, there is no space between the characters, so the end result is a completely solid line. Other ASCII block characters could be used to display a dotted line, or we could even use standard keyboard symbols, such as letters, to accomplish the same thing. A line of Xs from 0 to 100 indicates the same value as a solid bar covering the same screen positions. However, when computers are used to display chart information, most persons expect a solid bar which looks much more professional.

Figure 5-3 shows another basic program, which will generate a bar graph using the IBM

Fig. 5-2. Screen printout of previous bar graph program run.

monochrome display. The previous program placed bars horizontally on the screen. This one does basically the same thing, except the bars are vertical, running from the bottom to the top. This program allows you to input three different values, each of which must be 19 or less. Again, this is a basic program, and later versions of it will allow for the inputting of more conventional values up to 100 or so.

In the previous program, ASCII block characters were printed in any of the 80 positions across the screen. Here, they are printed vertically, starting at a base of position 20 and moving up the scale to a minimum of 1. In order

```
10 CLS
20 KEY OFF
30 INPUT"A=";A
40 INPUT "B=";B
50 INPUT"C=";C
60 CLS
70 FOR A=0 TO A
80 I=20-A
90 LOCATE I,5:PRINT CHR$(219)+CHR$(219)+CHR$(219)+CHR$(219)
100 NEXT A
110 FOR B=0 TO B
120 J=20-B
130 LOCATE J,15:PRINT CHR$(219)+CHR$(219)+CHR$(219)+CHR$
    (219)
140 NEXT B
150 FOR C=0 TO C
160 K=20-C
170 LOCATE K,25:PRINT CHR$(219)+CHR$(219)+CHR$(219)+CHR$
    (219)
180 NEXT C
190 FOR X=1 TO 78
200 LOCATE 21,X:PRINT CHR$(223)
210 NEXT X
220 FOR Y=1 TO 20
230 LOCATE Y,1:PRINT CHR$(219)
240 NEXT Y
250 PRINT
260 PRINT
```

Fig. 5-3. Vertical bar graph program in text mode.

to get the display to print from bottom to top, the input values are given different assignments in lines 80, 120, and 160.

Let's assume for the purposes of this discussion that you input a value of 10 for A. Line 70 is the beginning of a for-next loop which counts from 0 to the value of A, or 10 in this case. The input value is reassigned in line 80 using the variable I. Therefore, during the first cycle of the loop, I will be equal to 20, or 20 - 0. During the next cycle, I will be equal to 20 - 1, and so forth. The maximum value I can have in this example is 10 (20 - 10). The locate statement in line 90 positions the cursor at 20,5 on the first cycle of the loop. This is the bottom position in the first bar. During the next cycle, the write position will be 19,5, and so on to 10,5. The second statement in line 90 orders the machine to print ASCII characters at the various positions. Four ASCII characters are added together to obtain a larger bar width. You could use only one character, but the width of the bar would then be one-fourth of the one obtained when using the program as written. Since this graph displays only three values, you can get away with greater bar widths. If we were to display forty or more values, the width would have to be cut down considerably to avoid running out of page space. Figure 5-4 shows the screen display of a vertical bar graph.

The process just described takes place for the input values of B and C in lines 110 and 150, respectively. This program also provides base and reference lines, which are set up in lines 190 through 240. Line 190 begins the action

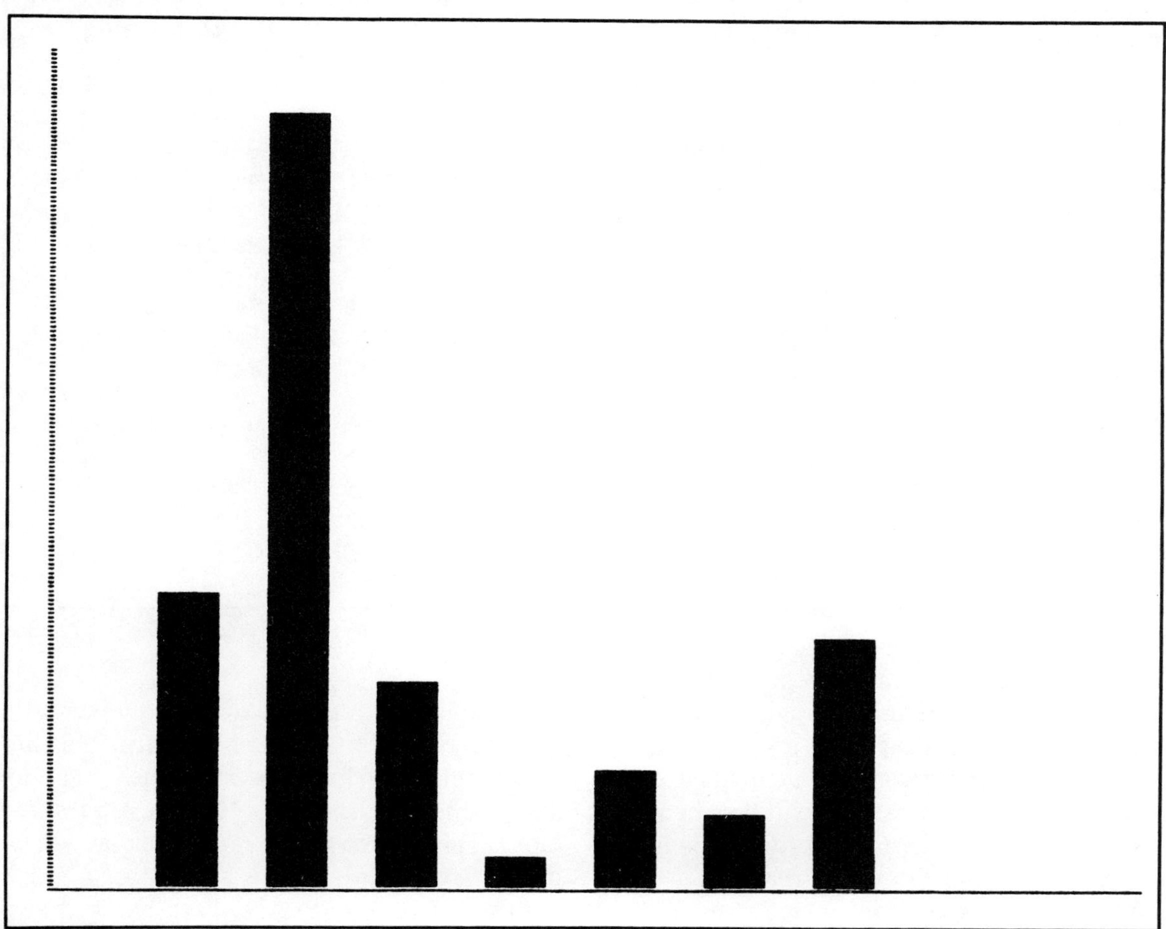

Fig. 5-4. An example of a vertical bar graph.

which causes the solid line to be drawn across the bottom of the screen. This is composed of ASCII character 223. Lines 220 through 240 cause a vertical line to be drawn at the left-hand side of the screen from position 1,1 to 20,1. More sophisticated programs will allow coordinate markings to be displayed on these lines and key values to be input at the beginning of the program run.

COLOR/GRAPHICS IN THE TEXT MODE

Most of our discussions regarding text mode graphics programming have been centered around the IBM monochrome display and its adapter board. However, some persons elect to forego this combination and simply purchase the color/graphics board and use a color television receiver as their single monitoring source. This is more in line with the graphics mode, but text statements and commands work just as well, and you have the advantage of being able to use color statements to produce all fifteen visible colors on the receiver. Text mode programming, then, may be thought of as programming which does not use the special color/graphics statements such as circle, pset, put, get, etc. Figure 5-5 shows a program that will allow the input of up to fifteen different values, each of which will be represented on a graph in a different color. Line 10 sets the mode of operation. It indicates the text mode with color. This same program may be used with the IBM monochrome display, but of course, the color statement will not mean the same thing. Therefore, this program is useful only when a color television receiver or RGB color monitor is used in conjunction with the color/graphics adapter board.

```
10 SCREEN 0,1,0,0
20 Y=1
30 WIDTH 40
40 INPUT"MAXIMUM SCALE VALE:
   ";V
50 CLS
60 LOCATE 1,1:INPUT "VALUE"
   ;N
70 N=N*(20/V)
80 FOR A=0 TO N
90 COLOR Y,0:LOCATE 22-A,7+Z
100 PRINT CHR$(219)
110 NEXT
120 Y=Y+1
130 Z=Z+2
140 FOR B=1 TO 21
150 LOCATE B,1
160 PRINT CHR$(219)
170 NEXT
180 FOR C=1 TO 40
190 LOCATE 22,C
200 PRINT CHR$(219)
210 NEXT
220 IF Y=16 THEN 240
230 GOTO 60
240 FOR E=1 TO 10
250 LOCATE 1,E
260 PRINT CHR$(0)
270 NEXT
```

Fig. 5-5. Program to print a color graph display in text mode using a color monitor.

This program, unlike those discussed previously, offers a scale set feature. This begins in line 40, where you input the maximum scale value. It can be 1, 10, 100, or even 1000 or more. This is a the maximum value that will be used for bar length. This is a vertical bar graph with up to fifteen vertical bars being drawn from the bottom to near the top of the screen.

Once the maximum scale value has been input, the screen is cleared and another prompt asks you to input the value of the first bar. This is assigned to the variable N. Line 70 allows this value to assume a proportional length in relation to the maximum scale value. This latter has been assigned to the variable V. Let's assume that you chose a maximum scale value of 100. Line 70 takes this into account and divides it into 20, which is the number of usable lines available on the screen using this program. In this case, the value you input for the first bar will be multiplied by one-fifth (20/100). If the bar value is 50, then N will equal 10, which is exactly half of the scale height. The value of 50 is also exactly half of the maximum scale value of 100. This program manipulates the input values for the bars but keeps all of them in proportion to the maximum scale value.

A for-next statement is used to draw the bars and scale on the screen. This begins in line 80. The variable A is assigned values from 0 to N. Remember that the value of N has been reassigned from its original value in line 70.

The color statement in line 90 assures that the screen will always have a black background. The foreground color is assigned to the variable Y. The next statement on this line takes the value of A and subtracts it from 22 in order to get a bar starting at 21 and ending at 10 (using our example in which the maximum value is 100, and the value entered is 50). The bars start at coordinates 21, 7 and are spaced two horizontal positions from each other. Line 100 causes the screen to display the vertical series of ASCII characters that make up the bar.

For the first bar, Y is assigned a value of 1 (in line 20), and Z has a value of 0, since it is unassigned. After the first bar is printed, however, lines 120 and 130 reassign the values of Y and Z. Two more for-next loops are then established at lines 140 and 180, respectively. These are used to draw the vertical and horizontal coordinate lines. Line 220 tests for the maximum value of Y. Line 230 returns the run to the portion of the program that will allow you to input the value of the second bar. This goes through the same routine as the first, except the color is changed by the reassigned value of Y. Also, the placement of this bar is moved to the right by the portion of the locate statement in line 90 that adds the value of Z (now 2) to 7.

The program repeats itself fifteen times, and then there is a branch to line 240, which is used to print a horizontal string of blanks to erase the value prompt at the top left corner of the screen. This removes all extraneous information and leaves you with only the bar graph displayed on the screen. The bars are displayed in blue, green, red, white, gray, yellow, and various other shades. Each color is distinctly different from the others and provides excellent definition of the various bars. As presented here, this shows the relative size of the various values that are input. It will be a simple matter, however, to mark each bar with an alphabetic designation by adding a print statement in the for-next loop contained in lines 80 through 110. Also, the vertical scale could be printed with numerical designations of from 0 to the maximum scale value by similar incorporation in the for-next loop, which begins in line 140. I think you will find this to be a very useful graph because at its use of color and its use of basic text mode programming in conjunction with the color/graphics adapter board and a color television receiver or RGB monitor.

GENERAL TEXT MODE PROGRAMS

Using text mode graphics and even text mode graphics animation, it is possible to program many different effects despite the limited graphics capability of this mode. I have been successful in programming several interesting action games that were run on the IBM monochrome display, and while they don't offer the quality of true graphics games, they are enjoyable. Any type of game program usually starts with a playing board or a structured background that establishes the scene upon which all action is to take place.

When programming automobile race games, you have the option of simply allowing two or more vehicles to travel across a blank screen, but you can also place a highway setting in the background with the program shown in Fig. 5-6. This causes the screen to display a two-lane highway with staggered line markings down the center. Program lines 20 through 70 draw the outside edges of the highway, while lines 80 through 110 draw the center markings. This can add realism to many racing games. The display is shown in Fig. 5-7.

A program in a later chapter allows you to draw a pine tree using statements that are executable only in true graphics mode. However, a simulated pine tree can also be produced in text mode, and it looks quite pleasing. Trees can add flavor to any graphics scene and can even serve as obstacles for graphic cars to run into. Figure 5-8 shows a simple program that will draw a sizeable tree on the screen. You can shrink it in size, however, by stringing together smaller numbers of ASCII characters. For-next loops are used to establish coordinates for the various parts of the tree, which is shown in Fig. 5-9. As you can see, the graphic image looks very much like a Christmas tree, albeit simply drawn. This is about all we can hope for when programming text mode

```
10  REM HIGHWAY
20  FOR X=1 TO 79
30  LOCATE 4, X
40  PRINT CHR$(219)
50  LOCATE 20, X
60  PRINT CHR$(219)
70  NEXT X
80  FOR Y=1 TO 79 STEP 8
90  LOCATE 12,Y
100  PRINT CHR$(223)+CHR$(223)+CHR$(223)+CHR$(223)
110  NEXT Y
```

Fig. 5-6. Program to generate a highway scene in text mode.

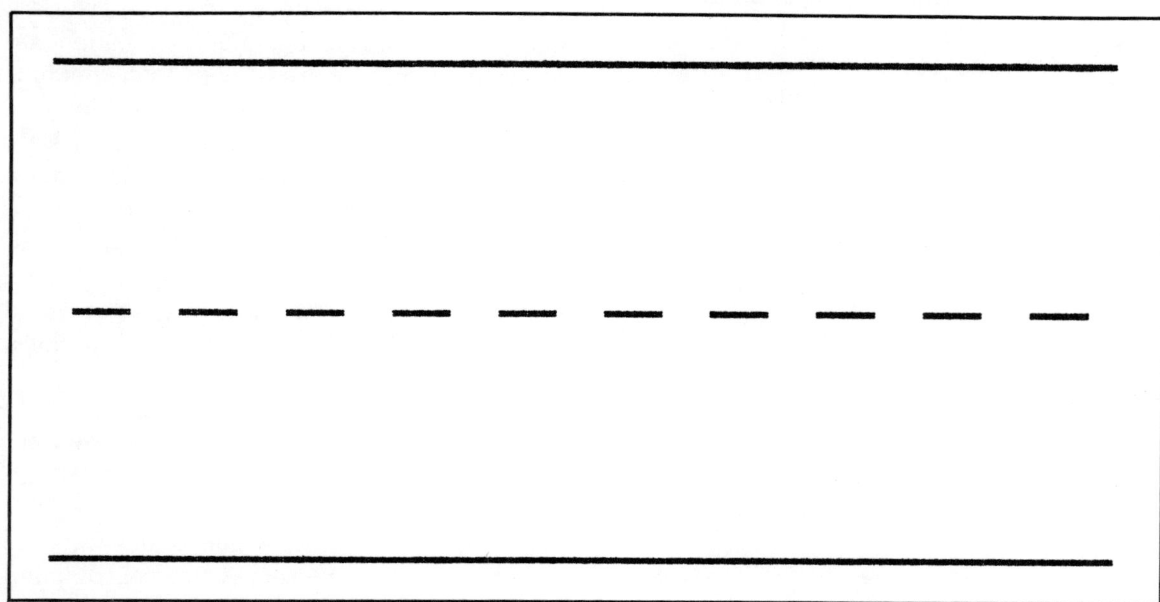

Fig. 5-7. Screen print of previous program run.

graphics. Some of the fine detail that is available in true graphics programming is just not possible in this restricted mode. The pine tree that is drawn using true graphics operation in a later chapter can be painted to simulate branches and a trunk. Of course, this program generates the object in green or white when using the IBM monochrome display. This text mode graphics tree program was extracted from a program entitled Bear Hunt. This was an action graphics game in text mode, and several trees were used to simulate a rural forest scene. Once you get the hang of it, text mode graphics are quite easy to produce, and a little programming can add tremendously to the effect of computer games.

I'm quite proud of this next program, although there's nothing especially complex about it. You may think of it as computer-controlled action graphics, in that there is apparent on-screen movement that is controlled by the computer rather than the real-time user. Shown in Fig. 5-10, this program draws a filter cigarette on the screen and causes smoke to rise from the end which contains the simulated graphic ashes. Lines 10 through 130 draw the cigarette by stringing ASCII characters 219 and 221 together. Lines 140 through 260 create the smoke effect. These are really parentheses, which are printed between the ash and the top of the screen. Immediately after each one is displayed, it is erased with a CHR$(0) statement before the next is written. When the for-next loop which is started in line 140, is completed, the GOTO statement in line 270 causes a branch back to the beginning of the smoke-generating routine. The program is thus on an endless loop, and the smoke will

```
10 REM TREE
20 CLS
30 KEY OFF
40 WIDTH 80
50 FOR A=6 TO 16
60 B=22-A
70 C=A+29
80 D=C+10
90 LOCATE A,D
100 PRINT CHR$(219)
110 LOCATE B,C
120 PRINT CHR$(219)
130 NEXT A
140 FOR E=35 TO 55
150 LOCATE 16,E
160 PRINT CHR$(222)
170 NEXT E
180 FOR F=17 TO 20
190 LOCATE F,45
200 PRINT CHR$(219)+CHR$
    (219)
210 NEXT F
220 FOR G=1 TO 79
230 LOCATE 21,G
240 PRINT CHR$(219)
250 NEXT G
```

Fig. 5-8. Graphics program which draws a pine tree.

continue to rise until execution is halted manually. You can use color statements if this program is to be run on a television receiver or other color monitor. These statements can color the filter a yellowish-brown, while the rest of the cigarette remains white. The smoke can be colored brown as well for a more natural effect. Creating this same graphic image using true graphics programming would be quite simple regarding the cigarette only, but generating the smoke effect would require approximately the same number of program lines. Occasionally, text mode animation can be handled even more simply than graphics animation, although the latter generally provides a more natural movement effect. Also, using true graphics language, it would be quite simple to make the cigarette ash advance toward the filter end and even bend down and fall away. This could be done with text mode graphics as well, but the difficulty factor would be substantially increased. Figure 5-11 shows the image.

The program in Fig. 5-12 generates a vase or a hanging lantern using text mode programming. This is simply a series of CHR$(219) characters strung together over and over again. As the progression gets under way, the length of the lines increases to a central point and then begins to taper off again. This results in an irregular hexagon or a Japanese lantern, if you use your imagination. The program is quite simple, but it took more than a little thought to work out. At first, I had difficulty getting the taper effect I needed. The top to bottom increase in line length is determined by the value of R in line 30. During the first half of the for-next loop cycles (established in line 20), R will be equal to the value of A - 2. This means R equals 0 to 7. During the remainder of the for-next cycles, the value of R is changed to 18 minus the value of A. The actual value of R, then, will be from 8 to 0. This is set up in line 40. The values of Y are established in the for-next loop begun in line 50, which uses the value of R to determine the number of cycles. The assigned variables A and Y are then inserted into a locate statement in line 60, and the vase or lantern is generated. This is technically a vase because the object rests on a flat

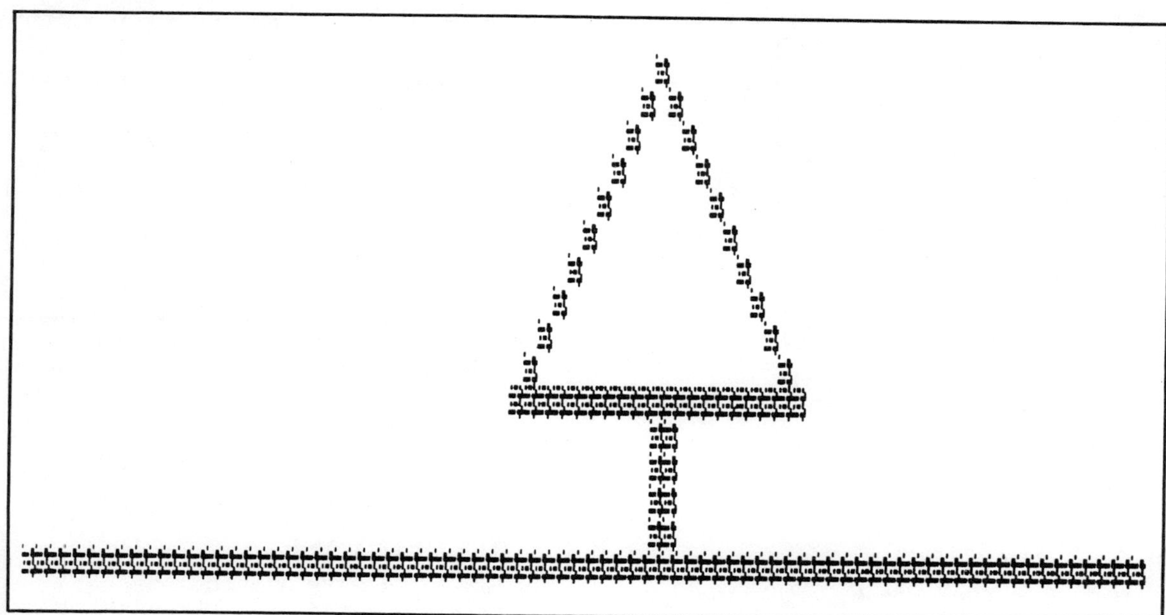

Fig. 5-9. An example of the tree image produced by the previous program.

surface, simulating a table. This surface is generated in lines 100 through 130. If you delete these lines, you can call it a Japanese lantern. Figure 5-13 shows the completed image.

The previous program was used as the basis for developing the one shown in Fig. 5-14. This is used to generate an alien face equipped with square or circular ears (depending on your perception). Such a face could be used in the introductory graphics of a game program involving spaceships and aliens. It's simply the vase with ears, eyes, nose, and mouth added. These were drawn over the filled-in area by inserting CHR$(0) blocks, and of course, the graphic platform the original vase rested on has been removed. Many of the faces generated by text mode graphics are square and robot-like, but the tapered effect is different and quite pleasing, especially when you've been accustomed to looking at all those square heads.

When tinkering with text mode graphic images, I'm continually amazed by what can grow out of a successful program and even more amazed at what can happen when a planned program goes awry. Figure 5-15 shows a program that will generate an excellent graphic image of a table lamp and shade. This image suddenly sprung out at me from the screen when I thought I had successfully programmed the vase image discussed earlier. As you can see from the screen print in Fig. 5-16, the vase program was a dismal failure, but I had successfully written the lamp program. Not one to scoff at fortunate misfortune, I im-

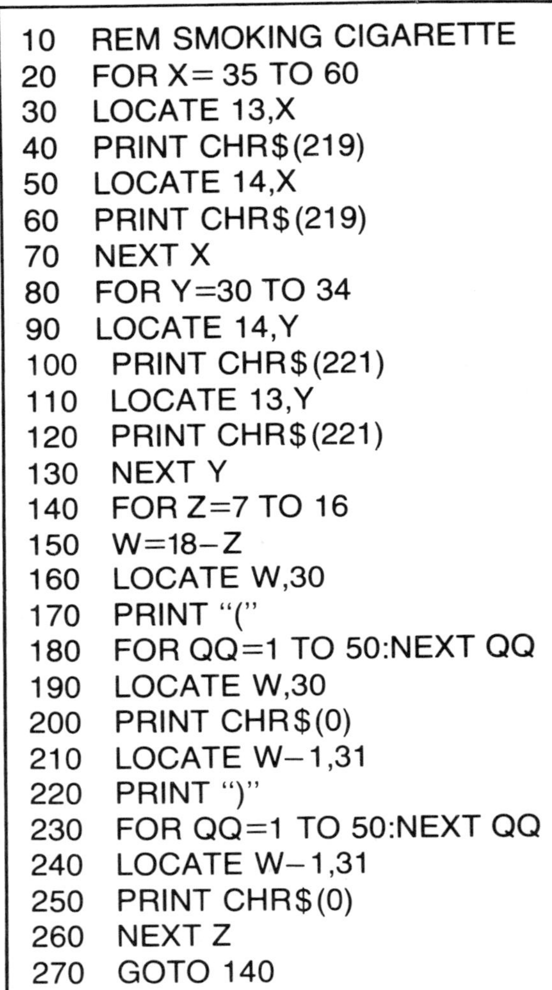

```
10   REM SMOKING CIGARETTE
20   FOR X= 35 TO 60
30   LOCATE 13,X
40   PRINT CHR$(219)
50   LOCATE 14,X
60   PRINT CHR$(219)
70   NEXT X
80   FOR Y=30 TO 34
90   LOCATE 14,Y
100  PRINT CHR$(221)
110  LOCATE 13,Y
120  PRINT CHR$(221)
130  NEXT Y
140  FOR Z=7 TO 16
150  W=18-Z
160  LOCATE W,30
170  PRINT "("
180  FOR QQ=1 TO 50:NEXT QQ
190  LOCATE W,30
200  PRINT CHR$(0)
210  LOCATE W-1,31
220  PRINT ")"
230  FOR QQ=1 TO 50:NEXT QQ
240  LOCATE W-1,31
250  PRINT CHR$(0)
260  NEXT Z
270  GOTO 140
```

Fig. 5-10. A program which will display a smoking cigarette on the IBM monochrome monitor.

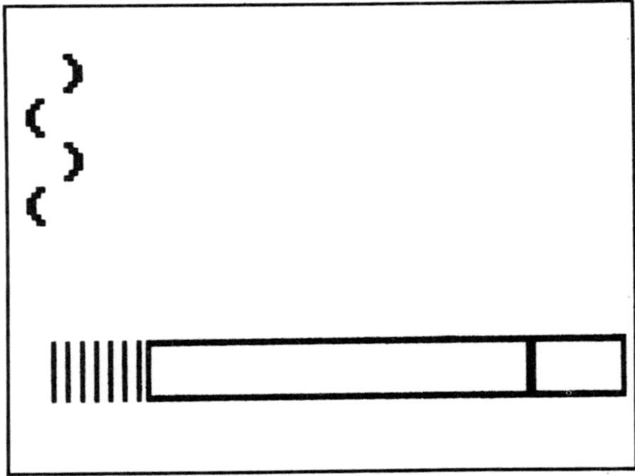

Fig. 5-11. Hard copy printout of the cigarette program run.

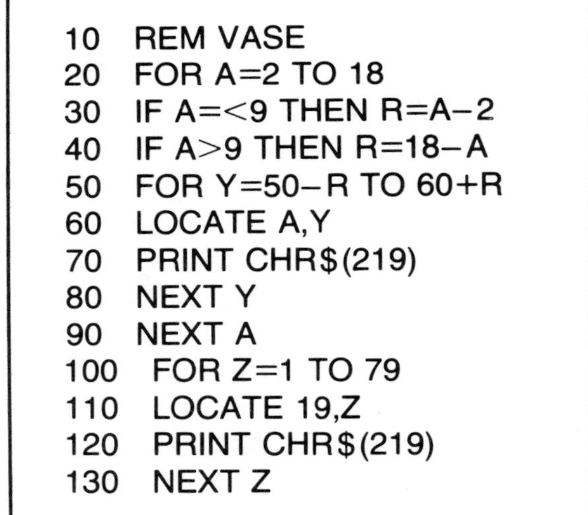

```
10   REM VASE
20   FOR A=2 TO 18
30   IF A=<9 THEN R=A-2
40   IF A>9 THEN R=18-A
50   FOR Y=50-R TO 60+R
60   LOCATE A,Y
70   PRINT CHR$(219)
80   NEXT Y
90   NEXT A
100  FOR Z=1 TO 79
110  LOCATE 19,Z
120  PRINT CHR$(219)
130  NEXT Z
```

Fig. 5-12. Program to write a graphic vase.

mediately committed the table lamp to disk and have used it several times in different graphics programs. The lamp image was generated because although I had successfully programmed the top taper for a vase, I messed up in the lines to provide the bottom taper. As soon as I had accidentally arrived at the table lamp, I added program lines 100 to 130 to draw a table for it to rest on. All in all, I ended up with a program that produced an image which was, I think,

Fig. 5-13. Result of the vase program run.

```
10  REM FACE
20  FOR A=2 TO 18
30  IF A=<9 THEN R=A-2
40  IF A>9 THEN R=18-A
50  FOR Y=50-R TO 60+R
60  LOCATE A,Y
70  PRINT CHR$ (219)
80  NEXT Y
90  NEXT A
100  LOCATE 8,50
110  PRINT CHR$(0)+CHR$(0)
120  LOCATE 8,59
130  PRINT CHR$(0)+CHR$(0)
140  LOCATE 11,54
150  PRINT CHR$(0)+CHR$(0)+
       CHR$(0)
160  FOR Z=51 TO 59
170  LOCATE 14,Z
180  PRINT CHR$(0)
190  NEXT Z
```

Fig. 5-14. Program to create an alien face.

```
10  REM LAMP
20  FOR A=3 TO 22
30  IF A=<13 THEN R=A-2
40  IF A>13 THEN R=7-A
50  FOR Y=20-R TO 60+R
60  LOCATE A,Y
70  PRINT CHR$(219)
80  NEXT Y
90  NEXT A
100  FOR W=1 TO 79
110  LOCATE 22,W
120  PRINT CHR$(221)
130  NEXT W
```

Fig. 5-15. Table lamp program.

even more interesting than the vase. To take this one step further in order to arrive at a base, I reversed a few variable assignments and ran the program again. The modified version is shown in Fig. 5-17, but again, I had failed to produce the sought-after vase. Instead, I had an upside down lamp which looked for all the world like an old-fashioned lemon squeezer. This image is shown in Fig. 5-18. It

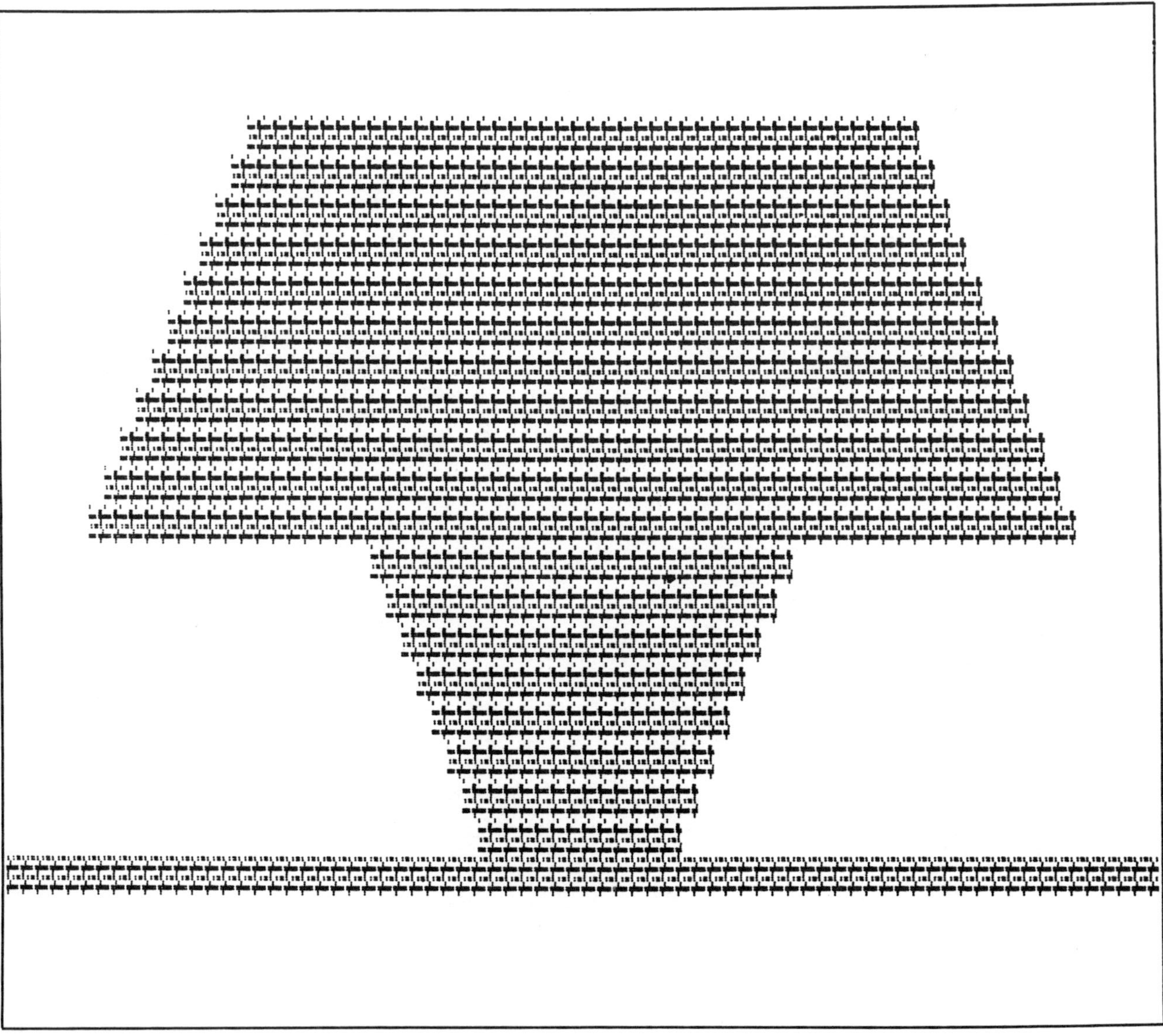

Fig. 5-16. An example of the image created by the previous program.

```
10  LEMON SQUEEZER
20  FOR A=1 TO 12
30  IF A=<6 THEN R=A-2
40  IF A>6 THEN R=22-A
50  FOR Y=50-R TO 60+R
60  LOCATE A,Y
70  PRINT CHR$(219)
80  NEXT Y
90  NEXT A
```

Fig. 5-17. Lemon squeezer program.

can be raised to the top of the screen and used as a helmet for the alien face discussed earlier. If it were tilted 90 degrees, it might even look like a ray gun. Again, the vase program was arrived at after a lot of trial and error, but the products from these errors were certainly useful, and the whole experience turned out to be quite productive.

To new programmers, these accidental programs might seem like a fairly rare occurrence, but as you become heavily involved in graphics, you will probably discover almost as much through accidents such as these as you

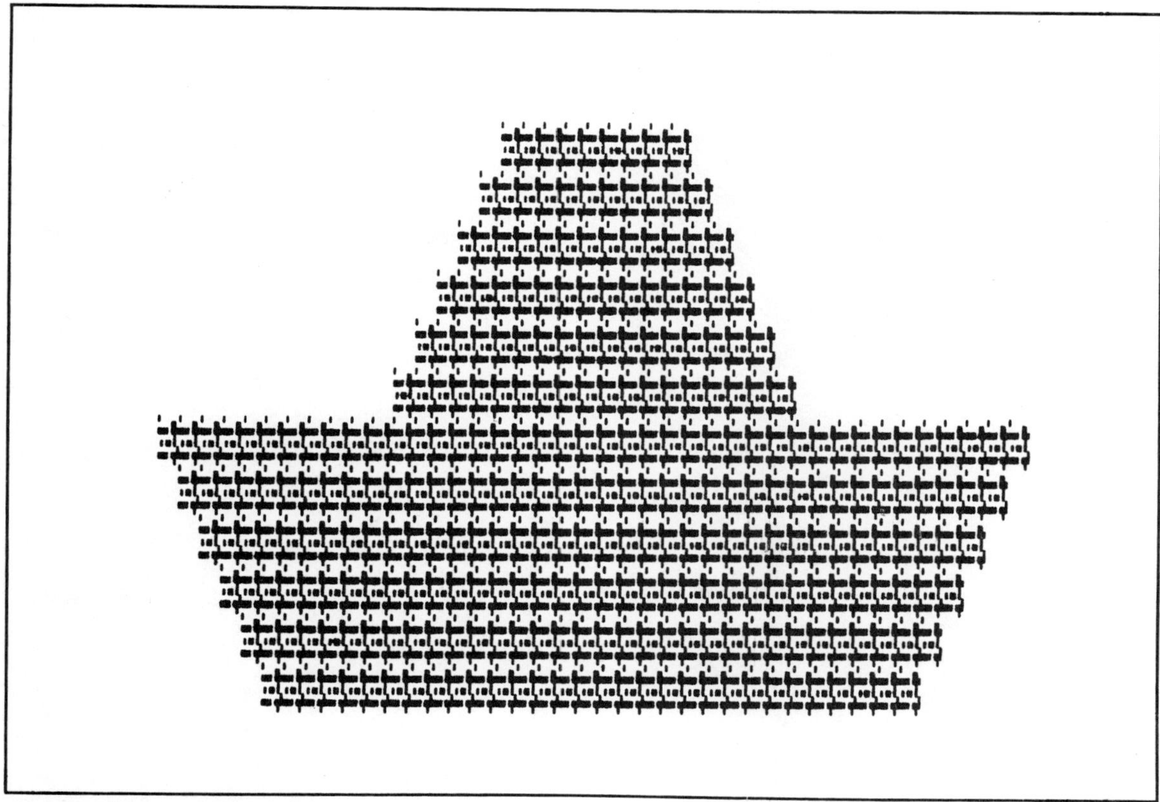

Fig. 5-18. Graphic lemon squeezer.

will through your successes. This points to the fact that learning graphics programming in either text or true graphics mode is partly a matter of inputting "something" and then noting the results. At this juncture, if I ever want to program another vase, I'll know exactly how to go about it. But due to the accidents, I will also know exactly how to program a table lamp, alien face, lemon squeezer, alien hat, or even a ray gun.

Chapter 6

High-Resolution Color/Graphics

In this chapter, we are at the point where many otherwise excellent programmers tend to become a bit paranoid. Text mode graphics are often less frightening because the programs used to write them are very similar to text programs. In most instances, we are just substituting ASCII block characters or letters. Everything else remains pretty much the same. However, when we hit high-resolution graphics, we also encounter some new statements, and apparently, a new way of doing things that seems to be quite different from text mode operations.

This is true in one way and false in another. High-resolution graphics are programmed in a manner similar to the way text mode graphics are programmed, but there are many more screen coordinates to deal with . In the text mode, we're talking about an 80 × 25 coordinate format, whereas in graphics mode, coordinates are specified in 320 or 640 × 200 points or positions. But let's simplify things a bit by saying that the special statements used in graphics programming overcome any added complexities which may be encountered due to the higher-resolution coordinate format. The upper left-hand corner of the screen in graphics mode is specified by the coordinates 0,0 as opposed to 1,1 in text mode. The lower right-hand corner is at 320,200 in medium-resolution graphics mode and 640,200 in high-resolution graphics mode. Actually, we do not use the last points, so from a practical standpoint, the positions are 319,199 and 639,199.

In graphics mode, we have the capability of writing more points on the screen than we do in text mode, and this is where our higher-resolution comes into play. IBM BASIC makes it very easy for us to draw circles, lines, and fairly complex objects, which are more true to life than is possible in text mode. For example, if we wish to draw a line from the left-hand side of the screen to the middle in text mode, the following program might be used:

```
10  FOR X = 1 TO 40
20  LOCATE 1,X
30  PRINT CHR$(219)
40  NEXT
```

This program connects a series of block characters, starting at the left-hand corner of the screen and traveling in a straight line to the top center of the screen. You will note that four separate statements are needed in text mode to accomplish this. However, in graphics mode, we can accomplish the same thing with only one line.

```
10  LINE(0,0)-(160,0)
```

Actually, it would also be necessary to include one line previous to this one which would set the screen to medium-resolution. **SCREEN 1** will accomplish this.

What line 10 tells the computer to do is to print a series of points from the 0,0 position to the 160,0 position. The result will be a continuous line. Using other statements in conjunction with numerical designators following the information in line 10, you can even draw the line in a certain color.

Now, if you want to draw a box from the left-hand side of the screen to the center, one line is still all that's required. It might read:

```
10  LINE(0,0)-(160,20),,B
```

This will draw a hollow box whose top line spans the coordinates 0,0 – 160,0 and whose bottom line is at 0,20 – 160,20. If you want to fill in the box, you simply type the letter "F" after the "B". To do this in text mode would require adding ASCII characters together and many more program lines.

One of the nicest things about the IBM Personal Computer and its language lies in the fact that there are many different ways to accomplish the same on-screen graphics. In many instances, programs written using the PSET statement may be accomplished more easily by using the line statement. You might also use the draw statement. Once you become more familiar with graphics programming on the IBM Personal Computer, you will undoubtedly mix these statements to form program combinations that accomplish what you're after with a minimum of keyboard input time.

Figure 6-1 shows a simple corridor scene. Each of the lines which make up this drawing are indicated with a letter. The program in Fig. 6-2 will draw this scene using 25 program lines. Line 10 sets the screen to the medium-resolution mode. The for-next loop in lines 20 through 70 establishes the length of vertical lines A, B, C, and D. The top of line A is at screen coordinate 20,50. The bottom is at 20,125. In each case, the second value of this coordinate structure is equal to the value of A. Starting in line 30, the PSET statement is used to draw the vertical lines. Each time the for-next loop cycles, another point is drawn on the screen. The first numbers in the PSET statement identify the horizontal position on the screen at which the point is to be written.

In line 80, another for-next loop is used to draw vertical lines E and F. This is handled in

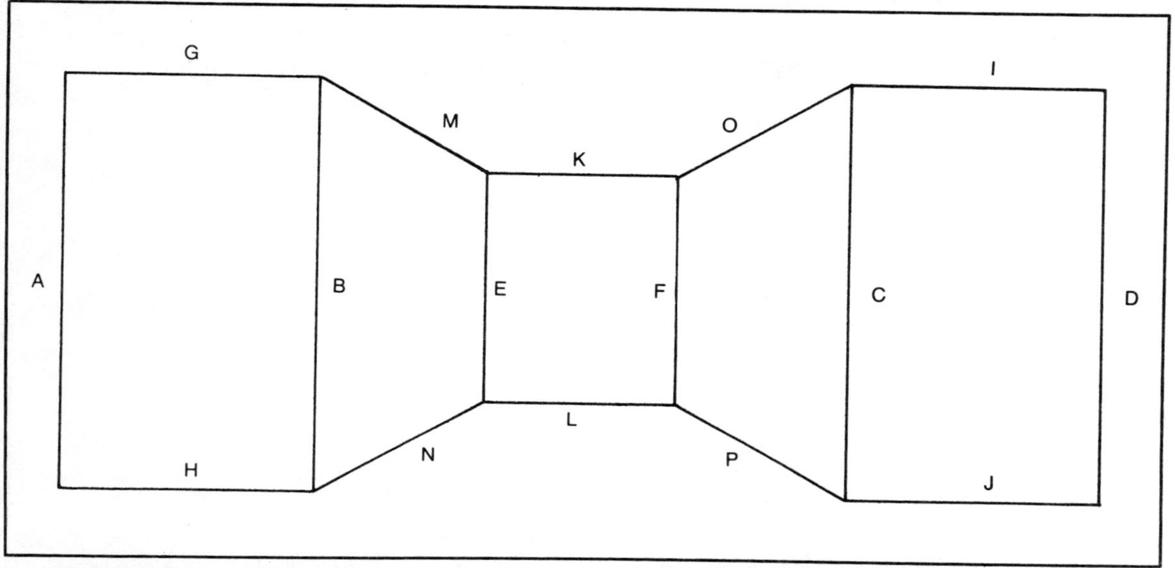

Fig. 6-1. A labeled corridor scene which may be reproduced graphically on the IBM Personal Computer.

the same manner as before, except with different coordinates. The for-next loop that begins at line 120 and ends at line 170 draws lines G, H, I, and J. The next four program lines draw graphic lines K and L.

The diagonal connecting lines are drawn by the last portion of the program. This is a bit more difficult than the preceding part. In this for-next loop, another variable, Y, has been entered, and it is assigned an ever-decreasing negative value. This changes the point-setting operation by adding or subtracting this value from the second coordinate designation. Line 230 in the program draws graphic line M, while program lines 240 through 260 draw N, O, and P, respectively.

The program shown in Fig. 6-3 draws the same corridor scene and is almost identical to the previous program, except that the diagonal graphic lines are drawn in a different and much simpler fashion. Basic line statements are used to connect the tops and bottoms of the various rectangular figures to form the corridor scene. Program line 220 draws line M, which begins at coordinates 60,50 (the top of B) and ends at 120,70 (the top of E). This process is repeated in the remaining program lines for the different coordinates. Using the line statements, only four lines are necessary to do what took seven lines in the previous program. Therefore, keyboard input time has been decreased. Figure 6-4 shows a screen print of the corridor scene.

Taking this one step further, we arrive at the best program for accomplishing the corridor program, which is shown in Fig. 6-5. This program consists of only eight lines, as compared to 28 lines in Fig. 6-2 and 25 in Fig. 6-3. Here, line statements are used with the box designator (B) to draw four graphics lines with

```
10 SCREEN 1
20 FOR A=50 TO 125
30 PSET(20,A)
40 PSET(60,A)
50 PSET(230,A)
60 PSET(270,A)
70 NEXT
80 FOR B=70 TO 105
90 PSET(120,B)
100 PSET(170,B)
110 NEXT
120 FOR C=19 TO 62
130 PSET(C,50)
140 PSET(C,125)
150 PSET(C+210,50)
160 PSET(C+210,125)
170 NEXT
180 FOR D=120 TO 170
190 PSET(D,70)
200 PSET(D,105)
210 NEXT
220 FOR X=60 TO 120
230 PSET(X,50-Y)
240 PSET(110+X,70+Y)
250 PSET(X,125+Y)
260 PSET(105+X,105-Y)
270 Y=Y-.35
280 NEXT
```

Fig. 6-2. *Corridor Scene* program.

```
10 SCREEN 1
20 FOR A=50 TO 125
30 PSET(20,A)
40 PSET(60,A)
50 PSET(230,A)
60 PSET(270,A)
70 NEXT
80 FOR B=70 TO 105
90 PSET(120,B)
100 PSET(170,B)
110 NEXT
120 FOR C=19 TO 62
130 PSET(C,50)
140 PSET(C,125)
150 PSET(C+210,50)
160 PSET(C+210,125)
170 NEXT
180 FOR D=120 TO 170
190 PSET(D,70)
200 PSET(D,105)
210 NEXT
220 LINE(60,50)-(120,70)
230 LINE(60,125)-(120,105)
240 LINE(170,70)-(230,50)
250 LINE(170,105)-(230,125)
```

Fig. 6-3. Modified version of the previous corridor program.

each single program line. Line 20 draws graphic lines A, B, G, and H. Line 30 handles graphic lines, E, F, K, and L; while line 40 draws C, D, I, and J. The remaining program lines are identical to those in the program shown in Fig. 6-3 and complete the graphic picture by drawing lines N, M, O, and P.

All three of these programs accomplish exactly the same on-screen graphic representation. It is obvious, however, that the last program is the best one to go with, simply because it takes far less time. Here, we've been able to cut the program lines to one-fourth of what was required using the first program. This should mean an approximately equivalent decrease in programming time. In previous programs, at least one statement was required for every line that was drawn on the

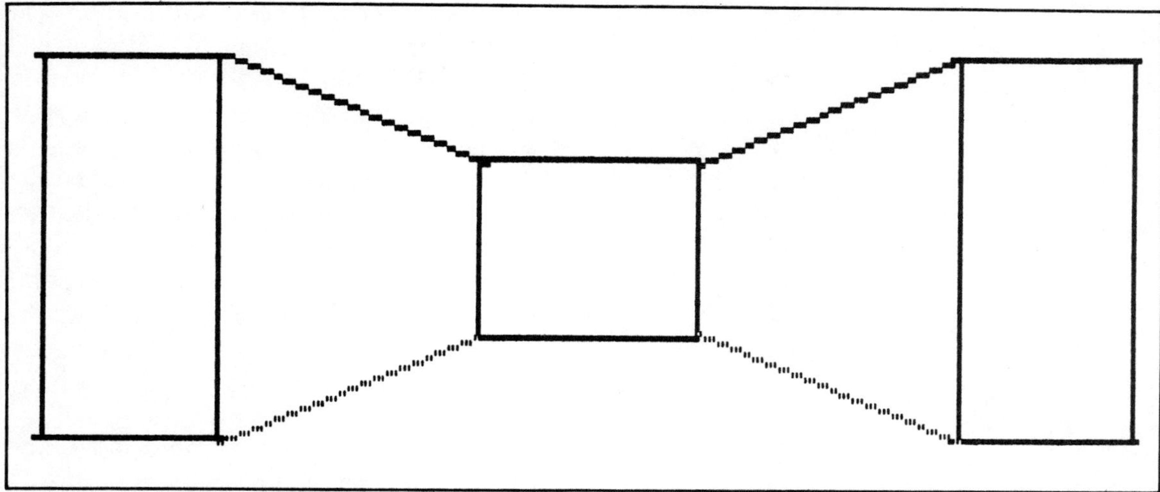

Fig. 6-4. Screen print of the completed corridor scene.

screen. With this last one, we were able to do far better by drawing whole rectangles or squares with a single statement. This is not to say that the PSET statement should not be used. The latter is a highly versatile statement. I mean only that there are many instances where one statement can be used to better advantage than another. Different situations dictate different statements or methods of drawing on-screen graphics, so you must become familiar with the different ways of

```
10 SCREEN 1
20 LINE(20,50)-(60,125),,B
30 LINE(120,70)-(170,105),,B
40 LINE(230,50)-(270,125),,B
50 LINE(60,50)-(120,70)
60 LINE(60,125)-(120,105)
70 LINE(170,70)-(230,50)
80 LINE(170,105)-(230,125)
```

Fig. 6-5. The final version of the corridor program is the simplest yet.

programming graphics before you can find the most efficient tactics to accomplish a particular assignment.

Let's return to an earlier subject, that of drawing on-screen graphs. The program shown in Fig. 6-6 will allow you to input up to six different values and have them displayed as a bar graph on the screen. This bar graph is presented in the vertical mode, with bars running from the bottom of the screen to the top. Once the values have been entered, line 110 establishes the width of each bar at 20 screen points. Again, for-next loops are used to draw each line, but instead of using PSET statement or line statements, the draw statement is brought into play. PSET statements are used in each for-next loop to establish a starting point for each bar. The input value is inserted in the for-next loop to establish maximum value (FOR A = 1 TO N, for example). For the sake of discussion, let's assume that you entered a value of 100 at line 40. Variable N

```
10 CLS
20 KEY OFF
30 SCREEN 1
40 INPUT"ENTER VALUE";N
50 INPUT"ENTER VALUE";O
60 INPUT"ENTER VALUE";P
70 INPUT"ENTER VALUE";Q
80 INPUT"ENTER VALUE";R
90 INPUT"ENTER VALUE";S
100 CLS
110 I=20
120 FOR A=1 TO N
130 PSET (80,150),1
140 DRAW"U=A;R=I;D=A;L=I;"
150 NEXT A
160 FOR B=1 TO O
170 PSET(110,150),2
180 DRAW"U=B;R=I;D=B;L=I;"
190 NEXT B
200 FOR C=1 TO P
210 PSET(140,150),3
220 DRAW"U=C;R=I;D=C;L=I;"
230 NEXT C
240 FOR D=1 TO Q
250 PSET(170,150),1
260 DRAW"U=D;R=I;D=D;L=I;"
270 NEXT D
280 FOR E=1 TO R
290 PSET(200,150),2
300 DRAW"U=E;R=I;D=E;L=I;"
310 NEXT E
320 FOR F=1 TO S
330 PSET(230,150),3
340 DRAW"U=F;R=I;D=F;L=I;"
350 NEXT F
360 LINE(40,10)-(40,152)
370 LINE (40,152)-(304,152)
```

Fig. 6-6. *Vertical Color Graph* program.

would then be equal to 100, and the for-next loop that starts in program line 120 would count from 1 to 100. The PSET statement in line 130 tells the computer that the starting coordinate for the figure it is about to draw is 80,150. This is followed by a comma and the number 1, which establishes a color for the bar.

Finally, the draw statement is encountered in line 140. This instructs the computer to draw a line on the screen which goes up (U) the value of A starting from the point at coordinates 80,150. During the first cycle of the loop, the first line consisting of one point will be drawn one coordinate position above the starting point. Line will be entered from A to 20 points to the right of A (R = I). Then, another line consisting of one point is drawn down the screen from the upper point established by A. The bar is completed by going 20 points to the left (L = I). Each instruction with the draw statement tells the computer to plot points in the direction indicated starting from the last point drawn on the screen.

This process is repeated until the first bar is completely drawn (and filled in) and repeated again for the next five input values. Program lines 360 and 370 use line statements to display the horizontal and vertical graph axes. Figure 6-7, which follows the color section, shows a screen print of the program run.

CIRCLES

Drawing circles on the display screen is very simple using IBM BASIC. The circle statement is followed by the numerical coordinates that describe where the center of the circle is to appear on the screen.

Text continues after the color section.

Color Section

This book describes graphics operations on the IBM Personal Computer, with a special emphasis on color graphics. Throughout this book, many of the designs and other screen displays have been represented by printouts of what is seen on the screen. However, these are in black and white only and do not give you a good idea of the beautiful colors that can be displayed by this machine. To overcome this limitation (at least partially), this section includes a number of actual color photographs of the screen display. Most of the displays here were produced by many of the programs presented in this book. A few have been generated by other programs that you can produce yourself using the information in this book.

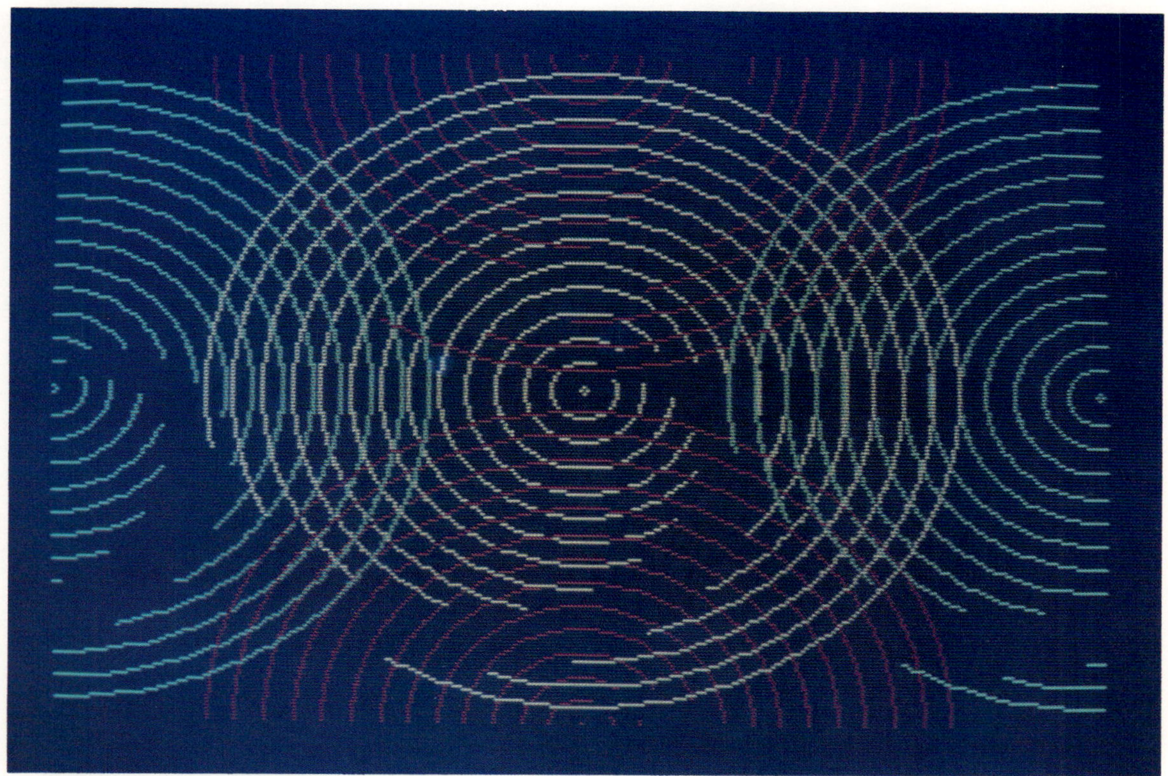

A pattern-generating program using five intermeshed circles.

The solar system showing the sun at its center and the orbits of the nine planets.

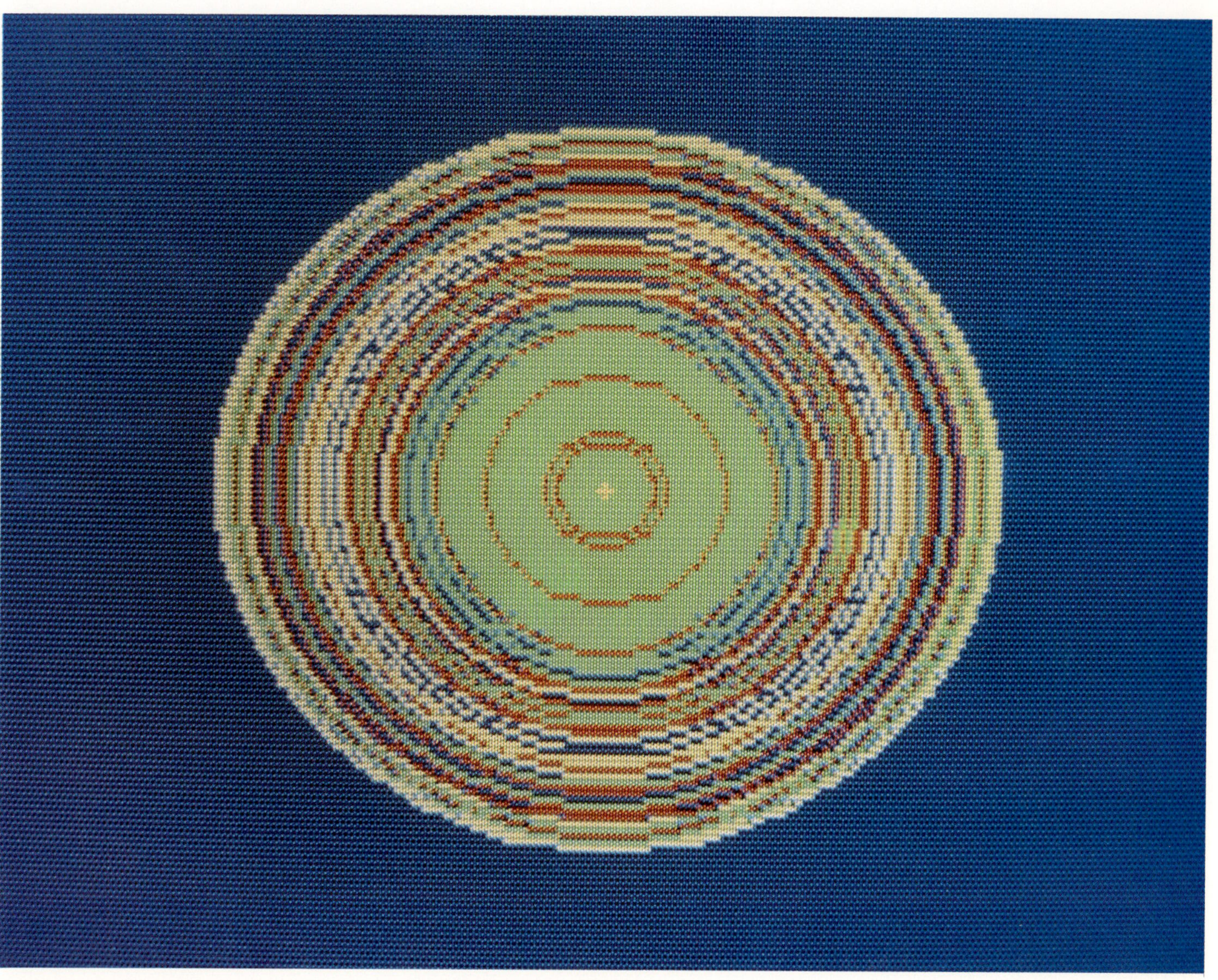

Randomized circle statements may be used to produce spectacular color displays.

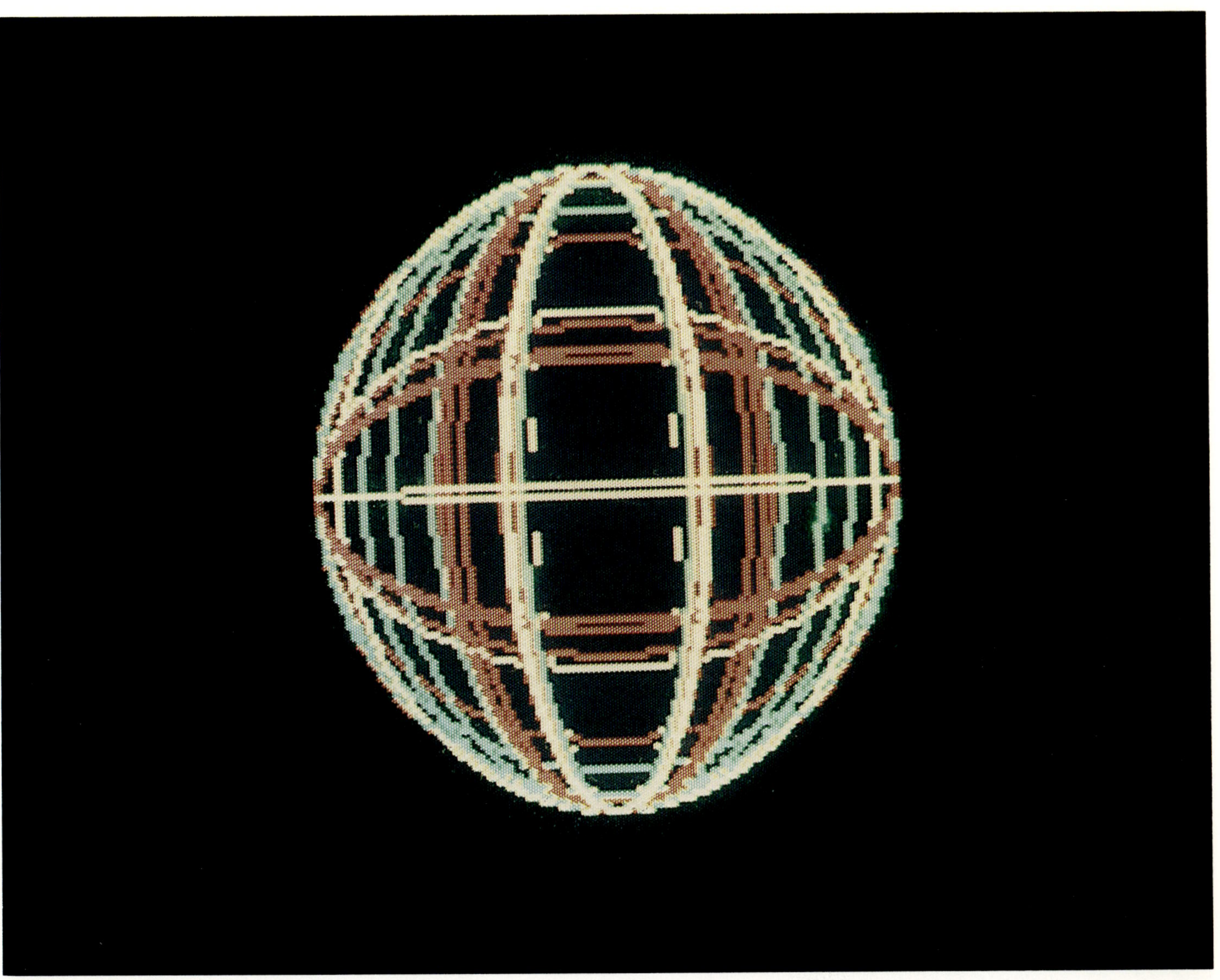

It is possible to achieve a 3-D effect using circle statements.

This display was produced by the *Traveling Circles* program, which uses put and get statements.

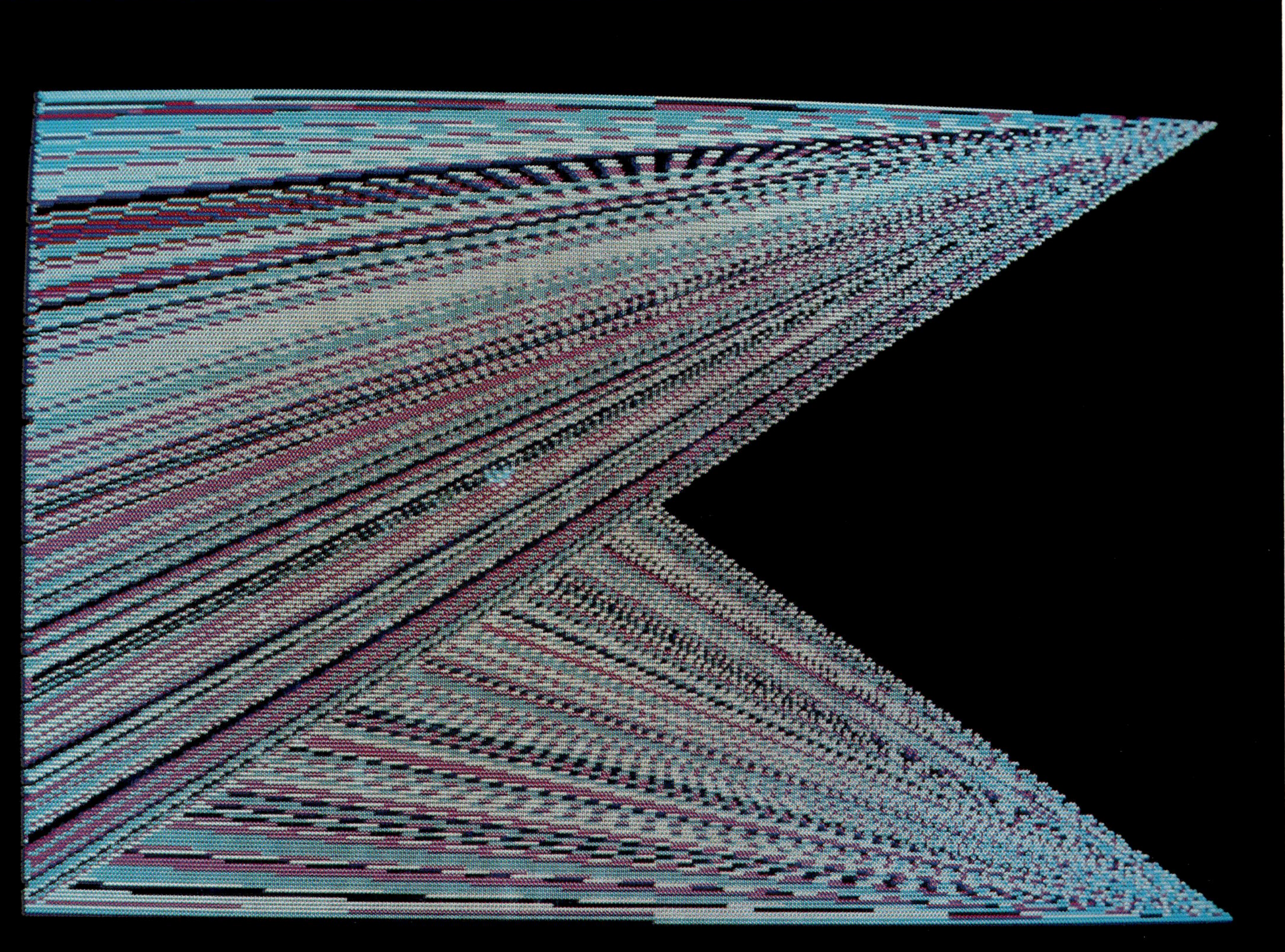

The *Drapes* program uses randomly spaced lines to produce a colorful hanging effect.

This display was produced by the *Modern Art* program, which combines line and circle statements.

It is easy to produce "Star Wars" games using IBM graphics.

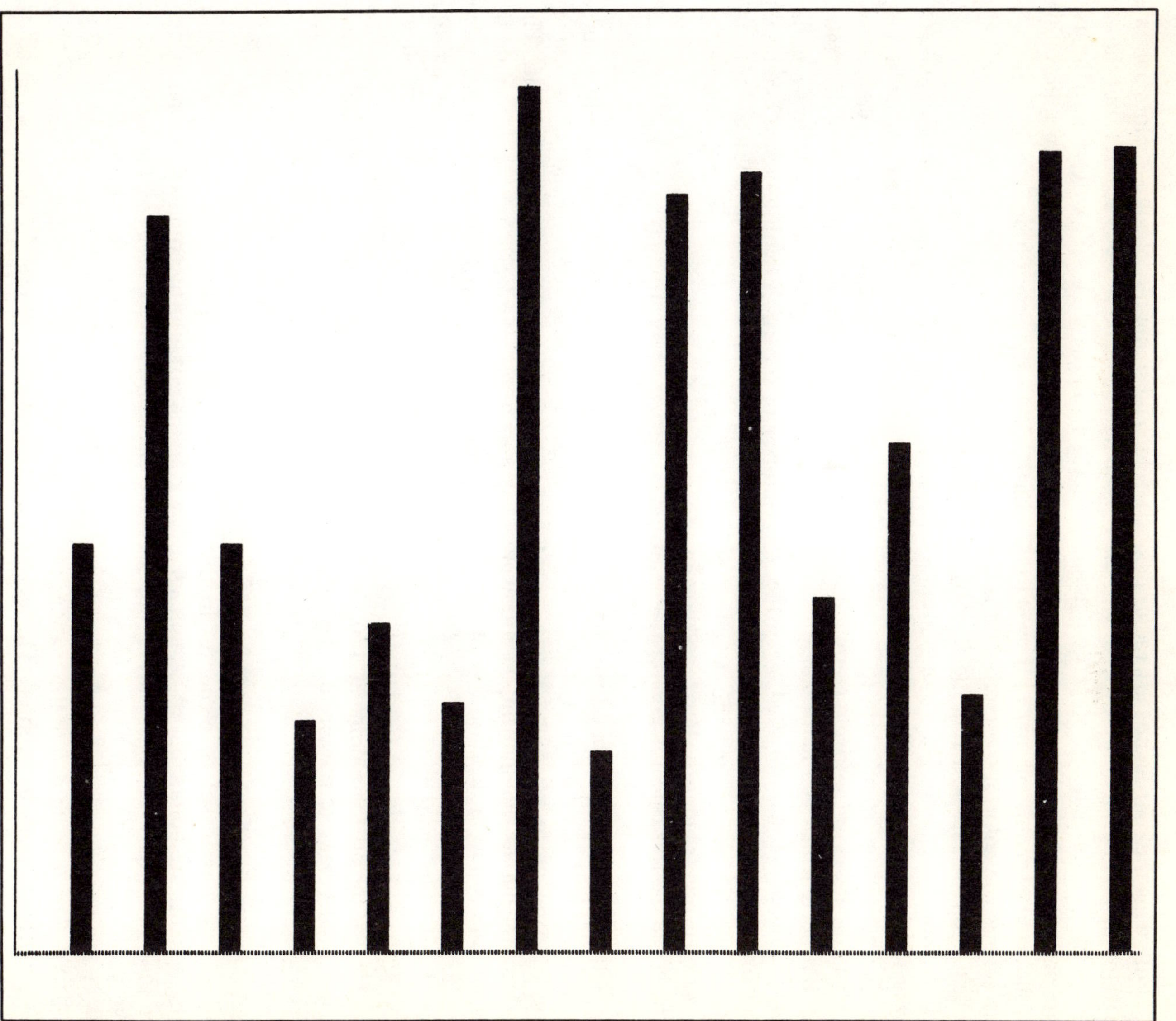

Fig. 6-7. Sample screen print of previous program run.

Following the coordinates is a radius designation, also numeric, and the circle will extend outward this number of screen points from the center. The radius numeral may then be followed by a color number of from 0 to 3. This selects the color of the circle and is dependent upon the palette that is specified by an earlier color statement. The color statement may be followed by a start—end set of designation that may range from −2 pi to +2 pi.

The final part of the circle statement can be the aspect, which is a numeric expression usually handled in fraction form. If the aspect is less than 1, the radius length is measured along on the X axis. This means that the radius can be measured in points along the horizontal portion of the screen. If the aspect is greater than 1, R is measured along the Y radius.

This sounds complex, but it isn't once you get the hang of it. As a matter of fact, you can draw a large, perfectly round circle at the center of the screen by inputting the following program line while in medium resolution:

```
CIRCLE(160,100),60
```

This designates the point at 160,100 to serve as the center of the circle. The radius will be 60 points, which is the distance from the center that the circle's circumference will be drawn. Put more simply, you can imagine a draftman's compass set to 60 units. In this case, the units are points, but you can imagine that they are really inches, centimeters, or whatever. The pointed tip of the compass is placed at the center point of the screen (160,100). The writing end of the compass is placed 60 units from the center. The entire instrument is rotated 360° to draw a perfect circle. The computer, of course, plots points a specified distance from the center, but the effect is about the same. We will get into the use of the other remarks which may follow this basic circle statement a bit later.

PAINTING

In IBM BASIC, the paint statement is used to fill in a specified area on the screen with a particular color. Since we have just discussed the circle statement and actually drawn a circle, we will now show how to *paint* the interior of the circle with a desired color. In order to do this, we must include a color designation with the circle statement, such as:

```
CIRCLE(160,100),60,3
```

The 3 stipulates one of four usable colors, which may be selected from the palette established by an earlier color statement. The number 3 was chosen at random. It could be any number from 0 to 3. This number is used to specify the color only of the points plotted around the center of the circle. It establishes a perimeter for the paint statement.

The paint statement that will follow this circle statement might read:

```
PAINT(160,100),2,3
```

The numerals in parentheses specify a point within the circle. Any point will do, and since the circle branches out 60 points either side of the center, we could as readily get by with the coordinates of 150,90. All that is necessary is to identify one point within the circle. The numeral which follows (2) specifies the color you wish the circle to be painted. The next number must be the same as the color designation that follows the circle statement, as this specifies the color of the boundaries that will enclose the area to be painted. For the sake of discussion, let's assume that a number 2 as the color designator will create the color pink and that number 3 is green. Without the paint statement, the hollow circle will take on a greenish tinge, but with the paint statement specified, the entire circle will be solid and will be colored pink.

Using these two program of lines, the paint statement searches for the area on the screen specified in the coordinates. It begins from this point and paints every portion of the screen pink until it encounters the boundary area specified. In this case, it is the color specified by the number 3. At this point, it stops. Now, if for some reason, you have specified a point outside of the circle, the entire screen will be painted, with the exception of the circle itself, since it is surrounded by limiting boundaries. If you accidentally leave off the color remark from the circle statement or don't properly match this number with the boundary number in the paint statement, the entire screen will be completely colored, and your circle will effectively disappear.

The following program will create a solid pink circle at the center of the screen

```
10  SCREEN 1
20  CIRCLE(160,100),60,3
30  PAINT(160,100),2,3
```

When you run this program, you will see the circle circumference formed first and almost immediately, it will be painted. The first painting trace will start at the exact center of the circle and rise upward, filling in the top half. Immediately after this, the bottom half will be filled in. This process takes place very rapidly, but you can see the actual painting operation as the circle area is filled in.

The paint statement is certainly not limited to circles. It may be used to fill in boxes, triangles, and any other graphic forms that are drawn on the screen. When writing programs that produce animation of an object on the screen. Problems can occur when the moving object is relatively large and must be painted. During the animation process, the object is moved and then painted many times, and due to its large size, a highly noticeable flicker occurs. This is due to the fact that the line drawing of the object is moved first and a half-second or so is required to paint it. This occurs again and again as the object is moved to the different screen positions. However, if the moving object is kept to a small size, the time required to paint it is shortened equivalently and the flicker is not so noticeable.

Figure 6-8 shows a simple program which will draw a circle on the screen and paint it. However, the radius of the circle is determined by a for-next statement that uses the variable X. Here, the radius will be a value from 1 to 100, so the circle starts out very small and increases its radius to a maximum of 100. Notice that the circle and paint statements contain the same starting coordinates (160,100). Each time the for-next loop cycles, the variable X increases in value. It is not necessary to insert this variable in the paint statement, as all this statement requires is a reference to one point within the circle, regardless of its overall size. The effect of this program is an ever-expanding circle, and due

```
10 REM CIRBLST
20 SCREEN 1
30 COLOR 8,2
40 FOR X=1 TO 100
50 CIRCLE(160,100),X,3
60 PAINT (160,100),2,3
70 NEXT
```

Fig. 6-8. *Concentric Circle* program.

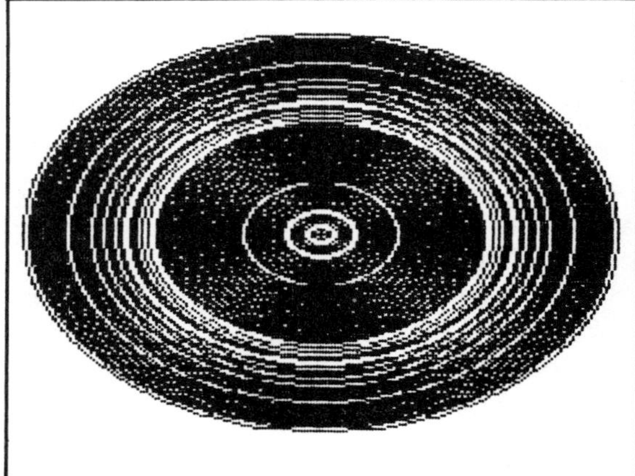

Fig. 6-9. Screen print of image produced by previous program.

to the multitude of radii, the painted interior is finely segmented to form a highly textured pattern. Figure 6-9 shows a screen print of the image.

3-D BOX

Using the IBM Personal Computer's graphics capability, you can write a myriad of geometric figures on the screen. One example of this is a 3-D box, which is generated by the program shown in Fig. 6-10. This program uses line statements to draw the image shown in Fig. 6-11. This is really a rectangle which is

```
10 REM 3-D BOX
20 SCREEN 1
30 LINE(120,80)-(200,80)
40 LINE(120,120)-(200,120)
50 LINE(120,80)-(120,120)
60 LINE(200,80)-(200,120)
70 LINE(160,60)-(240,60)
80 LINE(160,100)-(240,100)
90 LINE(160,60)-(160,100)
100 LINE(240,60)-(240,100)
110 LINE(120,80)-(160,60)
120 LINE(200,80)-(240,60)
130 LINE(120,120)-(160,100)
140 LINE(200,120)-(240,100)
```

Fig. 6-10. *3-D Box* program.

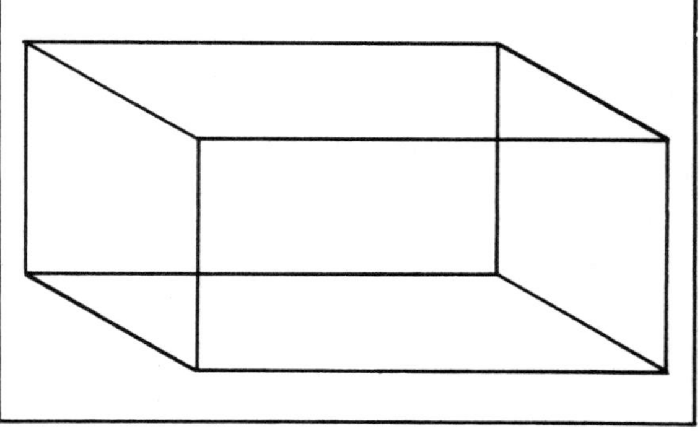

Fig. 6-11. *3-D Box* printout.

composed of twelve different lines. You will notice that the program in Fig. 6-11 contains twelve different line statements. Lines 30 and 40 draw two horizontal lines, and lines 50 and 60 draw the vertical connectors. Lines 70 through 100 draw an identical one-dimensional box on the screen, but this one is to one side of the one drawn earlier. The rest of the program lines form the diagonal connecting legs that

```
10 REM 3-D BOX(B-FORMAT)
20 SCREEN 1
30 LINE(120,80)-(200,120),B
40 LINE(160,60)-(240,100),B
50 LINE(120,80)-(160,60)
60 LINE(240,60)-(200,80)
70 LINE(240,100)-(200,120)
80 LINE(120,120)-(160,100)
```

Fig. 6-12. New version (shortened) of the *3-D box* program.

join the two one-dimensional boxes into a three-dimensional image.

While this program is not particularly complicated, we can cut down on the number of program lines required. This version is shown in Fig. 6-12. This program draws exactly the same image as before, but uses half the line statements. Program lines 30 and 40 follow their line statements with two commas and the letter B. This means that a box is to be formed on the screen and the computer writes this automatically. One program line, then, is used to do what required four in the previous program. Lines 50 through 80 connect the two boxes with diagonal lines to form the three-dimensional simulation.

Figure 6-13 shows another program that draws exactly the same image as the previous two. However, instead of using specific coordinates, an assigned variable has been incorporated. In this case, X is assigned the value of 200 to draw a 3-D figure that is the same size as those drawn by the previous program. All of the previous fixed coordinates are assigned a value that is a multiple of X. If X equals 200, then 0.6 times X is equal to 120. Take line 40, for example: the coordinates of the line statement are .6 times X, .4 times X and X,0.4 times X. Because X = 200, the computer interprets this line into the fixed coordinates of (120,80)–(200,80). If you will look back at the

```
10 REM 3-D BOX (RELATIVE COORDINATES)
20 SCREEN 1
30 X=200
40 LINE(.6*X,.4*X)-(X,.4*X)
50 LINE(.6*X,.6*X)-(X,.6*X)
60 LINE(.6*X,.4*X)-(.6*X,.6*X)
70 LINE(X,.4*X)-(X,.6*X)
80 LINE(.8*X,.3*X)-(1.2*X,.3*X)
90 LINE(.8*X,.5*X)-(1.2*X,.5*X)
100 LINE(.8*X,.3*X)-(.8*X,.5*X)
110 LINE(1.2*X,.3*X)-(1.2*X,.5*X)
120 LINE(.6*X,.4*X)-(.8*X,.3*X)
130 LINE(X,.4*X)-(1.2*X,.3*X)
140 LINE(.6*X,.6*X)-(.8*X,.5*X)
150 LINE(X,.6*X)-(1.2*X,.5*X)
```

Fig. 6-13. Another *3-D box* program using an assigned variable to vary scale size.

program in Fig. 6-10, you will see that it contains the same coordinates as found here, described in a different manner.

Now, anyone can see that this last program is more difficult to arrive at than the first, and since they both draw the same figure, why do it? The reason is simple. If you let X equal 100, and you get a figure which is onehalf the physical size of the first one. All lines will be of the same relative length, but you have the capability of making your geometric image larger or smaller. Figure 6-14 shows the same program with the substitution of for-next statements for a fixed value of X. Here, X will be equal to a value of from 100 to 200 in steps of 20. When the program is run, you will see a box advance from the left top portion of the screen to the center portion. As it advances, it gets larger. This gives the appearance of an approaching geometric figure that gets larger as it seems to get nearer, just as an approaching physical object seems to get larger as it gets closer to the viewer.

You can even use this basic program to draw an intricate design. Figure 6-15 is almost identical to the previous program, with line 170 (the CLS statement) removed. When this program is run, the previously written image is not erased and remains on the screen. You now see a series of boxes that begin at the upper left of the screen and advance past the center. These are all tied together and form one large screen pattern. Figure 6-16 shows the screen print.

You can certainly change the preceding program to draw geometric figures that contain lines of different proportions in relation to each other. You can make perfect square, flat

```
10 REM 3-D BOX(ADVANCING)
20 SCREEN 1
30 FOR X= 100 TO 200 STEP 20
40 LINE(.6*X,.4*X)-(X,.4*X)
50 LINE(.6*X,.6*X)-(X,.6*X)
60 LINE(.6*X,.4*X)-(.6*X,.6*X)
70 LINE(X,.4*X)-(X,.6*X)
80 LINE(.8*X,.3*X)-(1.2*X,.3*X)
90 LINE(.8*X,.5*X)-(1.2*X,.5*X)
100 LINE(.8*X,.3*X)-(.8*X,.5*X)
110 LINE(1.2*X,.3*X)-(1.2*X,.5*X)
120 LINE(.6*X,.4*X)-(.8*X,.3*X)
130 LINE(X,.4*X)-(1.2*X,.3*X)
140 LINE(.6*X,.6*X)-(.8*X,.5*X)
150 LINE(X,.6*X)-(1.2*X,.5*X)
160 FOR C=1 TO 500:NEXT
170 CLS
180 NEXT X
```

Fig. 6-14. Another version of the previous program using for-next statements to arrive at a scale factor value.

```
10 REM 3-D BOX(DESIGN)
20 CLS
30 SCREEN 1
40 FOR X=0 TO 220 STEP 10
50 LINE(.6*X,.4*X)-(X,.4*X)
60 LINE(.6*X,.6*X)-(X,.6*X)
70 LINE(.6*X,.4*X)-(.6*X,.6*X)
80 LINE(X,.4*X)-(X,.6*X)
90 LINE(.8*X,.3*X)-(1.2*X,.3*X)
100 LINE(.8*X,.5*X)-(1.2*X,.5*X)
110 LINE(.8*X,.3*X)-(.8*X,.5*X)
120 LINE(1.2*X,.3*X)-(1.2*X,.5*X)
130 LINE(.6*X,.4*X)-(.8*X,.3*X)
140 LINE(X,.4*X)-(1.2*X,.3*X)
150 LINE(.6*X,.6*X)-(.8*X,.5*X)
160 LINE(X,.6*X)-(1.2*X,.5*X)
170 NEXT
```

Fig. 6-15. *3-D Box Design* program.

rectangles, and even triangles and tetrahedrons, plus any geometric form you can think of. I have found that a good high school plane geometry book is a great help, because it not only shows the various figures, but will often give you relative dimensions and coordinates of the lines that are used to draw them. These can usually be input directly in BASIC using the special graphic statements found in the Advanced version of this language. Incidentally, while these figures are drawn using line statements, you can do the same thing using PSET. However, I find that using the line statement for this type of drawing greatly decreases input time and also cuts down on the confusion element. When a line is drawn with the PSET statement, it is necessary to establish for-next loops within the program, and these add at least two additional program lines to draw each screen line.

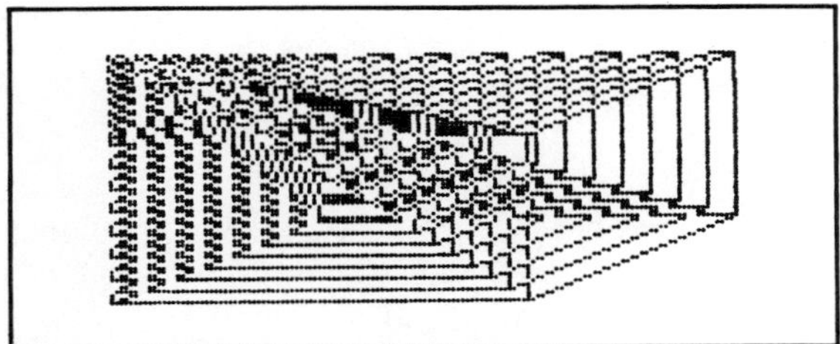

Fig. 6-16. Screen print of a *3-D box.*

A GRAPHIC PICTURE

We have already discussed in detail the various methods of drawing certain images on the screen. By combining these ideas into a single program, whole pictures that consist of lines, circles, and a number of colors may be drawn. A good example of this is shown in Fig. 6-17. This program displays an image of the planet Saturn with four orbiting moons. To arrive at this program, it was necessary to use circle statements, as well as line, PSET, and paint statements. Lines 20 through 40 set up

```
10 REM SATURN SPACE SCENE
20 CLS
30 SCREEN 1,0
40 COLOR 0,1
50 CIRCLE(1,100),100,2,3,2
60 PAINT(1,100),1,2
70 LINE(0,112)-(160,110),3
80 LINE(0,97)-(160,110),3
90 LINE (0,100)-(160,110),2
100 LINE(0,104)-(160,110),2
110 LINE(0,103)-(160,110),3
120 LINE(0,102)-(160,110),2
130 LINE(0,101)-(160,110),3
140 LINE(0,99)-(160,110),2
150 LINE(0,105)-(160,110),2
160 LINE(0,106)-(160,110),3
170 LINE(0,107)-(180,110),2
180 LINE(0,108)-(160,110),3
190 LINE(0,110)-(160,110),2
200 CIRCLE (280,70),10,2,1.1,1
210 PAINT(280,70),3,2
220 CIRCLE (260,100),5,2,2.3,2
230 PAINT(260,100),2,2
240 LINE (0,40)-(70,40)
250 LINE (0,30)-(55,30)
260 LINE (0,70)-(95,70)
270 LINE(0,120)-(99,120)
280 LINE(0,150)-(80,150)
290 CIRCLE(210,150),3,2
300 PAINT(210,150),1,2
310 CIRCLE (190,170),3,2
320 PAINT (190,170),1,2
330 FOR X=1 TO 200
340 PSET(RND*320,RND*199)
350 NEXT
```

Fig. 6-17. Program to generate a deep space scene.

the screen, and line 50 draws the large circle which will represent the planet. Due to the center coordinates of this statement, only about half the circle will actually appear on the far left-hand side of the screen. Line 60 paints the circle a light green. Program lines 70 through 190 draw lines on the circle which are supposed to represent the colorful bands of

Saturn. Our first moon is drawn and painted in lines 200 through 210. Lines 220 and 230 draw another. Program lines 240 through 280 draw a simulation of the rings of Saturn, while lines 290 through 320 add more moons. At this point, the scene looks pretty good on the display, but there is an obvious lack of stars. To get a starry background, a for-next loop is set up in lines 330 through 350. The PSET statement is used in line 340 to write random dots on the screen. These are the stars. Since it's impractical and not even desirable to plot the coordinates of each of 200 stars, the coordinates with the PSET statement consists of random numbers that correspond to any point that can be plotted on the screen. Using these three lines, 200 stars can be displayed, although the number can be increased or decreased by altering the maximum value for X in line 330. Figure 6-18 shows the screen print.

There you have it—a complete deep space picture which requires only 35 program lines and uses four different specialized graphic statements in Advanced BASIC. Believe it or not, you could write this same program in text mode for display on the IBM monochrome monitor. However, the circles would not be nearly as good, and you would need a large number of for-next statements to plot the various coordinates. While I have not written this program for text mode, I would imagine that it could easily take up several hundred program lines. This points to the distinct advantage which the IBM graphics language gives to the serious programmer.

RANDOM GRAPHICS

One of the most entertaining aspects of computer programs which draw graphics on the screen involves letting the computer decide what it wants to draw. This is an apt description of a program which uses the RND statement to determine screen coordinates. You never know just what will be displayed when these statements are successfully used, and random patterns can be entertaining for hours on end. I know one owner of the IBM Personal Computer who has six or eight simple programs which do nothing but display a series of random images on a color television receiver. He uses these for atmosphere at parties and other gatherings. The television set is simply turned on and a program which is written in "endless loop" form is run. Invariably, guests will drift toward the television receiver and stand mesmerized for long periods as the various patterns occur.

Figure 6-19 shows a program which will generate random lines. This is an endless loop type because a GOTO statement in line 50 continually branches to line 30 and line 40, the latter of which actually writes the line on the screen. The program will continue to execute until it is manually halted.

The most important line in the program contains a line statement. While previous line statements have consisted of two sets of coordinates, this one seems to contain only one. Notice that the hyphen is placed in front of the random coordinates contained within parentheses. This tells the computer to write a line from the last coordinate to those specified. This program actually draws random boxes on the screen, since the line statement is followed by the letter B. Another random statement is used to denote color. Depending upon the number output by the random number gen-

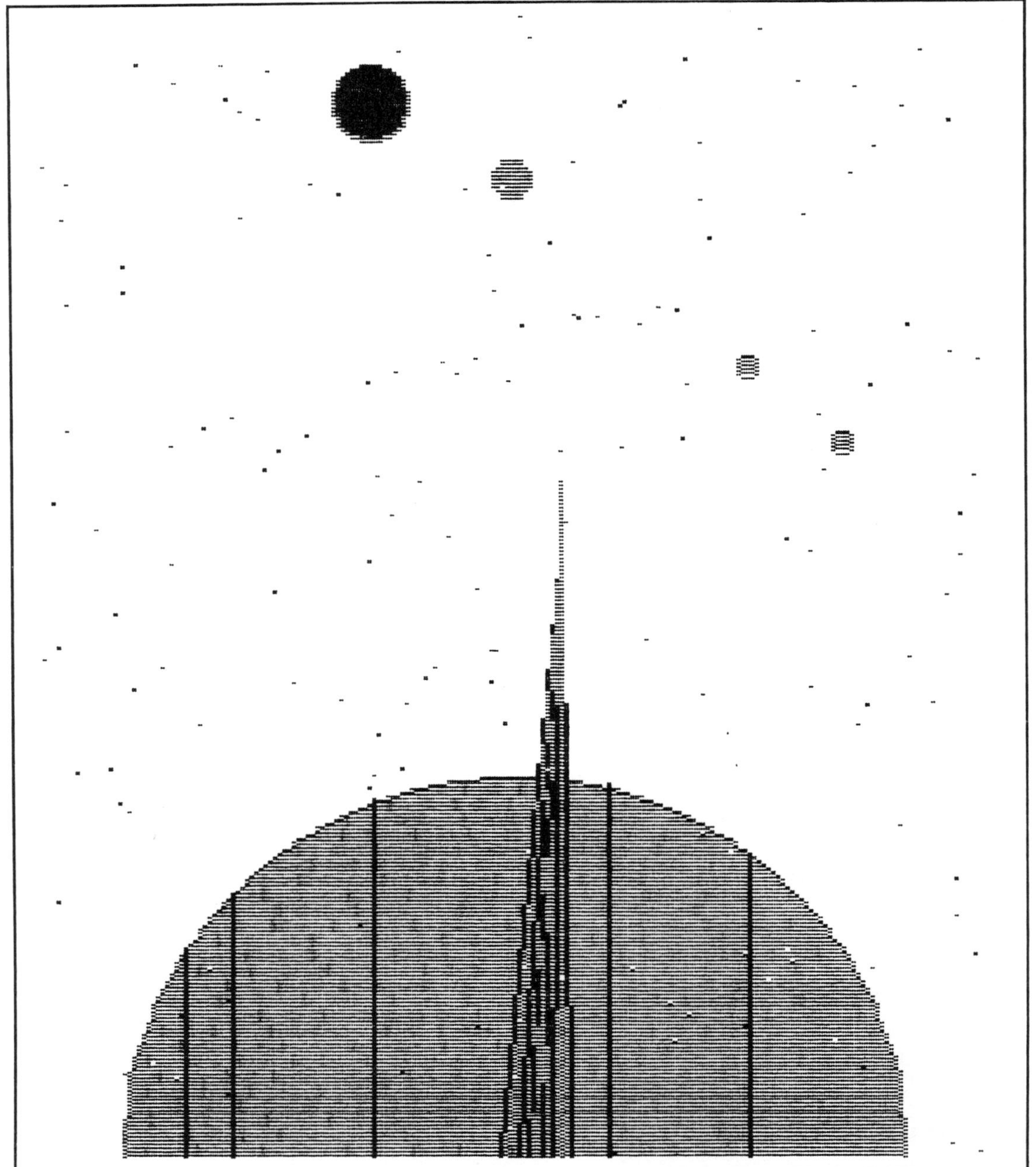

Fig. 6-18. Screen print of results from the last program.

```
10 REM RANDOM LINES
20 CLS
30 SCREEN 1,0:COLOR 0,0
40 LINE -(RND*319,RND*199),RND*4,B
50 GOTO 40
```

Fig. 6-19. A simple program to generate random lines or boxes.

erator, the lines that make up the boxes will be composed of one of four colors (0-3). The random number generated will always be less than 1, so the color number will have a maximum value of 3.

This program does not erase a randomly placed box to make room for the writing of another. The display information builds up on the screen, and after a few minutes, you will have an almost solid combination of lines from top to bottom and from side to side. The coordinates specified in line 40 can be at any place on the screen, so you never know just where a box will appear.

Of course, after enough boxes have been written, the screen becomes very crowded, so it might be more advantageous to use the program shown in Fig. 6-20. Here, a for-next loop is established which will write 100 boxes on the display screen. When this loop times out, the GOTO statement in the next line returns the program to line 20, which clears the screen and begins the printing operation all over again for another hundred boxes. You get the same effect here without the screen congestion. You can alter the for-next loop to print as few or as many boxes as desired before the screen clears itself. Another slight alteration will cause the screen to display filled boxes. Simply add the letter F immediately after the letter B in the program line that contains the line statement. You can fool around with the color palette and the random coordinates to get just about anything you want—of a random nature.

If you would like to draw circles, the program shown in Fig. 6-21 will accomplish this for you. The screen will slowly display an ever-enlarging circle, which contains many

```
10  REM RANDOM LINES
20  CLS
30  SCREEN1,0:COLOR 0,0
40  FOR X = 1 TO 100
50  LINE – (RND*319,RND*199),RND*4,B
60  NEXT X
70  GOTO 20
```

Fig. 6-20. The modified random line program avoids screen congestion.

```
10  SCREEN 1: COLOR RND*15, RND*8
20  CLS
30  FOR X = 1 TO 60
40  CIRCLE(160,100),X,1
50  NEXT X
60  GOTO 20
```

Fig. 6-21. *Random Circle* program.

smaller circles within its area. After a point, the circle will disappear and a new version will begin to build in the space the old one occupied.

To make the program even more interesting, you can add other circle statements to cause several circles to be drawn on the screen at the same time. These patterns will take many different forms and colors as well, because of the random portion of the color statement.

The idea with all of these programs is to remove the computer from human control. A properly written random program will allow for indefinite periods of untended operation, and you can simply sit and watch your color monitor to see all that is displayed.

Now, what purpose do random programs serve? Other than the entertainment value, they can offer a high degree of education. For example, you may have tried for hours on end to draw a certain type of geometric form on the screen, only to have your efforts end in failure. Suppose, however, that you find one of your random programs happens to produce just what you're looking for. You can discover the correct combination which was used to arrive at this form by adding the program lines needed to get the computer to display the random coordinates that were used to generate the screen write. Using the program previously shown in Fig. 6-20 as an example, we can add a few lines to get it to display information after every write. The program is shown in Fig. 6-22.

All that is different about this program is the addition of the information contained in lines 50 through 80. Line 40 will draw a box on the screen. Then, lines 50 through 70 will print the line coordinates and the color numeral which was used to generate the geometric figure. Line 80 simply stops the program run until you press the enter key. At this point, the program will repeat itself, using a different set

```
 10  CLS
 20  SCREEN 1,0:COLOR 0,0
 30  FOR X = 1 TO 100
 40  LINE – (RND*319,RND*199),RND*4,B
 50  PRINT RND*319
 60  PRINT RND*199
 70  PRINT RND*4
 80  INPUT A$
 90  NEXT X
100  GOTO 10
```

Fig. 6-22. This program prints random lines and displays random numbers used to generate them.

of coordinates which will again be displayed. This procedure can be very useful in random programs which generate complex figures. The needed lines are inserted into a simple program for clarity of explanation only. The program used to generate random program lines is so simple that in most instances, the coordinate and color information will not need to be extracted as shown. However, in a program which generates random circles and other highly complex geometric forms, the extracted information may be invaluable.

Random graphics programs are quite simple to write and take a minimum of input time. Basically, they use one or more of the special graphics statements. Only their position and color numerals are randomized. Most programs are written in endless-loop form to allow for untended operation.

A good example of this is shown in Fig. 6-23. I call this one the *Circular Maze*, and it uses the circle and paint graphics statements. The radius of the circle is randomized, as is the color numeral of the paint statement. The color statement is also randomized, and this three-way combination provides a very colorful on-screen graphic display.

Line 30 sets up the foreground and background colors, which are dependent on the random number which is output. A major loop is then entered in line 40, which will be discussed a bit later. A nested loop (loop within a loop) is found in line 50. This draws the circle using 20 different radius figures. As soon as the circle has been drawn 20 times, the program advances to a paint statement in line 80, which fills in a portion of the circle just generated. The major loop next statement is encountered in line 90. This returns the program to line 40 and allows 20 more circles to be drawn over or inside the ones already displayed on the screen. All in all, the graphic image may contain up to 200 circles within circles. When the loop begun in line 40 is finished, the screen is cleared (line 100), and there is a branch back to the beginning of the program, where the entire sequence of events is repeated. Due to the random numbers, however, the next sequence will be completely different from the first.

The maximum radius of the circle gener-

```
10 REM CIRCULAR MAZE
20 SCREEN 1
30 COLOR RND*15,RND*8
40 FOR A=1 TO 10
50 FOR X=1 TO 20
60 CIRCLE(160,100),RND*70,RND*4
70 NEXT
80 PAINT (160,100),RND*4,RND*4
90 NEXT
100 CLS
110 GOTO 30
```

Fig. 6-23. *Circular Maze* program.

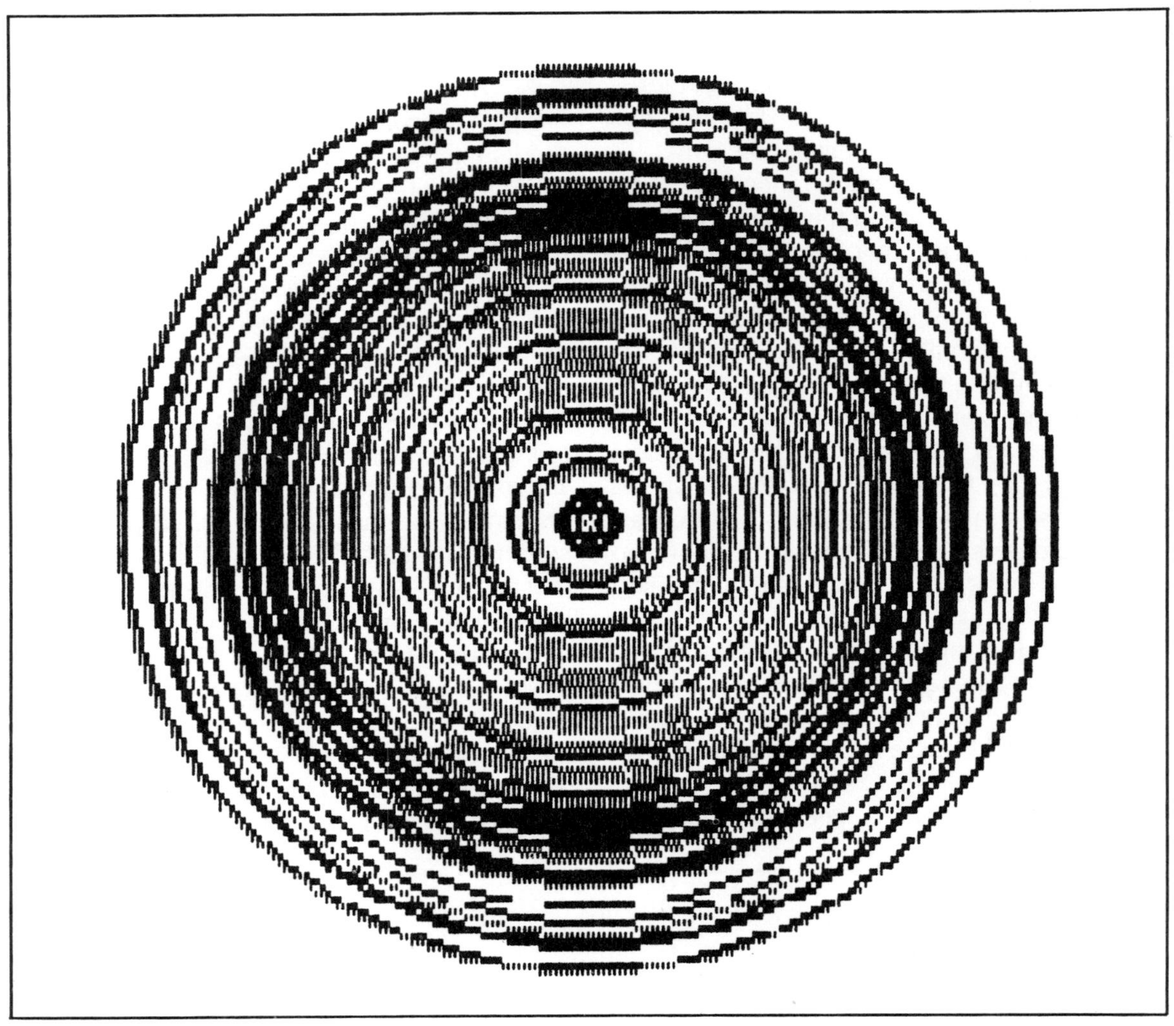

Fig. 6-24. Screen display of previous program run.

ated by this program will always be less than 70 screen points. All of the many circles generated will appear inside the circle created at the maximum radius. At first, the circle is quite simple, but as each second ticks by, it becomes more and more complex. After a short time, it seems to be completely filled in by rings, and the rings themselves then seem to be moving. If you use your imagination, it may seem like a vast circular stadium with millions of people moving around inside. You can increase or decrease the maximum radius of the circle by changing the number 70, which follows the circle statement, to a higher or lower number. Figure 6-24 shows the screen display when the program is run.

Figure 6-25 shows another random graphics program which revolves around the circle statement. This one is handled in much the same way as the one discussed previously. However, put and get statements are used to move the circle a different point on the screen. As it is moved, it leaves trace lines behind, and the end result is two colorful circles, one on the left and one on the right, with a string of colorful lines in between. The put and get statements are discussed in detail in a later chapter on animation. These are used to store a screen image in an array and place it at different points on the screen. When used in one way, the old image will be erased. In this program, the old images are left intact, so the display is a combination of many different circles being created at the same vertical point on the screen over a linear number of horizontal points. Figure 6-26 shows the screen display when this program is run.

Figure 6-27 shows a program that will generate a bowtie type of graphic figure on the screen. This, again, is a random graphics program, and each screen write will be a bit different. The first four lines have been seen in other programs. It is necessary to define the dimensions of an array (J) because the put and get statements are used to move a small dot on the screen. This is set up in line 50, which causes a point to be plotted at coordinates 319,100 on the far right-hand side of the screen. The put and get statements found in lines 60 and 70 commit this point to the array. A for-next loop is then entered. Line 90 assigns the value of X, which is used in the next put statement. Effectively, this causes the dot to travel from the right-hand side of the screen to the left-hand side. We may think of the position of the dot as being represented by the variable

```
10 REM TRAVELING CIRCLES
20 DIM J(1000)
30 SCREEN 1
40 COLOR RND*15,RND*10
50 FOR X=1 TO 30
60 CIRCLE(60,100),RND*50,RND*4
70 NEXT X
80 GET(10,50)-(110,150),J
90 PUT(10,50),J
100 FOR X=10 TO 200
110 PUT(X,50),J:FOR S=1 TO 100:NEXT
120 NEXT
130 CLS
140 GOTO 40
```

Fig. 6-25. *Traveling Circles* program.

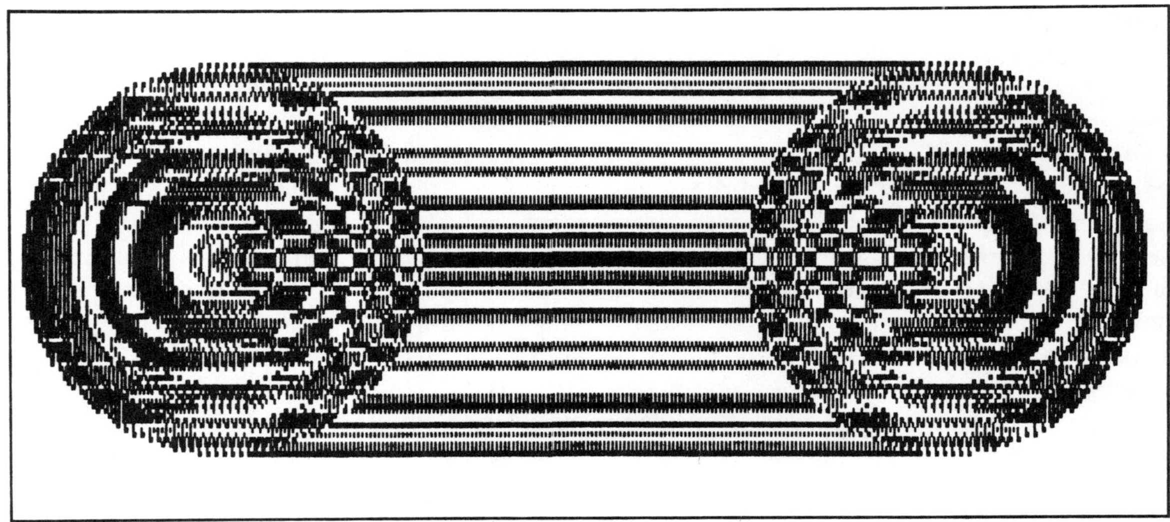

Fig. 6-26. *Traveling Circles* monitor display.

X. The line statements in program lines 110 through 140 find the location of X and plot a series of points to the four corners of the screen. Line 110 plots from X to the top right-hand side of the screen, line 120 to the bottom right-hand side, and lines 130 and 140 to the bottom left and top left, respectively. Each time the dot moves to the left, a line is drawn from its position to the four corners. The end effect is two triangles connected at their tips to form the appearance of a bowtie.

As soon as the dot has traveled to the left-hand side of the screen, the loop is finished, and the screen is cleared in line 160. Line 170 then branches to the start of the writing portion of the program, and the process is repeated over and over again. You will note that there is a random portion of the for statement found in line 80. This establishes the movement of the point from which all lines are drawn. Sometimes, it will move in steps of two screen coordinates; sometimes, it will move in steps of fifteen or more. This can provide a bowtie pattern of closely-spaced or widely-spaced lines.

Each of the line statements is followed by a random color designator, which determines the color each line will assume during each cycle of the loop. This serves to provide a very colorful display which has many thousands of different combinations. The display is shown during a portion of the run in Fig. 6-28.

Figure 6-29 shows a modification of the previous program, which plots only two corners of the screen from X. Here, the point plotted in line 60 moves from the top left of the screen to the bottom left. The distant points to which lines will be plotted from X and located in the top and bottom right-hand portions of the screen. This produces a drapery effect and is an appealing graphic display. Again, screen colors and line colors have been randomized.

However, the for-next loop that begins at line 90 cycles in even steps of one, so the pattern of the graphic drapes will always be very fine. This is a very simple program, but it is one of my favorites for producing random graphic patterns on the screen. Figure 6-30 shows the screen display.

At this point in our discussion, we have gotten into random lines, random circles, and even random rectangles, so maybe it's about time we combined a few of these to come up with an even more colorful and unusual pattern. One might think that combining two types of programs would require twice as many program lines, but this is simply not so. In most cases, one or two for-next loops control the printing of on-screen patterns, and we can fit many different graphic commands in a single loop.

The program shown in Fig. 6-31 is about the same length as others presented thus far and may be thought of as the previous drapery program combined with a modified version of the random circle program. After the for-next loop is established in line 40, line 50 plots points that are based upon the value of X. The point begins in the extreme upper left-hand corner and moves horizontally to the right as it moves vertically downward. A line is plotted from this point to the upper right-hand corner of the screen. When the loop times out, the point is at the center of the screen. The next loop which begins at line 80, then takes over. The value of Y is subtracted from 199, and this value is assigned to the variable Z. Note that the values of Y take over where the maximum value of X left off. The value of Y will take the point to the bottom of the screen, and the value

```
10 REM RANDOM BOWTIE GENERATOR
20 DIM J(500)
30 SCREEN 1
40 COLOR RND*15,RND*5
50 PSET(319,100)
60 GET(318,100)-(319,100),J
70 PUT(318,100),J
80 FOR A=0 TO 318 STEP RND*20+2
90 X=318-A
100 PUT(X,100),J
110 LINE(X,100)-(319,0),RND*4
120 LINE(X,100)-(319,199),RND*4
130 LINE(X,100)-(0,199),RND*4
140 LINE(X,100)-(0,0),RND*4
150 NEXT
160 CLS
170 GOTO 40
```

Fig. 6-27. *Random Bowtie Generator* program.

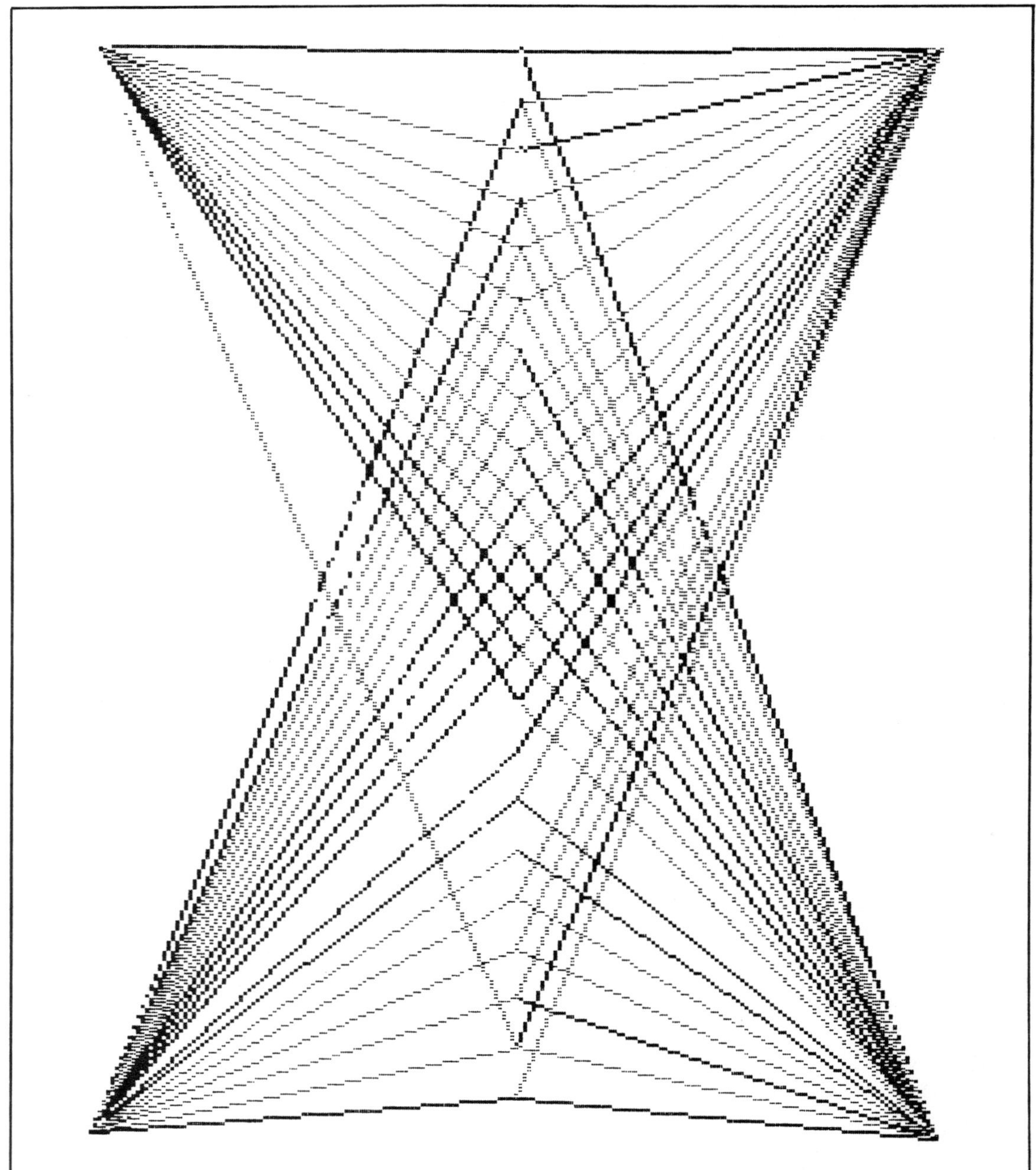

Fig. 6-28. An example of one of several thousand possible screen displays created by the previous program.

```
10 REM GRAPHIC DRAPES
30 DIM J(500)
40 SCREEN 1
50 COLOR RND*15,RND*5
60 PSET(1,0)
70 GET(0,0)-(2,1),J
80 PUT(0,0),J
90 FOR X=0 TO 198
100 PUT(0,X),J
110 LINE(0,X)-(319,0),RND*4
120 LINE(0,X)-(319,199),RND
    *4
130 NEXT
140 CLS
150 GOTO 50
```

Fig. 6-29. Modified version of the previous program provides a different graphics picture.

of Z will cause the point to move horizontally to the left as it advances vertically downward to the bottom of the screen. At this midway position, another line is plotted from the moving point to the bottom right-hand corner of the screen. At the same time, a circle is drawn based upon the information found in line 120. Note that the radius of the circle (and thus, its circumference) is determined by a randomized number. The loop then repeats itself, and each time, the bottom line pattern gets wider and the circle begins its own internal action as more circles are added. When this last loop is finished, line 150 branches back to the start of the writing process, so the patterns continue on an endless basis. The screen display is shown in Fig. 6-32.

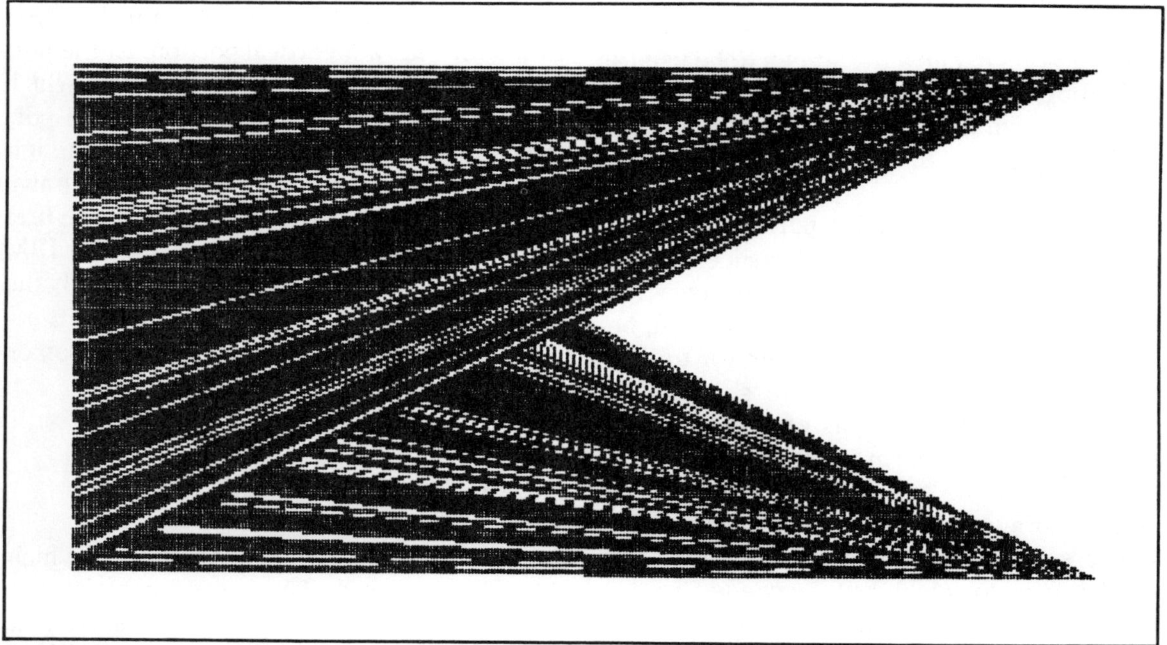

Fig. 6-30. Screen display using previous program.

```
10 REM MODERN ART
20 SCREEN 1
30 COLOR RND*15,0
40 FOR X=0 TO 100
50 PSET(X,X)
60 LINE(X,X)-(319,0),RND*4
70 NEXT X
80 FOR Y=101 TO 199
90 Z=199-Y
100 PSET(Z,Y)
110 LINE(Z,Y)-(319,199),RND*4
120 CIRCLE(210,100),RND*30,RND*4
130 NEXT Y
140 CLS
150 GOTO 30
```

Fig. 6-31. *Modern Art* program.

AUTHENTIC ARTWORK

Among its many other capabilities, the IBM machine offers the language and machine configuration to allow the screen to be used as a drafting board or even as a canvas. Images may be drawn in a similar manner to drawing them on paper with a pencil, pen, or even a paintbrush.

The statement used to perform these operations is available only in Advanced BASIC (BASICA), which is contained on your DOS disk. The draw statement is aptly named, because it is used to allow the operator to draw highly complex images on the screen. The word draw is used here as opposed to other statements that perform an entire graphic function. For example, the circle statement is used solely to draw a circle or a portion of a circle on the screen. The draw statement, on the other hand, is used to quickly put the needed lines on the screen in a fashion that will eventually write a completed figure. For example, if you want to draw a one-dimension box on a piece of paper, you might start by drawing the top horizontal portion. At the right end of this line, you would then draw a vertical portion. At the bottom of this, another horizontal portion, which is the same length as the top horizontal portion, would be drawn to the left. From the left side of this line, a vertical line would be drawn upward to meet with the beginning of the first line. Using the draw statement and the IBM Personal Computer, you would do basically the same thing.

The program to accomplish such a box on the screen would look like this:

```
10   SCREEN 1
20   DRAW "R15 D15 L15 U15"
```

It consists of only two lines, the first of which sets up the screen. The second contains the needed graphic information. Let's assume that each side of the box is to be 15 screen positions

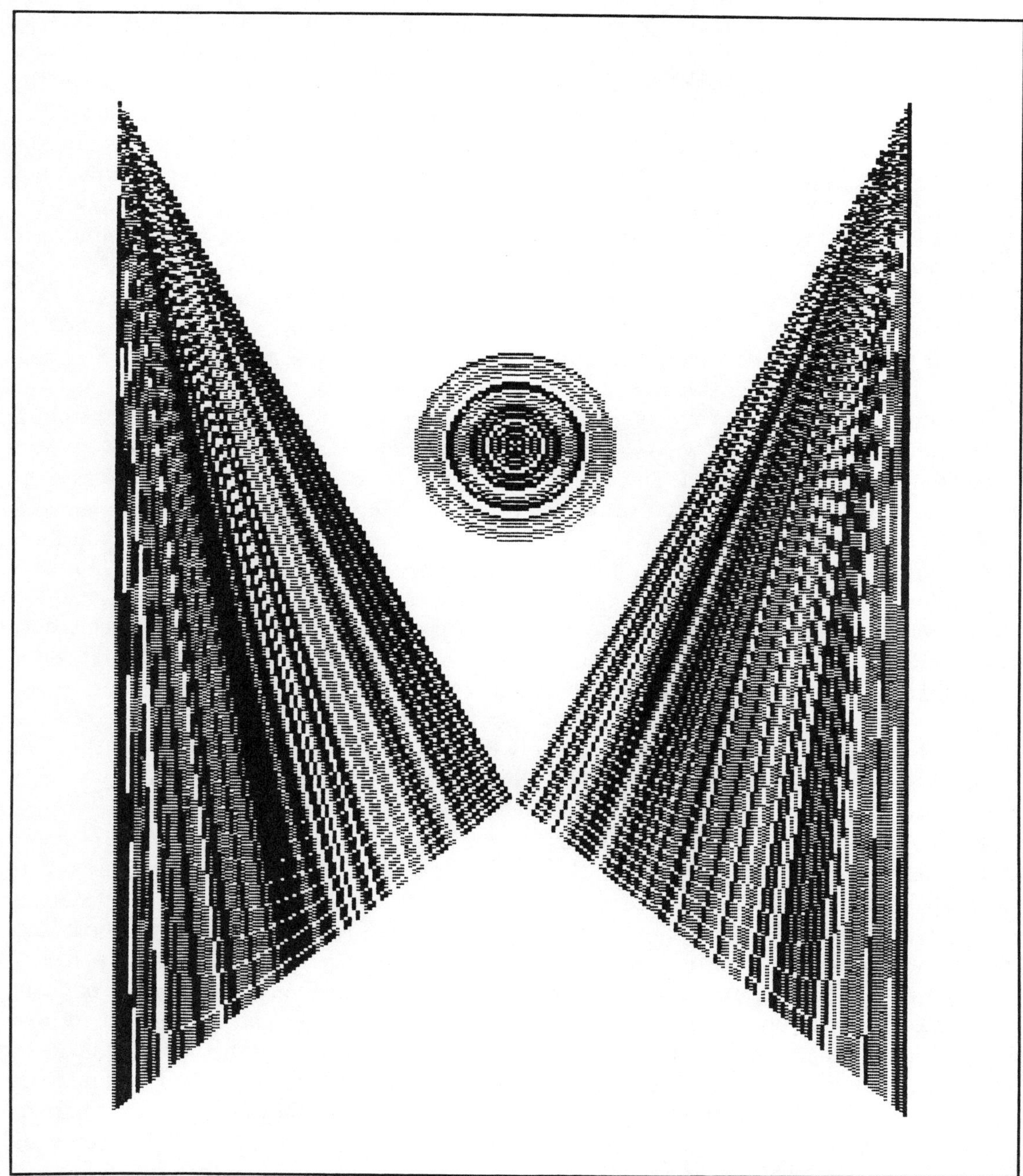

Fig. 6-32. *Modern Art* screen display.

in length or height. In explaining this program, we will go through the same routine used to draw the box previously discussed on paper. The draw statement begins with R15. This instructs the machine to display a line from coordinates 0 to 15 on the screen. The letter R means move right. We have now drawn the top horizontal portion of the box. The next command in the draw statement is D15, which tells the machine to draw a line down from the last point drawn on the top line. This forms our right vertical side. Imagine now that your pencil is still on the paper at the point where you completed this vertical line. You now must move to the left, and the draw statement matches this with an L15 command. The box is completed with a U15 command, which draws a line "up" from the ending point of the last completed line. You now have a perfect box on the screen.

If you wanted to draw a rectangle instead of a box, the R command might be followed by a value of 30. This would also be reflected in the L command. The other two commands could remain the same, since you will always begin drawing at the point from where you last stopped and in the direction indicated by the alphabetical designator. Boxes and rectangles are easy, but, of course, writing them on the screen can be greatly simplified by using a line statement followed by a B. The real magic of the draw statement is realized when it is necessary to draw a fairly complex figure such as an automobile, a freight train, or for that matter, any other shape that can be machine-simulated through the use of straight lines. The draw statement allows you to move up, down, back and forth, as well as diagonally, and the figure is drawn in what would be identical to one continuous motion if you were drawing the same figure with paper and pencil. In other words, the computer's pencil never leaves the drawing board. When it finishes a certain command, it holds its electronic stylus ready at the ending point to draw some other line upon command. Of course, you will undoubtedly reach a point where you will want to move to another section of your drawing to add a line or two. When you make this move, you certainly won't want a line drawn to it from the last position. There is a command which is represented by the letter B, which tells the electronic stylus to move without plotting points. This will help you position the stylus to begin another drawing maneuver. You may even draw different lines in different colors using the "C" command, which is part of the draw statement.

Before moving on to the actual drawing of pictures on the screen, let's start out a bit more simply by discussing the letter "H". This discussion may seem like a throwback to the popular television show, Sesame Street, but it will help get the point across regarding the draw statement and how it is used.

Figure 6-33 shows the capital letter "H" surrounded by the commands that are required to produce it on the screen in conjunction with draw statements. Assume that our starting point is at X. From this point, it will be necessary to draw up a certain number of places to write the left-hand vertical leg. The command used for this is U4. I could just have easily used U10 or even U40, but all that's important as far as the numerals are concerned within these commands is that they all bear a certain relationship to each other. The U4 command draws the left vertical leg. It is then necessary

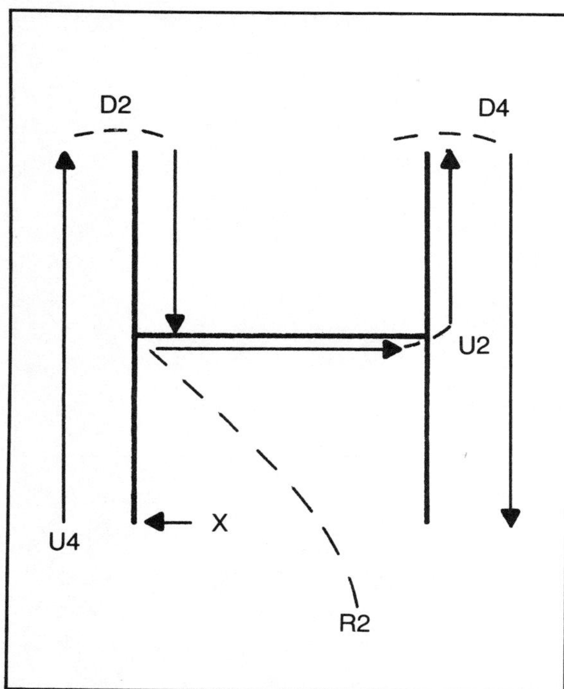

Fig. 6-33. Capital letter H surrounded by the draw commands needed to produce it graphically. The letter X is the starting point.

to get back to the center of this leg in order to draw the horizontal portion. Therefore, a D2 command is used. What happens here is a line is drawn over the top half of the vertical leg and back to the center point. This line is not actually seen, since it simply traces over the one that is already there. To draw the horizontal crossbar, an R2 command is used. This takes us to the center portion of the right vertical leg, which will be drawn by the next series of commands. A U2 command draws the top half of the right vertical leg, and this is followed by a D4 command which traces over the last line drawn and extends to the bottom. This is how the letter H may be drawn.

There are many other ways of drawing this same letter using the draw statement. For example, the D2 command could be replaced by BD2. With the addition of the B, this command tells the computer to move down two positions, but not to plot any points. It's not necessary to do this, since the line which is drawn by the original D2 command is not really seen. We could use the same method at the point where the D4 command is shown on the drawing. We could replace this with two commands. The first would be BD2, which would move down two places without plotting any points, since a line is already drawn here. The second command would be D2, which draws the bottom portion of the right vertical leg.

The program shown in Fig. 6-34 takes the former discussion into account in order to produce the commands needed to spell the word "HELLO" on the screen. As a matter of fact, in the latter part of program line 40, you will see the same series of commands just discussed, U4 D2 R2 U2 D4, which form the letter H. REM statements are provided throughout this program to indicate which letter will be drawn by the next line.

There are a few other commands used with the draw statement that need further discussion. At the beginning of line 40, you will find a BL100 command. Without this, the first letter would start near the center of the screen. This command starts the printing of the first letter 100 points to the left of screen center. Remember, the letter B means move, but don't plot any points. The BL100 means move to the left 100 spaces, but don't plot any points.

Each draw statement also uses an S command. In each case, S is equal to the variable X. The letter S denotes the scale favor that de-

```
10 SCREEN 1
20 INPUT X
30 REM H
40 DRAW "BL100 S=X;U4 D2 R2 U2 D4 "
50 REM E
60 DRAW"S=X;BR2 U4 D2 R2 L2 U2 R2 L2 D4 R2"
70 REM L
80 DRAW"S=X;BR2 U4 D4 R2"
90 REM L
100 DRAW"S=X;BR2 U4 D4 R2"
110 REM O
120 DRAW"S=X;BR2 U4 R2 D4 L2"
```

Fig. 6-34. Program to print the word HELLO in large letters.

termines the overall size of each line which the draw statement produces. This number may be anywhere from 1 to 255, and in each case, the scale number is divided by 4. In otherwords, if X equals 1, the scale factor will be ¼ and each line will be drawn ¼ of the length specified by the actual number in the draw statement commands. Again, assuming a value of 1 for X, this would mean that the U command in line 40 would be drawn for only one screen point.

Line 20 allows you to input the value of X, which means that you can increase or decrease the size of the word "HELLO" when printed on the screen. After the letter H is drawn in line 40, the next executed line is 60. Here, we find the scale factor designator and a BR2 command. This latter command spaces the next letter to be drawn two relative screen places from the ending of the previous letter. The plotting point is moved two relative places to the right before the next letter is begun. This same command could just as easily have been placed as the last command in the draw statement of line 40. Without these spacing commands, all of your letters would run together. Line 60 draws the letter E, and the remaining draw statements complete the word "HELLO".

When you run this program, nothing will happen until you input a value for X. This variable may assume a value up to approximately 50 before the letters run off the screen due to their size. Each time you run the program, you can input a different value for X and watch the size of the word become enlarged or shrink down to almost nothing.

There is one other thing that must be pointed out here. Looking at line 120, you will see that the last command moves the plotter two relative places to the left. This means that the letter is finished at a point which is inside or to the left of another line which makes up the same letter. These are the commands which form the letter O; and effectively, the starting and ending points are the same. If you wanted to follow this letter with another letter in the same word, you must begin the next draw statement with a BR4 command instead of BR2, which was used in all the other lines. A BR4 takes you four places to the right of the ending point. The first two places already contained a portion of the letter O. The two additional places allow you the same relative spacing as with the previous letters. In most instances, I try to end all my letters at a point that is on the far right-hand side (of the letter) and at the bottom. By the same token, if your plotter is not on the bottom line when one letter is finished, it is necessary to command it to go there and then command the proper spacing before moving on to the next letter. Remember, when using the draw statement, all commands specify movement from the last place on the screen that the plotter has assumed.

A modification of this program is shown in Fig. 6-35. Here, the value of X is represented by a for-next loop that steps from 1 to 35. This program will draw "HELLO" 35 times, and with each cycle of the loop, the word gets larger. It seems to be coming by you on an angle and getting nearer as it enlarges. Again, REM statements are provided to specify the letter drawn by each line. Line 130 contains a time delay for-next loop, which allows each word to establish itself for a short time on the screen before the next word is printed. After the printing of each word, the screen is cleared and the next word is printed. Line 140 tests for the value of X, and when it equals 35 (the loop maximum), the program is ended. This precedes the CLS statement in line 150, so the final word remains on the screen.

Figure 6-36 shows a similar program, but in this case, the word "COMPUTER" is spelled out on the screen. Again, you may

```
10 SCREEN 1
20 FOR X=1 TO 35
30 REM H
40 DRAW "S=X;U4 D2 R2 U2 D4 "
50 REM E
60 DRAW"S=X;BR2 U4 D2 R2 L2 U2 R2 L2 D4 R2"
70 REM L
80 DRAW"S=X;BR2 U4 D4 R2"
90 REM L
100 DRAW"S=X;BR2 U4 D4 R2"
110 REM O
120 DRAW"S=X;BR2 U4 R2 D4 L2"
130 FOR C=1 TO 500:NEXT
140 IF X=35 THEN END
150 CLS
160 NEXT
```

Fig. 6-35. Program to display the word HELLO in 35 different sizes.

```
10 REM "COMPUTER"
20 SCREEN 1
30 COLOR 8,0
40 INPUT X
50 REM C
60 DRAW"BL100 S=X;U4 R2 BD4 L2"
70 REM O
80 DRAW"BR4 S=X;U4 R2 D4 L2"
90 REM M
100 DRAW"BR4 S=X;U4 F2 E2 D4"
110 REM P
120 DRAW"BR2 S=X;U4 R2 D2 L2 BD2"
130 REM U
140 DRAW"BR4 S=X;U4 BR2 D4 L2"
150 REM T
160 DRAW"BR6 S=X;U4 L2 R4 BD4"
170 REM E
180 DRAW"BR2 S=X;U4 R2 BD2 L2 BD2 R2"
190 REM R
200 DRAW"BR2 S=X;U4 R2 D2 L2 R1 F1 D1"
210 END
```

Fig. 6-36. Program to generate the word COMPUTER in giant letters.

specify the value of X to vary the size of the word. In this program, I have used the B command in many instances to move without plotting points. In line 60, the BL100 command moves the plotter to the left center of the screen. To draw the letter C, the Plotter moves up four places and then to the right two places. The BD4 command moves the plotter down to the bottom line (two places to the right of the beginning) without plotting points. The L2 command then completes the bottom horizontal section of the letter C. However, this is an example of the ending point being identical to the starting point, so line 80 includes a BR4 statement to arrive at a two-point spacing between the right side of the letter C and the next letter. You will see several other examples of this situation throughout the remainder of the program. Sometimes a BR2 is required; sometimes a BR4. In line 160, it was necessary to use a BR6 to provide proper spacing between the letter T and the letter E.

I did have a few aesthetic problems with the letter R, which is drawn in line 200. The diagonal leg just didn't look right at first. Many computer printouts draw the letter R in much the same manner as the letter A, replacing the diagonal leg with a vertical one. I fiddled with this for a few minutes and finally came up with a combination that was pleasing to me. You may wish to do otherwise. While the draw statement does offer diagonal lines, you are somewhat limited in the angles at which they will exit a previous line section. For the most part, drawing large alphabetic figures with this statement is limited to block form. In other words, no curves.

Using the draw statement, all 26 letters in the alphabet may be easily reproduced on the screen, and you also do numerals using the same basic techniques. Producing the entire alphabet is good practice before moving on to more complex artwork.

Figure 6-37 shows a line drawing that is known as a block graph. In this case, each of the blocks represents a different portion of an electronic circuit. The alphabetic designators in each section have been removed here, as all that we're interested in for this exercise is the line drawing itself. This is a simple one-dimensional drawing, but it will take a bit of time to write into a program using the draw statement. Admittedly, we could use line statements to draw the same picture and could probably do so more quickly. However, when we move further into more complex artwork, this won't be possible. Assume for now that the only graphic statement available to us in draw and that this simple piece of artwork is to be reproduced exactly as shown in Fig. 6-37. How do we begin?

First, it is necessary to establish a relationship for each line within the drawing. This is done quite simply by using a finely graduated straight edge to measure the length of each line and each line segment between intersections occur. Figure 6-38 shows my mockup of the drawing in Fig. 6-37. This is just a freehand sketch that serves as a chart for later programming. I simply sketched in a rough draft of the original in much larger form to allow for the insertion of the relative values of each line. These values were garnered by applying the straight edge to each line in the original drawing. You will want to choose a straight edge that is graduated in very small values. In this particular case, the values given are in millimeters, but remember that these are ralative values, so small fractions of an inch work as well. It is only necessary that each line be given a value that is proportional to every other line in the drawing. I chose the starting point for this drawing to be at the left-hand side, as indicated by Fig. 6-38. You could just as easily choose the right-hand side, but we Americans are accustomed to the tradition of working from left to right.

While it would be possible to include all of the commands to reproduce this artwork graphically in one draw statement, I will divide the assignment up into several draw statements for clarification purposes. You may wish to proceed on a basis that will require less program lines once you have mastered the basic structure.

Since the first command in the draw statement generally starts at the center of the screen, we would first insert a BL100 to move our plotter to a point near the left-hand side. Now, beginning at the point marked START, we would input an R10 command to draw a line 10 relative points to the right. The next command would be U4, moving upward 4 relative points. This is where an intersection occurs. My intentions here are to draw the intersecting line first and then proceed onward. The

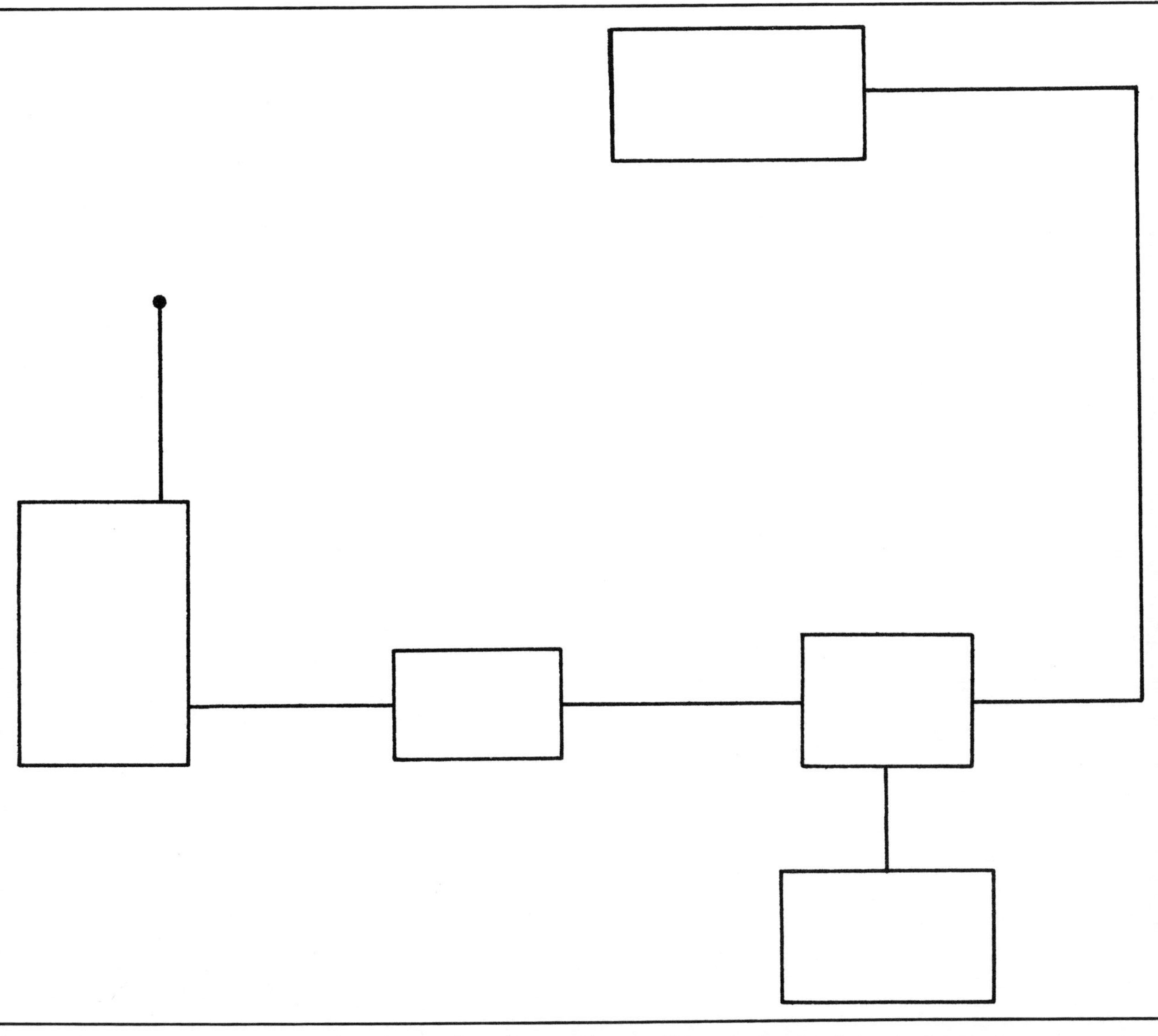

Fig. 6-37. A schematic block diagram such as the one shown here may be accurately reproduced on the computer screen.

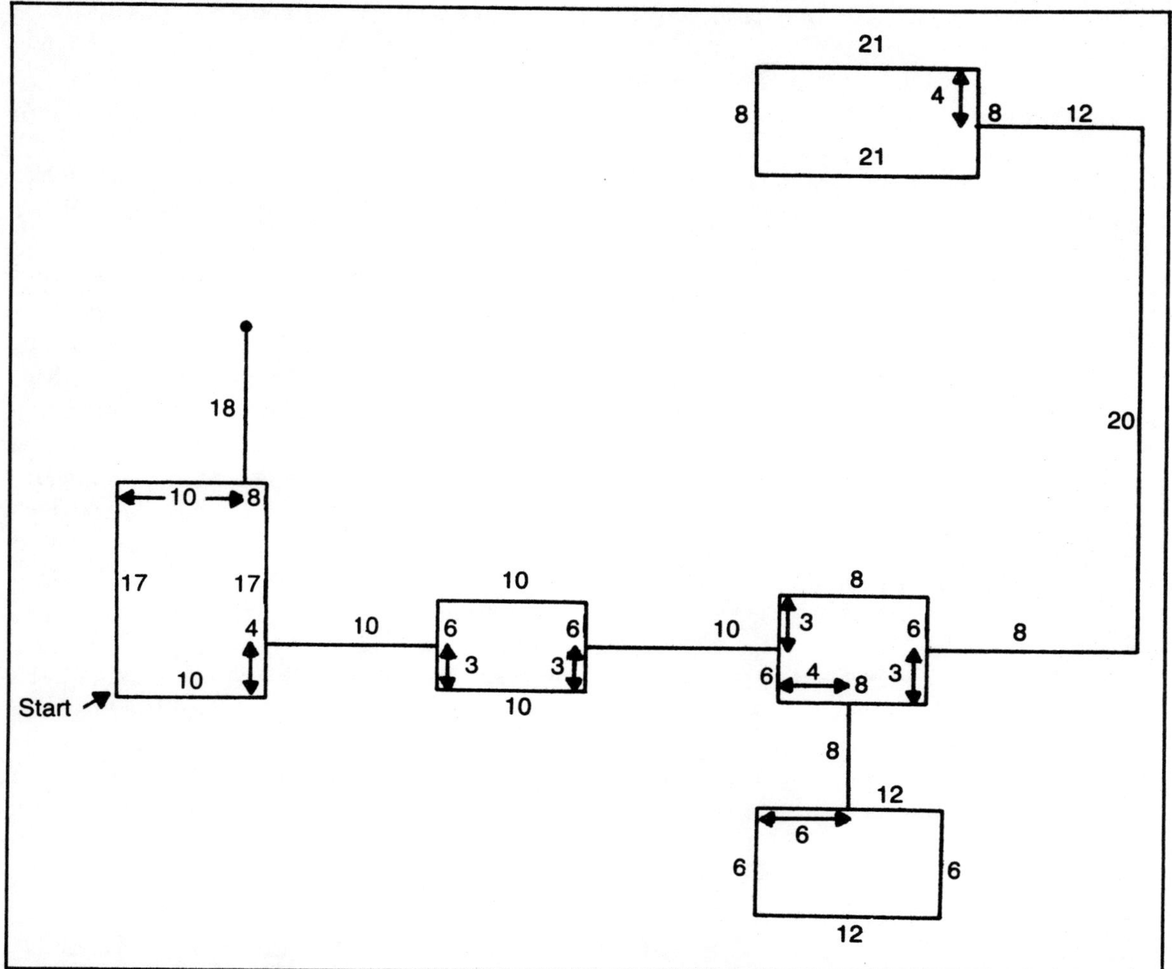

Fig. 6-38. Mockup drawing of the previous diagram indicates relative length of each line.

next command, then, is R10, but now, I'm out of the first rectangle which must be completed. Therefore, I retrace my steps with a BL10 command, which moves 10 places to the left doesn't plot any points. This gets me back to the original point of intersection. This side of the rectangle is 17 relative points in length, but the first 4 have already been drawn by a previous command, so I used a U13 (17 – 4) command, which completes the long side. It is now necessary to move 10 points to the left, but there is another intersection 2 points in, so the next command is L2. This is followed by a U18, which draws the outstanding vertical line. I arrive back at the intersection point with a BD18 and complete the rest of the top horizontal portion with an L8. The remaining vertical side is drawn with a D17. At this point, the plotter is back at the start, and it is necessary to move on to the second rectangle. This is at the end of the horizontal line which was drawn earlier. Perhaps the least confusing way to get there is with this combination:

BR10 BU4 BR10

The plotter is now at the point of the second block which is intersected by the connecting line from the first. This side of the new block is 6 relative units in height, and the intersection point is at the center. The next combination draws the second block and the outgoing horizontal line that connects it to the third block:

U3 R10 D6 L10 U3 BR10 R10

What I've done here is draw up 3, then write 10, down 6, left 10 and up 3. This takes me back to the beginning point for this block, but I'm on the wrong side to continue further. The BR10 moves the plotter from the center of the leading block edge to the center of the trailing edge. This last command does not plot any points. The final command draws the horizontal line which intersects with the next block.

I think you will agree with me when I say that this is a very simple process once you understand the use of the draw statement and have mapped yourself out a graphic guideline by means of a rough sketch. The complete program to draw this image is shown in Fig. 6-39. In this program, line 20 draws the first rectangle and its connecting line. Program line 30 draws the next block and connects it to the third. Line 40 draws the third and connects it to the one on the bottom, which is drawn in line 50. Line 60 draws the line which exits block 3 and extends upward to the overhead block. This last block is drawn in line 70. The entire program is only eight lines long, including the end statement which is not mandatory.

Admittedly, the original drawing was quite simple, but it probably would take you much longer to draw it neatly with pencil and

```
10  SCREEN 1
20  DRAW "BL100 R10 U4 R10 BL10 U13 L2 U18 BD18 L8 D17 BR10 BU4
         BR10"
30  DRAW "U3 R10 D6 L10 U3 BR10 R10"
40  DRAW "U3 R8 D6 L8 U3 BD3 BR4 D8"
50  DRAW "R6 D6 L12 U6 R6 BU8 BR4 BU3"
60  DRAW "R8 U20 L12"
70  DRAW "U4 L21 D8 R21 U4"
80  END
```

Fig. 6-39. Program to reproduce the block diagram graphically.

paper and a graduated straight edge than using this method and a computer. It took approximately five minutes to prepare the freehand sketch used to write this program. This includes the measurement time. Once the chart was completed, only a few minutes were required to input the program to the machine via the keyboard. In a drawing this simple, it's usually not necessary to check each line that contains a draw statement after it is written by running the partial program. The method is so simple that you expect it to work the first time, and it often does. Of course, if you make an error or two, the debugging process is usually a matter of shifting a few commands, which takes only a few additional minutes.

You might think, "Sure, this was pretty easy, but it must be much more difficult to draw a really complex piece of art." This is not really true. As long as the complex artwork is limited to straight lines and angles of 0°, 90°, 180°, and 270°, the process is handled in exactly the same manner. Certainly, it will take you more time to mock up your sketch and get the relative lengths in complex drawings, especially those which contain a much larger number of lines. The programming process will take more time as well because more commands will be needed to draw these lines. The fact is, however, that once you have your chart mapped out, you proceed in exactly the same way as with a simple block drawing. The IBM BASIC language surrounding the draw statement is common sense in nature. If you want to go up 10 places, you input a U10. If you want to go down the same number, a D10 will do the job. We can safely, say, then, that complex artwork certainly takes longer, but it's no more difficult from a mental or mathematical standpoint than drawing a simple square.

When programming complex art, you may find it necessary to run a partial program after every two or three draw statements are input because there is more chance of error. Debugging a program to draw a simple geometric figure is, of course, simpler than debugging one which is complex and consists of possibly several hundred different lines. Programming complex art can be tedious, but only because of the time element involved. The more you program in this mode, the more you will realize that drawing art on the IBM Personal Computer is like having a magical pencil which draws at your command . . . and it never draws a crooked line.

Going back to our on-screen reproduction of the block drawing, let's assume that you want to enlarge it by several times. As presented, the program will reproduce it at about the size shown in the original drawing. However, this appears very small on the large screen. All that is necessary to blow up the image is to include factor commands. The modified program is shown in Fig. 6-40. The scale factor designators are placed at the beginning of each draw statement. In this program, X is given a value of 10, which causes the graphic representation to be written much larger than before and at the center of the screen. When it is necessary to produce artwork for pamphlets, magazines, books, etc., all that is required is to input the figure using relative length commands and then arrange the factor commands to allow the image to be produced at exactly the size you desire. Then, with a good graphic printer, you can usually

```
10 SCREEN 1
20 X=10
30 DRAW"S=X;BL20 R10 U4 R10 BL10 U13 L2 U18 BD18 L8 D17
   BR10 BU4 BR10"
40 DRAW"S=X;U3 R10 D6 L10 U3 BR10 R10"
50 DRAW"S=X;U3 R8 D6 L8 U3 BD3 BR4 D8"
60 DRAW"S=X;R6 D6 L12 U6 R6 BU8 BR4 BU3
70 DRAW"S=X;R8 U20 L12"
80 DRAW"S=X;U4 L21 D8 R21 U4"
90 END
```

Fig. 6-40. Modified program to reproduce block schematic.

reproduce the display in hard copy form, ready to go to the printer. Incidentally, you won't be able to do this with the IBM 80 CPS printer, since it reproduces in text mode only. A later chapter describes a modification to the printer that will allow it to plot points and, with a suitable "screen dump" program, reproduce graphic images directly from the screen.

There is yet another specification that may be used in draw statements that has not been discussed in detail to this point. It would come in handy in creating the previous block drawing by shortening programming time. This new command is represented by the letter N and means to move in the direction indicated and to plot the points along the way, but then to return to the original starting position when the line has been plotted. Looking at the program in Fig. 6-40, we can see how this move/return command could be put to good use. In line 30, the R10 command draws the bottom horizontal line in the first block. The U4 command draws a vertical line to the intersecting point of the horizontal connecting line which travels to the next block. Referring to Fig. 6-38, as well as the program, will help you understand this a bit better.

In the original program, I used a R10 command to draw the horizontal connecting line followed by a BL10 to return the plotter to the starting position for this line. I could have eliminated this last command by using an NR10 instead of the R10. By the use of NR10, the horizontal connecting line would automatically be drawn, and the plotter would then return to the starting point. The U13 command would then be used to complete the right vertical side of the first block. An N command could also have been used to replace the U18 command in the original program. Using an NU18 here, the following BD18 would not have been necessary, as the plotter would have been automatically returned to the starting point of this last line. Sometimes you will find it advantageous to use the move/return command, while at other times, it may not speed programming at all. There are many different situations that could occur with any piece of artwork, so it is nearly impossible to establish any set rules that will apply generally. Figure 6-41 shows the screen display of the original block diagram.

Figure 6-42 shows a program that will produce a colorful display. I call this Shooting Star, and a draw statement is used to produce a six-pointed graphic star at the center of the screen. The star does not actually move, but everything around it constantly changes. The color statement has been randomized, and a color command is inserted within the draw statement. This is the second command within the statement, which is "C=Y". Y is previously assigned a value of RND*8. The draw statement produces the six-pointed star from what

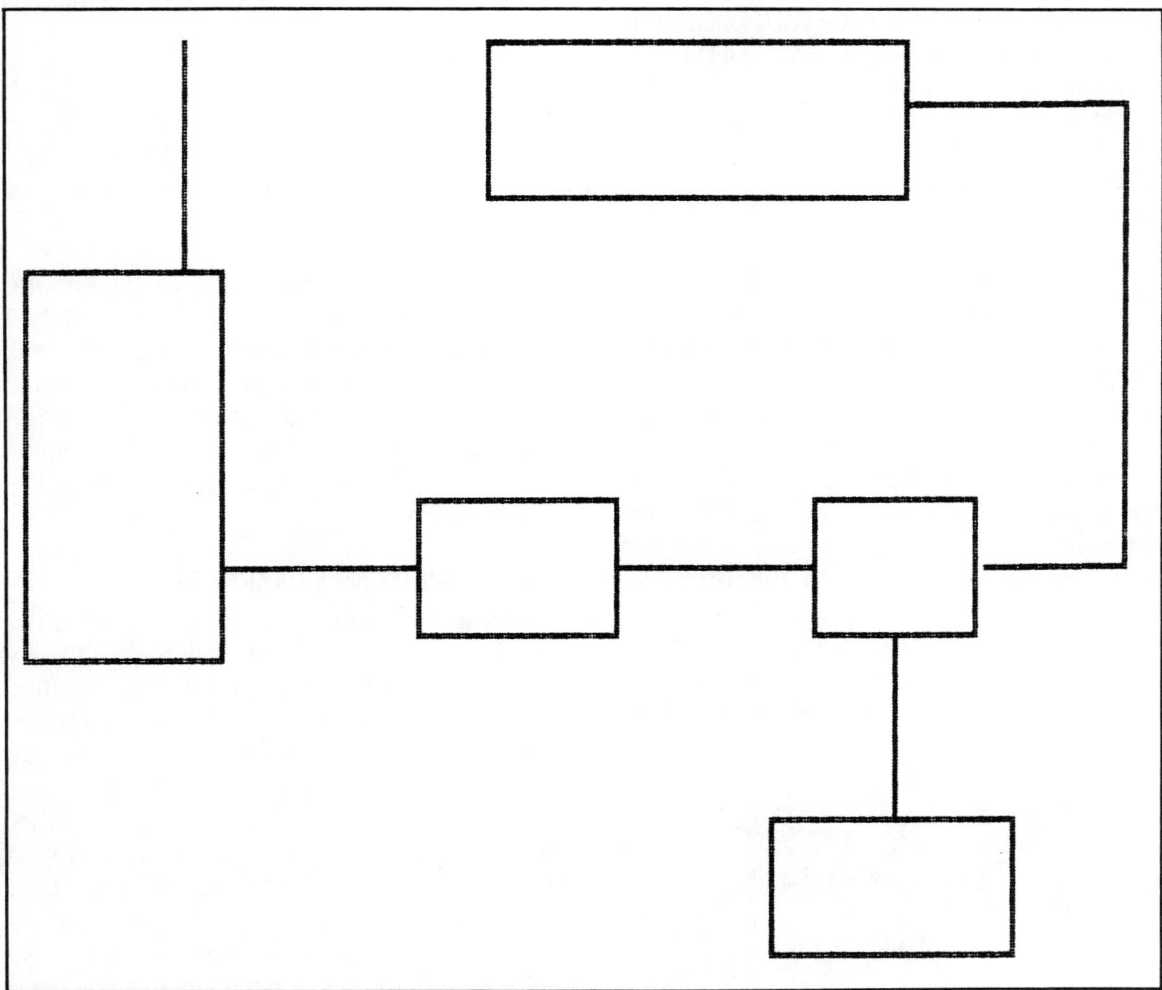

Fig. 6-41. Computer display of the original block diagram.

```
10 REM SHOOTING STAR
20 CLS
30 SCREEN 1
40 COLOR RND*15,RND*8
50 X=10
60 Y=RND*8
70 DRAW"S=X;C=Y;BL20 BD10 E10 BE10 E10 F10 BF10 F10 L20
   BL20 L20 BU20 R20 BR20 R
20 G10 BG10 G10 H10 BH10 H10
80 PAINT(160,100),1,Y
90 FOR X=1 TO 200:NEXT
100 GOTO 40
```

Fig. 6-42. *Shooting Star* program.

can best be described as a well-laid out series of triangles. As soon as the star has been drawn, the paint statement in line 80 fills in the graphic image with everchanging colors. The background will change as well. switching from red to blue to green, etc. A time delay loop is established in line 90 to allow the image to remain on the screen for a short period of time. After this, the screen is cleared and the same image appears again with a different color combination.

In drawing the star which is the "star" of the show, I simply opened up an art book, found what I needed, and went through the routine previously described. The star was sketched out on paper and a graduated straight edge was used to measure the dimensions of the original drawing. This entire program was written in about ten minutes, and this included measurements and sketches. Figure 6-43 shows the screen display.

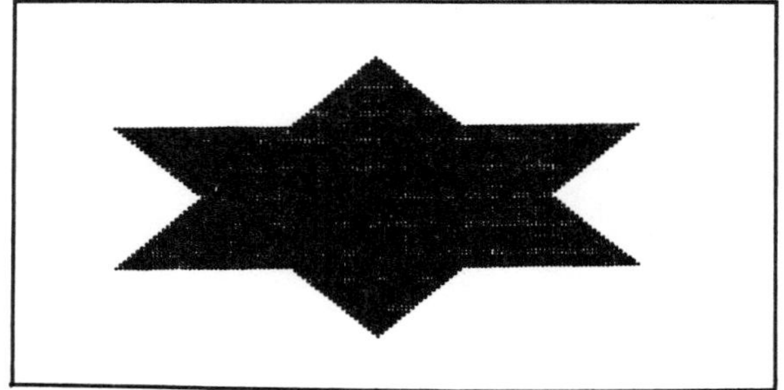

Fig. 6-43. *Shooting Star* display.

THREE-DIMENSIONAL DRAWINGS

Producing simple two-dimensional drawings (height and width, but no depth) is a fairly simple thing to do using the routines outlined previously. However, when it is necessary to simulate a three-dimensional drawing, the process becomes a bit more complex. This is not true so much from a programming standpoint as it is from knowing how to obtain the dimensions you need to insert in the draw statement commands. Let me first say that it is impossible to draw a true three-dimensional figure on a flat piece of paper unless you want to include the microscopic height of the graphite on this medium. Three-dimensional drawings, then, are really simulations of three-dimensional objects using a medium which is limited to only two dimensions. This applies to drawings on paper and as well as graphic representations on a computer screen, since both mediums are limited to two dimensions.

Figure 6-44 shows a three-dimensional drawing of a house. The extra rectangles are there to represent solar collectors. These give us more objects to reproduce on the computer screen. At first glance, the assignment may look simple. To draw the bottom front of the house, you would simply place your graduated straight edge between the beginning and ending of this line and arrive at a relative figure of about 50 units. Assuming that you start at the left front corner of the house, you would then input a command of R50 to get this line. This is an absolutely correct assumption. But how about drawing the bottom of the left side of the house? This line is about 35 units long, but it travels away from the front bottom edge at an obtuse angle. If you return to the start point and input an L35 command, you would simply add length to the first line drawn, making one long line which would be a total of approximately 85 relative units in length. You can't easily use any form of the draw command here (A), because the angle needed isn't a right angle or a 45 degree angle. How do you overcome this? The answer is you don't, at least within the framework of the draw statement. However, we are not limited to draw statements alone. We have a whole bevy of graphic statement at our disposal in IBM Advanced BASIC (BASICA).

Let's take another look at what we're

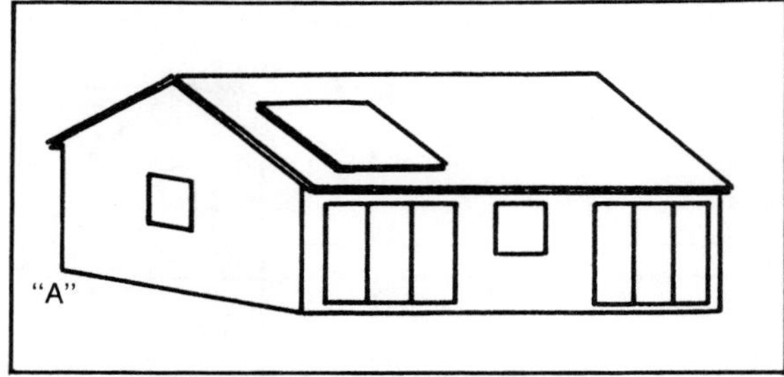

Fig. 6-44. Three-dimensional drawing of a house.

faced with by referring to Fig. 6-45. This is the same house as before, but horizontal lines have been drawn through the house parallel to the bottom of the screen. We can see that the far end of the left side of the house (A) is elevated by a short distance from the left corner of the front of the house (B). Once the front is drawn, a line statement could be used to draw a line from the coordinates of A to the coordinates of B. We don't have to worry about angles here, only about the coordinates of the two points.

For the sake of discussion, let's assume that point B is located at coordinates (140,130) on the screen. Let's also assume that the height from the reference line that is drawn from border to border through point B is 4 relative units. This means that the vertical coordinate of A will be equal to the vertical coordinate of B minus 4 units. In this example, the vertical coordinate of A would be 126 (130 – 4). The horizontal coordinate of point A is derived by measuring the distance from point B to the dotted line emanating from A. This line was drawn parallel to the edges of the frame. In the example shown, the distance between point B and the dotted line is approximately 23 relative units. Therefore, the horizontal coordinate of point A is equal to the horizontal coordinate of point B minus 23. (If

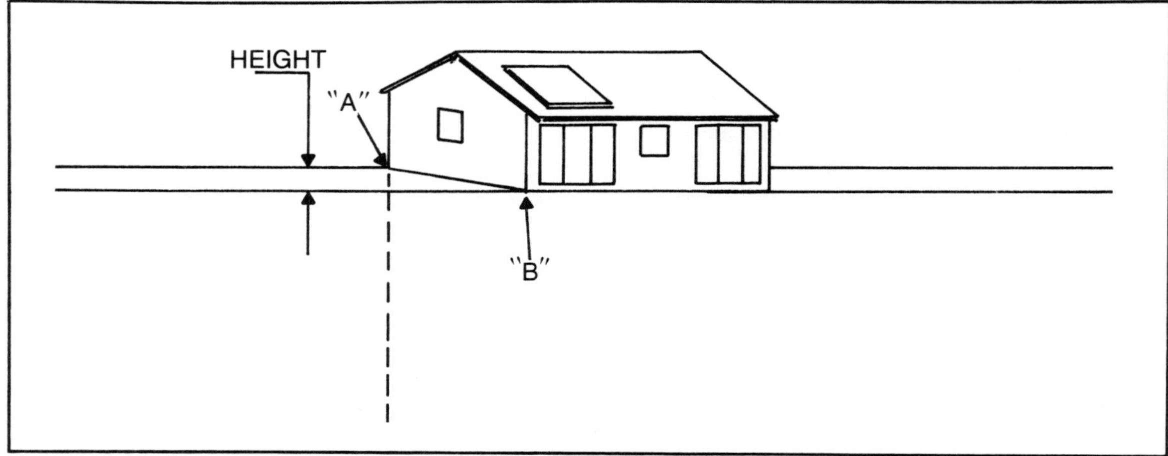

Fig. 6-45. The same drawing with a few horizontal lines added.

we were trying to figure a coordinate that was to the right of point B, we would add the unit figures to point B's coordinates instead of subtracting.) By using a little simple mathematics, we can easily arrive at the coordinates of point A, which are (140 – 23,130 – 4), or (117,126).

To draw the bottom line of the left side of our house, then, we would first draw the reference line (the front bottom portion of the house) and then include another program statement (on a separate line) which would read:

```
LINE (117,126) – (140,130)
```

This accomplishes exactly what we wanted to. This method will be used to generate any lines that approach any other lines (which may be produced using draw statements) at an angle. Note that it is only necessary to measure physical line lengths with a graduated straight edge when the draw statements are used. The length of the lines generated in line statements is determined by the distance between the sets of coordinates and may be calculated through the extrapolation process using the borders as guides.

Of course, there are many objects in this scene that are formed by horizontal and vertical lines. These can be detected by laying a straight edge horizontally or vertically across the drawing and observing which of the lines fall across its length. Each time you find a line that conforms to the straight edge, pencil in a line across the entire picture. This will tell you exactly which lines can be generated by the draw statement.

The drawing in Fig. 6-46 shows our house after the search has been completed. We see here that the top of the roof, the lower roof edge, the bottom front of the house, and the tops and bottoms of the windows and solar panels conform to our horizontal lines. We also see that the vertical window sections and the three visible vertical edges of the house conform to the vertical lines. All of these may also be drawn using the draw statements. Anything excluded from this graphlike pattern must be produced using other graphic commands.

The way I normally proceed at this point is to produce everything I can using draw statements. This involves measurement of the physical lines on the original drawing. If possible, it is best to make a copy of the drawing (several in fact) and then draw your borders. Naturally, you will measure the distance from your last drawn point to the start of the next portion you wish to draw and use B commands to move the plotter to this latter point without drawing a line. The elements that fit our two-dimensional category are drawn in exactly the same manner as the examples shown previously in this chapter.

When all of the draw statements have been completed, you can make a test run to make certain everything is included on the screen. You should see all of the lines that have been marked with vertical and horizontal lines.

Now the hard part begins. To draw the diagonal lines, it is necessary to treat each one as a separate entity altogether. Let's refer to Fig. 6-45 again, with the assumption that all portions of the program that can be created using the draw statement have already been input. In order to draw the bottom left-hand edge of the house, we must again arrive at point B. You will therefore input another draw statement, which in this case would be:

```
DRAW "BM140,130"
```

These were the original coordinates of point

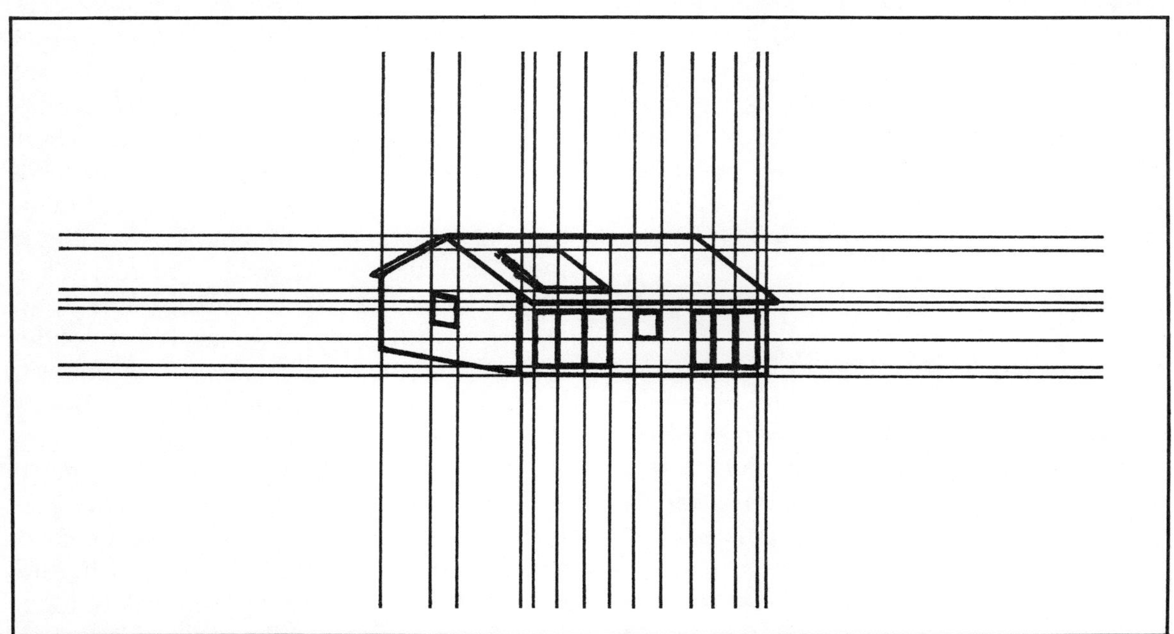

Fig. 6-46. The same drawing with all necessary horizontal and vertical lines added.

B. The process for determining the coordinates of A when those of B are known has already been discussed, but reread these directions again if you don't have them clear in your mind.

The new draw statement has returned the plotter to the coordinates specified, so all that's necessary now is to input the following line:

```
LINE (117,26) – (140,130)
```

Actually, the new draw statement just discussed is not mandatory, nor even desirable from a programming point of view. It is not necessary to return the plotter, since both coordinates (A and B) are specified in our new line statement. The new draw statement was used because it better explains what we're trying to do here, and it can also be put to good use, if you're trying to learn graphics programming rather than just using previously written programs. Let's assume that you have input the new draw statement. If you desire, you may now shorten the new line statement to:

```
LINE –(117,26)
```

This line statement will create a plotted line from the last position referenced on the screen to the coordinates specified within the parentheses. The new draw statement returns the plotter to point B, and the abbreviated line statement then plots a series of points from B to the coordinates of A.

This explanation should show you that there is more than one way to skin a cat, or in this case, plot a line. I have found that using draw statements with the BM command in conjunction with abbreviated line statements often speeds total programming time simply because it gives the programmer a constant reference point. Inputting a new draw statement to return to a certain point and then an abbreviated line statement does take a bit longer from the standpoint of actually feeding information to the computer, but if the human thinking process is slowed by using the other method, then the total time required for writing the entire program may be lengthened by several times. You have both resources at your command. Use the one you think best for your individual programming routines.

All right, we have now been successful in connecting the left edge portion of the house with the bottom edge, so let's move on to another problem. Assume that we want to connect the left ends of the horizontal solar panel lines. How do we determine the coordinates of the left end of each line? Technically, the information is contained in the draw statements used to generate these lines, but you will have to go back through the program and begin adding and subtracting to get the numbers. Another method is shown in Fig. 6-47. We already know the coordinates of point B, so let's figure the coordinates of the left end of the top solar panel line, which we will call point C. Again, key horizontal and vertical lines are drawn. We first measure the distance from point B to the vertical line which is labeled W in the drawing. You may find that this is equal to approximately 4 relative units. Then measure the height (H) from the bottom line to point C. This will be roughly equivalent to 20 relative units. Then, we subtract these from the coordinates of point B, because the new

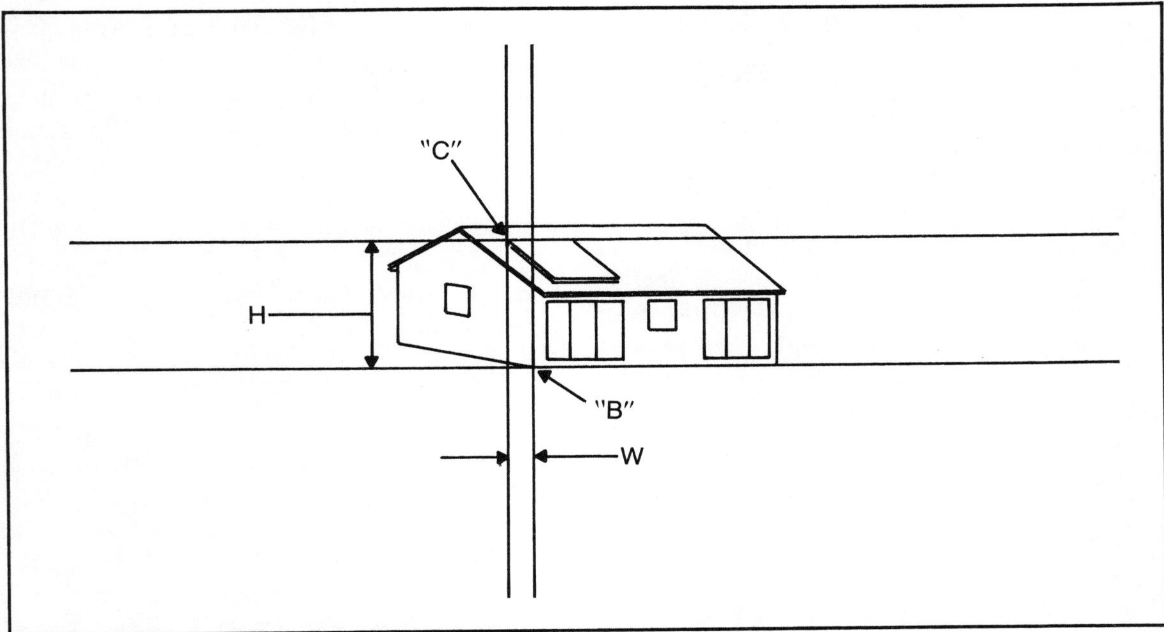

Fig. 6-47. Another method of determining coordinates.

coordinates lie to the left of and above point B.

This will give us the coordinates of point C, which are equal to:

140-4,130-20, or 136,110

It's now necessary to figure out the coordinates of the left end of the bottom line. This is accomplished by drawing a vertical line through the left end of the bottom line. In this case, the end point lies to the right of the horizontal coordinates of point B, which means the horizontal distance, approximately 3 relative units, must be added to coordinate 140. This point also lies above point B, so the vertical distance, approximately 14 relative units, will be subtracted from 130. The new coordinates are 143,116. Our original purpose was to connect the left ends of both lines, so the statement that will get this is:

LINE (136,110) – (143,116)

Eureka! Our diagonal line is drawn.

Now, to connect the nights ends of the two horizontal lines, the process is much simpler. Since the coordinates of the left ends of these lines are known, all you have to do is locate the R commands in the draw statement originally used to produce these horizontal lines. These should be R12 or thereabouts. The right ends of the lines will still be at the same vertical coordinates as the left ends. All you do is add 12 relative positions to the horizontal coordinates of the left ends. In this case, the following command will connect the two:

LINE (148,110) – (155,116)

The drawing of every other diagonal line in this picture is handled in the same manner, so proceed as before, always remembering to draw horizontal and vertical lines where necessary.

There is one other problem that occurs when draw statements are used in conjunction with line statements, or for that matter, with any other graphics commands. In previous drawings, the scale command was used in draw statements to vary the relative size of the object to be produced. However, varying the scale of the draw commands will affect the size of the lines that are produced by the draw statements only. The line statement coordinates will remain the same. For this reason, the two must be coordinated. Within each draw statement should be an S = X command, with a previous line specifying the value of X as 4. When a 4 is used, the draw *command numerals*, (that is, the lengths indicated in the draw statements) correspond exactly with screen points. If you want to enlarge the object, try doubling or tripling the value of the command numerals. You must then make the appropriate changes in the line statements. By this, I do not mean that you double the coordinates numbers in the line statement each time you double the draw command numerals. This only means that you have to add or subtract the new command numerals within the line statements. For example, in Fig. 6-47, it was established that the horizontal distance between point B and point C was 4 relative units. If you want to double the size of the drawing, this distance would be 8. Therefore, 8 must be subtracted from the horizontal coordinate of point B.

You can figure the coordinates in a slightly simpler manner by making all of your line statement coordinates relative. For instance, instead of typing the coordinates for a line starting at point C as:

LINE (136,110)

you would use the original coordinates of point B (140,130) as follows:

LINE (140-4,130-20)

This last line assumes that you used the actual line lengths in the original drawing. Then let's say that you want to double the size of the overall drawing. To accomplish this within the draw statements, you would input an S = X command, along with a previous line, X = 8. The value of X in this case doubles the values of the command numerals. Then, you would go back to your line statement and edit as follows:

LINE (140-(4*2),130–20*2))

The following lines will modify your basic program into a form in which all coordinates in the line statements should automatically correspond to the coordinates at the end points of the lines created using the draw statements, regardless of the scale factor used in the latter. Again, these lines represent only a portion of the program and are used for explanation purposes only.

```
10  SCREEN 1
20  INPUT X
30  Y = X/4
```

```
40  DRAW"BM140,130 S=X;U4 R4 D8
    R16....etc.
50  LINE (140-(4*Y),130-(20*Y))
```

Line 20 allows you to input a different value for X each time the program is run. This value is then inserted into the draw statement in line 40. Obviously, many draw statements will be required to produce the picture under discussion. Only one is shown here for illustration purposes. The same may be said of the line statement. The one shown, however, multiplies the differences between each of the coordinates for the point of origin (point B) and the coordinates for point C by the value of Y. If S is equal to 4 (X = 4), this amount will be divided by 4 in line 30. The value of Y will then be 1, and the line coordinates designated will not change. However, if the value of X changes to 8 (in effect doubling the command numeral in each draw statement), the value of Y will be 2, so the line coordinates will be modified accordingly. Using this system, however, it is necessary to reference all line statement coordinates to the starting point of B. This means that in some instances, it will be necessary to add to or subtract from the horizontal coordinates only, from vertical coordinates only, or from both. It is quite difficult, or at least timeconsuming, to draw a line on the right side of the screen based upon the coordinates of point B on the left. You can, however, use partial line statements, as discussed previously, to start a line at the last point drawn on the screen. This is a case of mix and match, and no two computer artists will arrive at the same picture in exactly the same way. There are just too many ways of accomplishing the same purpose. After a bit of experience, you will find that you are leaning toward one particular method or set of methods, and if you feel comfortable with this method, fine. If not, you may want to experiment a little more until you arrive at a system which is better suited to your thinking processes.

The program shown in Fig. 6-48 draws the original figure. You may input this directly to your IBM Personal Computer in order to end up with an on-screen display which can be varied in size, depending on the amount you input for the variable X. Again, this is certainly not the only way to draw this picture, and possibly not even the best way. It uses programming methods that I am personally comfortable with, but you may wish to experiment a bit to see if you can develop a shortcut or two that aids you in writing similar problems.

Figure 6-49 shows my first attempt at producing this three-dimensional graphic house with the unmodified version of the program shown in Fig. 6-48. This is what was produced on the first run, all coordinates having been worked out on paper with the aid of the original artwork and the horizontal and vertical lines. For a first stab, this is not bad at all. Note that a few lines are slightly out of kilter, but remember that this is what was produced on the first run, and no previous partial runs were conducted to determine just where I was. The window on the left side of the house is slightly misaligned, as are both sides of the roof. Other than this, everything seems to be fine. Figure 6-50 shows the results of the debugged version, which cleans up the problem areas mentioned.

Line 20 in the program in Fig. 6-48 allows you to input a scale factor between 1 and 10. If the scale factor goes above 10, the screen is

```
10 REM 3-D HOUSE
20 INPUT"TYPE IN THE SCALE FACTOR(1-10):";X
30 IF X>10 THEN 20
40 CLS
50 SCREEN 1,0
60 A=140
70 B=130
80 Y=X/4
90 COLOR 8,1
100 DRAW"S=X;BM140,130 R51 U12 L50 BL2 D12 NU13"
110 LINE(A+2*Y,B-12*Y)-(A-8*Y,B-24*Y)
120 DRAW"S=X;R50"
130 LINE(A+42*Y,B-24*Y)-(A+52*Y,B-12*Y)
140 DRAW"S=X;BM140,130 BL21 BU4 U12 L1"
150 LINE(A-24*Y,B-16*Y)-(A-8*Y,B-24*Y)
160 LINE(A-22*Y,B-4*Y)-(A,B)
170 LINE(A+8*Y,B-1*Y)-(A+20*Y,B-11*Y),,B
180 LINE(A+23*Y,B-6*Y)-(A+28*Y,B-11*Y),,B
190 LINE(A+32*Y,B-1*Y)-(A+44*Y,B-11*Y),,B
200 DRAW"BM140,130 S=X;BR36 BU1 NU10 BR4 NU10"
210 DRAW "S=X;BM140,130 BR12 BU1 NU10 BR4 NU10"
220 DRAW"S=X;BM140,130 BL8 BU7 U5 BL4 BU1 D5"
230 LINE(A-8*Y,B-7*Y)-(A-13*Y,B-8*Y)
240 LINE(A-8*Y,B-12*Y)-(A-12*Y,B-13*Y)
250 DRAW"S=X;BM140,130 BU14 BR7 NR10 BU6 BL4 R10"
260 LINE(A+7*Y,B-14*Y)-(A+3*Y,B-20*Y)
270 LINE(A+17*Y,B-14*Y)-(A+12*Y,B-20*Y)
```

Fig. 6-48. This program reproduces the original house drawing.

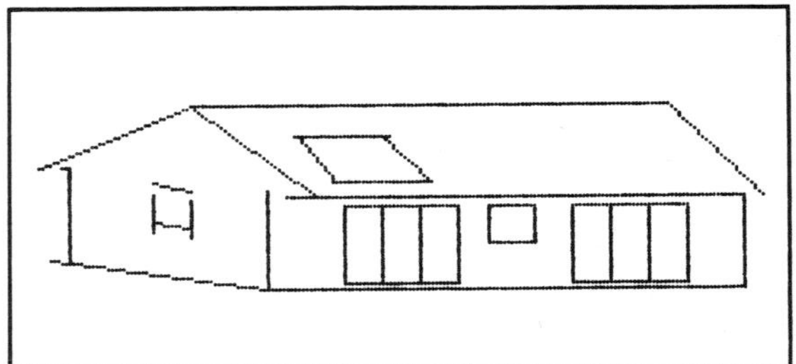

Fig. 6-49. An example of the first screen write while developing the program.

not able to contain the entire image. Therefore, a test line is found in program line 30. If the input value of X is greater than 10, there is a branch back to line 20. The program will not run unless the scale factor input is 10 or less.

In order to coordinate the two statements used to actually draw the house (DRAW, LINE), I assigned the major coordinate values to variables A and B in lines 60 and 70. These are the only coordinates which do not change

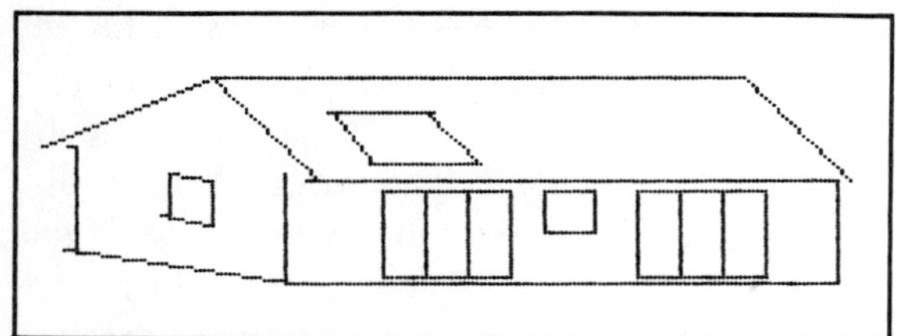

Fig. 6-50. The finished screen write of the three-dimensional house.

with the scale factor, since this is the point on the screen where all drawing begins. Assigning these values to variables greatly shortens programming time. Note in line 80 the assignment of a value to the variable Y which is equivalent to X divided by 4. This last variable will be used as a multiplier within the line statement as explained earlier.

Our first draw statement is encountered in line 100. The starting coordinates are specified by the BM command. The R50 command draws the front bottom portion of the house, while U12 draws the vertical section of the far end. The next command draws the top front of the house, and the next series of commands cause the left vertical edge to be drawn. The line statement in program line 110 draws the diagonal left edge of the roof. Note that the coordinates are based on A and B, which are the coordinates for our beginning point. The Y variable is used to increase or decrease the coordinate value to keep it in scale with the draw statements, which are controlled by scale factor X. The rest of the program pretty much continues to follow the pattern outlined a bit earlier in this discussion. I have thrown in a few shortcuts, however. Lines 170 through 190 draw the front window and the two panels on either side. You will notice here that I have used line statements followed by the B command, which causes a box or rectangle to be created. Line 170 draws the outline of the solar panel on the left side of the front of the house. Line 180 draws the small window at the center, and line 190 draws the outline of the right-hand solar panel. Then, lines 200 and 210 incorporate draw statements to segment the two panels, giving the appearance of three smaller panels in each.

Now, I could have used draw statements alone to produce these last three portions of the drawing, but using the line statements followed by the B commands was much simpler. If I'd used a draw statement to produce the left solar panel, for instance, four separate commands would have been required, in addition to the two required to produce the segmenting lines. Using the line statement, however, I simply filled in the coordinates of the left bottom edge of the box and the right top corner, and a box was automatically formed. Some persons may argue that the line statement includes four coordinate values, which could be equated with the four commands in the equivalent draw statement. This is certainly true, but I found it easier to write my program in this manner and elected to go the most comfortable route. If you feel another way is better, then by all means, do what I did and program comfortably.

I would "guestimate" that total programming time was about thirty minutes work on my part. It may take you a longer period of time or even a shorter period. The main thing is to be able to keep track of what you're doing. While not shown in this program, it would be a good idea to include REM statements before every write line just to indicate what each line is doing. In this manner, you can label your program lines to match the segments of the artwork they produce. The only problem I encountered was during the modification process to straighten out the few erratic screen lines. Since I did not include REM statements, I got a bit confused as to which program line did what. I attempted to identify the problem area by inserting a very large coordinate value in a line statement. When the program was run, the screen line which was affected by the altered program line was much longer, and through this trial and error process, I was finally able to coordinate the on-screen information with the program itself. Unfortunately, I switched a value and then couldn't remember where it was located, or for that matter, what the original value was. Add to this the fact that I had not committed the original program to memory, and you can begin to realize my quandry. I finally located the problem line by placing end statements at various points on the program. Eventually, the problem was located and the coordinate value was reset as before. This should be a good lesson for everyone. As soon as you get a program that is close to being what you want, immediately store it on disk. You can then go through the debugging process without fear of messing up what you've worked so hard to obtain. If you mess up the program in current memory, you simply reload the stored version and start again. This should be no great revelation to anyone, but even those of us who are programming on an almost-constant basis slip up now and then and forget the rule of thumb.

ASSORTED COLOR PROGRAMS

Now that we've gone through most of the statements used in color/graphics programming, it's time to have some fun. The following portion of this chapter includes a number of programs that have been written specifically for the IBM Personal Computer. Admittedly, many of these were conceived while I was miles away from my own computer. They were quickly jotted down on paper in program line form. Once you become familiar with the IBM computer and especially with the language used to create on-screen graphics, you will find ideas popping into your head almost constantly. Unfortunately, the IBM Personal Computer is a rather bulky system and certainly could not be considered portable. Therefore, when ideas crop up when you are away from your normal operating position, you often have to write your programs from your knowledge of the computer and then test them out later.

While many of these programs were conceived and written without the aid of a computer, be assured that each of them has been input and run just to make certain no errors have occurred. All of the programs in this book were output from the computer and retained in hard copy form using the IBM printer. While it is possible to produce graphic programs that will run on a certain machine without the direct use of the machine, the images are often off center, and invariably, a bit of cleaning up is dictated to produce a good machine run. I think you will find that most of the programs in this book are very clean, and while you may wish to make modifications to suit your personal tastes, all programs will run as shown.

Figure 6-51 is a simple program I call *Stars*. It may be used for background in programs that display deep space scenes. The

```
10 STARS
20 CLS
30 SCREEN 1,0,0
40 COLOR 8,0
50 X=RND*319
60 Y=RND*(199)
70 PSET (X,Y)
80 GOTO 30
```

Fig. 6-51. Program to generate stars, which are really random points on the screen.

```
10 REM WHEEL
20 SCREEN 1
30 COLOR 8,0
40 CIRCLE(160,100),60,1
50 CIRCLE(160,100),10,3
60 LINE(170,100)-(220,100)
70 LINE(160,110)-(160,150)
80 LINE(150,100)-(100,100)
90 LINE(160,90)-(160,50)
100 LINE(168,105)-(203,135)
110 LINE(117,135)-(152,107)
120 LINE(115,68)-(152,95)
130 LINE(167,95)-(207,68)
140 PAINT(160,100),2,3
```

Fig. 6-52. *Color Wheel* program.

stars are simply random points of light that will appear all over the screen. This program is written in endless-loop form, so the stars will continue to increase in number until the entire screen is filled. In practical application, you will probably want to insert a for-next loop around the portion of this program that accomplishes the actual screen write. If your for-next loop counts from 1 to 100, you will have a maximum of 100 stars on the screen. You can increase or decrease the number of stars by adjusting the for-next loop accordingly.

You will most likely want to play around with the color statement and possibly even adjust the random numbers assignments in lines 50 and 60. In some graphic space scenes, it may not be desirable to have stars all over the screen but rather, to one side or the other. Line 50 controls the horizontal placement of stars on the screen, while line 60 controls vertical placement. If you change line 60 to Y = RND*(100), all of the stars will be confined to the top half of the screen. This might be advantageous in writing a program which displays the surface of a planet with the stars overhead. The PSET statement uses the coordinates of X and Y to print a single point of light on the screen. Since X and Y are given random values, no fixed patterns occur and the display will be ever-changing.

Figure 6-52 shows a program which will draw a colorful spoked wheel on the screen. The wheel rim is created by the circle statement in line 40, while the hub is created by the one in line 50. Once the rim and hub have been programmed, it is then necessary to create the spoke. I used line statements to accomplish this, and these are contained in program lines 60 through 130. A total of eight spokes are drawn from the hub to the rim. These are spaced symmetrically around the circumference. To fill in the hub, a paint statement is used in line 140. Figure 6-53 shows a sample printout of this program run.

By reducing the dimensions of the circles and lines, the wheel image could easily be

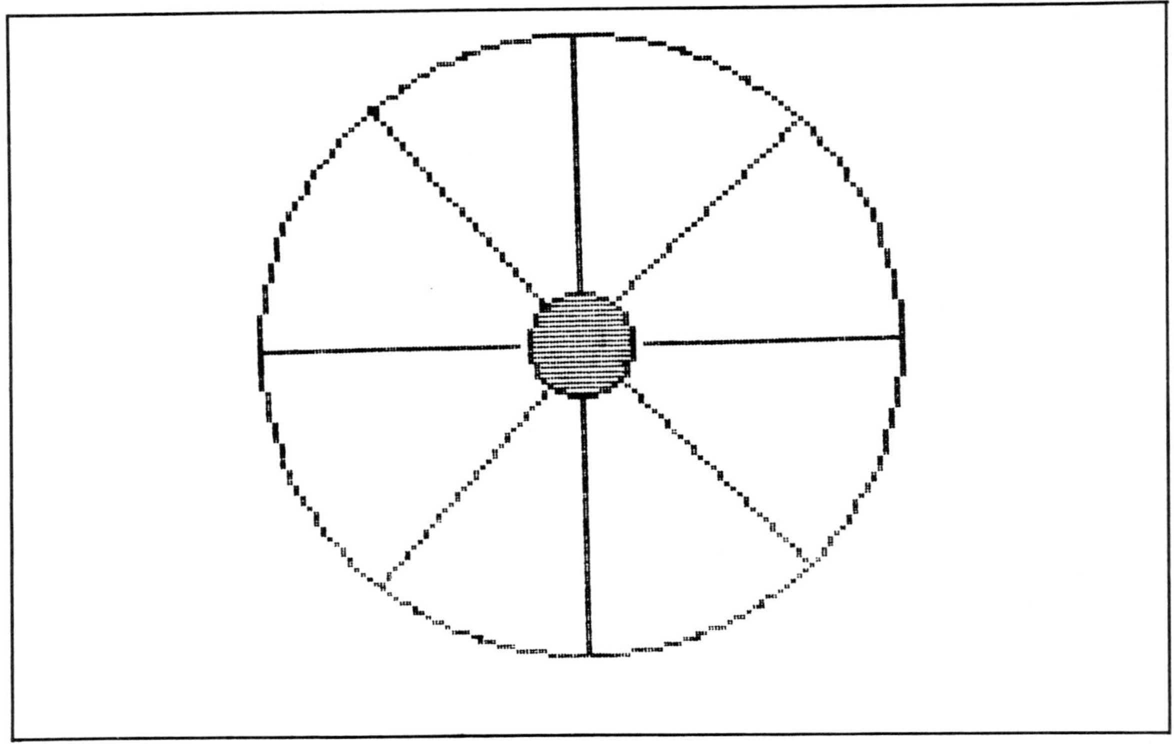

Fig. 6-53. Sample printout of the *Color Wheel* program run.

```
10 REM PINWHEEL
20 SCREEN 1
30 COLOR RND*15,RND*4
40 FOR X=1 TO 70 STEP RND*
   6+1
50 CIRCLE(160,100),X,1
60 NEXT
70 FOR X=100 TO 155
80 PAINT(161,X),RND*4,1
90 NEXT
100 FOR TS=1 TO 600:NEXT
110 CLS
120 GOTO 20
```

Fig. 6-54. *Pinwheel* program.

incorporated in a graphics program used to draw a wagon or even an automobile. By tagging the line statements with appropriate color designators, additional paint statements could be used to fill in each spoke section with a different color. This would present a fixed kaleidoscopic effect.

Figure 6-54 is a program which creates a pinwheel effect. A circle with a variable radius is created in line 50, and paint statements are used to fill in the spaces as the concentric circles are completed. The number of circles created depends on the quantity issued from the random number generator, and therefore, each image is a bit different. The time delay

```
10 REM FUNNEL
20 SCREEN 1
30 COLOR 8,RND*3+1
40 FOR X=80 TO 150 STEP RND
   *10
50 CIRCLE(X,250-X),X-60,RND
   *3+1
60 NEXT
70 CLS
80 GOTO 20
```

Fig. 6-55. This program generates an attractive funnel on the color monitor screen.

loop in line 100 allows for one image to fully establish itself before the screen is cleared to prepare for the printing of the next series. The randomized color statement in line 30 produces a very colorful on-screen effect.

The program in Fig. 6-55 produces a sort of funnel on the display monitor. This is accomplished by drawing circles which partially overlap. The placement of each circle is determined by the for-next loop which begins at line 40. The first circle will be printed in the left-hand bottom portion of the screen. The next will be slightly higher and to the right. This process continues toward the righthand top of the screen. The step command in line 40 will vary the amount of space between each circle and the one written previously, so a multitude of different combinations is available When the funnel first appears, it may seem that you're looking at it from the small end or that you're looking down the wide section toward the small end. As the funnel continues to grow, your relative perspective seems to change. As the circles travel from left to right, they get larger. The first circle created will have a radius of 20, which is set up by the X − 60 designator following the circle coordinates in line 50. The next circle will have a radius that is slightly larger. The actual value is determined by the random number used with the step command. Circle colors will also change, because of the random color command at the end of the circle statement. You can easily reverse the direction the circle takes by rearranging the circle coordinates in relation to the value of X. Figure 6-56 shows a screen write of the program run.

The program shown in Fig. 6-57 draws a schematic diagram of a simple electronic circuit that consists of two series resistors in parallel with two other series resistors. This program uses draw statements to produce all on-screen images, since the schematic symbols for resistors and conductors are composed solely of vertical, horizontal, and diagonal lines. More complex schematic diagrams may be produced by using circle statements, PSETs, and others. Some companies are even offering special electronic schematic programs

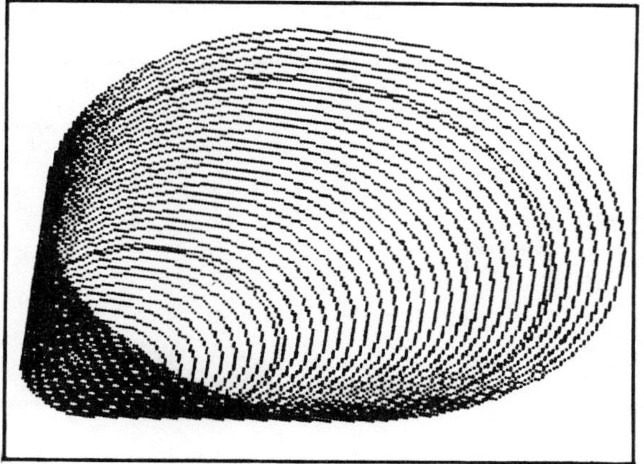

Fig. 6-56. Screen write of the funnel program run.

```
10 REM SCHEMATIC DIAGRAM
20 SCREEN 1
30 CLS
40 KEY OFF
50 X=8
60 DRAW"B150 S=X;R8 U10 R10 E1 F3 E3 F3 E3 F3 E1 R24 E1 F3
   E3 F3 E3 F3 E1 R10 D1
0 NR8 D10 L10 G1 H3 G3"
70 DRAW"H3 G3 H3 G1 L24 G1 H3 G3 H3 G3 H3 G1 L10 U10"
```

Fig. 6-57. This program draws a simple schematic diagram.

that will run on the IBM Personal Computer and can be used to draw on-screen schematics in a much simpler manner. Such programs simply act as an easy go-between and allow for simpler input instructions to bring about more complex machine functions. For example, the portion of the program just discussed that draws the resistor symbol would be committed to a file in an electronic diagram operating system. The user might input a single command such as "R" to access this file, and the more complex information needed for the IBM Personal Computer to draw a resistor symbol would automatically be input to the machine. Figure 6-58 shows the graphic schematic diagram.

By using the graphics capability of the IBM Personal Computer, it is quite easy to produce professional-appearing schematic diagrams from rough circuit sketches. You can even build your own operating system, which will allow you to easily call up the series of commands needed to produce transistors, diodes, and many other electronic components in schematic symbol form. Such a system would not be tremendously difficult to design. It would simply consist of a large number of small programs each of which could be accessed by a

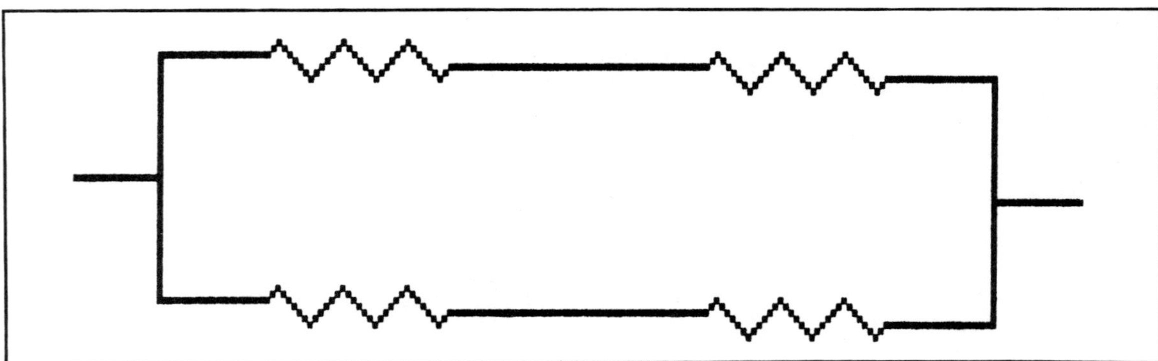

Fig. 6-58. Graphic schematic diagram.

single command. However, there are many different electronic symbols, and a separate program would be required for each one. You would also have to devise a method of specifying the coordinates at which each symbol is to be placed. You could even build in variable length, angle and radius factors, which would allow you to vary the size of your computer-generated schematic diagrams.

From a practical standpoint, most schematic diagrams are drawn in very simple form. Even the complex ones can be broken down into their basic, simple elements, and if you have the capability of drawing each of these, then you have the capability of drawing many different electronic circuits on the monitor screen by varying the size of each graphic symbol. It is conveivable, then, that whole schematic diagrams of a sophisticated piece of electronic equipment could be commited to memory and recalled when needed for troubleshooting purposes.

```
10 REM ROTATING BOX
20 SCREEN 1,0
30 CLS
40 X=10
50 A$="S=X;U15 R15 D15 L15"
60 DRAW"A0"+A$
70 GOSUB 160
80 DRAW"A1"+A$
90 GOSUB 160
100 DRAW"A2"+A$
110 GOSUB 160
120 DRAW"A3"+A$
130 GOSUB 160
140 DRAW"A0"+A$
150 GOTO 40
160 FOR Y=0 TO 10:NEXT Y
170 X=10
180 CLS
190 RETURN
200 CLS
```

Fig. 6-59. *Rotating Box* program.

Figure 6-59 shows a program which uses the A command within the draw statement to angularly rotate a box around a central axis. Line 50 commits the draw information to a string variable, and the next series of lines uses the angle command with this string variable to draw the box at various locations on the screen. The lower left-hand corner of the box as drawn originally will serve as the axis around which the box will rotate. Line 60 causes the computer to write the box on the screen. The A0 designation means that the angle is zero and is really included here for explanation purposes. There is a branch in line 70 that accesses a for-next time delay loop to allow each write to establish itself before being erased. When the loop times out, the screen is cleared by the CLS in line 180, and the return statement in line 190 branches to line 80. Here, we have a similar draw statement, but the angle command is dictated by A1. This specifies a 90° angle, so the box is rotated 90°. After another GOSUB and return, line 100 is accessed. The A2 command specifies a 180° rotation, so the box will be printed at a 180° angle from its origin. Line 120 specifies a 270° rotation, and finally, line 140 returns the box to its original position. There is a GOTO statement in line 150, which causes the program to act on an endless loop basis. The branch here causes the program to start all over again.

The on-screen effect this program produces is a complete 360° rotation of a box. The rotation is accomplished in steps of 90° each.

The box will continue to spin around the central axis until the program is manually halted.

The angle command can be used to speed programming time when using a number of draw statements. If, for example, you wanted to print two boxes that were connected at a common point and opposed by 180°, you would commit the basic box information to a string variable and insert an A0 command in one line and an A2 command in another, both using the same string variable. It would be necessary to input the information needed to draw the box two times. Figure 6-60 shows what such a program would yield. The two images remain on the screen simultaneously, because a CLS statement is omitted.

Figure 6-61 is a variation on previous programs that you draw concentric circles starting from a small radius at a point near the center of the screen and expanding outward. This program, however, goes one step further. As soon as the circle has reached a maximum circumference, it begins to implode. In other words, the circle reaches a maximum size and then begins to shrink back to nothingness again.

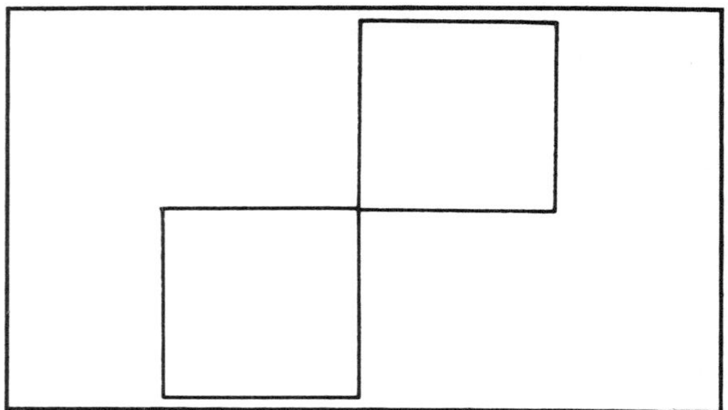

Fig. 6-60. An example of the screen print during the *Rotating Box* program run.

```
10 REM CIRCLE EXPLODE/
   IMPLODE
20 SCREEN 1,0
30 COLOR RND*15,RND*4
40 CLS
50 FOR X=0 TO 100
60 CIRCLE(160,100),X,RND*4
70 NEXT X
80 FOR Y=0 TO 100
90 CIRCLE(160,100),100-Y,0
100 NEXT Y
110 GOTO 30
```

Fig. 6-61. This program creates concentric circles which then slowly disappear.

The first circle is generated in line 60 using values from 0 to 100 for its radius. As soon as the for-next loop that is begun in line 50 times out (reaches 100), line 80 begins another for-next loop. The circle statement in line 90 is the same as before, except the value of Y is subtracted from 100. The first circle generated, then, will have a radius of 100 – 0, or 100. The color command that follows the radius command is a 0, which means that the circle will be printed in the background color. This effectively erases the last circle generated in line 60. The first circle statement generated a series of ever-widening circles. The last circle statement produces a series of ever-narrowing blank circles, in effect erasing the concentric circles in reverse order. This program is on an endless loop, so as soon as the first set of circles are written and then erased, another set will begin. The randomized color statement in line 30 and the color command in line 60 create a wide variation of screen color backgrounds and circle colors. If you really get wrapped up in this display, it may appear that you're falling down a shaft toward an opening at the lower end. However, as the circle begins to decrease, it might seem like you're falling down a chimney with the opening above seeming to get ever smaller as your distance from it increases. It's a grand display, and this program may be input to the IBM Personal Computer in just a few minutes.

Figure 6-62 is a program that produces a fairly intricate bit of lacework on the screen. Draw statements are used to produce the lines required to draw what appears to be an intricately tied rope consisting of four loops which cross over or under other image segments. This image is quite common in the computer graphics world and has been duplicated in many interesting ways. I got the idea from an Epson printer manual. This was the figure that was used to demonstrate the graphics capability of their MX-80 model. Theirs was a bit more intricate than the one this program produces, and a considerable number of write commands were required because it was necessary to graphically simulate a wide piece of rope. Two parallel lines are required for each segment to give the impression of width.

```
10 REM INTERLACE
20 SCREEN 1
30 A=RND*10+1
40 B=RND*3+1
50 COLOR A,B
60 X=RND*3+1
70 R=20
80 DRAW"S=R;C3 BM100,150U12BU4U12R12BR4R12D12BD4D12L12BL4L
   12"
90 DRAW"S=R;C3 BM100,150U12R8BR4R16D4BL4L12BL4L4D4R4BR12R4
   U4"
100 DRAW"S=R;C3 BM100,150R12U16BU4U8L8BD4D4BD12D4R4U12BU4U
    4L4"
110 DRAW"S=R;C3 BM100,150U12BU8BR4R12BR4R4U4L4D12BD4D4R4"
120 DRAW"S=R;C3 BM100,150BR16U8BU4U16"
130 DRAW"S=R;C3 BM100,150BU16R16BR4R8"
140 X=RND*3+1
150 PAINT(101,38),X,3
160 PAINT(185,48),X,3
170 PAINT(185,145),X,3
180 PAINT(101,145),X,3
190 FOR TS=1 TO 600:NEXT TS
200 CLS
210 GOTO 30
```

Fig. 6-62. *Interlace* program.

After the outline is produced by the draw statements, paint statements are used to fill in the various sections. Originally, I filled in each of the four loop sections with a different color, but I later modified the program to paint the entire piece of lacework the same color, which is constantly changing due to the randomized color command. A randomized color statement changes the screen background and the foreground palette each time the design is drawn. This statement is found in line 50. A time delay loop is found in line 190. As soon as it times out, the screen image is cleared and the program branches back to line 30, where new random color numbers are inserted for a completely different screen display.

Sometimes the lacework produced by this program will seem to be perfectly flat; other times, it will appear to be three-dimensional depending on which random colors are output. If the right color combinations come up (or perhaps I should say the wrong combinations), there will be no image at all on the screen for a few seconds. This occurs when the background color, the foreground color, and the line color are all the same. The point is, you never know

Fig. 6-63. An example of one of the many screen displays created using the Interlace program.

```
10 REM PINE TREE
20 SCREEN 1
30 X=25
40 COLOR 8,0
50 DRAW"S=X;BM140,150 C3U4L8E4L3E4L2E4L1E4F4L1F4L2F4L3F4L
   16BR8D4L5"
60 LINE(0,150)-(319,150)
70 PAINT(152,70),1,3
80 PAINT(160,140),3,3
```

Fig. 6-64. A graphic pine tree is created with this program.

what to expect from such a display. Figure 6-63 is an example of one of the many screen displays produced during this program run.

The program shown in Fig. 6-64 draws a simple piece of artwork on the screen. This is one of the first programs I wrote using the draw statement, and it was originally conceived and written at a point far removed from the computer. I wanted to draw a simple pine tree and quickly jotted down what I thought would do the job. When I was finally able to input this program to the computer, I found that it worked perfectly. I did, however, include some additional commands to increase the size of the tree and to paint some colors. Looking at the commands within the draw statement in line 50, U4 is the first one that writes anything on the screen. I imagined that I was starting at the bottom of the trunk on the left-hand side. The U4 command draws the left side of the trunk. Then the L8 command draws the left bottom portion of the branches. E4 draws a diagonal line upward and to the right for a distance of 4 relative screen positions. Then we move left again for 3 screen positions, and so forth to the top of the tree. The taper effect is controlled by the values in the L commands, and you will notice that they decrease to 1 at the very top. At this point, the entire left side of the tree has been drawn, so we begin down the other side. The F4 command moves down to the right diagonally, and I then simply matched my previous L commands in reverse order. The right side of the tree starts from a minimum value and increases to a maximum of L16. This last command draws a single line from the right side of the tree branches to the left side of the trunk. This completely separates the branch section from the trunk. A BR8 command moves back to the right side of the tree without plotting points, where a D4 command completes the right side of the trunk. The last command draws a horizontal line across the bottom of the trunk. It was necessary to completely enclose the branch section and the trunk section because these were to be painted different colors. The line statement in program line 60 draws the base for the tree, which simulates the ground.

The paint statements in lines 70 and 80 fill in the two tree sections with colors. The first one paints the branch section green, while the second paints the trunk a brownish color.

No, the tree doesn't look true to life, but it does look like the simple Christmas trees we all drew as children. Using some line and PSET statements, it would be possible to draw in some branch details for a more lifelike appearance. However, most computer graphics programs are used to simulate objects, not to depict them exactly as they appear in real life. Anyone who uses the display from this program will have no difficulty whatsoever in determining that this is indeed a pine tree. To go a step further, you might want to include some colorful circle statements to simulate ornaments to turn our pine tree into an authentic Christmas tree. You can even use a modified version of a simple program presented earlier in this chapter for drawing random points on the screen. These would make good simulations of colorful Christmas tree lights. If you want your tree to be larger or smaller, simply increase or decrease the value of X in line 30 until you get what you're looking for. Figure 6-65 shows the graphic image of the pine tree.

At this point, let me give you a little tip on speeding up programming time. Let's assume that you've input the program shown here and produced a tree on the screen. Let's also assume that you want to draw another one just like it, so that two trees will appear on the screen. Obviously, you will have to change the BM command to move the first tree further to the left or right to make room for another, which would also use a different BM command. This is simple, but you still have to type in all of the other commands in the draw statement. To speed up programming time, you can use this trick. The draw statement is located in line 50, so all you need to do is type in LIST and press the enter key. The screen will then display all eight program lines. Now, using the editing keys, move the cursor under the 5 in 50, press the INS key and type 1. Then press the enter key again. Now, clear the screen and type LIST

Fig. 6-65. Pine tree image.

again. You will see the same program as before. Line 50 will have been unchanged, but there will now be an additional line, 150, which contains the same program information as the original line 50. Instead of retyping this line in its entirety, you have duplicated it and can now use the editing functions again to change the BM command values to produce the on-screen images you desire. You can do this over and over to easily produce more trees through simple editing of computer reproduced program lines.

The program shown in Fig. 6-66 allows the computer to display a simplistic nighttime scene that includes a house, a green lawn, two trees, the moon overhead, and numerous stars in the sky. In many ways, it is a combination of several other programs that were presented and discussed previously. For the most part, this is a two-dimensional display, but it is quite colorful and will really attract attention. In writing this program, I started out to draw a simple house with two windows, a door, and a chimney. This was accomplished rather rapidly, so I began playing around to add more images to the display. As I added more images, I was spurred on to include even more and decided to quit with the program presented here.

Program lines 50 through 200 draw the basic structure of the house using line statements, some of which contain the familiar BF command for filled boxes. Line 170 draws the ground the house rests on, and line 180 paints in the green grass. The circle statement in line 150 draws the doorknob.

At this point, I decided to add a couple of trees to the lawn, and these are produced by the draw statements in lines 210 through 260. The paint statements in lines 270 and 280 fill in the tree images.

The statements in line 190 and 200 draw the moon overhead and fill it in. The only thing lacking at this point is a sky full of stars. This is produced in lines 290 through 330. The value of X is used to limit the number of stars to 20 per PSET statement, or a grand total of 60. I couldn't use a general randomized PSET, because this would have filled in the entire screen. I caused the program to print three sets of random stars. Line 300 involves the stars directly overhead and across the entire width of the screen. The maximum vertical value that any star can assume will be less than 30. In the middle of the screen, the house comes into play, and I certainly didn't want stars printed all over the roof. The PSET statement in line 310 prints random stars to the left of the house, while the one in line 320 prints them to the right. These coordinates and the actual number of stars (as defined by the value of X) were arrived at by trial and error. The entire process, however, took less than ten minutes.

The on-screen effect when this program is run is that of a rural home bathed in intense moonlight on a clear, starry night. By using some animation techniques, it should be possible to simulate an entire 24 hours in this screen. Using put and get statements, the moon could be made to move off the screen, after which the sunlight rises from the left-hand side and the stars could be dimmed. This gets much more involved, however, and it would be necessary to reduce the overall size of the house to allow more room for the moving heavenly bodies.

Note the use of 0 for color statements in

```
10 REM HOUSE SCENE AT NIGHT
20 CLS
30 SCREEN 1,0
40 COLOR 8,0
50 LINE(90,180)-(212,90),2,BF
60 LINE(90,90)-(148,48)
70 LINE(212,90)-(148,48)
80 LINE(177,140)-(203,112),0,BF
90 LINE(190,140)-(190,112)
100 LINE(177,126)-(203,126)
110 LINE(97,140)-(123,112),0,BF
120 LINE(97,126)-(123,126)
130 LINE(110,112)-(110,140)
140 LINE(132,140)-(164,180),,BF
150 CIRCLE(156,160),2,1
160 LINE(120,72)-(134,48),,BF
170 LINE(0,180)-(319,180),1
180 PAINT(2,181),1,1
190 CIRCLE(280,40),15,2
200 PAINT(280,40),3,2
210 DRAW"C2 BM250,180 U4 L8 E4 L3 E4 L2"
220 DRAW"C2 E4 L1 E4 F4 L1 F4 L2 F4 L3"
230 DRAW"C2 F4 L8 D4 L4"
240 DRAW"C2 BM60,180 U4 L8 E4 L3 E4 L2
250 DRAW"C2 E4 L1 E4 F4 L1 F4 L2 F4 L3
260 DRAW"C2 F4 L8 D4 L4"
270 PAINT(251,179),3,2
280 PAINT(61,179),3,2
290 FOR X=1 TO 20
300 PSET(RND*319,RND*30)
310 PSET(RND*80,RND*150)
320 PSET(319-RND*100,RND*150)
330 NEXT
```

Fig. 6-66. Program to draw a nighttime house scene.

lines 80 and 110. These serve to blacken the windows behind the lines that make up the pane crosspieces, giving the appearance of a darkened interior. The house roof is the same color, matching that of the darkened portion of the screen display. You can increase the complexity of this scene by adding more stars or even more windows to the home. There is also room for several more trees if you wish to take the time to write them into the program. Once you have programmed the basic scene, you can then begin to make the modifications necessary to personalize your on-screen display. By changing the background color, you can instantly convert the program as shown to produce a daytime scene. In this case, the moon is converted to the sun and the BF commands that color the interior of the windows would be altered to produce a light color to simulate interior illumination. Figure 6-67 shows the completed scene.

ELECTRONIC GRAPHS

An oscilloscope is an electronic test instrument that will visually display various electronic operations and parameters. These devices are often used to display the waveform of an ac signal. We can simulate the same effect on the IBM Personal Computer through appropriate programming. The computer does not actually read or measure the output from an electronic device, but we can build in certain parameters by means of software. Figure 6-68 shows a program which will generate a sine wave on the monitor screen. A sine wave is constantly changing polarity, with equal portions of the curve on the positive and negative sides of the graph. Figure 6-69 shows the graphic display. When this program is run, the solid horizontal line represents the value 0, while the upper portion of the scale is positive and the lower portion is negative. The graph shows a perfect sine wave, in that those wave portions which lie in the upper portion of the scale are mirror images of those which lie below.

The reference line is drawn in program line 50. This line spans the entire horizontal width of the screen and is situated at its center. Line 60 establishes the value for pi, while lines 70 and 80 determine the starting and ending points of the sine wave display. Line 90 divides the difference between B and A into 638, which is exactly twice the maximum screen width (319). Line 100 establishes the spacing between each point plotted on the graph. Here, I'm using a step of .1. Line 120 uses the SIN function to cause the plotted points to be displayed as a true sine wave. The sine of the value of D is multiplied by P. The latter variable determines the maximum value of each wave section, or the distance of each peak from the horizontal line. Line 130 performs the actual plotting function.

Due to the small step in line 100, it will take thirty seconds or so for the entire graph to be completed. You can use larger step factors, although each waveform will not be displayed as finely. We could say that this is a sine wave that represents a value of 60 volts ac, since we chose a value of 60 for P. This assumes that the value of P is to directly represent potential difference. Any other value could be assigned to P, as long as it does not exceed 100. For the display actually shown, the value of P is unimportant, at least in regard to it representing some true electronic value. However, if such a graph were to be used for the comparison of sine waves of different voltage values, P's value would be all-important.

A program which will allow you to compare sine waves of different voltage values is shown in Fig. 6-70. This is basically the same as the previous program, except line 40 allows you to input a peak ac value of up to 220 volts. This peak value is scaled for graphing purposes

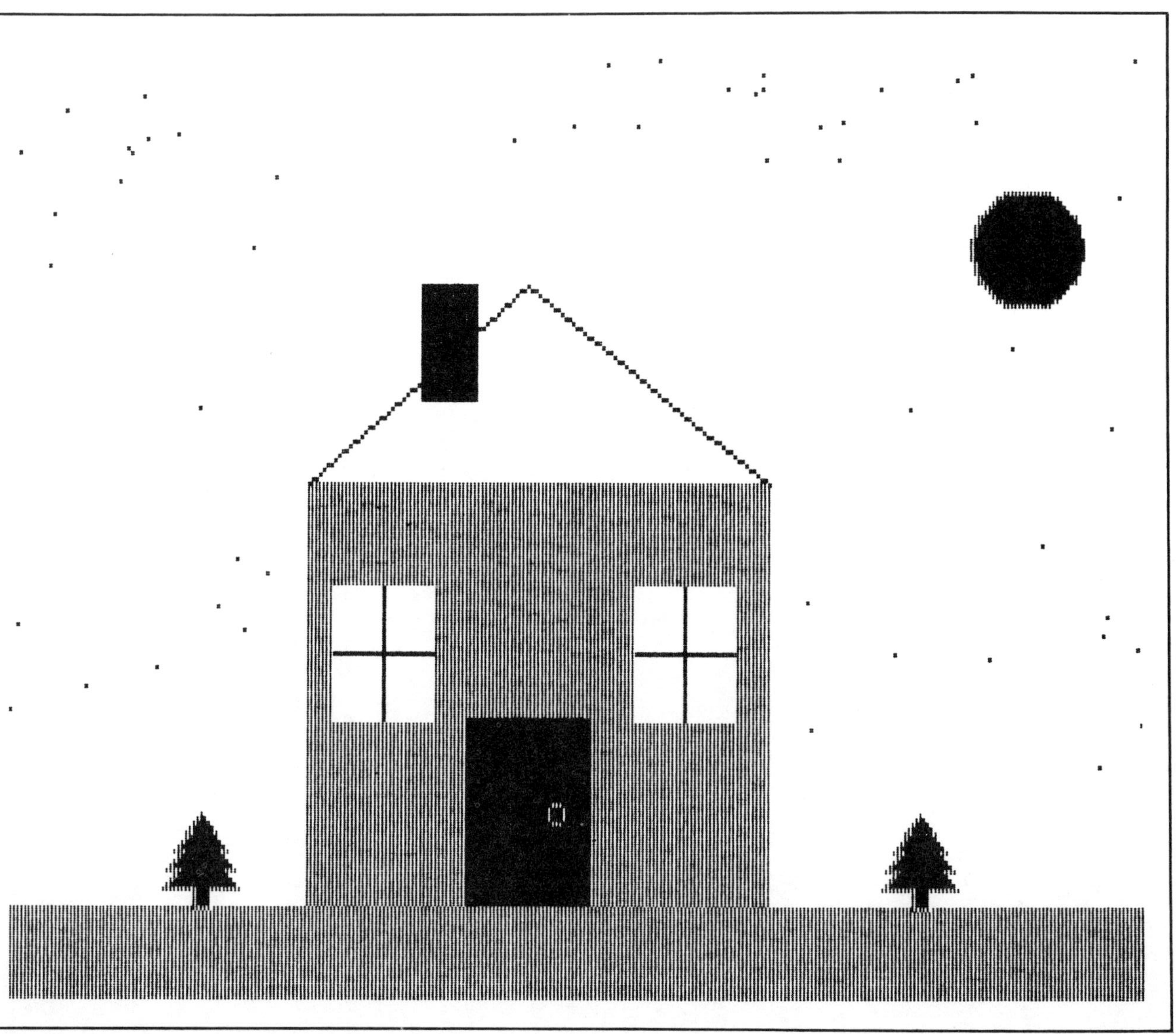

Fig. 6-67. This screen display of the nighttime house scene is much more attractive in color, as the various elements of the scene are better differentiated.

```
10 REM SINE WAVE
20 CLS
30 P=60
40 SCREEN 1
50 LINE(0,100)-(319,100)
60 PI=3.14159
70 A=-11*PI
80 B=7*PI
90 C=638/(B-A)
100 FOR D=A TO B STEP .1
110 X=D*C
120 Y=SIN(D)*P
130 PSET(X+60,100+Y)
140 NEXT D
150 END
```

Fig. 6-68. This program generates a sine wave on the monitor screen.

by the formula in line 50, and it is subsequently plotted on the graph. The remainder of the program is identical to the previous one, although there is a GOTO statement in line 170, which constantly returns the program to its beginning so that more waveforms may be displayed.

Figure 6-71 shows the plot of three different sine waves valued at 200, 100, and 50 volts, respectively. The largest swings represent the highest value. This graph, then is a comparison of three different sine waves. You're certainly not limited to three. The program is on an endless loop, so you may plot as many as you desire. Again, this program limits the maximum peak value to 220 volts, but a slight modification will allow you to set any maximum value desired. You can then input any peak values that are equal to or below the maximum graph value. The modifications are:

```
31  INPUT "MAXIMUM VALUE: ";M
32  CLS
....
....
50  P = P*(80/M)
```

When you run this modified version of the program, you will first be prompted to input the maximum value, which is then assigned to the variable M. The rest of the program runs as

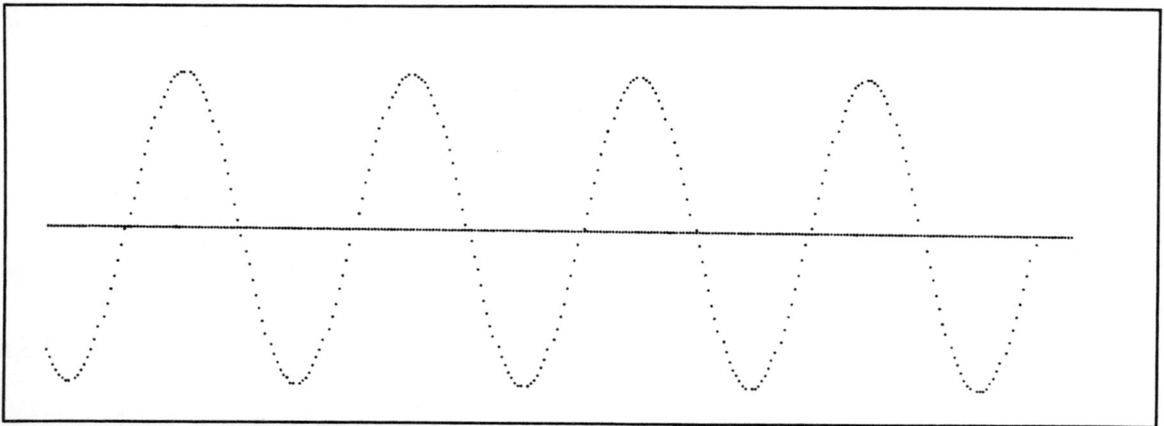

Fig. 6-69. Sample print from the *Sine* program.

```
10 REM WAVEFORM GRAPH
20 CLS
30 LOCATE 1,1
40 INPUT"PEAK VALUE: ";P
50 P=P*(80/220)
60 SCREEN 1
70 LINE(0,100)-(319,100)
80 PI=3.14159
90 A=-11*PI
100 B=7*PI
110 C=638/(B-A)
120 FOR D=A TO B STEP .12
130 X=D*C
140 Y=SIN(D)*P
150 PSET(X+60,100+Y)
160 NEXT D
170 GOTO 30
```

Fig. 6-70. This graphics program allows you to compare sine waves of different potentials.

before, except you can now input any value up to that of M. If you're plotting relatively low values, insert the anticipated maximum when prompted to do so. Any values near this point will then be displayed near the top and bottom of the screen. By being able to vary the maximum value, it is much easier to arrive at a display which is spread out enough to be meaningful. In the original program which contained a maximum value of 220 volts, displaying a low value of 1 or 2 volts would give you a waveform trace that was so close to the horizontal line that it would be difficult to clearly see the spacing. However, in this last program, if you choose 5 as a maximum value, a 1 or 2 volt plot will fill up 20 to 40 percent of the vertical space allotted to the display.

Figure 6-72 shows another type of graphics display that is based on this same program.

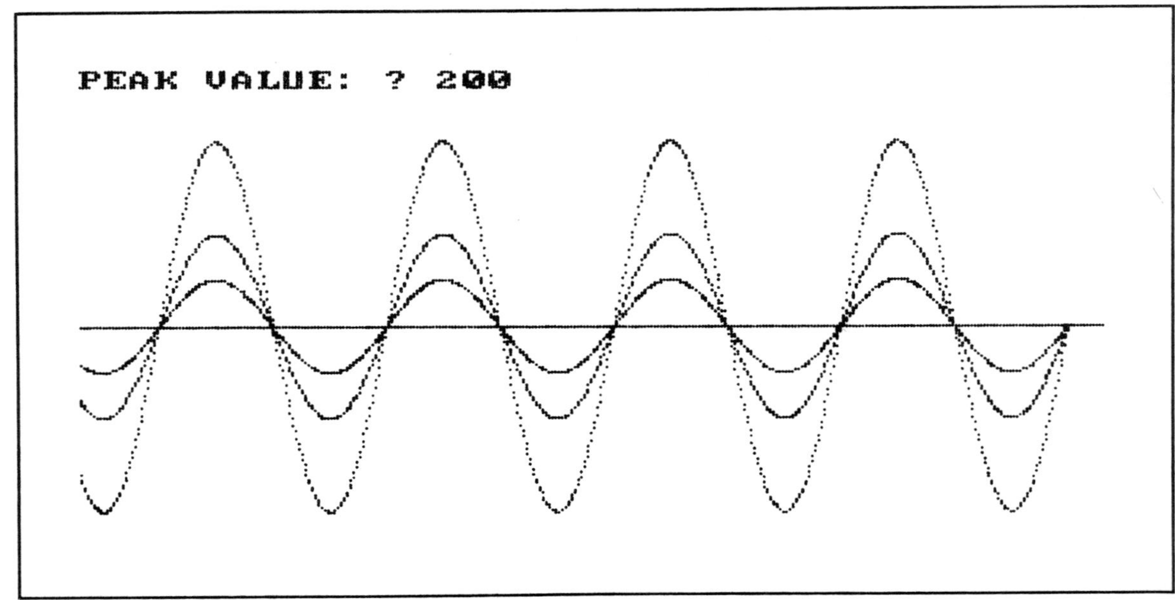

Fig. 6-71. Screen print of three sine waves, each of a different value.

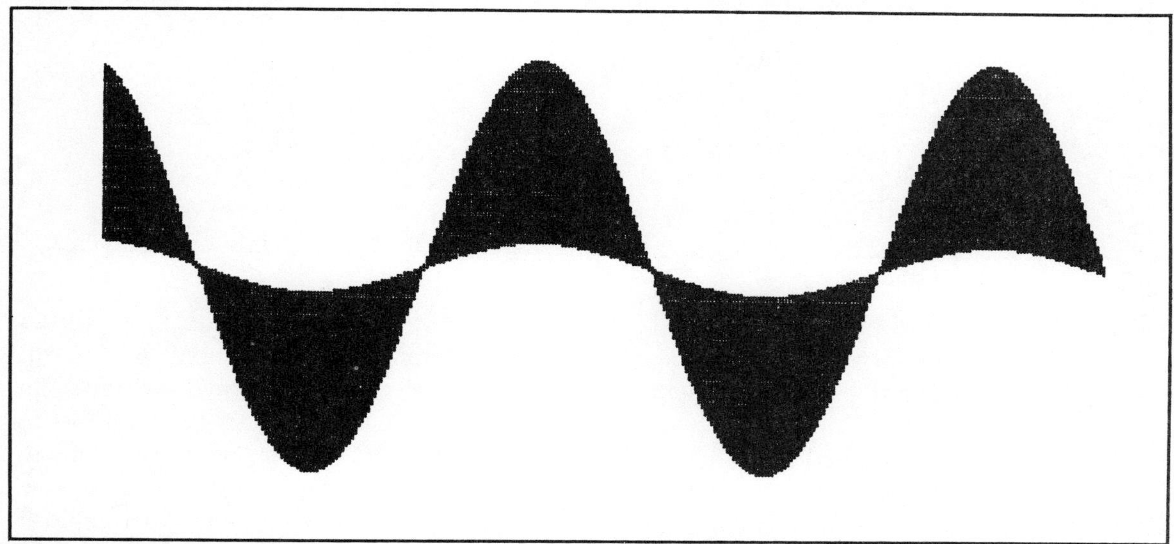

Fig. 6-72. A Ribbon image is generated by filling each half cycle of the sine wave.

Here, the waveforms have been completely filled in and the horizontal line is removed. This program is used to simulate a twisted ribbon. The program shown in Fig. 6-73, is basically the same as before, but there are different starting and ending points, as established in lines 60 and 70. The filled-in appearance is created in line 90, where the step factor is reduced to a very low value. When this program is run, line 30 steps the value of P by 1 during each cycle. This is another major factor in creating the filled-in appearance. Seventy different values of P cause the computer to plot seventy different sine waves. They are so close together that they blend on the screen and give us the ribbon effect. Unfortunately, it takes a tremendous amount of time for the program to complete the screen write. While I didn't time it closely, I think you can figure about a half hour to complete your ribbon. This could be speeded up to a minute or so completion time by writing the first trace and the last trace only and filling in with paint statements. Either way, you will get a highly attractive screen write which can be enhanced with color statements.

```
10 REM RIBBON
20 CLS
30 FOR P=10 TO 80
40 SCREEN 1
50 PI=3.14159
60 A=-6*PI
70 B=3*PI
80 C=638/(B-A)
90 FOR D=A TO B STEP .02
100 X=D*C
110 Y=SIN(D)*P
120 PSET(X+100,100-Y)
130 NEXT D
140 NEXT P
```

Fig. 6-73. Ribbon generating program.

```
10 REM RANDOM BOXES
20 SCREEN 1
30 COLOR 0,0
40 LINE -(RND*319,RND*199),RND*3,BF
50 GOTO 20
```

Fig. 6-74. *Random Box* program.

MORE RANDOM PROGRAMS

By randomizing statement commands, you can form any different graphic objects on the screen, some of which will resemble (quite accidently) true-life objects. You can think of these programs as a computerized version of the Rorschach Test, which involves inkblot designs used by psychiatrists for personality and intelligence testing.

Figure 6-74 shows a program that will draw random boxes on the screen. Line 40 uses the line statement with randomized coordinates and a randomized color command. The BF that ends this line causes filled-in boxes to appear at the spots indicated by the random coordinates. No CLS statement is used, so the boxes pile up. Figure 6-75 shows an example of what was printed on my screen after about 15 run-throughs. The program is on an endless loop, so you can stop execution by hitting the

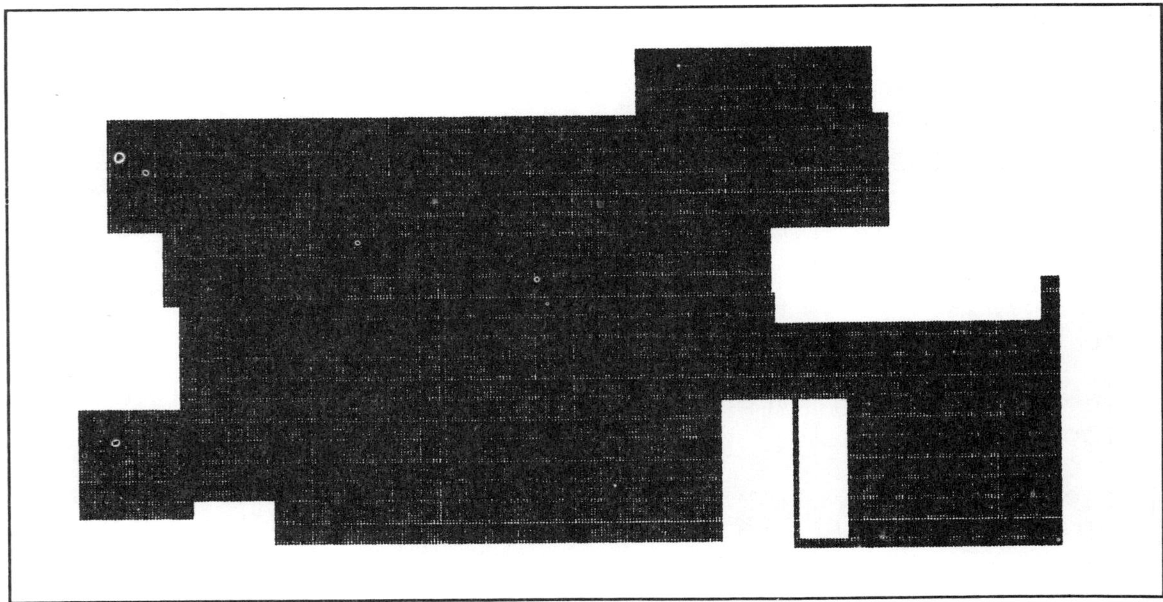

Fig. 6-75. This portion of the output from the *Random Box* program resembles a shopping mall.

control and break keys whenever the screen write pleases you. I think this figure resembles a complex shopping mall, but you may perceive it as something else. Undoubtedly, the psychiatrists in my readership will have learned a great deal about me by my perception of this as a shopping mall.

On a more serious note, if you allow the program to run for quite some time, the entire screen will be filled with multi-colored blocks of various sizes. When this occurs, you may wish to stop the program and run it again or to allow it to continue. When the screen is filled, additional blocks are simply written over the top of the ones already there. This is one of those entertainment programs that can keep an audience spellbound for quite some time.

I call this next program *Stained Glass*, because it simulates the stained glass windows found in many churches. Shown in Fig. 6-76, the program uses the circle statement to draw random circles within a confined area of the screen near its center. Other programs of this nature have drawn patterned concentric circles, but this one uses put and get statements to move them around a bit (again, within a confined area of the screen). This creates the

```
10 REM STAINED GLASS
20 DIM J(1000)
30 CLS
40 SCREEN 1,0
50 COLOR RND*8,RND*4
60 FOR X=0 TO 100 STEP 3
70 CIRCLE(160,100),X,RND*4
80 GET(110,50)-(210,150),J
90 PUT(130,50),J:PUT(90,50)
   ,J
100 NEXT X
110 GOTO 30
```

Fig. 6-76. This program simulates a stained glass window.

effect shown in Fig. 6-77. Your display should show a perfectly round circle. The specialized screen dump program I used to allow me to display graphic writes on my printer tends to compress the top and bottom of any circle, giving it more of an ellipsoid appearance. The rectangular block at the center of the circle is made from other circles as well. The get statement in line 80 commits the circle that is drawn in line 70 to an array. Then, the put statement in line 90 moves it to two different coordinates on the screen. The circles that are generated are of varying random sizes, and they begin to intermesh, forming the designs in rectangular block shown in Fig. 6-77. This figure shows just one of many thousands of different combinations that may be displayed on the screen. You won't always get a perfect circle, nor a perfect rectangle, but whatever is generated will be finely detailed, colorful, and quite interesting. Feel free to play around with the coordinate values and the randomized values in order to obtain a completely different screen write.

With the concentration now on circles, the program shown in Fig. 6-78 is quite appropriate and is different from all the rest, in that it will allow you to create a graphic display that simulates a three-dimensional ball. Again, randomized commands have been used...but not to vary the size or radius of the circle. This is fixed in line 50 to 60 units. Following this command, however, you will see two randomized commands, one for color and the other for aspect. The aspect determines the actual shape of the circle. At one value, the aspect may cause the display of a flat ellipsoid. Other values can create perfect circles or circles that are viewed from one edge. By randomizing the

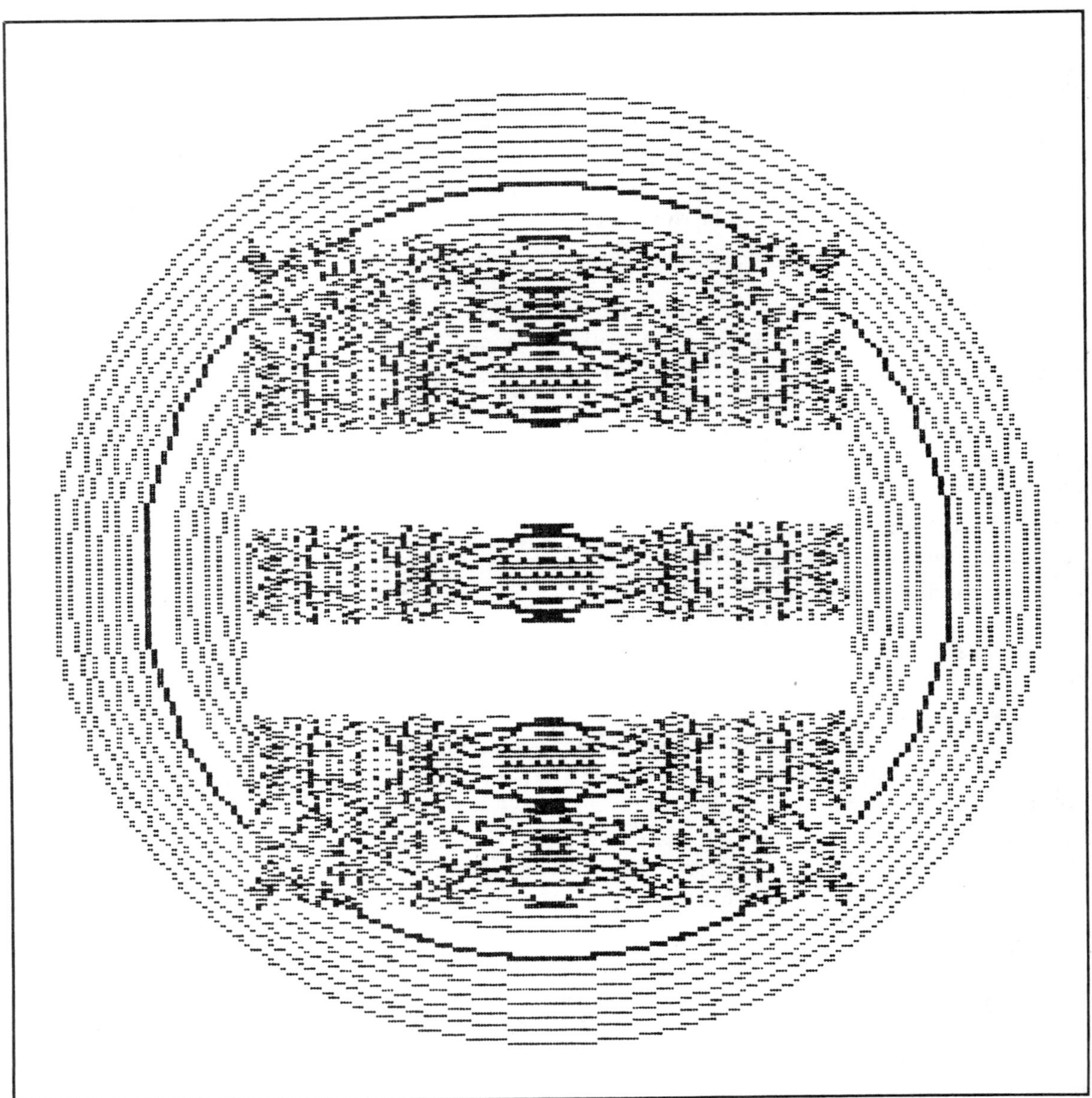

Fig. 6-77. Screen print from the previous program.

aspect command, many different types of circles are written on the screen, but they all have the same radius. Therefore, the completed write results in a single ball. The three-dimensional effect is created by this method, which seems to display brightly colored bands along the circumferences. The bands may be any of three different colors for any one

```
10 REM 3-D CIRCLE
20 SCREEN 1,0
30 CLS
35 COLOR RND*8,RND*4
40 FOR X=1 TO 35
50 CIRCLE(160,100),60,RND*4,,,RND*4
60 NEXT X
70 FOR Y=1 TO 2000
80 NEXT Y
90 GOTO 30
```

Fig. 6-78. This program generates a three-dimensional sphere.

palette, but this is changed for each ball with the randomized color statement in line 35. Therefore, your ball may assume many different colors, as may the screen background. Figure 6-79 shows the result of one of the random screen writes. This program is on an endless loop. However, the for-next loop established in lines 40 through 80 will keep each ball from becoming too congested. When this loop times out after completing 35 different circles, the screen is cleared and another ball is written.

When I wrote this program, I found the display to be quite colorful and interesting, but there simply wasn't enough of it. Therefore, I added more circle statements and arrived at the program shown in Fig. 6-80. This one also produces a three-dimensional ball pattern, but there are six patterns, each of which is different from the others. The circle statements contained in lines 60 through 110 are identical, with the exception of the changed coordinates. At least, they appear identical in program line form. Actually, the randomized commands in each circle statement will mix and match color and aspect values, and the results should be similar to what is seen in Fig. 6-81. Again, my printer version of what is seen on the screen compresses the balls a bit, and it's difficult to get the full impact because of the black and white reproductions here. On the screen, the myriad of colors in each ball produce a very striking effect.

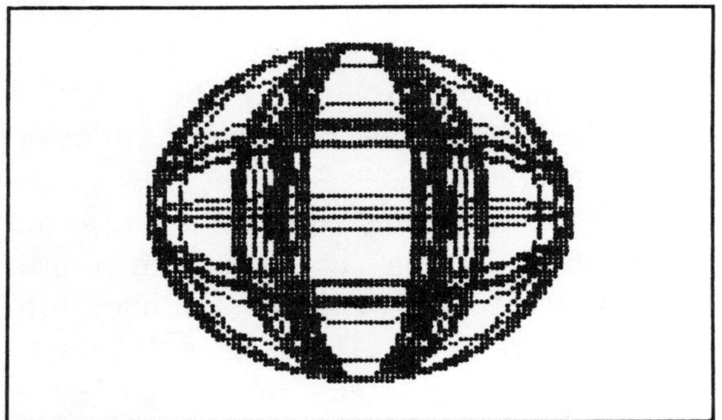

Fig. 6-79. An example of the monitor display using the previous program.

While randomized circles are quite interesting, the same can be said of randomized squares or rectangles. Figure 6-82 shows a program which will generate mirror-image boxes on the display screen. These are the equivalent of concentric circles, in that smaller boxes (or portions thereof) are generated within two larger boxes on the screen. There are many ways of accomplishing this effect, and

```
10 REM 3-D MULTI-CIRCLES
20 SCREEN 1,0
30 CLS
40 COLOR RND*8,RND*4
50 FOR X=1 TO 35
60 CIRCLE(60,50),40,RND*4,,,RND*4
70 CIRCLE(170,50),40,RND*4,,,RND*4
80 CIRCLE(270,50),40,RND*4,,,RND*4
90 CIRCLE(60,150),40,RND*4,,,RND*4
100 CIRCLE(170,150),40,RND*4,,,RND*4
110 CIRCLE(270,150),40,RND*4,,,RND*4
120 NEXT X
130 FOR Y=1 TO 2000
140 NEXT Y
150 GOTO 30
```

Fig. 6-80. *3-D Multi-Circle* program.

most programmers elect to use line statements with randomized coordinates. I elected to take a different route and use draw statements, which are seen in lines 70 and 80. Each draw statement forms a box on the screen. The two boxes are offset 180°. Instead of randomizing coordinates, I elected to partially randomize the scale factor, which is represented by the S command in each draw statement and by the variable Y. The for-next loop which begins in line 50 uses a RND*5 command to create random steps. These random steps are subtracted from 35 and assigned to the value of Y in line 60. During each cycle of the loop, the value of Y will get smaller. Therefore, the scale factor in each draw statement is also altered. In each case, the two blocks will be written using the same scale factor. Thus, one is always a mirror image of the other. As with the previous program, a CLS statement is used to cut down on screen congestion after the for-next loop in line 50 times out. Lines 100 and 110 form a time delay loop to allow each write to establish itself before the screen is cleared and the next write is begun. Figure 6-83 shows the result of two different on-screen writes.

I tried to improve on this program and ended up with the modification shown in Fig. 6-84. This program looks quite different from the previous one, but it uses the same programming concept. I included the for-next loop that is begun in line 50 to allow for six sets of squares. As this loop cycles, the value of Q is detected in lines 80 through 130. The GOSUBs in these lines then branch to other portions of the program, which use additional draw statements to define where the squares are to be written on the screen. Following the return statements, the draw statements in lines 140 and 150 are executed. These draw the semi-random boxes at the screen coordinates designated in the GOSUB branches.

Figure 6-85 shows one of the screen

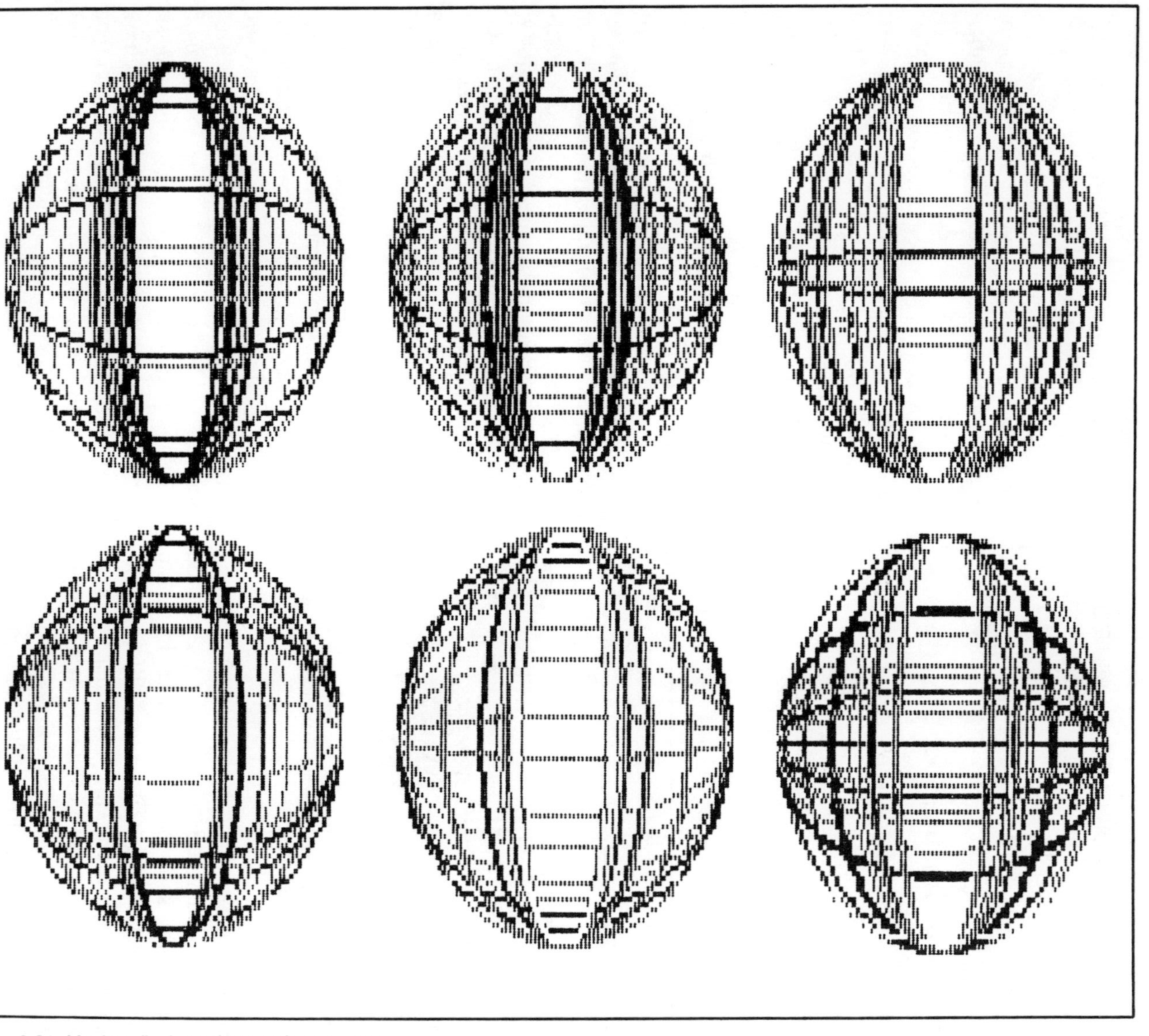

Fig. 6-81. Monitor display using previous program.

```
10 REM MIRROR IMAGE BOXES
20 CLS
30 SCREEN 1
40 COLOR 8,1
50 FOR X=0 TO 30 STEP RND*5
60 Y=35-X
70 DRAW"BM150,100 S=Y;R5 U5
   L5 D5"
80 DRAW"BM150,100 S=Y;L5 D5
   R5 U5"
90 NEXT X
100 FOR A=1 TO 600
110 NEXT A
120 CLS
130 GOTO 30
```

Fig. 6-82. *Mirror Image Box* program.

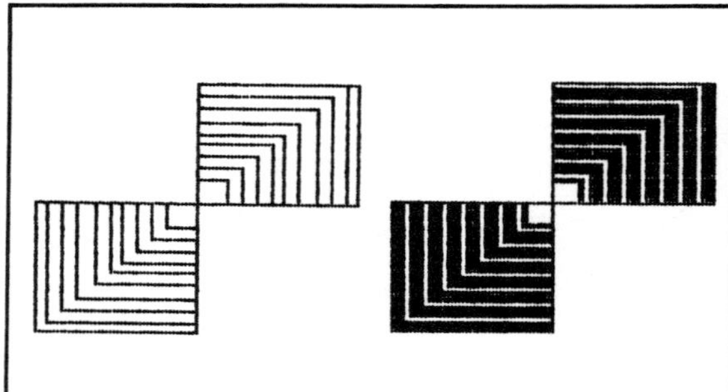

Fig. 6-83. Two examples of what may appear when the previous program is run.

writes. This one looks a lot more interesting on the screen when you can see the colors. Figure 6-86 shows another write from the same program, which includes a different patterned configuration. This program is not on an endless loop and will end after drawing the six sets of mirror image blocks. Running the program again should yield a different combination.

PIE CHARTS

This chapter has presented several different types of graph programs. However, these involved printing rectangles or bars of certain lengths on the screen. Another type of graph program, which is quite popular, is called a pie chart. It displays values in sections of a complete circle. The program shown in Fig. 6-87 will allow you to input up to ten different values and will give each of them a designation that will later be printed on the screen. All values input are relative. To explain this further, let's assume that you want to input two values, one to be labeled Mortgage and the other to be labeled Automobile. If you give the first a value of 100 and the second a value of 50, the Mortgage section of the circle will be twice as large as the section designated Automobile. If you used values of 10 and 5, respectively, for these two categories, the circle would be written in exactly the same manner. If you input the maximum of 10 values to this program, ten separate circle sections will be displayed. If all values are the same, then each segment of the circle will be the same size.

Figure 6-88 show a chart printout using five different values and categories. It is best to keep the category names as short as possible, using abbreviations if necessary. In some case, long category names will be written over some circle sections. When the program is first run, you will be prompted to input the number of values you wish to insert. This number is committed to the variable T, which determines the number of cycles in the for-next loop that begins in line 130. You will then be prompted to input the name of the item and its assigned value. When the last value has been input, the screen will clear and the pie chart will be

```
10 REM SYMMETRICAL TIER
20 CLS
30 SCREEN 1
40 COLOR 8,1
50 FOR Q=1 TO 6
60 FOR X=0 TO 30 STEP RND*5
70 Y=35-X
80 IF Q=1 THEN GOSUB 190:GOTO 140
90 IF Q=2 THEN GOSUB 210:GOTO 140
100 IF Q=3 THEN GOSUB 230:GOTO 140
110 IF Q=4 THEN GOSUB 250:GOTO 140
120 IF Q=5 THEN GOSUB 270:GOTO 140
130 IF Q=6 THEN GOSUB 290:GOTO 140
140 DRAW"S=Y;R5 U5 L5 D5"
150 DRAW"S=Y;L5 D5 R5 U5"
160 NEXT X
170 NEXT Q
180 END
190 DRAW"BM55,40"
200 RETURN
210 DRAW"BM95,40"
220 RETURN
230 DRAW"BM135,40"
240 RETURN
250 DRAW"BM 175,40"
260 RETURN
270 DRAW"BM215,40"
280 RETURN
290 DRAW"BM255,40"
300 RETURN
```

Fig. 6-84. The *Symmetrical Tier* program is a modification of the previous program.

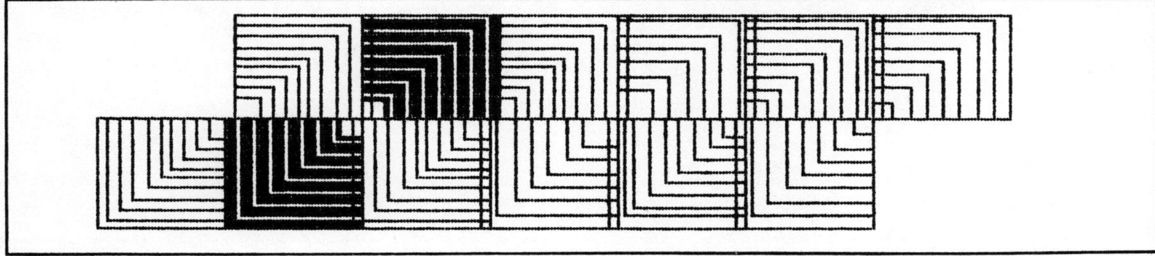

Fig. 6-85. One example of the output from the *Symmetrical Tier* program.

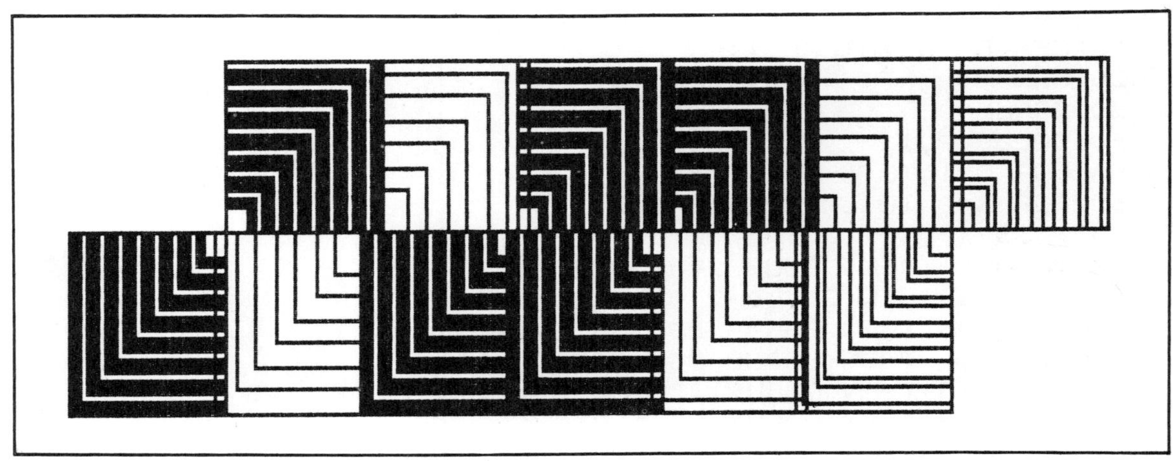

Fig. 6-86. When the program is automatically run again, the screen is erased and a different tier image appears.

```
10 REM PIECHART(10 VALUE MAXIMUM)
20 DIM J(10),J$(10)
30 SCREEN 1,0
40 COLOR 1,0
50 INPUT"NEED INSTRUCTIONS(Y/N)";Q$
60 IF Q$="N"THEN 90
70 IF Q$="Y" THEN GOSUB 430
80 IF Q$<>"Y" AND Q$<>"N" THEN 50
90 CLS
100 INPUT "NUMBER OF CHART VALUES(10 MAX.)";T
110 IF T>10 THEN 100
120 CLS
130 FOR U=1 TO T
140 INPUT"THE NAME OF THIS ITEM IS:",J$(U)
150 CLS
160 PRINT"THE VALUE ASSIGNED TO "J$(U)" IS:";
170 INPUT J(U)
180 CLS
190 PI=3.14159
200 C=C+J(U)
210 NEXT
220 FOR Q=1 TO T
```

Fig. 6-87. The *Pie Chart* program.

```
230 J(Q)=J(Q)/C
240 NEXT Q
250 CLS
260 FOR X=1 TO T
270 ZZ=XX:XX=XX+J(X)*(PI*2)
280 XY=.5*(ZZ+XX)
290 AB=165+COS(XY)*10
300 RQ=100-SIN(XY)*10
310 CIRCLE (AB,RQ),40,1,-ZZ,-XX,5/6
320 V=RQ-SIN(XY)*70
330 W=AB+COS(XY)*70-4*LEN(J$(X))
340 LOCATE 1+(V*.12),1+(W*.12):PRINT J$(X);
350 NEXT X
360 LOCATE 1,1
370 INPUT EC$
380 CLS
390 INPUT"DO YOU WISH TO PLOT ANOTHER GRAPH(Y/N)?";ASK$
400 IF ASK$="N" THEN CLS:END
410 IF ASK$="Y" THEN 90
420 IF ASK$<>"Y" AND ASK$<>"N" THEN 390
430 CLS
440 PRINT"THIS IS A GRAPH PROGRAM WHICH"
450 PRINT"WILL DISPLAY UP TO TEN DIFFER"
460 PRINT"ITEMS AND THEIR VALUES IN A PIE-"
470 PRINT"CHART. SIMPLY INPUT THE NAME"
480 PRINT"OF EACH ITEM WHEN PROMPTED TO DO"
490 PRINT"SO. IMMEDIATELY AFTERWARD, YOU"
500 PRINT"WILL BE ASKED TO INPUT A VALUE"
510 PRINT"FOR THIS ITEM. ALL VALUES ARE"
520 PRINT"RELATIVE, SO YOU CAN INPUT THESE"
530 PRINT"IN ANY FORM AS LONG AS ALL VALUES"
540 PRINT"ARE DEFINED IN ONE TYPE OF NUMBERS"
550 PRINT"SYSTEM(I.E. METRIC,AMERICAN, ETC.)."
560 PRINT
570 PRINT
580 INPUT"PRESS <ENTER> TO BEGIN";R$
590 RETURN
```

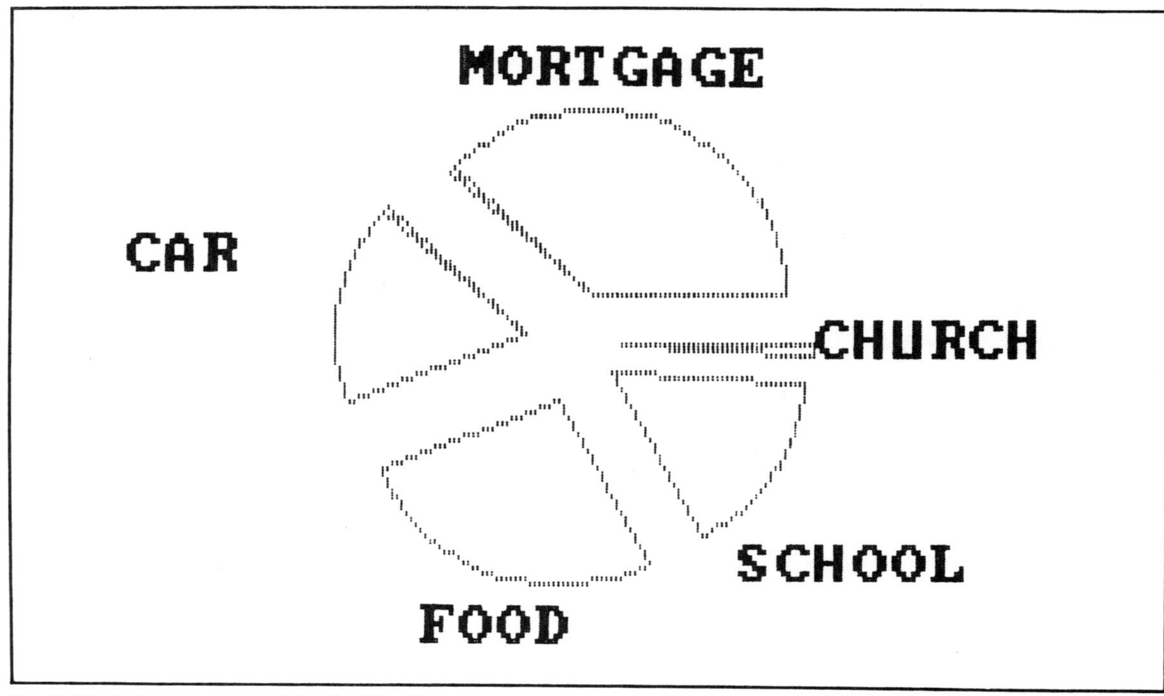

Fig. 6-88. A display produced by the *Pie Chart* program.

drawn, along with the category names placed outside the appropriate segments. Lines 440 through 550 provide an explanation during the program run. This subroutine is accessed by lines 50 through 80. You will be asked if you need instructions, and if you input a Y, there is a branch to line 430. If you do not need instructions, you input an N, and the branch is to line 90. You must input either a Y or N, or the prompt will stay on the screen.

This pie chart can be used to display household expenditures, energy consumption, and even an overall business picture. It is often easier to understand than are many of the bar graphs.

The graphics capabilities of the IBM Personal Computer are limited only by your imagination. Just about anything you can think of or see can be simulated on the screen. In IBM BASIC, you have several highly powerful statements at your disposal, many of which can accomplish the same thing. The trick here is to learn as much as you can about the language and decide which method of arriving at a graphic display is best suited to your particular style. When you combine programs to create these objects using animation routines such as those discussed in the next chapter, the machine's capabilities are expanded tenfold or more.

Chapter 7

Color Graphics Animation

Now we come to the fun part—true graphics animation. Some programs have been presented and discussed in the chapter on text mode animation, but at best, animation in the text mode is something we can put up with. It is not highly desirable when much better quality is available in graphics mode.

Unlike many other dialects of BASIC, IBM Advanced BASIC (BASICA) is heavily oriented toward graphics operation and especially animation. Here, you won't be bugged by the afterglow of the screen. When a figure is drawn and then animated, its movement is very true to life.

IBM BASIC uses put and get statements to handle high quality graphics animation. In IBM graphics programming, the get statement is used to read points from a specified area of the screen. It causes the information that creates these points to be held in an array. When the put statement is used, the information is retrieved from the array and put on the screen at a different location. The two statements may actually be thought of in a backward sort of way, in that the get statement puts information into the array after getting it from the screen. The put statement gets the information from the array and then puts it on the screen.

When programming to produce graphics animation, the first task is to draw an object on the screen. After this is done, the get statement is used, along with the coordinates of the object, to commit the information to the array. Then, the put statement pulls this information back out of the array and causes the object to be printed at another place. To erase the image from its new place and put it back into the array again requires an identical put statement. In other words, the first time you put an image, it appears; the second time, it disappears. To demonstrate this, I'll use the program shown in Fig. 7-1. Line 10 sets the screen up for medium-resolution graphics, and line 20 establishes an array to hold the image. The array is assigned to the variable J and is given a value of 800 bytes. This is far more than should be needed for the image that is to be drawn. A later discussion will tell you how to figure out just how much space to set aside for the array.

Our image is to be a rectangle, which is drawn by the line statement in program line 30. The BF remark following the line statement specifies a filled box, or in this case, a rectangle.

We now move to the start of the animation procedure by "getting" the image information from the screen. The get statement is followed by the same coordinates as those specified for the rectangle. These are followed by a comma and the letter J, which is the name of the array to which this information is to be committed.

```
10  SCREEN 1

20  DIM J(800)

30  LINE(40,75)-(70,100),,BF

40  GET (40,75)-(70,100),J

50  PUT(40,75),J

60  PUT(40,150),J
```

Fig. 7-1. This program draws a rectangle on the screen and then moves it to a different location.

Line 50 uses the put statement to erase the image from the screen at its original location, and line 60 then uses another put statement to put the same image back on the screen at different coordinates. Notice that the array designator follows all of the put statements.

When you run this program, you will see the filled rectangle near the top of the screen, and it will then immediately jump toward the bottom. The first image position is established by line 30. It is erased from this position by line 50 and rewritten at another coordinate by line 60. At this point, the program is over, and the image will remain. We could erase the final image by using a put statement identical to the one in line 60.

A problem may arise here, in that the image is drawn, erased and redrawn again so quickly that unless you're very attentive, you may not even see the first image near the top of the screen. Figure 7-2 shows the same program as before, but an extra line has been added to slow up the computer. The for-next statement contained in line 50 causes the computer to count from 1 to 500 before it erases the original image with the put statement in line 60. Line 30 draws the image, line 40 commits it to an array, the computer counts to 500, and the original image is then erased. Immediately upon erasure, the put statement in line 70 rewrites the original image at a new screen position near the bottom. You could even delay the rewrite process by including a similar for-next loop between lines 60 and 70. With such a program, the image would be displayed at one set of coordinates; a pause would occur; the image would be erased from those coordinates; another pause would occur; and finally, the image would be rewritten at its new position.

```
10 SCREEN 1
20 DIM J(800)
30 LINE(40,75)-(70,100),,BF
40 GET (40,75)-(70,100),J
50 FOR X= 1 TO 500:NEXT X
60 PUT(40,75),J
70 PUT(40,150),J
```

Fig. 7-2. The same program as shown previously with the addition of a time delay loop in line 50.

In many instances, a time delay loop is desirable before the image is erased, but it is rarely used to create a delay in the rewriting of the same image. Whether or not time delay is used, and if so, for what amount of time, will be determined by the purpose of the program itself. It takes only a few seconds to input a time delay via the keyboard and an even smaller amount of time to take it out, so this is something that you may wish to write into the program after it has been pretty much completed. This can be part of the debugging process.

Now that I've explained how to create simple animation in graphics mode using put and get statements, it is appropriate to address the topic of more complex movements. The program shown in Fig. 7-3 will cause our graphic rectangle to race across the screen from left to right. It is very similar to the previous program, except a for-next loop is incorporated to cut down on programming time.

First of all, the screen is set up and the boundaries of the array to hold the graphic information are established. Next, the image is drawn and the get statement is used to commit this data to the array. Line 50 uses the put statement to erase the original image and the for-next loop, which sets the values for the horizontal positions of the rectangle, is then entered. Line 70 contains the put statements to place the image on the screen at the coordinates determined by the value of X. X changes each time the loop cycles. Therefore, the image progresses across the screen, from left to right. A for-next time delay loop is also included in line 70 to control the speed at which the object travels. Line 90 allows the image to remain on the screen in the final position. Without this line, the image would be erased by the last put statement in line 70. This is the

```
10 SCREEN 1
20 DIM J(1000)
30 LINE(5,80)-(20,100),,BF
40 GET(5,80)-(20,100),J
50 PUT(5,80),J
60 FOR X=5 TO 280 STEP 5
70 PUT(X,80),J:FOR Y= 1 TO 100:NEXT Y:PUT(X,80),J
80 NEXT
90 PUT(X,80),J
```

Fig. 7-3. This program draws a graphic rectangle and then races it across the screen from left to right.

```
10 SCREEN 1
20 DIM J(1000)
30 LINE(5,80)-(20,100),,BF
40 GET(5,80)-(20,100),J
50 PUT(5,80),J
60 FOR X=5 TO 280 STEP 5
80 PUT(280-X,80),J:FOR Y= 1 TO 100:NEXT Y:PUT(280-X,80),J
90 NEXT
100 PUT(280-X,80),J
```

Fig. 7-4. The program does the same thing as the previous program, except the image is moved from right to left.

basic routine used in auto race programs. Instead of a rectangle, a graphic automobile is presented, but the steps to move it from one side of the screen to the other are the same.

If you need to write the program so that the image moved in reverse (from right to left), the program shown in Fig. 7-4 provides the basis for this. This one is nearly identical to the previous program. However, the value of X is subtracted from 280 in each case to establish coordinates. This program is simply a modification of the previous one, so the image will first appear on the left-hand side of the screen and will almost instantly appear again on the right-hand side before making its way to the far left. In practical applications, the coordinates of the line statement would be changed to draw it originally at the right side of the screen. The coordinates of the get statement in line 40 would reflect this change.

The basic program can also be modified to bring about a diagonal path of travel from the upper left to the lower right of the screen. The program shown in Fig. 7-5 does this by inserting variables in the put statements contained in line 80. Here, the vertical position of the object

```
10 SCREEN 1
20 DIM J(1000)
30 LINE(5,80)-(20,100),,BF
40 GET(5,80)-(20,100),J
50 PUT(5,80),J
60 FOR X=5 TO 280 STEP 5
70 XX=X-(X/2)
80 PUT(X,XX),J:FOR Y= 1 TO 100:NEXT Y:PUT(X,XX),J
90 NEXT
100 PUT(X,80),J
```

Fig. 7-5. A program to produce diagonal animation.

```
10 SCREEN 1
20 DIM J(1000)
30 LINE(5,10)-(20,20),,BF
40 GET(5,10)-(20,20),J
50 PUT(5,10),J
60 FOR X= 5 TO 175 STEP 5
70 XX=X-5
80 PUT(XX,X),J:FOR Y=1 TO 150:NEXT:PUT(XX,X),J
90 NEXT
```

Fig. 7-6. This program produces the same results as the preceding program, but uses different programming methods.

through each cycle of the for-next loop is determined by the variable XX, which is equal to X - ½ X. As the object travels from left to right, it descends toward the bottom of the screen. Figure 7-6 shows another program that does the same thing, but uses different coordinates.

If you simply want the object to move from top to bottom while holding its horizontal screen position, use the program in Fig. 7-7. The horizontal position is given the coordinate 5, while the vertical position is determined by the for-next loop beginning at line 60. When this program ends, the final image will be erased by the last put statement in line 70.

A final modification to this program involves the insertion of a color statement to set the foreground and background colors. In the program shown in Fig. 7-8, the color statement is contained in line 11. The first number following this statement determines the background color, while the next number determines the foreground, which can best be thought of as the color of the object. This combination will give you a red background with a snow-white image traveling across it from left to right. Different numerals within the color statement can produce green, pink, and many other background and foreground colors.

The put and get statements have been used here in their simplest form. The put

```
10 SCREEN 1
20 DIM J(1000)
30 LINE(5,10)-(20,20),,BF
40 GET(5,10)-(20,20),J
50 PUT(5,10),J
60 FOR X= 5 TO 175 STEP 5
70 PUT(5,X),J:FOR Y=1 TO 150:NEXT:PUT(5,X),J
80 NEXT
```

Fig. 7-7. This program moves an object from top to bottom on the screen.

```
10 SCREEN 1
11 COLOR 4,1
20 DIM J(1000)
30 LINE(5,80)-(20,100),,BF
40 GET(5,80)-(20,100),J
50 PUT(5,80),J
60 FOR X=5 TO 280 STEP 5
80 PUT(X,80),J:FOR Y= 1 TO 100:NEXT Y:PUT(X,80),J
90 NEXT
100 PUT(X,80),J
```

Fig. 7-8. This program uses the color statement in line 11 to set background and foreground colors. This provides an attractive setting for the movement.

statement is often followed by an action command, which in turn, is followed by the array designation. These actions include PSET, PRESET, XOR, OR, and AND. If no action is designated, the computer automatically defaults to XOR, which is the special mode used for graphics animation. The other commands have been discussed in a previous chapter, but they will be reviewed again and explained through simple programs.

CIRCLE ANIMATION

Using the circle statement found in Advanced BASIC, circles of various circumferences can be drawn on the screen using a single program line. We can also animate these circles in much the same manner as we animate lines, rectangles, and other graphic images. However, it is necessary to interpolate a bit to arrive at the proper section of the screen to be placed in an array and then pulled out again using put and get statements. Figure 7-9 shows a program that draws a circle at one location on the screen and moves it to a different location. The DIM statement in line 10 sets up the size of the array to contain the circle information. The circle statement in line 40 creates a circle with a center at coordinates 100,100, a radius of 20, and a color designated by the number 3. The paint statement in line 50 fills in this circle with the color designated by the numeral 2.

Animation starts to take place in line 60, where the get statement is used. Here is where the differences crop up. We must get the

```
10 DIM J(500)
20 SCREEN 1
30 COLOR 8,2
40 CIRCLE(100,100),20,3
50 PAINT(100,100),2,3
60 GET(60,60)-(140,140),J
70 PUT(60,60),J
80 PUT(180,100),J
```

Fig. 7-9. This program draws a circle and moves it to a different location in much the same manner as a previous program moved a rectangle.

entire section of the screen which encompasses the circle. Since the circle has a radius of 20, we know that the area of the screen encompassing the circle will be twice 20. This is due to the fact that the radius extends 20 positions from the center. The diameter of the circle will be 40 screen coordinates. Therefore, to be safe it is necessary within the get statement to specify the range of coordinates which begin at the circle's center minus forty screen coordinates and extending to the center plus 40 screen coordinates. Thus, the get statement specifies coordinates (60,60)–(140,140),J. The put statement in line 70 includes only the first set of coordinates. The second put statement in line 80 redraws the circle at coordinates 180,100. Using this method, the circle is drawn and painted, committed to an array, and then erased from the screen. It is then put back on the screen at the new coordinates specified in line 80.

The program in Fig. 7-10 illustrates circle animation using the popular Pac-Man figure. What is actually done here is to draw two circles which correspond to the Pac-Man. One circle shows the figure with mouth closed; the other shows it with the mouth open. Lines 60 and 70 draw the first figure. Line 80 is another

```
10 REM PMAN SIMULATION
20 DIM J(1000):DIM K(1000)
30 SCREEN 1
40 COLOR 8,0
50 PI=3.141593
60 CIRCLE(160,100),12,2
70 PAINT(160,100),2,2
80 CIRCLE(158,94),1,0
90 GET (138,88)-(172,112),J
100 FOR X=1 TO 100:NEXT
110 PUT(138,88),J
120 CIRCLE(160,100),12,2,-PI*1.25,-PI/1.34
130 PAINT(161,101),2,2
140 CIRCLE(158,94),1,0
150 GET(138,88)-(172,112),K
160 FOR X= 1 TO 100:NEXT
170 PUT(138,88),K
180 FOR A=15 TO 300 STEP 15
190 B=300-A
200 PUT(B,100),J:FOR X=1 TO 100:NEXT X:PUT (B,100),J
210 PUT (B,100),K:FOR X=1 TO 100:NEXT X:PUT(B,100),K
220 NEXT
```

Fig. 7-10. The popular video game character preceding, Pac-Man, is simulated using this program.

circle statement which draws the tiny eye. The large circle has a radius of 12, and the get statement commits the entire image to array J. A for-next loop begins at line 100, and line 110 does the actual array placement. Line 120 uses another circle statement specifying the same radius, but the starting and ending points of the circle are established by the pi designators following the color numeral. This draws the Pac-Man with mouth open, and line 130 paints it the same color. Line 140 is just a copy of a previous line which draws the Pac-Man eye. The resulting image is shown in Fig. 7-11. Get and put statements retrieve the information from the screen, assign the Pac-Man with open mouth to array K, and erase the original image. Lines 100 and 160 are simple time delay loops which provide for cleaner animation. Another for-next loop beginning at line 180 causes the Pac-Man to travel across the screen from right to left. The values of A are subtracted from 300, and this latter value is assigned to the variable B. Line 200 puts the closed-mouth image on the screen. There is then a time delay loop. The second put statement in line 200 erases the image from the screen. Line 210 puts the open-mouthed image on the screen for a period of time determined by the following for-next loop. The second put statement erases this image. Line 220 causes the loop to repeat itself, and this process continues over and over until the loop times out with the image at the lefthand side of the screen. The closed-mouth and open-mouth image are placed in the same position. As soon as the closed-mouth version is erased, the open-mouth rendition appears at the same location. Then both figures are advanced across the screen. The drawing and erasing of these figures occur rapidly, and result in the appearance of two types of motion. First, there is the right-left motion of what aipears to be a single figure. Second, there is the up-down motion, which simulates the opening and closing of the mouth. This latter motion is basically the same thing that is encountered when you flip book pages very rapidly while looking at the page numbers. The numbers seem to step up in count, but are displayed at the same location.

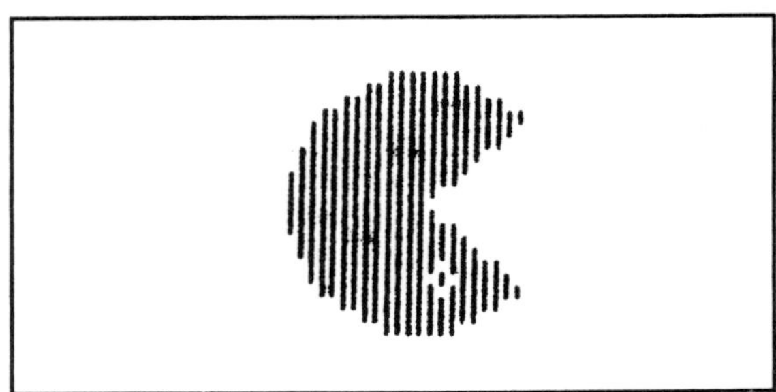

Fig. 7-11. Pac-Man as seen on the IBM Personal Computer screen.

It would be very easy to control direction of the Pac-Man figure, as is done in the video game of the same name through the use of key on statements. When a certain key is depressed, the parameters of the for-next loop might be changed to include vertical movement rather than horizontal. Using this program as a basis, a Pac-Man simulation could be written for the IBM Personal Computer, although this would be a very lengthy program.

CALCULATING ARRAY SIZE

At this point, we'll pause in the discussion of actually doing graphics animation and discuss how to determine the size of an array needed to store the on-screen information

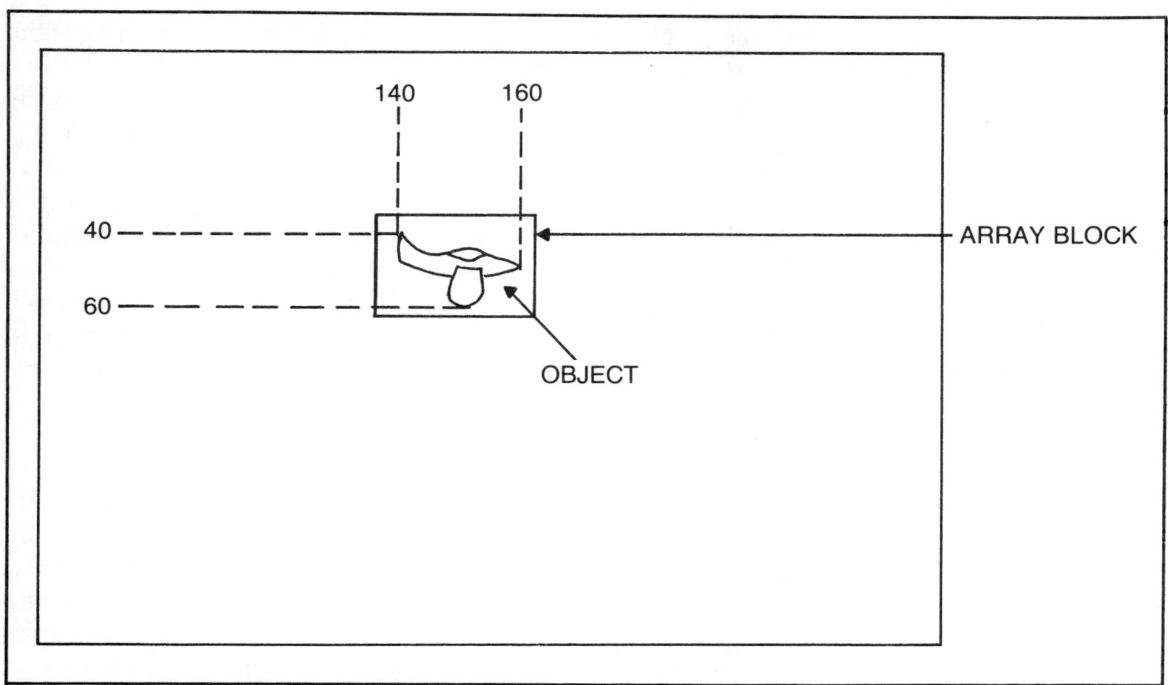

Fig. 7-12. A graphic image is committed to an array by pulling a graphic block section from the screen. The size of the array is determined by the dimensions of the graphic block.

Before the get statement can be used and the array size must be established by means of DIM statements. Figure 7-12 shows a graphic image that we wish to get from the monitor screen. Let's assume that the image spans the vertical coordinates of 40 to 60. Let's also assume that the horizontal coordinates are 140 to 160. If we had to square things off, this would mean that the image occupies a screen "block" which is 20 by 20 (20 points by 20 points). To be on the safe side, we might want to get an area which is 22 by 22. The specified coordinates of the object, then, would be 140,40 - 160,60. In order to get a slightly larger area that is sure to encompass our graphics object, we might use the statement:

```
GET(139,39) - (161,61)
```

This gets the array block that encompasses the image and the block measures 22 points by 22 points. Now, how large of an array do we need to hold this block? This is the value that will be inserted in the DIM statement.

In their manual on BASIC, IBM provides a formula for determining the array needed to hold any image. It is:

```
4+INT((x*bitsperpixel+7)/8)*y
```

At first glance, this formula looks a bit frightening, but it's not difficult at all. In this formula, the variables x and y are simply the number of horizontal and vertical points in the block. In our case, both x and y are equal to 22. How about that word "bitsperpixel"? Don't worry about it! In medium-resolution mode, this is equal to 2; in high-resolution graphics mode, it's equal to 1, so you can forget about it completely in this latter mode. However, since most of our color/graphics work will be done in medium-resolution, simply change bitsperpixel to the number 2. Put in plain language, the formula means that the array size is equal to the number of horizontal points times 2, plus 7. This value is then divided by 8, and the result is multiplied by the vertical point value. You then add 4 to this number, and you've arrived at your array size. The following formula shows how the array size is obtained for the screen image under discussion:

```
4+INT((22*2+7)/8)*22 = array size
          or
4+INT(6.375)*22      = array size
```

The integer of 6.375 is 6. Therefore, we arrive at:

```
4+(6*22) = array size
      or
4+ 132 = 136 = array size

array size = 136
```

If you're not accustomed to working with formulas, be sure to perform all of the work within the parentheses first. Take the integer of the value in the parentheses (the whole number with all decimal places removed) and multiply it by y, and then add 4 to this value. The addition of 4 is done at the very end, even though it originally falls at the beginning of the equation.

From this formula, then, we know that the array size must be at least 136 bytes. This is the minimum we can get away with. Of course, most graphic images that are to be used with get and put statements do not require a lot of array space. To commit the entire screen to an array would take a little over 16K bytes, which is still far short of maximum capacity, assuming a 64K byte minimum machine configuration. Even if your program is quite long, there is a good chance that you will be nowhere near maximum memory capacity. After a bit of practice, you can pretty much judge the size of the array needed, and I usually play it safe by using a figure of 1,000 in the DIM statement for most graphic blocks. If it won't work, go back and add another thousand. Of course, if you've got a lot of arrays and a long program, space may be dear, so you may have to do a bit of fancy figuring in an exceptionally complex animation program. However, if you had to go through that formula each time you wanted to commit something to an array, graphics programming would be quite a tedious affair.

It may be a help to you to know of my "cheap and dirty" formula for figuring array size. Simply multiply the horizontal points by the vertical points and divide the result by 3.5. Using this formula to figure array size for the 22 by 22 example under discussion gives us:

```
(22*22)/3.5 = array size
           or
484/3.5     = 138 (approx.)
array size  = 138 bytes
```

This formula assures that you have enough

array space set aside and doesn't involve any complicated mathematics. Using the IBM formula, an entire screen could be stored in an array with a total size of 16,004 bytes. Using my formula, it comes out to a little over 18,000 bytes, and of course, the difference increases in proportion to the size of the block that must be committed. However, in every case, you are assured of having enough room for the array, as long as the blocks are at least 20 by 20. When they fall below this value, you'll have to taper off and divide by 2.5. This is a good rule of thumb equation and can usually be worked in your head. Assume you have a block which is 40 by 40. We can multiply the width and height and arrive at 1,600 in our heads. Since it may be difficult to divide this by 3.5, play it safe and divide by 3, and you come up with about 530 or so bytes. If you work the same thing with the accurate formula, you'd come up with an exact value of 404 bytes. In most instances, we can spare many thousands of bytes of storage, so going over by 20% or 30% is no big deal, especially when we're talking about relatively small array sizes. If you get into a situation, however, where you have to store very large arrays and storage is at a premium, then get your calculator out and use the complex formula. Even better, run it in direct mode on the IBM machine. Simply input:

```
PRINT 4+INT((x*bitsperpixel+7)/8)*y
```

Naturally, you will insert the values for x, y, and bitsperpixel. As soon as you press the enter key, your answer will be displayed on the screen. This is sometimes a hassle when you're right in the middle of a program, so use the method you are most comfortable with. If you figure wrong and try to commit too large a block to an array that just can't handle it, the screen will display the error message "Subscript out of range". This means you've got to go back to your DIM statement(s) and set aside more array space. Of course, if you're like most programmers, you'll just set aside a thousand bytes or so for each small image and let it go at that. With the storage capability of the IBM Personal Computer in its minimum graphic configuration (48K), memory space will probably not be a major concern. Of course, if you've decided to simulate a game like Pac-Man or Donkey Kong in every detail, you may have to figure very closely.

GUNNERY GAME

Video games that use joysticks are extremely popular today. Many of these simulate wars, both on the earth and in the vast reaches of outer space. Most are quite complex, at least in regard to programming them in BASIC. However, using the IBM Personal Computer and its animation capabilities, we can simulate many of the video game actions on the color monitor. Due to the relatively slow speed of BASIC when compared with video games which are programmed on a machine level, there will be a noticeable flutter in many moving objects, which is very difficult to get around. This is especially true when paint statements are used to fill in larger graphics objects. The program draws the object first and then fills it in. The larger objects require longer periods of time, both during the writing and the paint operation. With smaller objects, however, the effect is not so noticeable.

Figure 7-13 shows a program which will

```
10 REM GUNNERY GAME
20 SCREEN 1
30 CLS
40 KEY OFF
50 INPUT"NEED INSTRUCTIONS(YES/NO)?";A$
60 IF A$="YES" THEN GOSUB 500
70 IF A$="NO" THEN 90
80 IF A$<>"YES" AND A$<>"NO" THEN 50
90 CLS
100 X=10
110 XX=15
120 DRAW"BM160,199 S=XX;R5U3L2U2L1U1L1D1L1D2L2D3R2"
130 DRAW"BM160,100 S=X; C3 F1 L2 G1 L1 H1 L2 H2 R2 F1 R5"
140 PAINT(156,102),2,3
150 DIM J(100)
160 DIM K(100)
170 DIM L(100)
180 GET (130,96)-(165,106),J
190 PUT(130,96),J
200 DRAW"BM160,100 S=X; A3 C3 F1 L2 G1 L1 H1 L2 H2 R2 F1 R5"
210 GET(150,76)-(165,102),K
220 PUT(150,76),K
230 KEY(1) ON
240 ON KEY(1) GOSUB 440
250 FOR X=10 TO 280
260 PUT(X,5),J:PUT(X,5),J
270 IF X=145 AND POINT(169,9)>0 THEN 280 ELSE 300
280 LOCATE 1,19:PRINT CHR$(0)+CHR$(0)+CHR$(0)
290 LOCATE 2,19:PRINT CHR$(0)+CHR$(0)+CHR$(0)+CHR$(0)
300 NEXT
310 FOR X=1 TO 300:NEXT
320 GOTO 250
330 CIRCLE(X+15,5),20,2
340 SOUND 3000,2
350 PAINT(X+15,5),2,2
360 GET(X-5,0)-(X+35,25),L
370 FOR T=1 TO 100:NEXT T
380 PUT(X-5,0),L
390 FOR Y=2 TO 170 STEP 4
```

Fig. 7-13. A graphics program game that simulates antiaircraft combat.

```
400 PUT(X,Y),K:PUT(X,Y),K
410 NEXT Y
420 FOR G=1 TO 400:NEXT G
430 RETURN
440 FOR B=180 TO 0 STEP -20
450 SOUND 250,.35
460 CIRCLE(165,B),2,1:CIRCLE(165,B),2,0
470 IF X>137 AND X<147 THEN GOTO 330
480 NEXT
490 RETURN
500 CLS
510 PRINT"THIS IS A GAME OF SKILL WHERE"
520 PRINT"THE PLAYERS ATTEMPT TO SHOOT"
530 PRINT"DOWN AN AIRCRAFT. YOU MUST STRIKE"
540 PRINT"THE AIRCRAFT AT A CERTAIN SPOT"
550 PRINT"NEAR THE TAIL SECTION. WHEN"
560 PRINT"YOU SCORE A CORRECT HIT, THE"
570 PRINT"PLANE WILL EXPLODE AND FALL"
580 PRINT"TO EARTH. KEY F1 IS THE FIRING"
590 PRINT"BUTTON. GOOD LUCK!!"
600 PRINT
610 PRINT
620 INPUT"PRESS <ENTER> TO BEGIN";B$
630 CLS
640 RETURN
```

simulate a fixed artillery station or antiaircraft gun. This is a simple program, so the gun is fixed in place and can only fire along a certain path. A miniature airplane flies across the top of the screen from left to right, and the idea is to shoot it down. I'm certainly not presenting this as a game that will entertain you for hours on end, although it's a bit more difficult to shoot the plane down than one might imagine because you have to hit it with the graphic projectile at a single spot near the tail section. Of course, after a few successful attempts, you begin to get the hang of it and the game becomes a bit boring.

This program, then, is presented as an exercise or a basic building block, if you will, for more complex programs that might include several airplanes and a movable cannon. Figure 7-14 shows the basic screen setup. The plane is in the upper left-hand corner, while the fixed cannon rests at the bottom center of the screen. When the plane flies directly over the cannon, it is fired at by depressing the F1 Soft Key on the keyboard. You will then see the

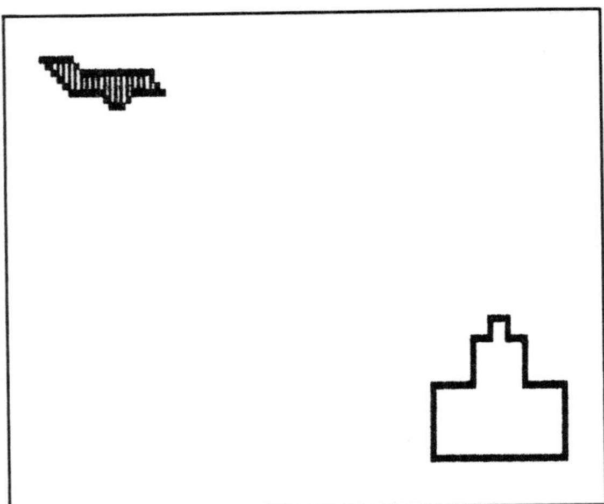

Fig. 7-14. The screen display provided by the gunnery program.

projectile quickly made its way toward the plane. If a hit is scored (in the correct location), the plane bursts into flames and suddenly makes a vertical dive toward the ground, where it explodes. This is a simple program, but the graphics display is not bad at all. The program didn't take very long to write, but there were a few bugs in it that involved an hour or so of rewriting.

Figure 7-15 shows an enlarged version of the tiny jet aircraft which will appear on the screen. This was produced using a single draw statement, although it is repeated elsewhere in the program. This will be explained a bit later. Line 130 in the program (Fig. 7-13) was used to produce this plane. When the program first runs, you will see this object at the center of the screen, and it will then be nabbed by the get statement and erased from the screen by the put statement. These are found in lines 180 and 190 of the program. Most game programs using color mode graphics don't take full advantage of all the graphics capabilities available. These capabilities are quite good on the IBM Personal Computer, and once the basic program has been input, a little extra time can yield a much more impressive effect. I was not content to simply have the airplane disappear (as if it had disintegrated) when struck by the projectile. I wanted it to dive vertically for the ground. I accomplished this by another draw statement, which is found in line 200. Once my basic program had been written, I listed line 130, erased the line designator, and changed it to 200. When the entire program was listed once again, I had identical lines at 130 and 200. I then inserted one additional command in the latter line. This is the A3 which falls immediately after the scale command. This causes the original image to be inverted 270°. Effectively, this produces a 90° pitch downward (at the nose). At this point, I actually had two graphic images, both identical as far as lines were concerned, but one depicted the airplane in the normal flying configuration and the other produced the appearance of a nose dive. The latter figure was placed in a separate array (K). At this point, I had the capability of displaying the plane in either of the two configurations. I then drew the gun using the statement that is now found in line 120 of the program. Of course, the gun is useless unless you have the projectile. I decided to use a very tiny circle, which is set up in line 460. This will be discussed a bit later.

Of course, when an aircraft is struck by antiaircraft artillery, it usually bursts into flames. I wanted to simulate this as well, and I did this with a circle statement in line 330. This circle is painted red, and during the program run, it will be written over the aircraft when it is struck. This produces the graphic equivalent of a fireball explosion. I chose also to paint the aircraft in its normal flying configuration, but to leave it blank in the crash configuration. The crashing aircraft object travels faster, and I wanted to avoid flicker. I feel this combination produced the best possible effect. The painted circle that represents the explosion was committed to array L, so that it could be erased shortly after it was written. We now have three arrays. The nose dive configuration is designated by array K, J is the jet in its normal flying configuration, and L is the fireball explosion.

Now that all the graphic images had been devised and committed to arrays, it was time to figure out the movement pattern. The normal flight configuration is handled in lines 250 through 300. The changing value of X is inserted in the two put statements in line 260, so the airplane flies from left to right across the screen at positions 10,5 through 280,5. The lines that control the vertical descent of the crashing plane are 390 through 410. As soon as the plane is struck, the old image is erased and the vertical plane is put on the screen at the same position. It travels from the top to the bottom of the screen. The path of the bullet from the gun is controlled by lines 440 through 480. Instead of using put and get statements here, I shortened programming time by writing a circle on the screen and then writing over it with another circle. How can that be? Wouldn't that just leave a trail of circles from the gun to the airplane? The answer is yes it does, but you can't see them. The first circle in line 460 is written in the color green, as designated by the 1 following the radius designator. Immediately thereafter, another circle of exactly the same size is written over the one that already appears on the screen. Note here, however, that the color designator is 0, which is the same as the background. When this second circle is written, it simply blends with the background, for all intents and purposes, erases the first from the screen. These circles are rewritten as a for-next loop advances. The path of the

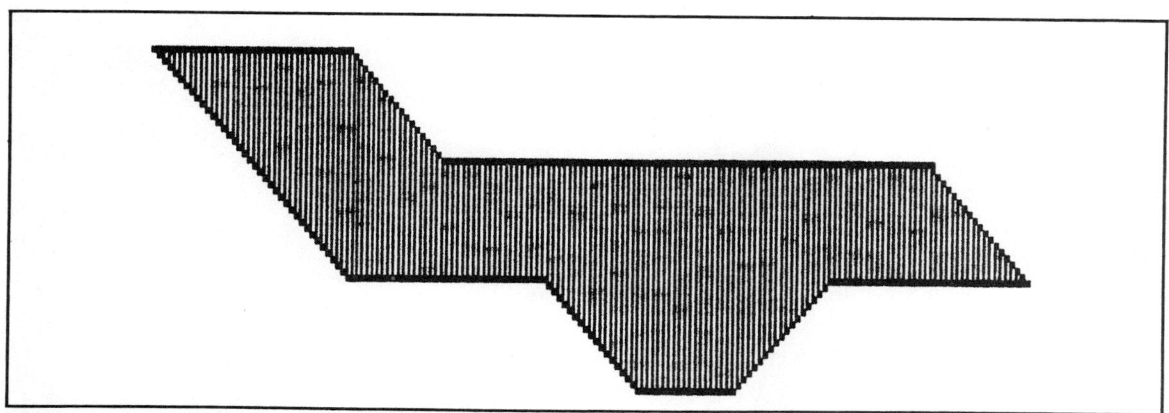

Fig. 7-15. Enlargement of the graphic jet airplane.

circle/projectile, then, is from the muzzle of the gun (165,180) to the airplane strike position (165, 0).

In order to be able to activate this projectile subroutine, the F1 key is turned on in line 230. Line 240 specifies the branch to line 440 (the start of the projectile routine) when F1 is depressed. You will also see a sound statement in the projectile firing loop (line 450). This transmits a short low-frequency beep each time the loop cycles. This produces the "ack" effect, which adds more realism to the game. Line 470 checks for a hit, which occurs if the X coordinate of the flying plane is between 138 and 146. If the projectile strikes the plane at these coordinates, there is a branch to line 330. If it does not, the plane continues on its path.

Line 330 starts the crash sequence. First, a circle appears at the coordinates of the plane. I simply could not reproduce the sound of an explosion, so I chose a short duration, high-frequency beep instead. The beep is created in line 340. The paint statement in line 350 colors the entire circle red, and this image is then committed to array L in line 360. I didn't want the fireball circle to disappear too suddenly, so a time delay loop is found in line 370. The put statement in line 380 simply erases the circle from the screen. I could have used a previous trick and used another circle statement here instead of the put-get routine. The second circle would have been drawn over the first and painted with the screen background color to erase it. But remember, it takes longer to draw and paint a circle in the background color than it does to remove it from the screen using put. The difference here is only a fraction of a second, but I think this method produces a slightly better effect.

Now, our plane has been hit, the explosion has occurred, and it's time for the crash. This is handled by the for-next loop in lines 390 through 410. The value of Y establishes the downward path and the rate of the aircraft. We now pull the crash configuration plane from array K with the put statement in line 400. The second put statement erases it and the loop then recycles, drawing the image again at a lower point on the screen. This process continues until the loop times out, at which time the last put statement has removed the plane completely from the screen. Line 420 contains another time delay loop (dramatic effect) and the return statement in line 430 then branches back to the execution point where soft key F1 was available to be pressed.

I ran into a problem here because one never knows exactly at what point in execution the F1 key is going to be pressed. If it is pressed during the split-second when the flying plane is being erased, when the normal sequence starts again after the crash, a fixed image of the plane remains on the screen while an identical moving image constantly flies through it. I solved this in a simple manner by inputting line 270. This reads the screen at a point where the plane would be located when struck by the projectile. If the point value is 0 (the screen background color), no written image exists here and the program runs normally. If, however, the point value is greater than 0, this indicates a screen write, and there is a branch to line 280 and 290. These lines contain locate statements that access the area on the screen where the bogus image appears and simply wipe it out by printing a string of blanks. When the program is run, you can sometimes view the unwanted write and its near-instantaneous erasure, but you've got to look closely.

Figure 7-16 shows the screen display when the plane is hit. Figure 7-17 shows a portion of the crash sequence. As was stated previously, this program will probably not hold an adult's attention for more than fifteen minutes or so, but it is an interesting exercise in the basics of programming a graphics action game. It is quite easy to control the speed at which the airplane flies across the screen by means of time delay loops in the controlling for-next loops. The elevation at which the airplane flies can be varied by using random numbers to establish the vertical screen position. You can even arm the airplane by using the projectile routine discussed here in reverse. This way, the plane could randomly drop bombs, hoping to hit the artillery station, or you could even key the bomb drop with another soft key for a two-player version. Here, one player is the pilot and the other is the gunner. All of these modifications could take place without having to introduce more than one additional graphic image to the screen (the bomb).

OTHER ANIMATION PROGRAMS

While the get and put statements are very powerful and highly useful for many types of animation, in some cases, they are not desirable. Animation programs that depict a figure apparently traveling directly away from you in a straight line on the screen often do not use put and get statements. They could, but only at the expense of many more program lines. For example, let's suppose you want to display a ball traveling down the center of the road. Assuming that you are on the same level as the ball, the roadway will be displayed as a V, and

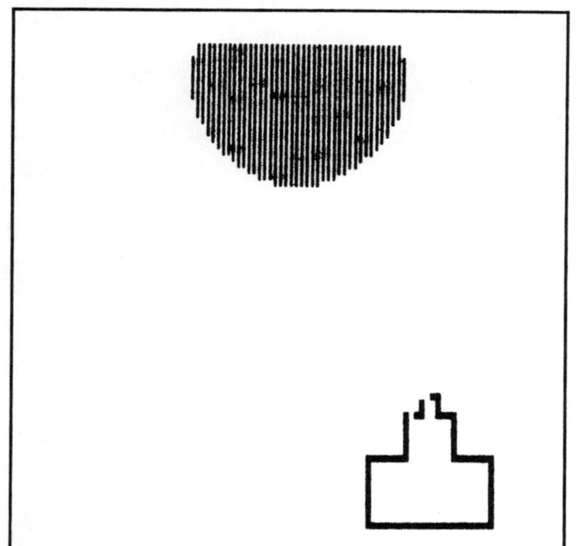

Fig. 7-16. Screen display when a hit is scored.

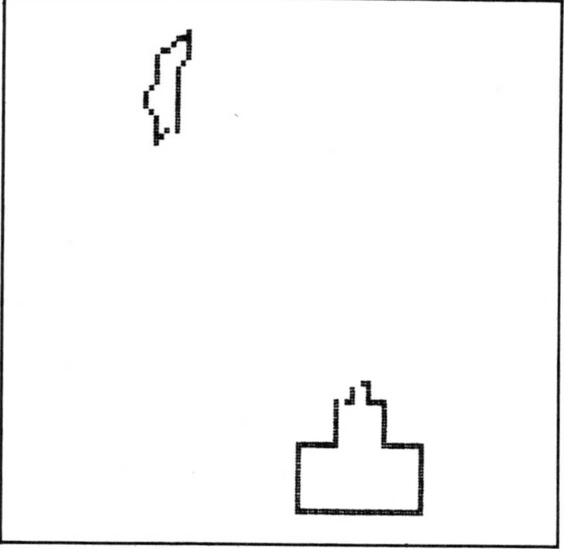

Fig. 7-17. Screen display during crash sequence.

```
9 REM BALL/ROAD SCENE
10 CLS
20 SCREEN 1
30 COLOR 8,0
40 LINE(0,109)-(160,100),3
50 LINE(319,109)-(160,100),3
60 FOR X=30 TO 1000 STEP 10
70 CIRCLE(160,100),1000/X,2
80 PAINT(160,100),2,2
90 CIRCLE(160,100),1000/X,0
100 PAINT(160,100),0,0
110 LINE(0,109)-(160,100),3
120 LINE(319,109)-(160,100),
    3
130 NEXT X
```

Fig. 7-18. Moving Ball program.

the ball will not actually move from its original location. It will simply get smaller as it travels farther away from you. Figure 7-18 shows a program that will set up the moving ball sequence. Figure 7-19 shows the program run at its start. The slanted lines on either side of the ball depict the roadway. From this angle, you are viewing the ball at eye level and looking straight down the center of the road along the path the ball is traveling. As mentioned before, in a real-life situation, the ball will seem to get smaller as it travels further from you. We could use get and put statements to accomplish this, but we would have to draw the ball, probably in several hundred different sizes, each a bit smaller than the one before, using the circle statement. This involves a lot of circle statements and an equal number of put and get pairs.

The program, however, takes a tip from the previous one and uses a for-next loop to determine the radius and thus, the size of the ball. Looking at the program, lines 40 and 50 set up the initial roadway scene. Line 60 begins the for-next loop which will determine circle size. The initial circle is drawn and painted in lines 70 and 80. The circle is then erased by another circle/paint combination in lines 90 and 100. The latter two statements have used color designation numbers of 0, which paints over the original circle in the screen background color. This causes it to disappear from the screen. The radius of the circle in line 70 (and line 90) is determined by the formula 1,000/FK. As X gets larger, the circle gets smaller. When X reaches a value of 1,000, the radius is 0, and therefore, the circle no longer exists.

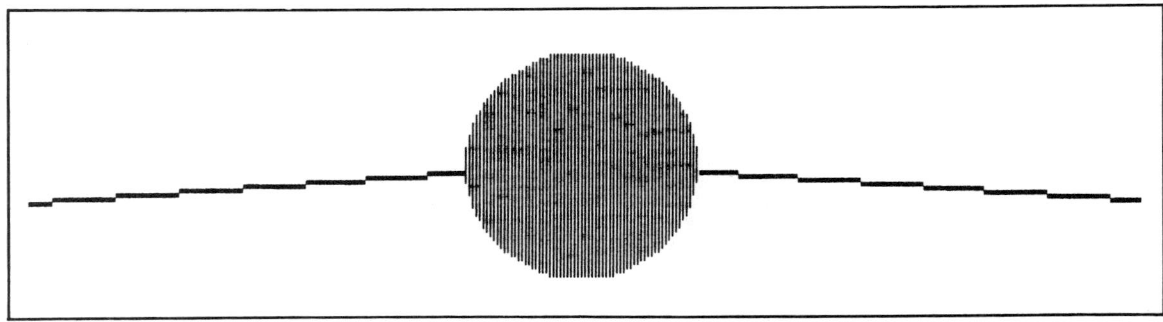

Fig. 7-19. Screen display from the Moving Ball program.

When the program is run, the erasing of the circle also erases portions of the diagonal lines that depict the roadway. Therefore, lines 110 and 120 are inserted in the for-next loop to redraw these lines during every cycle. When the program is run, the ball will seem to be moving away from you until it travels such a distance that it disappears.

Many popular video game programs are based upon the movie Star Wars, which depicted small spaceships traveling through a three-dimensional trough during bombing runs. It is quite easy to simulate this on the IBM Personal Computer, and the program shown in Fig. 7-20 does just this. This program is presented here for demonstration purposes, and a circle is used instead of a "tie-fighter" or other such fictional spaceship/fighter. Figure 7-21 shows the on-screen display. You may not get as much of a three-dimensional effect when viewing this black and white reproduction of what appears on the screen in color. The actual on-screen display paints the floor of the trough a different color from the sides, which adds to the three-dimensional realism.

The basic trough was produced using the draw statement in line 60. The diagonal lines that separate the floor from the walls are produced in lines 70 through 100. While you only see two lines in the drawing, each is really composed of a pair of lines placed very close together. This separates the various sections, allowing the paint statements found in lines 110 through 130 to fill in the sides and floor. This program uses get and put statements for animation, along with the ever-decreasing circle routine discussed in the previous program. Four different circles are initially drawn in lines 190 through 340. The first circle has a radius of 10, while the last one committed to a get statement has a radius of 2. The four circles are different sizes to allow for the image to shrink as it seems to get farther away. Four arrays are established to hold these images (J through M).

A for-next loop is created in lines 350 through 400. This puts the various circles on the screen. The largest circle is committed to array J, and line 360 tests for the value of X to determine when this large circle is to be placed on the screen. The value of X also determines where it will be placed. The circle is placed on the screen and then immediately blotted out using the two put statements in line 360. When the value of X becomes larger than 50, line 370 detects this and puts the next smaller-sized circle on the screen. This circle continues to travel down the trough until X reaches a value of 90, at which time the next circle is placed on the screen. The smallest circle is written when X reaches a value of 120.

At this point, the circle is near the center of the trough at its far end. Another for-next loop reprints the circle at this same location and then causes it to apparently shift course by flying straight away from you. Lines 420 and 440 use the same routine as the previous program to cause the circle to hold its position while shrinking in size. At this point, the program is over.

Since an object which moves down a trough in this manner will seem to maintain the same relative distance from the diagonal corner of the trough, it is necessary to cause it to gain altitude in relation to the bottom of the screen. The if-then statements in lines 360 through 390 subtract a small portion of he value of X from the line position (150). As X in-

```
10 REM BALL IN TROUGH
20 CLS
30 SCREEN 1
40 COLOR 8,0
50 X=50
60 DRAW"BM0,90 S=X; C3 R9 D4 C1 R6 C3 U4 R9 D8 C1 L24 C3 U8"
70 LINE(0,189)-(111,140),1
80 LINE(0,188)-(111,139),3
90 LINE(300,189)-(185,140),1
100 LINE(300,188)-(185,139),3
110 PAINT(160,180),1,1
120 PAINT(10,170),2,3
130 PAINT(280,170),2,3
140 DIM J(100)
150 DIM K(100)
160 DIM L(100)
170 DIM M(100)
180 SCREEN 1
190 CIRCLE(160,100),10,3
200 PAINT (160,100),3,3
210 GET(150,90)-(170,110),J
220 PUT(150,90),J
230 CIRCLE(160,100),7,3
240 PAINT (160,100),3,3
250 GET(150,90)-(170,110),K
260 PUT(150,90),K
270 CIRCLE(160,100),4,3
280 PAINT (160,100),3,3
290 GET(150,90)-(170,110),L
300 PUT(150,90),L
310 CIRCLE(160,100),2,3
320 PAINT (160,100),3,3
330 GET(150,90)-(170,110),M
340 PUT(150,90),M
350 FOR X=5 TO 130
360 IF X<=50 THEN PUT(X,150-(X*.4)),J:PUT(X,150-(X*.4)),J
370 IF X>50 AND X<90 THEN PUT(X,150-(X*.4)),K:PUT(X,
    150-(X*.4)),K
```

Fig. 7-20. Ball in Trough program.

```
380 IF X>=90 AND X<120 THEN PUT(X,150-(X*.4)),L:PUT(X,
    150-(X*.4)),L
390 IF X>=120 THEN PUT(X,150-(X*.4)),M:PUT(X,150-(X*.4)),M
400 NEXT X
410 FOR Y=2 TO 0 STEP -.05
420 CIRCLE(145,105),Y,3
430 PAINT(145,105),3,3
440 CIRCLE(145,105),Y,0
450 PAINT(145,105),0,0
460 NEXT Y
```

creases in size, the object increases in altitude, again in relation to the bottom of the screen. In other words, the object follows the path which parallels the left diagonal line.

You can play with this program all you want, and you will probably want to add some wings to the ball in order to make it appear more like a tie fighter. Using sound or play statements within the for-next loop which begins at line 350, you can also produce some startling sound effects that will add audio excitement to an interesting visual display.

The possibilities for animation programming using the IBM Personal Computer are just about infinite. This chapter has dealt specifically with animation techniques, so the in-

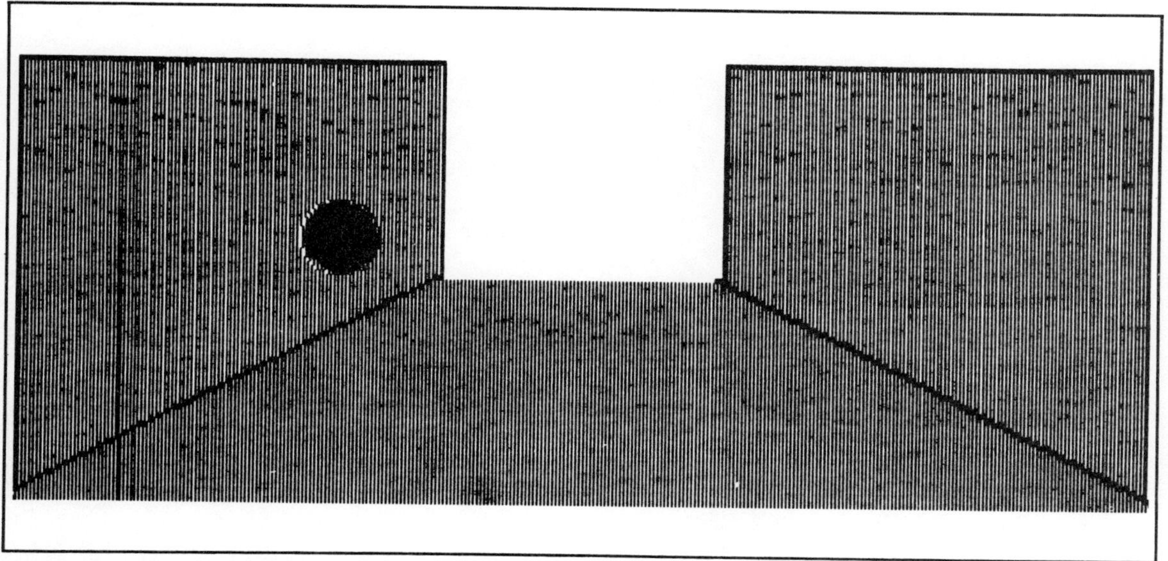

Fig. 7-21. Screen display from the ball in trough program.

formation found in the previous chapter on how to draw various types of figures is also required reading. Once you know how to draw any graphic object you desire, you can then use the information in this chapter to animate it. Anything you can draw on the screen can also be animated. Most programmers begin by drawing a basic object on the screen and will then decide how they want it to be animated. In some cases, the object may be drawn several times from several different angles. Each is committed to an array with the get statement and then placed at the various screen positions using put. For-next loops are quite useful in cutting down on the number of put statements by assigning ever-changing coordinate values for variables in the put statements. You will want to stay away from the paint statement as much as possible, especially for large objects, since painting takes a relatively long time. This will cause on-screen flicker, which is unavoidable when programming in BASIC. The true video games paint their objects in machine language, which is much faster. This latter method of programming is a whole new subject and is not dealt with in this book. However, I think you will find that the powerful graphics and animation language of IBM BASIC will be quite adequate for most of your programming needs.

Printer Graphics

In recent years, the interest in hard copy graphics has been on the rise. Most business type printers do not have the capability of plotting points. Thus, you are limited to printing alphabetic and numeric figures, as well as a few ASCII block characters. Most of the time, the ASCII block characters used for text mode graphics will not appear the same when a print of the screen is made. Solid lines drawn with connective strings of ASCII blocks are displayed by the printer as broken lines or as an almost solid line with several holes in it.

THE IBM PRINTER

The IBM printer is really the Epson MX-80. This is probably the most popular printer ever made for small computers. Recently, however, Epson America, Inc. in Torrance, California has offered point plotting graphics capability through a modification known as GraftraxPlus. This allows the printer to display many of the characters it would not before and gives you high-resolution capability from the printer.

As of this writing, the IBM printer is the old model MX-80 without the Graftrax option. A check with Epson America, Inc. supplied me with the fact that this graphics option, which is sold as a kit for the older machines, is compatible with the IBM printer. However, when the modification is made, you will lose the ability to print the hard copy version of the ASCII block characters. In most applications, this will be of little concern, and a technician at Epson America, Inc. indicated that, in his opinion, the Graftrax modification would certainly be advantageous for most users. He also informed me that it has been rumored that IBM is coming up with their own modification which adds the graphics capability. He was not aware of the exact nature of this PROM package. He conjectured that if the IBM modification allows for the same capabilities as Graftrax but also retains the ASCII block graphics print ability, perhaps the IBM option might be more advantageous for owners of the IBM Personal Computer.

The IBM printer with the Graftrax modification will still display program lines as before, but any on-screen block characters will come out as other symbols when a screen print command is given. The Epson technician explained that his company had tried to build in the graphics capabilities that were most needed by the computerist and those which are most difficult to perform on a standard printer.

Those of you who are interested in making the Graftrax modification may contact Epson directly, or, more than likely, you can pick a kit up from your local computer store. I purchased mine from Frederick Computer Products in Frederick, Maryland, and was sent a small package that consisted of three ROMs. Also included was the MX printer manual, which explains the installation of the ROM kit in one of the appendices.

The IBM printer contains three sockets for the dual-in line package ROM integrated circuits. In the standard version, only the first socket is occupied (by a 2332 ROM). The other two sockets are empty. The conversion process is quite simple and can probably be performed within a half hour or certainly within an hour. Basically, it involves removal of the top printer cover, removal of the single ROM, and the insertion of the three replacement ROMs in sockets that are already provided on the circuit board.

I found Epson's instructions to be quite helpful and experienced little difficulty in making the conversion. For those of you who might wish to make this conversion to your present IBM printer, I will tell you my experiences in making this new installation.

The first step involves removing the setscrews from the bottom of the printer case. To do this, I removed the paper rack and turned the printer upside down on a soft surface. The four screws are located at the corners of the case and can be quickly removed with a medium-sized Phillips screwdriver. When the screws are out, grip the case by the sides, holding the top and bottom sections together. Then, flip the printer over and rest it on a solid work surface. The soft surface was initially used to avoid scratching the unprotected top cover.

The next step requires you to remove the platen knob, which is located on the right side of the printer. All you do is grasp it firmly and pull outward. It may be a bit tight, so a firm but gentle hand is necessary. For goodness sake, don't pull in any direction except straight out. The knob is friction-fitted and comes off in much the same manner as the tuner knob on your television set.

When the knob is off, gently raise the left-hand side of the top cover. Then, slide the entire cover toward the right in order to clear the platen knob shaft. Caution: There is a multi-conductor cable that exits the electronics of the printer and connects to the right-hand side of the top printer case section. Don't be confused into thinking that the cover is completely free of the printer or you may rip out some wires. When the cover is partially cleared, simply tilt it on its right side. It should stay in place with little difficulty, but you can rest the right edge of the printer on the edge of the cover to more firmly secure it. When looking at the printer from the front, you will see two empty IC sockets near the rear. To the right of these is a third socket which contains a single IC. Your first job is to remove the original IC, and this is not as easy as it sounds, especially if you don't have a handy tool known as an IC puller. Like most people, I didn't have one, but a small flathead screwdriver can be used in its place. Starting at the rear of the IC, insert the screwdriver in the thin slot between it and the socket. Make sure you don't get the screwdriver up under the socket, as this is firmly soldered in place. Gently pry the back of the IC up a bit. This component should come up vertically. Don't allow it to wiggle from side to side, or you will place a strain on the socket and the component itself. Incidentally, the board on which the socket is mounted does not seem to be secured on all four sides, so it will tend to raise a bit through your prying operation. To avoid any problems here, place your hand on the circuit board itself at a location that does not contain any electronic components and apply a slight downward pressure. This will offset the upward pressure applied while removing the IC.

Unfortunately, it is extremely difficult to gain access to the front of the IC. I tried to pry this end up with a very tiny screwdriver, but just couldn't manage it. What I ended up doing was prying the back edge up and then slipping a fingernail under the IC at the front edge and applying more pressure here. Admittedly, it was a tricky process, but after a few minutes, the IC finally popped free. You should now set this IC aside in a safe spot, because there may come a time when you would like to reconvert your printer to its original condition in order to have the capability of printing ASCII block characters.

Now, look to the right of the large IC which is mounted in front of the three sockets previously mentioned. It should carry an 8049 designation. On the right-hand side of this device is a tiny jumper wire that is soldered directly to the circuit board. It's quite small, so look carefully. It is identified on the circuit board as J1. With a small pair of diagonal cutters, snip this wire near its center and bend back the two sections so that it is impossible for them to touch.

It is now time to install the Epson-supplied ROMs. In my kit, each was identified by a separate color dot (red, yellow, and blue) and also by printed markings of 1B, 2B, and 3B. If you look at the back of the IC sockets, you will see the same markings on the circuit board, but in reverse order. Socket 3B is on the left-hand side, while 1B is on the right. The original IC should have been installed in socket 1B. All you do at this point is match the IC designation with its socket. Start with 1B on the far right. Make sure you have the IC marked 1B, and be absolutely certain that you install it with pin 1 facing toward the front of the printer. My ROMs were not marked with pin numbers, but each did contain a half-moon cutout in the plastic surface on one end. If you look at the IC sockets, you will see a matching half-moon cutout at the end that is nearest the front of the printer. Match these up, and you're in good shape. In all three cases, the end which contains the half-moon cutout is installed nearest the front of the printer.

Now, most people will tell you that it's a very simple matter to install an IC in its socket.

Sometimes this is true; often it is not. Each ROM contains 28 pins (14 to a side) and every pin must be properly aligned with its appropriate socket slot. The standard procedure written up in many books is to place the IC evenly over the socket, allowing each pin to rest in its slot. Then, press with gentle but even pressure until the component snaps in place. Don't you believe it! There's generally a fair amount of aligning and even bending of the pins slightly to get everything to match. Ideally, you want to push all the pins in the same distance at the same time, but you will probably end up having to "rock" the IC into place. I had little difficulty with the first IC, but the second one took me about ten minutes. The third was medium-difficult. You must make certain that one or two pins don't accidentally bend out or under. If such cases, these pins do not make contact with the rest of the circuit, and the printer won't work . . . at least not properly. After each IC is installed, examine all the pins carefully to make certain they are indeed properly fitted in place. Then move on to the next IC. When making these installations, be absolutely sure that you are mounting the correct IC in each socket and that the half-moon cutouts are pointing toward the front of the printer. When all three are installed, reexamine the pin connections. If it is necessary to remove an IC due to improper placement, pry it up using the directions given in an earlier part of this discussion. If you should bend the pin out or under, it's usually a simple matter to straighten it after the IC is freed once again. Don't bend the pins too much though, or they may break, making replacement necessary.

The final step involves resetting the small DIP switches, of which there are two. These are located to the left and slightly behind the left-hand IC and immediately behind the center IC. The large switch is at the center position and contains eight miniature switches. These will have to be reset for the new modification to work. Epson provides a function chart for these switches, but the normal positioning of those contained on the large switch is 8 on, 6 on, and all the rest off. Switch 2 is the smaller one and contains only four miniature switches. All of these should be in the off position.

When you have completed the switch assignments, double-check to make certain the ICs are properly positioned and installed and that the small jumper wire has been cut. Also, make sure you have not inadvertently dropped any screws or other small pieces of hardware onto the circuit board. You may then re-install the top cover by sliding it over the platen knob shaft and aligning it with the bottom cover. Gripping the printer from its sides again, flip it over and allow it to rest on a soft surface. Replace the four setscrews and the conversion is complete.

The Self-Test Function

The success of your modification can be checked by actuating the self-test function. The original printer contained one as well, but with the Graftrax modification also comes a change in this test pattern. It is not necessary to connect the printer to the IBM computer. Simply plug it into a power outlet and press the line feed button while simultaneously turning the printer power switch to the on position. Figure 8-1 shows the proper test pattern. This will consist of approximately 2½ lines of numbers, letters, and figures. At this point, the

```
 !"#$%&'()*+,-./0123456789:;<=>?@ABCDEFGHIJKLMNOPQRSTUVWXYZ[\]^_'abcdefghijklmno
pqrstuvwxyz{|}~Ø£¨'`§┌┐├┤┬└┘|─┴┼!"#$%&'()*+,-./0123456789:;<=>?@ABCDEFGHIJKLMNOP
QRSTUVWXYZ[\]^_'abcdefghijklmnopqrstuvwxyz{/}~Ø
```

Fig. 8-1. Self test function of the IBM printer with the Graftrax Plus modification.

printer will stop. The original self-test went on for quite some time, but this one is much shorter.

You may now connect the printer to the IBM Personal Computer using the same interface cable originally supplied. The printer should work as before with the exceptions previously noted regarding the ASCII block characters. I would strongly suggest that you read the MX printer manual. As I stated earlier, this was provided with my kit, although this may be done in every case. In any event, you will certainly need one to complete the modification and to check out the operation of your printer. The manual is excellent and provides several programs that you may wish to input. My version did not have any specific information on programs for the IBM Personal Computer, but most of the programs will work.

If you experience difficulties with operation after the modification has been completed, I would suggest that you again remove the top cover and reexamine your work. Are all ICs correctly installed and in the right sockets? Has the small jumper lead been clipped and its wires separated? Are the switch positions set as specified? If this inspection doesn't provide any answers, refer to the troubleshooting guide contained in the Epson manual.

Using the Modified IBM Printer

My main reason for converting the original IBM printer to the Graftrax Plus version was to have the capability of copying my screen graphics onto computer printer forms. When the modification is complete, the printer has this capability, but unfortunately, the computer doesn't have the ability to output the graphic information on the screen directly to the printer. What you need here is what is commonly known as a screen dump program. This bit of software reads all of the points on the screen and dumps this information to the printer. A version of this type of utility program is contained in the on-board ROM of the IBM Personal Computer, but it operates only in text mode. This is the function which is called up by pressing the uppercase (arrow) and PrtSc keys simultaneously. In graphics mode, however, these keys won't do anything. What you need is a screen dump program that you can input to the computer and save on disk. Whenever you want to copy an on-screen graphics display, this program will be merged with the one you want to copy. When this merged program is run, the graphic information will appear on the screen. The screen dump program will then automatically be run, and eventually, the printer will get the needed information and reproduce in printed form a close equivalent of what is displayed on the screen. You can program graphics directly to the printer. Here, there is no on-screen display, and the sole output of the program is committed to the printer. This type of programming involves substantial modification of program techniques and will not be dealt with in this book. The Epson manual that was supplied to me with the modification chips deals with this subject in detail.

I prefer to stick with on-screen graphics. In this manner, I can see exactly what I have programmed before committing it to hard copy using a screen dump program. When program information goes directly to the printer instead of from the screen to the printer, making corrections can be a lengthy process, and you never know exactly what you've got until the entire printout is complete. When complex graphics are involved, this can take a fair amount of time and reams of printer paper.

SCREEN DUMP PROGRAMS

But where do I get a screen dump program? This is the question I asked myself upon completing the modification. I checked with Epson, and a technician there told me that he was not aware of any that had been written for the IBM Personal Computer. He went on to say that there were probably several out there, or there would be shortly, and to keep my ear to the ground, so to speak. I next called a fellow author, Rich Ingram, who is presently enrolled at the University of Indiana at Bloomington. Rich is completing his doctorate in psychology, but he is also part of a high-level computer program there and has access to many exotic machines, including the IBM Personal Computer. He told me he was not aware of any screen dump programs for the IBM machine, but would see if he could locate one. A few days later, I received a copy of a page from *Creative Computing Magazine*, in which author Will Fastie described his screen dump program for the IBM Personal Computer. Here was just the program I needed, and it required only 50 or so program lines. Will lives in Baltimore, Maryland, and a phone call to him got me the permission I needed to reprint the program, which is copyrighted to him, in these pages. Figure 8-2 shows the original program as it was published in Creative Computing Magazine. As you can see, most of the lines are taken up by explanatory remarks. The executable portion of the program itself involves about 50 lines. Will used the only true function in IBM advanced graphics language, which is point. This function reads the setting of each of the 64,000 dots that make up the medium-resolution image on the screen. The printer routine portion of the program sends a single character to the printer by outputting it directly to the hardware printer port. In line 1410 of this program, you can see that NR.ROWS = 200 and NR.COLS = 320. These are the row and column variables that correspond with the 320 × 200 format of the medium-resolution screen. When a graphics image is on the screen, this program is keyed up and the computer begins to scan from 0,0 to 320,200, reading all 64,000 potential points. The information is then sent, a character at a time, to the printer port.

Will Fastie seemed to think the program had limited practical use because of the amount of time required to perform the scan and print operation. In his article in *Creative Computing*, he explained that the first version of the program took about forty minutes to print what was on the screen. The version shown here was modified considerably to cut the time down to about fifteen minutes or so. Approximately ten minutes of this time is required for the computer to read the entire screen. The next five minutes is taken up by the mechanical printing process. Will explained to me during our phone conversation that writing such a program in BASIC is bound to end in a retarded processing/print time factor. However, many persons involved in graphics work will now have the need to reproduce a lot of graphic screens. Therefore, the time factor may be less of a hindrance than the meticulous Mr. Fastie has concluded. Many of the graphics prints shown in previous chapters in this book were run using this program, or a slightly modified version that I developed to speed up the printing process.

This program is shown in Fig. 8-3. The only modification to the original program by Will Fastie involves the input statements starting at line 20. This allows you to input different values for NR.ROWS and NR.COLS. In the original program, all 64,000 points are scanned, regardless of the size of the graphic object to be reproduced. However, if your graphic display involves only a few objects, it's usually a simple matter to position them in the top half of the screen. Then, all that is necessary is to scan the first hundred rows or so instead of all 200. A single object might be placed in the top left portion of the screen. You could then cut down on the number of columns scanned as well. Processing time will be cut in half by scanning only half the rows. It's cut by another half if only 160 columns are scanned. When the input statements are added to this program, you can scan only the rows and columns needed to include the image produced on the screen. For small images, this cuts total scanning and printing time down to a few minutes. Of course, if your display fills the entire screen, you will have to count on the full fifteen minutes before the image is complete.

When this modified program is run, you must have first decided on the number of rows and columns which must be read in order to include the entire image on the screen. Most of the time, I simply placed the image in the top portion and still scanned 320 columns but only 100 rows. These values are input when prompted to do so by the input statements. Another modification to my version of Will Fastie's program is the deletion of lines 1320 and 1350. Many of the graphics programs included in this book are on endless loops, so what I do before committing them to the screen dump program is remove the GOTO statement that loops the program back to the start and replace it with the following line:

```
LOAD"SDP",R
```

SDP is the filename of the screen dump program. When the graphics program has completed its run, the above line loads the screen dump program from disk and then runs it. After a short time, you will hear a beep from the computer every few seconds. Will Fastie built this into his program using the beep statement. This lets the programmer know that the computer is reading screen points. After 200 beeps (assuming NR.ROWS = 200), there will be a short pause, and the printer is then activated as the information is output to its port.

Instead of using the load statement to pull the screen dump program out of memory and run it, you could simply merge the program that provides the graphics with the one that

```
1000 ' GPRINT - Graphics Dump Program for the IBM Personal Computer
1010 ' Will Fastie — Original version Feb 82, revised June 82
1020 '
1030 ' This program transfers the contents of the Color/Graphics Adapter
1040 ' memory to a GRAFTRAX-80 or GRAFTRAX-Plus equipped IBM 80 CPS or
1050 ' EPSON MX-80 printer, to an EPSON MX-100 printer, or to a new
1060 ' generation EPSON MX-80 or 100 printer (for which GRAFTRAX-Plus is a
1070 ' standard feature). Medium resolution images (200 × 320) are
1080 ' converted, whether in black and white or in color. Color
1090 ' images, which can be displayed using a 4 color set, are printed
1100 ' in black and white.
1110 '
1120 ' The program assumes that the program is executed on a machine
1130 ' equipped with the Color/Graphics Adapter only. If both
1140 ' display adapters are present, switch to the Color/Graphics
1150 ' adapter first, then run this program.
1160 '
1170 ' — Global program declarations
1180  DEFINT A-Z
1190  DIM PIN.MASKS (8)
1200  FOR PIN = 0 TO 7
1210    PIN.MASKS(PIN) = 2 ^ (7-PIN)
1220  NEXT PIN
1230  ESC = 27
1240  CR = 13
1250 '
1260 ' This section sould be written to suit your particular needs. For
1270 ' demonstration purposes, it loads a previously stored image from the
1280 ' disk into the memory of the Color/Graphics Adapter. You could
1290 ' generate the image here instead.
1300 '
1310  KEY OFF: CLS
1320  INPUT "Enter filename of image:  ",F$
1330  SCREEN 1,0          'Medium resolution, color enabled
1340  DEF SEG = &HB800          'Base address of CG/A memory
1350  BLOAD F$, 0
1360 '
1370 ' This section converts the image in memory to a numeric array
1380 ' containing the information required for the printer.
1390 '
```

Fig. 8-2. A screen dump program for the IBM Personal Computer. This was written by Will Fastie and originally appeared in the October 1982 issue of *Creative Computing*.

```
1400 ' — Declare an array to hold the data
1410  NR.ROWS = 200:   NR.COLS = 320
1420  ROWS.PER.PRINTED.LINE = 8
1430  NR.LINES = NR.ROWS/ROWS.PER.PRINTED.LINE
1440  DIM LINES(NR.LINES, NR.COLS)
1450 '
1460 ' — Initialize the array to 0
1470  FOR L = 0 TO NR.LINES-1
1480    FOR COL = 0 TO NR.COLS-1
1490      LINES(L, COL) = 0
1500    NEXT COL
1510  NEXT L
1520 '
1530 ' This section reads each point from the video memory, translates
1540 ' the points to a black and white representation, and builds
1550 ' the data for the printer.
1560 ' The ROW and COL variables are used to calculate the position in
1570 ' which the point value should be placed. The positions 0 through 7
1580 ' represent the printer's print head pins, from top to bottom. The
1590 ' value in each position in the array corresponds to these pin
1600 ' positions.
1610 '
1620  FOR ROW = 0 TO NR.ROWS-1
1630    L = ROW/ROWS.PER.PRINTED.LINE
1640    FOR COL = 0 TO NR.COILS-1
1650      IF POINT (COL, ROW) = 0 THEN GOTO 1670
1660        LINES(L, COL) = LINES(L, COL) OR PIN.MASKS(ROW MOD 8)
1670    NEXT COL
1680    BEEP
1690  NEXT ROW
1700 '
1710 ' This section prints the data by line to the printer. No assumption
1720 ' is made about the position of the paper.
1730 '
1740  GOSUB 2110          'establish line spacing
1750  FOR L = 0 TO NR.LINES-1
1760    N = NR.COLS:   GOSUB 2170          'put printer in graphics mode
1770    FOR COL = 0 TO NR.COLS-1
1780      C = LINES (L, COL): GOSUB 2000
1790    NEXT COL
```

```
1800    C = CR: GOSUB 2000        'advance the paper
1810  NEXT L
1820  LPRINT: LPRINT        'space between this and next
1830 '
1840  END
1850 '
1860 ' This routine transmits the value in C to the printer.
1870 ' A routine like this is necessary because PRINT in BASIC interprets
1880 ' some characters, and therefore cannot transmit arbitrary values.
1890 '
1900 ' This program uses the Printer Port on the IBM Monochrome Display
1910 ' and Parallel Printer Adapter. If you just have the Printer Adapter,
1920 ' you must change the port values in this routine according to this table.
1930 '
1940 '      Port Name          MD & PPA      Just PPA
1950 '      -----------        ------------  -----------
1960 '      DATA in/out        &H3BC         &H378
1970 '      Printer Latch      &H3BE         &H37A
1980 '      Status Register    &H3BD         &H379
1990 '
2000  OUT &H3BE, &H6
2010  IF INP(&H3BD) < > &HDF THEN 2010
2020  OUT &H3BC, C
2030  OUT &H3BE, &H3F
2040  IF INP (&H3BD) < > &HDF THEN 2040
2050  RETURN
2060 '
2070 ' Subroutine to set line spacing to 8/72 of an inch. Subsequent
2080 ' to this command, the printer moves the paper by this amount
2090 ' whenever a Carriage Return (13) is received.
2100 '
2110  C = ESC: GOSUB 2000: C = ASC("A"): GOSUB 2000: C = 8: GOSUB 2000
2120  RETURN
2130 '
2140 ' Subroutine to command the printer to consider the next N characters
2150 ' as Bit Image Graphics data.
2160 '
2170  C = ESC: GOSUB 2000: C = ASC("K"): GOSUB 2000
2180  IF N > 255 THEN C = N-256: GOSUB 2000: C = 1: GOSUB 2000
                 ELSE C = N:      GOSUB 2000: C = 0: GOSUB 2000
2190  RETURN
```

Fig. 8-2. A screen program for the IBM Personal Computer. This was written by Will Fastie and originally appeared in the Octoboer 1982 issue of *Creative Computing*. (Continued from page 191.)

does the printing. Here, it will be necessary to store the screen dump program in JSCII format. This is handled by the following command:

SAVE"SDP",A

This is executed when you have completed inputting the screen dump program. Naturally, the SDP filename may be replaced with any other you desire. The ASCII format storage is mandatory, or the program will not merge with the one that writes the graphics. You will still have to remove the endless loop from your graphics program, if one exists, and make sure that no CLS statements are inserted at points where they will erase the image from the screen before the screen dump program begins to run. During the scanning process, the image must be on the screen.

I am certain that slightly faster programs could be written using peek functions, but in this mode, the BASIC language is still going to be slow. Mr. Fastie's purpose in writing the program as shown was to provide a screen dump routine that could be easily programmed and would be easy to understand by a broad range of computer enthusiasts. In my opinion, his submission is quite relevant, and I have found it to be very useful.

Through Will's article in *Creative Computing*, I also learned that there are several commercial software outfits that are now offering screen dump programs for the IBM Personal Computer. One of these is Ratcom, Inc. in Miami, Florida. This is a part of the Software Division of Jack Strick & Associates. I called Jack, inquiring about the program, which is named Rattrax. He informed me they now have Rattrax-Plus, which is an improved version of the original and comes on a disk that is loaded under IBM DOS. This program requires an IBM Personal Computer with 48K memory, a single disk drive, and of course, the color/graphics board and printer. There are several versions available for several different printers. The one I ordered was compatible with the Epson MX-80 with Graftrax, which is the same as the IBM printer with the Graftrax modification discussed earlier.

Jack sent the program out immediately, and I was quite excited upon opening the package to find a fair amount of documentation with the disk. Several programs are contained on the disk to provide graphic samples and explain the operation of the entire system. Additionally, Ratcom provides a page which has been perforated to fit the spiral rings of the IBM BASIC manual. The page is formatted exactly like the pages in the IBM manual under the heading of "Statements." With this page properly inserted, you have a constant reference to the use of the Rattrax program.

The main programs of interest on the disk, in regard to obtaining hard copy prints of your graphics displays, have filenames of Rattrax and MX. Rattrax chains to MX, with the latter performing the functions specified in the former. For most purposes, or at least until you learn the full capabilities of Rattrax-MX Plus, you can use the Rattrax program by removing any endless loops from the graphics program to be copied. Then include the line:

LOAD"RATTRAX",R

After the graphics program writes its image on the screen, the Rattrax program provides all of

```
10 CLS
20 INPUT"NUMBER OF ROWS IS:";NR.ROWS
30 CLS
40 INPUT"NUMBER OF COLUMNS IS:";NR.COLS
50 CLS
60 MERGE"NAME OF PROGRAM TO BE COPIED",R
50000 DEFINT A-Z
50010 DIM PIN.MASKS(8)
50020 FOR PIN=0 TO 7
50030 PIN.MASKS(PIN)=2^(7-PIN)
50040 NEXT PIN
50050 ESC=27
50060 CR=13
50070 DEF SEG = &HB800
50080 ROWS.PER.PRINTED.LINE=8
50090 NR.LINES=NR.ROWS/ROWS.PER.PRINTED.LINE
50100 DIM LINES(NR.LINES, NR.COLS)
50110 FOR L=0 TO NR.LINES-1
50120 FOR COL=0 TO NR.COLS-1
50130 LINES(L, COL)=0
50140 NEXT COL
50150 NEXT L
50160 FOR ROW=0 TO NR.ROWS-1
50170 L=ROW\ROWS.PER.PRINTED.LINE
50180 FOR COL =0 TO NR.COLS-1
50190 IF POINT(COL,ROW)=0 THEN 50210
50200 LINES(L,COL)=LINES(L,COL) OR PIN.MASKS(ROW MOD 8)
50210 NEXT COL
50220 BEEP
50230 NEXT ROW
50240 GOSUB 50400
50250 FOR L=0 TO NR.LINES-1
50260 N=NR.COLS:GOSUB 50420
50270 FOR COL=0 TO NR.COLS-1
50280 C=LINES(L,COL):GOSUB 50340
50290 NEXT COL
50300 C=CR:GOSUB 50340
50310 NEXT L
50320 LPRINT:LPRINT
```

Fig. 8-3. My modification to the previous program to allow for the selection of the screen areas to be read.

```
50330 END
50340 OUT &H3BE,&H6
50350 IF INP(&H3BD) <>&HDF THEN 50350
50360 OUT &H3BC,C
50370 OUT &H3BE, &H3F
50380 IF INP(&H3BD) <> &HDF THEN 50380
50390 RETURN
50400 C=ESC:GOSUB 50340:C=ASC("A"):GOSUB 50340:C=8:GOSUB
      50340
50410 RETURN
50420 C=ESC:GOSUB 50340:C=ASC("K"):GOSUB 50340
50430 IF N>255 THEN C=N-256:GOSUB 50340:C=1:GOSUB 50340
      ELSE C=N:GOSUB 50340:C=0 :GOSUB 50340
50440 RETURN
```

the information needed for the printing process, specifying a form length of 11 inches. This program ends with a chain to the MX program (automatically), which then starts the scanning and printing process. If you want more than one copy or a longer or shorter print width, it will be necessary to use the common statement as on the insert page for the IBM BASIC manual. The process will be even clearer if you list the program lines of Rattrax. These contain a large number of explanatory remarks, and you can see how the various commands are inserted. It will serve no purpose to go into these in detail in this book. If you order the Rattrax-MS plus system from Ratcom, Inc., all of the information will be provided.

Rattrax-MX Plus offers eight different print modes. These are controlled by Soft Keys F1-F8. For standard printing, I use the F2 key. This is the 480 mode, which prints 2 dots for every vertical screen point. Other keys allow you to print up to four dots for every vertical screen point. The F2 print mode gives full size reproduction (13 inch screen) and little distortion.

Unlike some screen dump programs, Rattrax-MX Plus prints vertically. This is accomplished in all modes except one, and this exception will be discussed a bit later. This means that the lefthand portion of the graphic image on your display screen is printed at the top of the form. Instead of reading the screen from left to right, this program reads from bottom to top, starting at the left-hand side. When the form comes off the machine, you simply turn it 90°, as shown in Fig. 8-4. The top of this figure shows the screen display of a graphic IC chip. The bottom portion shows how this image is printed on the computer form. This is vertical printing, and the printed image is read by rotating the form 90°.

Again, vertical printing is handled in all print modes with the exception of the one accessed by depressing Soft Key F7. This causes one dot to be printed for every screen point, as

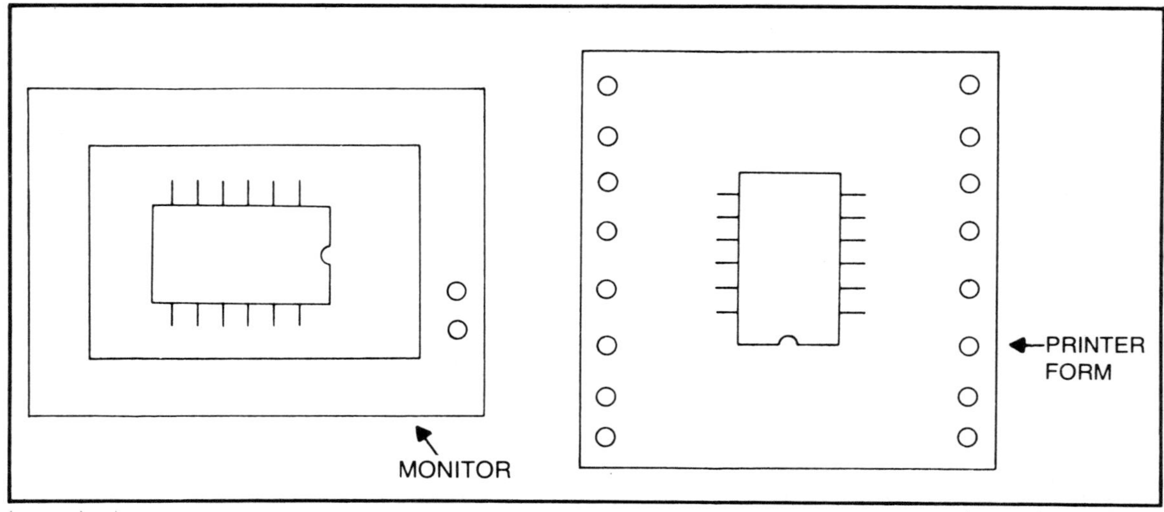

Fig. 8-4. At the top is a graphic figure on the monitor. At the bottom is the reproduction on the printer form. This is an example of vertical printing using the *Rattrax-MX Plus* program from Ratcom, Inc.

was the case with the F1 key, but the screen image is written in horizontal format, just as it appears on the monitor.

Soft Key F8 allows you to do some specialized graphic printing. This accesses the reverse image format. In this mode, any portion of the screen that contains graphic information will be displayed as a blank or "no print", while any area that does not contain graphic information will be filled in with printer points. This produces the reverse or negative image of what appears on the screen. For example, if your graphic display shows a hollow circle at the center of the screen, the reverse image printout will be a completely filled-in computer form, with the exception of the area occupied by the circumference of the circle, which will remain white.

Most or all of these features could be easily built into the Fastie program, but at the expense of more time. Many of the graphic drawings in this book were produced by the Rattrax program, and the quality is generally the same as those produced by the one written by Will Fastie although there are many more possible print variations. Rattrax-MX Plus really shines in the speed department, however, since it takes only a minute or so to produce an entire screen image as compared with about fifteen minutes for the Fastie program. Both screen dump routines tend to squash the circles a bit, but this type of compression is very difficult, if not impossible, to avoid in making the transition from an electronic display to a physical hard copy version.

Jack Strick has taken quite a few innovative steps in presenting his program. The disk contains a program which is the filename of HELP1. When this is loaded and run, you immediately see two graphic rat tracks near the center of the screen. After a few seconds, the complete Rattrax-MX + logo appears on the screen, and the internal speaker begins to play a computer version of Scott Joplin's "The Entertainer". Simultaneously, little rat tracks begin to walk up the screen, stepping on the logo. Figure 8-5 shows the screen display which was produced on my printer using this screen dump program. Jack Strick & Associates also offer many other programs for the IBM Personal Computer, one of which will do hard copy color/graphics using a color plotter. Further information on all of their products can be had by writing Jack Strick & Associates, 949 S. Southlake Drive, Hollywood, Florida, 33019.

I must have played with both screen dump programs for several hours. Figure 8-6 shows a line printout of a portion of one of my programs done in graphics mode. This printout was handled by plotting points and not by using the numerical and alphabetical functions of the print head. This figure is shown in the actual size it was in when it came off the printer and could easily be used in an advertisement for a computer business. Using a normal line printout, it would be necessary to blow the figures up considerably and quality would be lost.

Screen dump programs for the IBM Personal Computer and the IBM printer with the Graftrax Plus modification are available from several other companies, and I would imagine that more will be appearing almost every month. The Rattrax-MX Plus program on disk, which is compatible with IBM DOS, costs about $35. I feel this is a reasonable price, especially when you consider all of the print options.

In the past, many persons have been forced to program hard copy graphics in a manner that outputs the information directly to a printer and doesn't allow for on-screen testing. Alternately, a program might be written in screen version and greatly modified to access the printer. Either way, there's a lot of room for error. Using the IBM Personal Computer and a graphics printer, all of your programming is done with the on-screen display in mind. The printer can then copy the display information with a fair amount of accuracy. Such a system

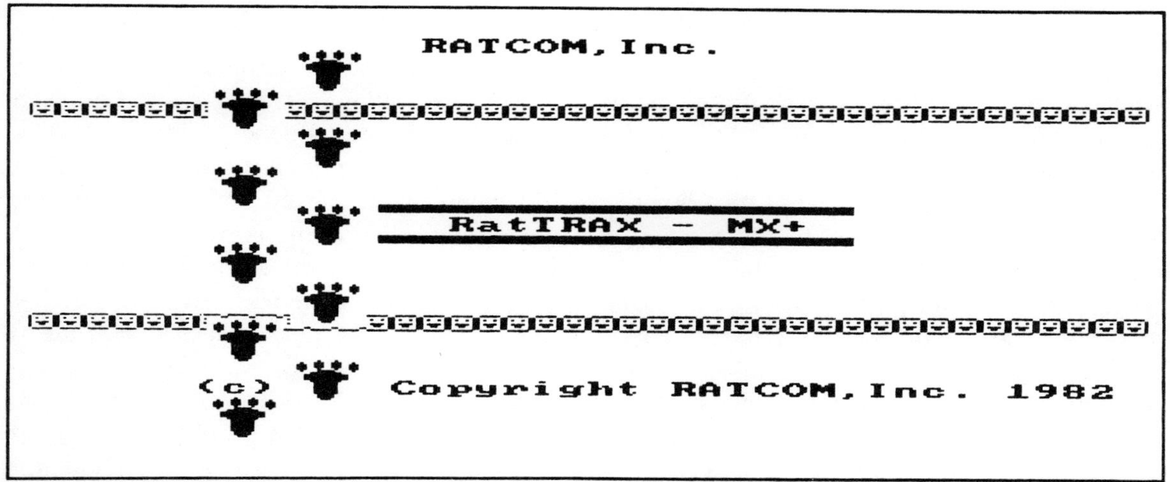

Fig. 8-5. The Ratcom logo is quite attractive and is reproduced here during the program run on the IBM Personal Computer.

```
70 PAINT(160,100),2,2
80 CIRCLE(158,94),1,0
90 GET (138,88)-(172,112),J
100 FOR X=1 TO 100:NEXT
110 PUT(138,88),J
120 CIRCLE(160,100),12,2,
-PI*1.25,-PI/1.
34
130 PAINT(161,101),2,2
140 CIRCLE(158,94),1,0
150 GET(138,88)-(172,112),K
160 FOR X= 1 TO 100:NEXT
170 PUT(138,88),K
180 FOR A=15 TO 300 STEP 15
190 B=300-A
200 PUT(B,100),J:FOR X=1 TO
100:NEXT X:P
UT (B,100),J
210 PUT (B,100),K:FOR X=1
TO 100:NEXT X:
PUT(B,100),K
220 NEXT
Ok
LOAD"C
Ok
RUN
```

Fig. 8-6. A full size replica of a computer printout using the Rattrax screen dump program.

serves to shorten overall programming time. True, you usually have to modify the tail end of graphics programs on endless loops to get them to run on the printer. What I do is write a screen graphics program only, commit it to storage, and then load it again. At this point, the endless loop is removed, and the single program line that accesses the screen dump program is added. You can also store this version under a different filename, but most of the time, I just clear it when I'm finished, and if I want another printout, I go through the same process again using the original program, which has been committed to disk. You can modify these procedures to suit your own operating requirements. The system is quite flexible and open to personal changes.

As was previously mentioned, the Rattrax-MX Plus screen dump program from Ratcom, Inc. offers eight different print modes. Each incorporates a different format, and all can be put to good use at various times, depending on what you want from a hard copy printout. Figures 8-7 through 8-14 show the actual prints obtained from the eight different modes. Again, the F8 key prints a reverse image of the graphics on the screen. This usually means that the printer must produce many more points than in the normal mode. Therefore, the print head will begin to heat up. This is a normal occurrence with any operation, but due to the higher percentage of on-time to off-time, the print head may reach intolerable temperatures if this mode is used for long periods. This can cause early print head failure. If you need to produce a large number of reverse image prints, it's a good idea to allow the print head time to cool down after each run.

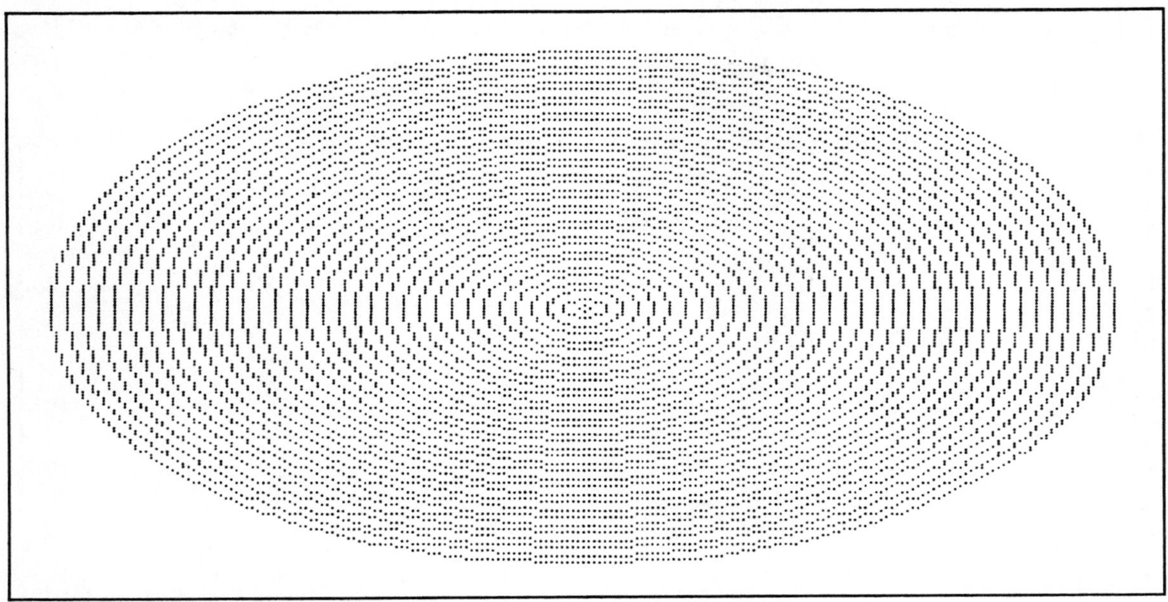

Fig. 8-7. Printer reproduction of screen contents using the F1 Soft Key mode.

I would imagine an off-time which is equivalent to the total on-time would be adequate. For example, if it takes two minutes to produce a reverse image picture, no other printing should be attempted for at least another two minutes, and preferably five minutes or more. This will allow the print head to endure for most of its expected operating life under more normal operating conditions. If you do a lot of reverse image printing, be prepared to replace a lot of ribbon cartridges. Other than these few requirements, reverse image printing can be handled very efficiently by the Rattrax program in conjunction with your IBM printer with the Graftrax Plus modification.

Figure 8-7 is the printer reproduction of a perfect circle on the display screen. Obviously, the F1 print mode does a lot of vertical compressing and the original circle displays itself as an ellipsoid. This effect may be advantageous in reproducing many screens that do not contain circular images, but in this case, it is not desirable. This circle has center coordinates on the screen of 160,100 and a radius of 100 points. You will find that the larger the circle's radius, the more compressed it will appear on the printout. This is due to the fact that the horizontal diameter of the circle will be reproduced at its normal width. The compression involves the height or vertical aspect of any screen object.

Figure 8-8 shows the same screen image printed using the F2 mode. Here, we have a perfect circle, which is identical to the one seen on the screen. While this circle appears to have a much wider horizontal diameter, it has exactly the same diameter as the printout in Fig. 8-7. Note, though, that the vertical diameter is identical to the horizontal diameter, making the circle completely uniform. The F2 mode is the one I normally use for the most accurate screen reproductions.

Figure 8-9 shows another version of the screen image using the mode accessed by the F3 Soft Key. Here, vertical compression is extreme, although the horizontal diameter is

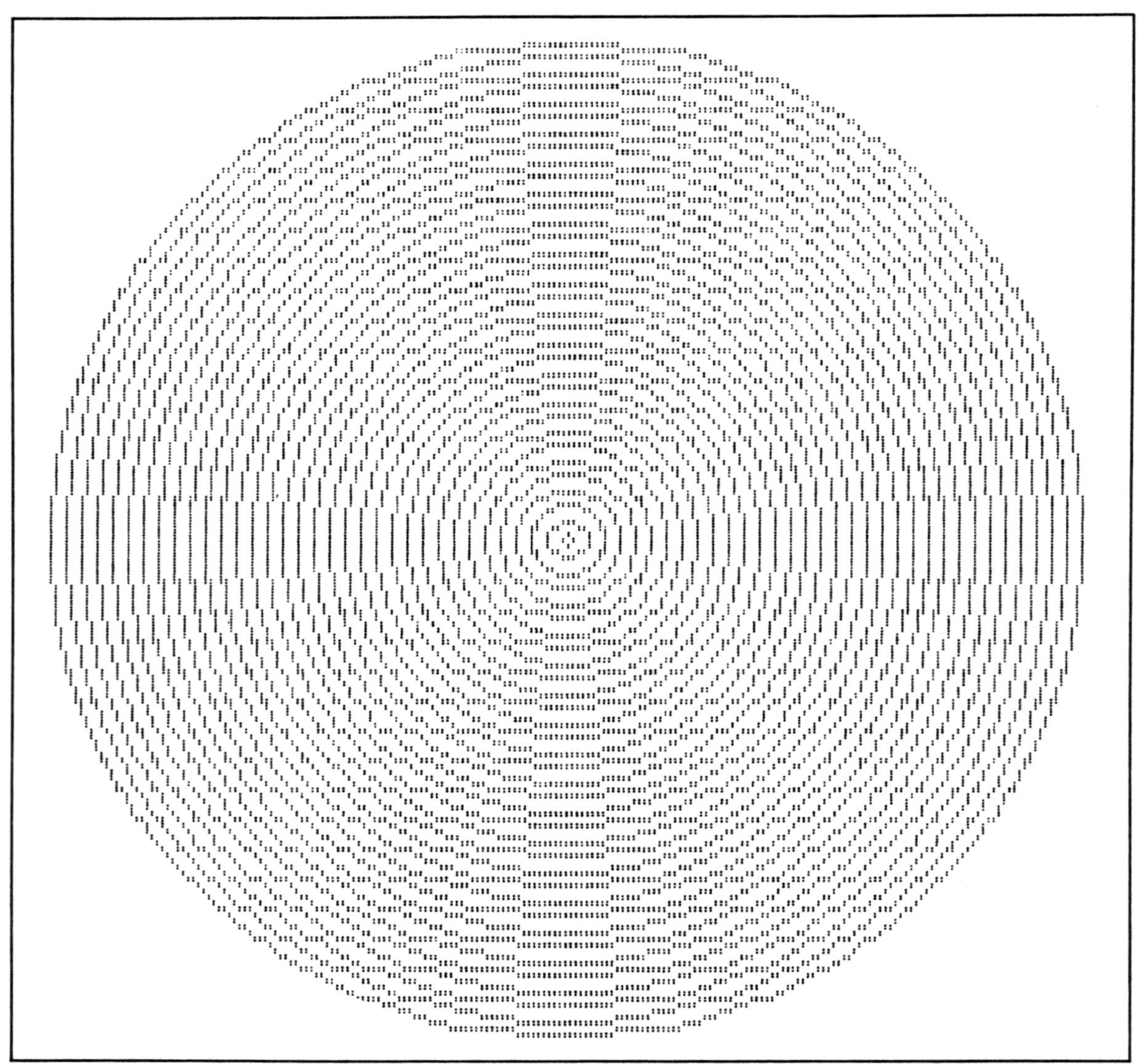

Fig. 8-8. Printer reproduction of screen contents using the F2 Soft Key mode.

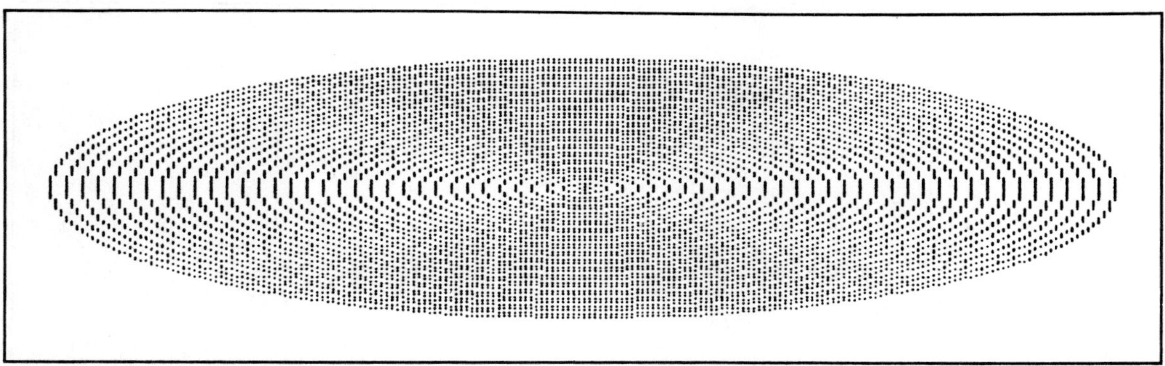

Fig. 8-9. Printer reproduction of screen contents using the F3 Soft Key mode.

identical to that in the previous two prints. Vertical compression is twice that obtained in the F1 Soft Key mode and four times greater than that obtained when in the F2 mode.

Figure 8-10 shows the F4 mode. This figure should look familiar, because it's identical to the printout obtained in the F1 mode with one exception. Twice as many dots are printed for each vertical screen point. This effectively means that Fig. 8-10 is identical to Fig. 8-7, but the former yields darker lines, and thus, more contrast. It uses up the ribbon faster as well. When I use this mode for reproduction, it is usually at a time when my ribbon is beginning

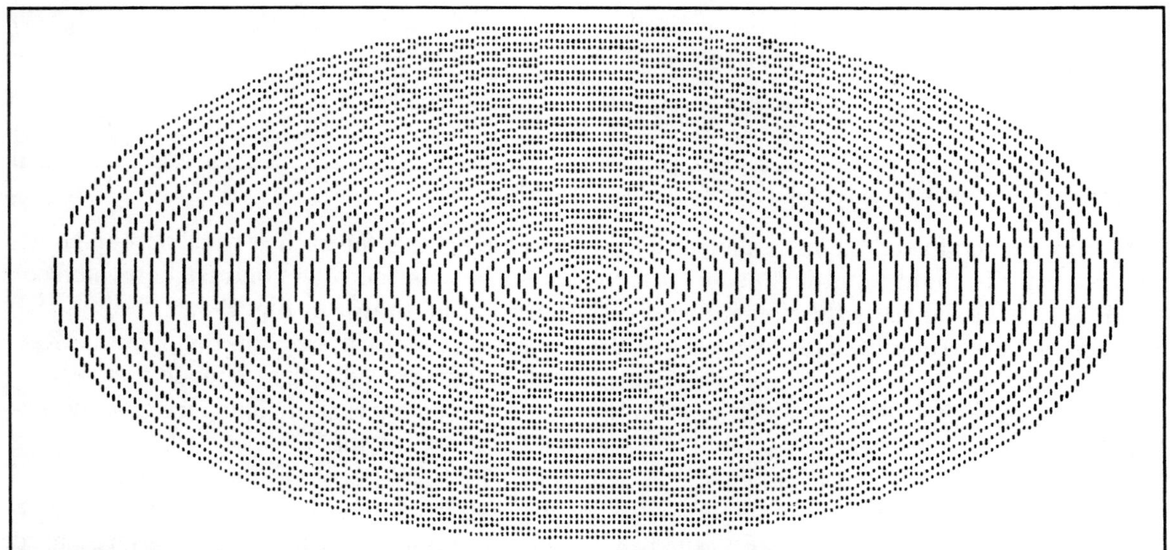

Fig. 8-10. Printer reproduction of screen contents using the F4 Soft Key mode.

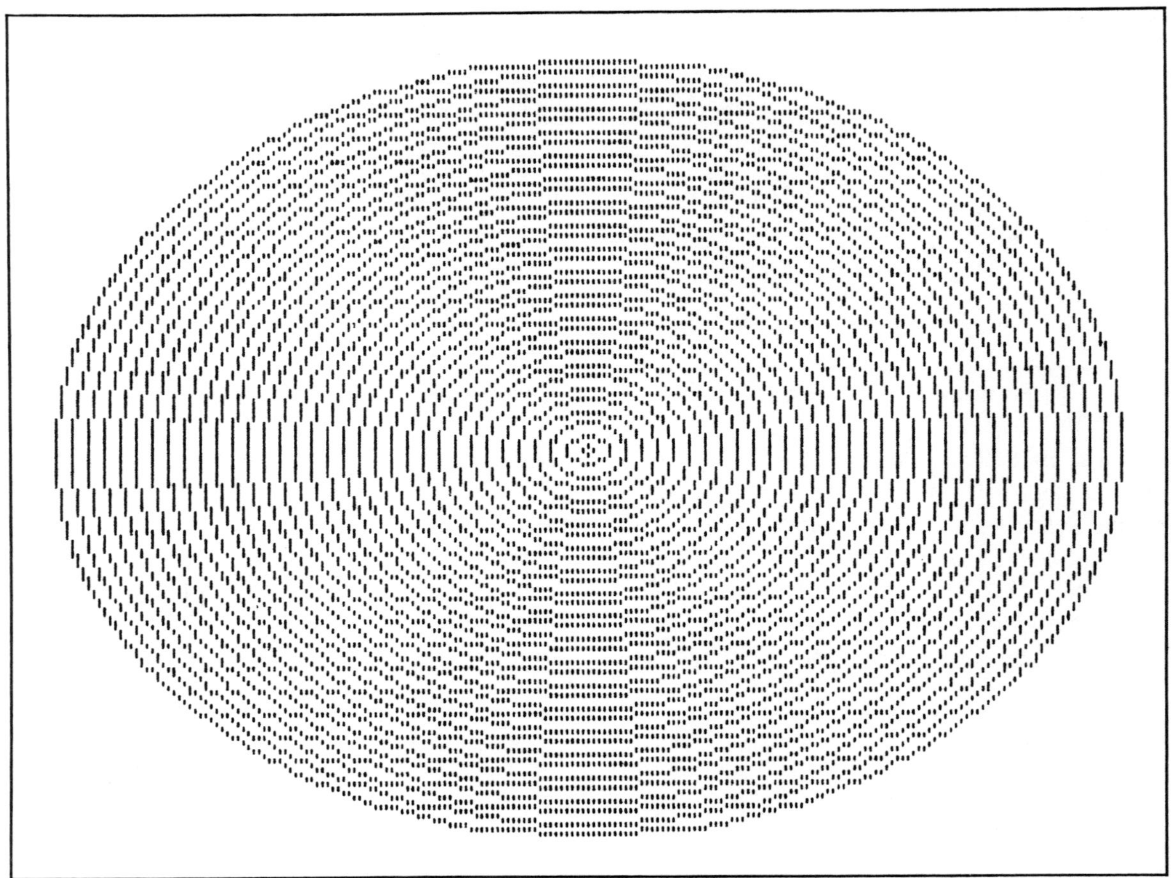

Fig. 8-11. Printer reproduction of screen contents using the F5 Soft Key mode.

to deteriorate and I need the increased or doubled dot print to yield reproducible results.

Figure 8-11 shows the F5 Soft Key mode. Here, three dots are printed for every vertical screen point. The compression is not as severe as with all of the previous modes (except F2). This mode may be thought of as lying somewhere between the F1 and F2 modes.

Figure 8-12 shows the reproduction of the circle in perfect form again. This F6 Soft Key mode is equivalent to F2, except twice as many dots are printed for each vertical screen point. This, then, is the high contrast equivalent of the F2 print shown in Fig. 8-8.

Figure 8-13 illustrates the F7 Soft Key mode. This is a reduced size mode that results in a bit of compression. This circle is the reduced image of the F5 mode shown in Fig. 8-11. The circle here is about 60% of the size of the previous circles. This is a good mode to use when it is not necessary to have a large hard copy print of the screen image. This is also the

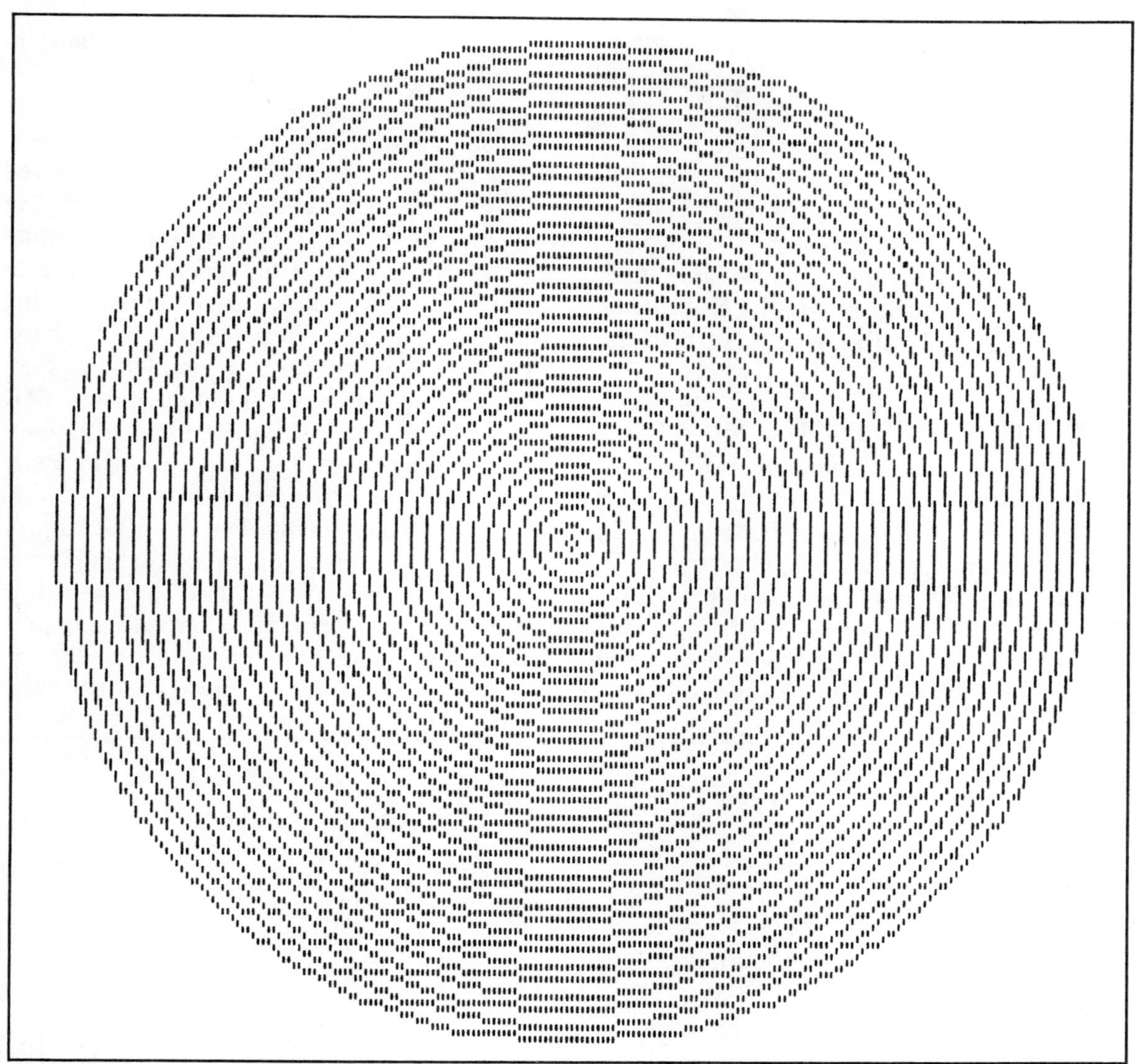

Fig. 8-12. Printer reproduction of screen contents using the F6 Soft Key mode.

only mode in the Rattrax program which prints horizontally. All of the others print vertically. The contrast is excellent, and this mode will allow you to save your ribbon as well as your paper, since the image is smaller and requires less printing space when operating in the horizontal mode.

The last figure (8-14) is an example of

reverse or negative printing. This is a handy feature to have. All the F8 key does is establish that the print will be in reverse form. It is then necessary to select which mode of operation you want. This is determined by Soft Keys F1 through F7. The F8 mode, then, is really a modification of any of the other modes. Figure 8-14 shows an example of reverse printing using the F8 key and the F1 key. This is the F1 mode, but in reverse. Any of the other modes may be operated with the reverse print feature.

GOING FURTHER WITH PRINTER GRAPHICS

Naturally, the screen dump program that accesses the IBM printer will create hard copies in one color only. Ribbons for this printer are available in black, blue, green, and red. Occasionally, you may find some other colors as well, but these are the ones most commonly available. While it is easy to see the outlines of each of the figures reproduced in this book using the IBM printer, a vast amount of information is lost due to the fact that you can't see the multitude of colors.

True color/graphics in printer form is available, but this requires specialized screen dump programs, and of course, a multi-colored plotter. Jack Strick & Associates does offer the ColorTRAX printer graphics program for the IDS Prism Printer. This enables the user to print screen contents on paper in color using this special printer. This program is a modified version of the Rattrax program. This system runs on the IBM Personal Computer with 64K memory, one disk drive, the color/graphics board, a color monitor, and the "Dot Plot" module for the Prism Printer.

I would imagine that the ColorTRAX program involves only a slight modification to the Rattrax program. While I have not seen this program in line form, most screen dump programs read the color of a point on the screen. The background color will always be 0. In stan-

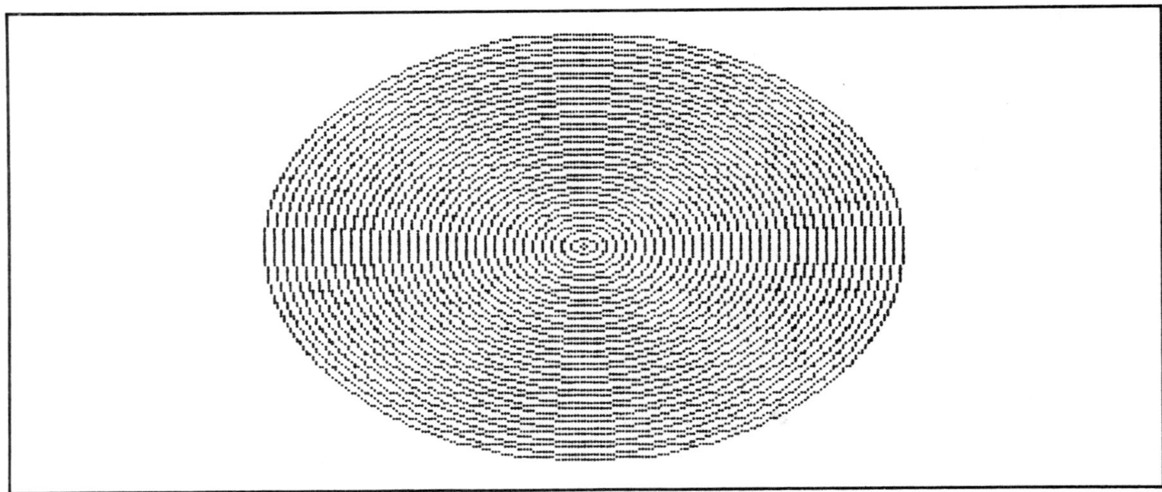

Fig. 8-13. Printer reproduction of screen contents using the F7 Soft Key mode.

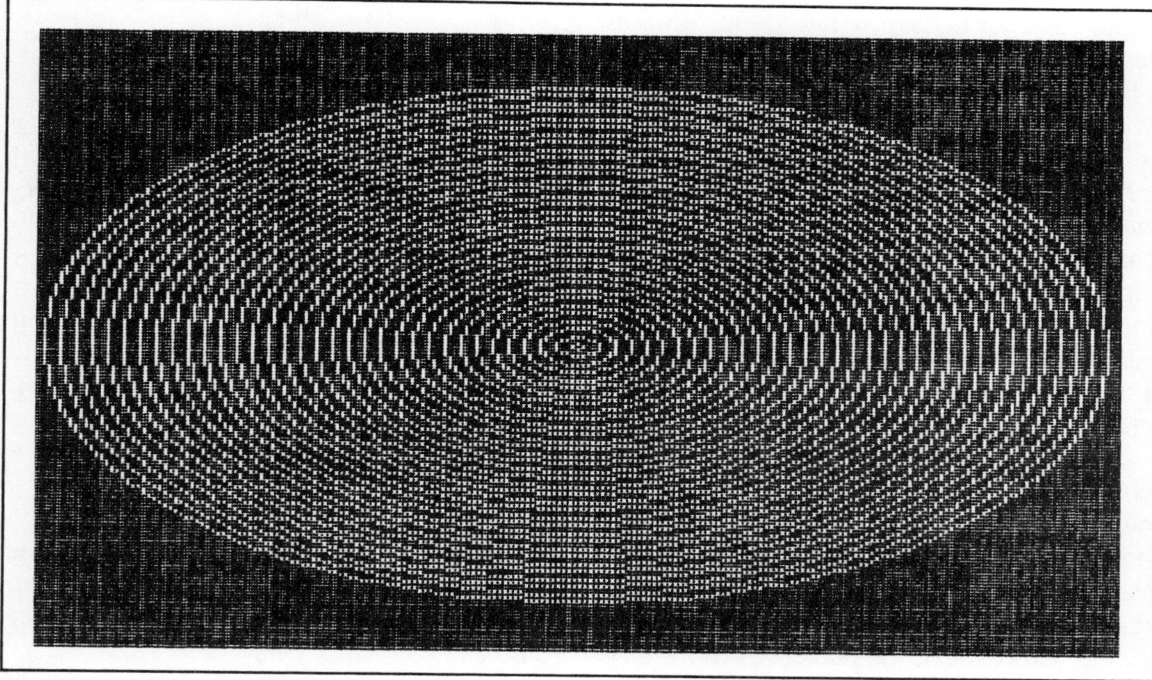

Fig. 8-14. An example of reverse or negative printing. This resulted from pressing the F8 and F1 keys. The F8 key sets up the reverse print mode and will copy in the negative fashion using any of the other modes. Note that this is the reverse image of Fig. 8-7.

dard mode, any time a 0 is encountered, no information is printed. If you think of the medium-resolution screen as being composed of a grid of 320 spaces (horizontally) by 200 spaces (vertically), the explanation is much simpler. When the screen is written by a graphics program, the background color is specified by a 0 at any point where this color is present. This is true regardless of whether the background color is black, white, blue, or any of the thirteen others. The foreground colors will be designated by a 1, 2, or 3. Again, these colors can vary and the palette is dependent on the background color selected.

The screen dump programs discussed here are concerned with only two color numbers. One is 0 and the other is any number that is greater than 0. Zero represents the background, so the printer simply places a space at this point when it is read from the screen. If the number is more than 0, this represents a write and a point is plotted. This is true whether the foreground color is 1, 2, or 3. Now, it is a fairly simply matter to modify the program to respond to the numbers 0, 1, 2, and 3 individually. The 0 still causes a space print in most instances, but a point color of 1 may activate the green channel in a color printer. The other two numbers will activate different channels.

If you will go back to the beginning of this

chapter and look at the program in Fig. 8-3, you may get a better idea of what I'm talking about. In line 50190, there is a test for the condition of screen 0. If the point read is 0, there is a branch to 50210, which simply starts the loop on its next cycle. If, however, the point read is not 0, line 50200 comes into play. This is part of the scanning routine which causes a space to be printed upon reading a point value of 0 and an actual dot to be printed when the number is more than 0. This process is repeated for each of the 64,000 points on the medium-resolution screen.

While I have not even attempted this, I could surmise that it would be possible to do color printing using the IBM printer with the Graftrax Plus modification by slightly changing this program. If the point read on the screen was 0, nothing would change. A space would be printed. However, if the number is more than 0, this is taken into account and an automatic stop is transmitted to the printer. You simply change to a different color ribbon then. Since the foreground colors used with an even numbered background are green, red, and brown, you could use green, red, and black IBM printer ribbons. I haven't quite figured out how the operator would be prompted as to which color was read on the screen because any information printed on the screen would then be read by the screen dump program. You could probably present a prompt using locate statements that would be positioned at the upper left-hand corner of the screen. This portion of the screen would not be used for writing any graphics. For example:

```
50 . . .   V = POINT
51 . . .   LOCATE 1,1
52 . . .   PRINT V
```

This little modification could be inserted somewhere within the screen read loop used to prompt the operator. Naturally, there would be a test for the value of 0, and if this were output, the printer would not stop but would plot a space. However, if the color red occurs at any point, the number 2 would appear in the top left corner of the screen, indicating that you should switch to a red ribbon, since the number 2 represents red.

A few other modifications could allow the printer to keep on writing information after a stop until the color number that caused the stop changes again (to either a 1 or 3 in this case). When a 1 is encountered, you would then insert a green ribbon and start the printer again, and so forth.

Such a program and hardware setup would be awkward, to say the least, but it could be marginally useful for reproducing simple graphics figures that do not contain a lot of interlaced colors. Naturally, for any serious color/graphics hard copy reproduction, it is absolutely mandatory that you have a good color printer or printer/plotter. At present, these have not really caught on with the majority of microcomputer hobbyists, but new products are being introduced every month, and undoubtedly, they are the wave of the future. This discussion about using the IBM printer, different colored ribbons, and modifications to existing screen dump program is more practicum than practical.

Appendix A

Decimal-Hexadecimal Equivalents

The following decimal-hexadecimal conversion table is provided for the convenience of those programmers who wish to go on to assembly language programming, a topic that is beyond the scope of this book, but which provides the ambitious programmer with yet another approach to IBM graphics.

256 - 100	257 - 101	258 - 102	259 - 103	260 - 104	261 - 105	262 - 106	263 - 107
264 - 108	265 - 109	266 - 10A	267 - 10B	268 - 10C	269 - 10D	270 - 10E	271 - 10F
272 - 110	273 - 111	274 - 112	275 - 113	276 - 114	277 - 115	278 - 116	279 - 117
280 - 118	281 - 119	282 - 11A	283 - 11B	284 - 11C	285 - 11D	286 - 11E	287 - 11F
288 - 120	289 - 121	290 - 122	291 - 123	292 - 124	293 - 125	294 - 126	295 - 127
296 - 128	297 - 129	298 - 12A	299 - 12B	300 - 12C	301 - 12D	302 - 12E	303 - 12F
304 - 130	305 - 131	306 - 132	307 - 133	308 - 134	309 - 135	310 - 136	311 - 137
312 - 138	313 - 139	314 - 13A	315 - 13B	316 - 13C	317 - 13D	318 - 13E	319 - 13F
320 - 140	321 - 141	322 - 142	323 - 143	324 - 144	325 - 145	326 - 146	327 - 147
328 - 148	329 - 149	330 - 14A	331 - 14B	332 - 14C	333 - 14D	334 - 14E	335 - 14F
336 - 150	337 - 151	338 - 152	339 - 153	340 - 154	341 - 155	342 - 156	343 - 157
344 - 158	345 - 159	346 - 15A	347 - 15B	348 - 15C	349 - 15D	350 - 15E	351 - 15F
352 - 160	353 - 161	354 - 162	355 - 163	356 - 164	357 - 165	358 - 166	359 - 167
360 - 168	361 - 169	362 - 16A	363 - 16B	364 - 16C	365 - 16D	366 - 16E	367 - 16F
368 - 170	369 - 171	370 - 172	371 - 173	372 - 174	373 - 175	374 - 176	375 - 177
376 - 178	377 - 179	378 - 17A	379 - 17B	380 - 17C	381 - 17D	382 - 17E	383 - 17F
384 - 180	385 - 181	386 - 182	387 - 183	388 - 184	389 - 185	390 - 186	391 - 187
392 - 188	393 - 189	394 - 18A	395 - 18B	396 - 18C	397 - 18D	398 - 18E	399 - 18F
400 - 190	401 - 191	402 - 192	403 - 193	404 - 194	405 - 195	406 - 196	407 - 197
408 - 198	409 - 199	410 - 19A	411 - 19B	412 - 19C	413 - 19D	414 - 19E	415 - 19F
416 - 1A0	417 - 1A1	418 - 1A2	419 - 1A3	420 - 1A4	421 - 1A5	422 - 1A6	423 - 1A7
424 - 1A8	425 - 1A9	426 - 1AA	427 - 1AB	428 - 1AC	429 - 1AD	430 - 1AE	431 - 1AF

432 - 1B0 433 - 1B1 434 - 1B2 435 - 1B3 436 - 1B4 437 - 1B5 438 - 1B6 439 - 1B7
440 - 1B8 441 - 1B9 442 - 1BA 443 - 1BB 444 - 1BC 445 - 1BD 446 - 1BE 447 - 1BF
448 - 1C0 449 - 1C1 450 - 1C2 451 - 1C3 452 - 1C4 453 - 1C5 454 - 1C6 455 - 1C7
456 - 1C8 457 - 1C9 458 - 1CA 459 - 1CB 460 - 1CC 461 - 1CD 462 - 1CE 463 - 1CF
464 - 1D0 465 - 1D1 466 - 1D2 467 - 1D3 468 - 1D4 469 - 1D5 470 - 1D6 471 - 1D7
472 - 1D8 473 - 1D9 474 - 1DA 475 - 1DB 476 - 1DC 477 - 1DD 478 - 1DE 479 - 1DF
480 - 1E0 481 - 1E1 482 - 1E2 483 - 1E3 484 - 1E4 485 - 1E5 486 - 1E6 487 - 1E7
488 - 1E8 489 - 1E9 490 - 1EA 491 - 1EB 492 - 1EC 493 - 1ED 494 - 1EE 495 - 1EF
496 - 1F0 497 - 1F1 498 - 1F2 499 - 1F3 500 - 1F4 501 - 1F5 502 - 1F6 503 - 1F7
504 - 1F8 505 - 1F9 506 - 1FA 507 - 1FB 508 - 1FC 509 - 1FD 510 - 1FE 511 - 1FF
512 - 200 513 - 201 514 - 202 515 - 203 516 - 204 517 - 205 518 - 206 519 - 207
520 - 208 521 - 209 522 - 20A 523 - 20B 524 - 20C 525 - 20D 526 - 20E 527 - 20F
528 - 210 529 - 211 530 - 212 531 - 213 532 - 214 533 - 215 534 - 216 535 - 217
536 - 218 537 - 219 538 - 21A 539 - 21B 540 - 21C 541 - 21D 542 - 21E 543 - 21F
544 - 220 545 - 221 546 - 222 547 - 223 548 - 224 549 - 225 550 - 226 551 - 227
552 - 228 553 - 229 554 - 22A 555 - 22B 556 - 22C 557 - 22D 558 - 22E 559 - 22F
560 - 230 561 - 231 562 - 232 563 - 233 564 - 234 565 - 235 566 - 236 567 - 237
568 - 238 569 - 239 570 - 23A 571 - 23B 572 - 23C 573 - 23D 574 - 23E 575 - 23F
576 - 240 577 - 241 578 - 242 579 - 243 580 - 244 581 - 245 582 - 246 583 - 247
584 - 248 585 - 249 586 - 24A 587 - 24B 588 - 24C 589 - 24D 590 - 24E 591 - 24F
592 - 250 593 - 251 594 - 252 595 - 253 596 - 254 597 - 255 598 - 256 599 - 257
600 - 258 601 - 259 602 - 25A 603 - 25B 604 - 25C 605 - 25D 606 - 25E 607 - 25F

608 - 260 609 - 261 610 - 262 611 - 263 612 - 264 613 - 265 614 - 266 615 - 267
616 - 268 617 - 269 618 - 26A 619 - 26B 620 - 26C 621 - 26D 622 - 26E 623 - 26F
624 - 270 625 - 271 626 - 272 627 - 273 628 - 274 629 - 275 630 - 276 631 - 277
632 - 278 633 - 279 634 - 27A 635 - 27B 636 - 27C 637 - 27D 638 - 27E 639 - 27F
640 - 280 641 - 281 642 - 282 643 - 283 644 - 284 645 - 285 646 - 286 647 - 287
648 - 288 649 - 289 650 - 28A 651 - 28B 652 - 28C 653 - 28D 654 - 28E 655 - 28F
656 - 290 657 - 291 658 - 292 659 - 293 660 - 294 661 - 295 662 - 296 663 - 297
664 - 298 665 - 299 666 - 29A 667 - 29B 668 - 29C 669 - 29D 670 - 29E 671 - 29F
672 - 2A0 673 - 2A1 674 - 2A2 675 - 2A3 676 - 2A4 677 - 2A5 678 - 2A6 679 - 2A7
680 - 2A8 681 - 2A9 682 - 2AA 683 - 2AB 684 - 2AC 685 - 2AD 686 - 2AE 687 - 2AF
688 - 2B0 689 - 2B1 690 - 2B2 691 - 2B3 692 - 2B4 693 - 2B5 694 - 2B6 695 - 2B7
696 - 2B8 697 - 2B9 698 - 2BA 699 - 2BB 700 - 2BC 701 - 2BD 702 - 2BE 703 - 2BF
704 - 2C0 705 - 2C1 706 - 2C2 707 - 2C3 708 - 2C4 709 - 2C5 710 - 2C6 711 - 2C7
712 - 2C8 713 - 2C9 714 - 2CA 715 - 2CB 716 - 2CC 717 - 2CD 718 - 2CE 719 - 2CF
720 - 2D0 721 - 2D1 722 - 2D2 723 - 2D3 724 - 2D4 725 - 2D5 726 - 2D6 727 - 2D7
728 - 2D8 729 - 2D9 730 - 2DA 731 - 2DB 732 - 2DC 733 - 2DD 734 - 2DE 735 - 2DF
736 - 2E0 737 - 2E1 738 - 2E2 739 - 2E3 740 - 2E4 741 - 2E5 742 - 2E6 743 - 2E7
744 - 2E8 745 - 2E9 746 - 2EA 747 - 2EB 748 - 2EC 749 - 2ED 750 - 2EE 751 - 2EF
752 - 2F0 753 - 2F1 754 - 2F2 755 - 2F3 756 - 2F4 757 - 2F5 758 - 2F6 759 - 2F7
760 - 2F8 761 - 2F9 762 - 2FA 763 - 2FB 764 - 2FC 765 - 2FD 766 - 2FE 767 - 2FF
768 - 300 769 - 301 770 - 302 771 - 303 772 - 304 773 - 305 774 - 306 775 - 307
776 - 308 777 - 309 778 - 30A 779 - 30B 780 - 30C 781 - 30D 782 - 30E 783 - 30F

```
784 - 310 785 - 311 786 - 312 787 - 313 788 - 314 789 - 315 790 - 316 791 - 317
792 - 318 793 - 319 794 - 31A 795 - 31B 796 - 31C 797 - 31D 798 - 31E 799 - 31F
800 - 320 801 - 321 802 - 322 803 - 323 804 - 324 805 - 325 806 - 326 807 - 327
808 - 328 809 - 329 810 - 32A 811 - 32B 812 - 32C 813 - 32D 814 - 32E 815 - 32F
816 - 330 817 - 331 818 - 332 819 - 333 820 - 334 821 - 335 822 - 336 823 - 337
824 - 338 825 - 339 826 - 33A 827 - 33B 828 - 33C 829 - 33D 830 - 33E 831 - 33F
832 - 340 833 - 341 834 - 342 835 - 343 836 - 344 837 - 345 838 - 346 839 - 347
840 - 348 841 - 349 842 - 34A 843 - 34B 844 - 34C 845 - 34D 846 - 34E 847 - 34F
848 - 350 849 - 351 850 - 352 851 - 353 852 - 354 853 - 355 854 - 356 855 - 357
856 - 358 857 - 359 858 - 35A 859 - 35B 860 - 35C 861 - 35D 862 - 35E 863 - 35F
864 - 360 865 - 361 866 - 362 867 - 363 868 - 364 869 - 365 870 - 366 871 - 367
872 - 368 873 - 369 874 - 36A 875 - 36B 876 - 36C 877 - 36D 878 - 36E 879 - 36F
880 - 370 881 - 371 882 - 372 883 - 373 884 - 374 885 - 375 886 - 376 887 - 377
888 - 378 889 - 379 890 - 37A 891 - 37B 892 - 37C 893 - 37D 894 - 37E 895 - 37F
896 - 380 897 - 381 898 - 382 899 - 383 900 - 384 901 - 385 902 - 386 903 - 387
904 - 388 905 - 389 906 - 38A 907 - 38B 908 - 38C 909 - 38D 910 - 38E 911 - 38F
912 - 390 913 - 391 914 - 392 915 - 393 916 - 394 917 - 395 918 - 396 919 - 397
920 - 398 921 - 399 922 - 39A 923 - 39B 924 - 39C 925 - 39D 926 - 39E 927 - 39F
928 - 3A0 929 - 3A1 930 - 3A2 931 - 3A3 932 - 3A4 933 - 3A5 934 - 3A6 935 - 3A7
936 - 3A8 937 - 3A9 938 - 3AA 939 - 3AB 940 - 3AC 941 - 3AD 942 - 3AE 943 - 3AF
944 - 3B0 945 - 3B1 946 - 3B2 947 - 3B3 948 - 3B4 949 - 3B5 950 - 3B6 951 - 3B7
952 - 3B8 953 - 3B9 954 - 3BA 955 - 3BB 956 - 3BC 957 - 3BD 958 - 3BE 959 - 3BF
```

```
959 - 3BF 960 - 3C0 961 - 3C1 962 - 3C2 963 - 3C3 964 - 3C4 965 - 3C5 966 - 3C6
967 - 3C7 968 - 3C8 969 - 3C9 970 - 3CA 971 - 3CB 972 - 3CC 973 - 3CD 974 - 3CE
975 - 3CF 976 - 3D0 977 - 3D1 978 - 3D2 979 - 3D3 980 - 3D4 981 - 3D5 982 - 3D6
983 - 3D7 984 - 3D8 985 - 3D9 986 - 3DA 987 - 3DB 988 - 3DC 989 - 3DD 990 - 3DE
991 - 3DF 992 - 3E0 993 - 3E1 994 - 3E2 995 - 3E3 996 - 3E4 997 - 3E5 998 - 3E6
999 - 3E7 1000 - 3E8
1000 - 3E8 1100 - 44C 1200 - 4B0 1300 - 514 1400 - 578 1500 - 5DC 1600 - 640
1700 - 6A4 1800 - 708 1900 - 76C 2000 - 7D0 2100 - 834 2200 - 898 2300 - 8FC
2400 - 960 2500 - 9C4 2600 - A28 2700 - A8C 2800 - AF0 2900 - B54 3000 - BB8
3100 - C1C 3200 - C80 3300 - CE4 3400 - D48 3500 - DAC 3600 - E10 3700 - E74
3800 - ED8 3900 - F3C 4000 - FA0
10000 - 2710 10100 - 2774 10200 - 27D8 10300 - 283C 10400 - 28A0 10500 - 2904
10600 - 2968 10700 - 29CC 10800 - 2A30 10900 - 2A94 11000 - 2AF8 11100 - 2B5C
11200 - 2BC0 11300 - 2C24 11400 - 2C88 11500 - 2CEC 11600 - 2D50 11700 - 2DB4
11800 - 2E18 11900 - 2E7C 12000 - 2EE0 12100 - 2F44 12200 - 2FA8 12300 - 300C
12400 - 3070 12500 - 30D4 12600 - 3138 12700 - 319C 12800 - 3200 12900 - 3264
13000 - 32C8 13100 - 332C 13200 - 3390 13300 - 33F4 13400 - 3458 13500 - 34BC
13600 - 3520 13700 - 3584 13800 - 35E8 13900 - 364C 14000 - 36B0 14100 - 3714
14200 - 3778 14300 - 37DC 14400 - 3840 14500 - 38A4 14600 - 3908 14700 - 396C
14800 - 39D0 14900 - 3A34 15000 - 3A98 15100 - 3AFC 15200 - 3B60 15300 - 3BC4
15400 - 3C28 15500 - 3C8C 15600 - 3CF0 15700 - 3D54 15800 - 3DB8 15900 - 3E1C
16000 - 3E80 16100 - 3EE4 16200 - 3F48 16300 - 3FAC 16400 - 4010 16500 - 4074
```

16600 - 40D8 16700 - 413C 16800 - 41A0 16900 - 4204 17000 - 4268 17100 - 42CC
17200 - 4330 17300 - 4394 17400 - 43F8 17500 - 445C 17600 - 44C0 17700 - 4524
17800 - 4588 17900 - 45EC 18000 - 4650 18100 - 46B4 18200 - 4718 18300 - 477C
18400 - 47E0 18500 - 4844 18600 - 48A8 18700 - 490C 18800 - 4970 18900 - 49D4
19000 - 4A38 19100 - 4A9C 19200 - 4B00 19300 - 4B64 19400 - 4BC8 19500 - 4C2C
19600 - 4C90 19700 - 4CF4 19800 - 4D58 19900 - 4DBC 20000 - 4E20 20100 - 4E84
20200 - 4EE8 20300 - 4F4C 20400 - 4FB0 20500 - 5014 20600 - 5078 20700 - 50DC
20800 - 5140 20900 - 51A4 21000 - 5208 21100 - 526C 21200 - 52D0 21300 - 5334
21400 - 5398 21500 - 53FC 21600 - 5460 21700 - 54C4 21800 - 5528 21900 - 558C
22000 - 55F0 22100 - 5654 22200 - 56B8 22300 - 571C 22400 - 5780 22500 - 57E4
22600 - 5848 22700 - 58AC 22800 - 5910 22900 - 5974 23000 - 59D8 23100 - 5A3C
23200 - 5AA0 23300 - 5B04 23400 - 5B68 23500 - 5BCC 23600 - 5C30 23700 - 5C94
23800 - 5CF8 23900 - 5D5C 24000 - 5DC0 24100 - 5E24 24200 - 5E88 24300 - 5EEC
24400 - 5F50 24500 - 5FB4 24600 - 6018 24700 - 607C 24800 - 60E0 24900 - 6144
25000 - 61A8 25100 - 620C 25200 - 6270 25300 - 62D4 25400 - 6338 25500 - 639C
25600 - 6400 25700 - 6464 25800 - 64C8 25900 - 652C 26000 - 6590 26100 - 65F4
26200 - 6658 26300 - 66BC 26400 - 6720 26500 - 6784 26600 - 67E8 26700 - 684C
26800 - 68B0 26900 - 6914 27000 - 6978 27100 - 69DC 27200 - 6A40 27300 - 6AA4
27400 - 6B08 27500 - 6B6C 27600 - 6BD0 27700 - 6C34 27800 - 6C98 27900 - 6CFC
28000 - 6D60 28100 - 6DC4 28200 - 6E28 28300 - 6E8C 28400 - 6EF0 28500 - 6F54

28600 - 6FB8 28700 - 701C 28800 - 7080 28900 - 70E4 29000 - 7148 29100 - 71AC
29200 - 7210 29300 - 7274 29400 - 72D8 29500 - 733C 29600 - 73A0 29700 - 7404
29800 - 7468 29900 - 74CC 30000 - 7530 30100 - 7594 30200 - 75F8 30300 - 765C
30400 - 76C0 30500 - 7724 30600 - 7788 30700 - 77EC 30800 - 7850 30900 - 78B4
31000 - 7918 31100 - 797C 31200 - 79E0 31300 - 7A44 31400 - 7AA8 31500 - 7B0C
31600 - 7B70 31700 - 7BD4 31800 - 7C38 31900 - 7C9C 32000 - 7D00 32100 - 7D64
32200 - 7DC8 32300 - 7E2C 32400 - 7E90 32500 - 7EF4 32600 - 7F58 32700 - 7FBC
32800 - 8020 32900 - 8084 33000 - 80E8 33100 - 814C 33200 - 81B0 33300 - 8214
33400 - 8278 33500 - 82DC 33600 - 8340 33700 - 83A4 33800 - 8408 33900 - 846C
34000 - 84D0 34100 - 8534 34200 - 8598 34300 - 85FC 34400 - 8660 34500 - 86C4
34600 - 8728 34700 - 878C 34800 - 87F0 34900 - 8854 35000 - 88B8 35100 - 891C
35200 - 8980 35300 - 89E4 35400 - 8A48 35500 - 8AAC 35600 - 8B10 35700 - 8B74
35800 - 8BD8 35900 - 8C3C 36000 - 8CA0 36100 - 8D04 36200 - 8D68 36300 - 8DCC
36400 - 8E30 36500 - 8E94 36600 - 8EF8 36700 - 8F5C 36800 - 8FC0 36900 - 9024
37000 - 9088 37100 - 90EC 37200 - 9150 37300 - 91B4 37400 - 9218 37500 - 927C
37600 - 92E0 37700 - 9344 37800 - 93A8 37900 - 940C 38000 - 9470 38100 - 94D4
38200 - 9538 38300 - 959C 38400 - 9600 38500 - 9664 38600 - 96C8 38700 - 972C
38800 - 9790 38900 - 97F4 39000 - 9858 39100 - 98BC 39200 - 9920 39300 - 9984
39400 - 99E8 39500 - 9A4C 39600 - 9AB0 39700 - 9B14 39800 - 9B78 39900 - 9BDC
40000 - 9C40 40100 - 9CA4 40200 - 9D08 40300 - 9D6C 40400 - 9DD0 40500 - 9E34
40600 - 9E98 40700 - 9EFC 40800 - 9F60 40900 - 9FC4 41000 - A028 41100 - A08C
41200 - A0F0 41300 - A154 41400 - A1B8 41500 - A21C 41600 - A280 41700 - A2E4
41800 - A348 41900 - A3AC 42000 - A410 42100 - A474 42200 - A4D8 42300 - A53C
42400 - A5A0 42500 - A604 42600 - A668 42700 - A6CC 42800 - A730 42900 - A794

43000 - A7F8 43100 - A85C 43200 - A8C0 43300 - A924 43400 - A988 43500 - A9EC
43600 - AA50 43700 - AAB4 43800 - AB18 43900 - AB7C 44000 - ABE0 44100 - AC44
44200 - ACA8 44300 - AD0C 44400 - AD70 44500 - ADD4 44600 - AE38 44700 - AE9C
44800 - AF00 44900 - AF64 45000 - AFC8 45100 - B02C 45200 - B090 45300 - B0F4
45400 - B158 45500 - B1BC 45600 - B220 45700 - B284 45800 - B2E8 45900 - B34C
46000 - B3B0 46100 - B414 46200 - B478 46300 - B4DC 46400 - B540 46500 - B5A4
46600 - B608 46700 - B66C 46800 - B6D0 46900 - B734 47000 - B798 47100 - B7FC
47200 - B860 47300 - B8C4 47400 - B928 47500 - B98C 47600 - B9F0 47700 - BA54
47800 - BAB8 47900 - BB1C 48000 - BB80 48100 - BBE4 48200 - BC48 48300 - BCAC
48400 - BD10 48500 - BD74 48600 - BDD8 48700 - BE3C 48800 - BEA0 48900 - BF04
49000 - BF68 49100 - BFCC 49200 - C030 49300 - C094 49400 - C0F8 49500 - C15C
49600 - C1C0 49700 - C224 49800 - C288 49900 - C2EC 50000 - C350 50100 - C3B4
50200 - C418 50300 - C47C 50400 - C4E0 50500 - C544 50600 - C5A8 50700 - C60C
50800 - C670 50900 - C6D4 51000 - C738 51100 - C79C 51200 - C800 51300 - C864
51400 - C8C8 51500 - C92C 51600 - C990 51700 - C9F4 51800 - CA58 51900 - CABC
52000 - CB20 52100 - CB84 52200 - CBE8 52300 - CC4C 52400 - CCB0 52500 - CD14
52600 - CD78 52700 - CDDC 52800 - CE40 52900 - CEA4 53000 - CF08 53100 - CF6C
53200 - CFD0 53300 - D034 53400 - D098 53500 - D0FC 53600 - D160 53700 - D1C4
53800 - D228 53900 - D28C 54000 - D2F0 54100 - D354 54200 - D3B8 54300 - D41C
54400 - D480 54500 - D4E4 54600 - D548 54700 - D5AC 54800 - D610 54900 - D674

55000 - D6D8 55100 - D73C 55200 - D7A0 55300 - D804 55400 - D868 55500 - D8CC
55600 - D930 55700 - D994 55800 - D9F8 55900 - DA5C 56000 - DAC0 56100 - DB24
56200 - DB88 56300 - DBEC 56400 - DC50 56500 - DCB4 56600 - DD18 56700 - DD7C
56800 - DDE0 56900 - DE44 57000 - DEA8 57100 - DF0C 57200 - DF70 57300 - DFD4
57400 - E038 57500 - E09C 57600 - E100 57700 - E164 57800 - E1C8 57900 - E22C
58000 - E290 58100 - E2F4 58200 - E358 58300 - E3BC 58400 - E420 58500 - E484
58600 - E4E8 58700 - E54C 58800 - E5B0 58900 - E614 59000 - E678 59100 - E6DC
59200 - E740 59300 - E7A4 59400 - E808 59500 - E86C 59600 - E8D0 59700 - E934
59800 - E998 59900 - E9FC 60000 - EA60 60100 - EAC4 60200 - EB28 60300 - EB8C
60400 - EBF0 60500 - EC54 60600 - ECB8 60700 - ED1C 60800 - ED80 60900 - EDE4
61000 - EE48 61100 - EEAC 61200 - EF10 61300 - EF74 61400 - EFD8 61500 - F03C
61600 - F0A0 61700 - F104 61800 - F168 61900 - F1CC 62000 - F230 62100 - F294
62200 - F2F8 62300 - F35C 62400 - F3C0 62500 - F424 62600 - F488 62700 - F4EC
62800 - F550 62900 - F5B4 63000 - F618 63100 - F67C 63200 - F6E0 63300 - F744
63400 - F7A8 63500 - F80C 63600 - F870 63700 - F8D4 63800 - F938 63900 - F99C

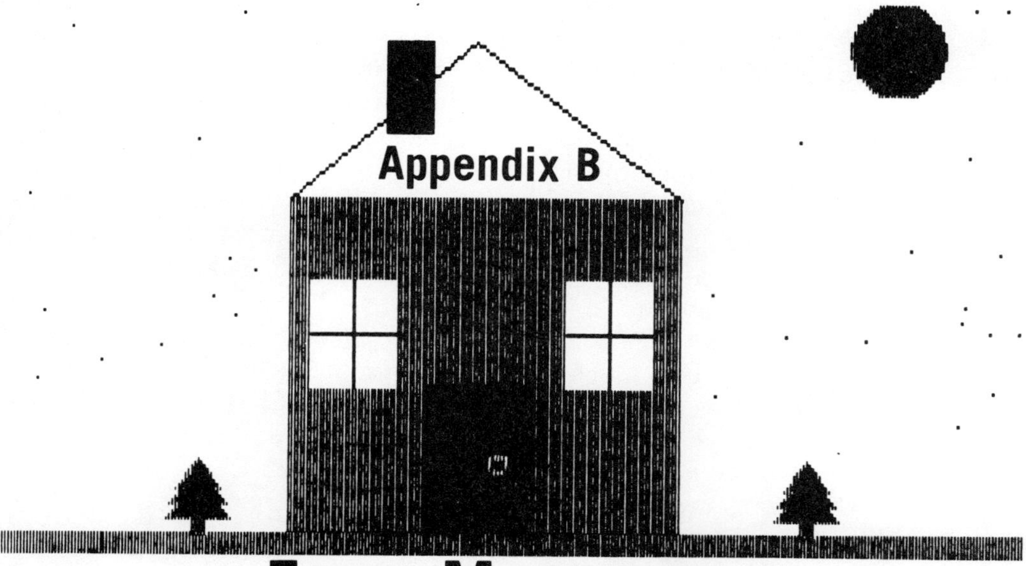

Error Messages

The IBM Personal Computer has the ability to detect certain errors that may occur when programs in BASIC are input. There are a total of 74 possible error messages, many of which apply directly or indirectly to graphics programming on this machine. The following is a list of error messages, along with a discussion of what each may mean.

Next without For. Often, points or multiple images on the graphic screen are generated by using a PSET or other statement within a for-next loop. Sometimes, loops are nested within other loops, and it is quite easy to become confused. This particular message indicates that a next statement has been encountered somewhere within the program for which there is no matching for statement, which should precede it. When several loops are needed, the next statement may be followed by a designator which ties into the for statement. As an example, FOR X = 1 TO 10 might be followed at a later point in the program by NEXT X. If the wrong designator (X) is inserted following the next statement, this error message may be generated.

Syntax Error. This message simply means that you have misspelled a word or entered a statement in a way that is not in correct IBM BASIC format. This might mean that you failed to include one or both parentheses around the coordinates in a graphics statement. When the syntax error message is displayed, it will usually be followed by the line number where the offense has occurred. This line will also be displayed on the screen, allowing you to immediately search for the problem.

Return without GOSUB. This message is very similar to the next without for error message and simply means that a return statement has been encountered without an appropriate GOSUB statement. This often occurs when a GOSUB is used to branch to a subroutine at the end of a specific program. Here, it is necessary to insert an end statement before the subroutine is entered by the straight-line program execution. Let's assume that the correct program termination point lies immediately after the execution of line 500, but that you have initiated a GOSUB to line 510. Also assume that the subroutine is composed of lines 510 through 560 and that 560 contains the return statement, which branches back to an earlier portion of the program. During the first run-through, the subroutine is accessed, executed, and execution is returned to the line immediately following the original GOSUB statement. Execution will then continue down to line 500. But if there is no end statement, lines 510 through 560 are accessed once again. The return statement is encountered in line 560, and the error message is displayed. By placing an end statement at line 505, you can prevent inadvertent entrance to the subroutine.

Out of Data. Data statements are often used to easily input point location information to a particular graphics program. This error message indicates that there is insufficient data information within these statements. In other words, the data has run out before full execution of the program can be completed. This is often due to the failure to insert a proper restore statement in the program or to an input error where an item or two of data was omitted.

Illegal Function Call. This occurs quite often in graphics programming and simply means that a parameter is encountered which is out of the range of capabilities of the machine. This can result when you attempt to run a graphics program in text mode.

Out of Memory. This can occur when you attempt to write a graphics program that is too large for the machine's capability. It can result from the use of too many for-next loops, subroutines, variables, or get/put arrays. Complex painting using paint statements is also another frequently encountered cause.

Undefined Line Number. This simply means that you have referenced a program line that does not exist. Check your branch statements when this error message occurs. You may have entered a GOSUB or GOTO that tells the program to execute a nonexistent line. This often occurs during the debugging procedure, when it may be necessary to change the branch line designations or to change line numbers themselves.

Subscript Out of Range. This means that an array element was used that contained a subscript that fell outside the dimensions of a particular array. Such arrays are established and referenced using put and get statements in graphics mode. This error message may also indicate an input typing error. For instance, in text mode graphics, CHR$ functions are used to draw ASCII block characters on the screen. When typing in a number of these functions, it's quite easy to omit the dollar sign and, for example, type CHR(15) instead of the correct CHR$(15). This will cause this error message to appear because the 15 is interpreted as a subscript rather than as a reference to a particular ASCII character.

Duplicate Definition. This means that

you have attempted to define the size of the same array two or more times. For example, assume you define an array to hold screen information for an animation program as: DIM R(100). Assume also that you establish another array using the R designator. You have effectively given two different arrays the same name. The duplicate definition message will appear. Each array must be given a different designation.

Type Mismatch. This simply means that you have not properly designated certain values. For example, if you input A$ = 4, a type mismatch error will occur. The A$ variable must be matched with a string value, which is specified in quotation marks. By the same token, if you input A = "HELLO", the same error message will occur due to the lack of the dollar sign ($) following the A variable.

String Too Long. This means that you tried to create a string that contains more than 255 characters. This is the maximum string length for the IBM PC.

Missing Operand. This means a program line contains an operator with no operand following it. This can be created by inputting A = 4*. The asterisk indicates multiplication, so you're effectively saying A = four times?. The program will run properly when an operand is inserted after the asterisk.

For without Next. When programming graphics, it is often necessary to use a number of for-next loops containing coordinate information. The for without next error message simply means that you forgot to end your loop with the proper next statement. (See also Next Without For.)

Out of Paper. This error message needs little explanation. It means that your printer has run out of paper or has simply not been turned on.

Internal Error. This message relates to hardware or to the disk you are using to read programs from. It indicates an internal malfunction.

Disk Full. This indicates that all disk storage space has been filled. Your disk can contain only so many files, and when this point is reached, the screen tells you of this condition so that you will not be under the impression that the program has been recorded. When this condition occurs, you may wish to erase any unneeded programs on the disk or use a fresh one.

Advanced Feature. This means that you have attempted to run a program in Disk BASIC that contains statements found only in Advanced BASIC (BASICA). All high-level graphics programs must be run in Advanced BASIC.

Appendix C
QuickDRAW

Shortly before this book went to press, I received a program from Jack Strick & Associates, who supplied other programs for the writing of this book. The program is called QuickDRAW and is copyrighted by Software America Division of American Computer Products, Inc. This program comes on disk and is written specifically for the IBM Personal Computer.

QuickDRAW allows the operator to draw a shape using the cursor control keys and the function keys. The cursor keys determine the position of the lines drawn. The function keys control the color and type of line drawn, along with the editing and storage of the finished shape. A grid is provided to help the operator determine the proper size and screen position of the shape.

The main menu gives the operator the choice of either drawing a new shape or editing and painting a previously drawn shape. If the operator wants to create a new shape, the program guides the operator through the file setup routine. Shape files follow the IBM file specification (DOS manual pages 3-6 and 3-7) and end with the extension, shp. Paint files have the same name as shapes that they paint and end with the extension, pnt. After the files have been set up, the program asks the user to select the resolution of the new shape. Medium-resolution uses Screen 1 (BASIC manual page 4-222) with four colors and 320 × 200 screen points. High-resolution uses Screen 2 (BASIC manual page 4-222) with only black and white and 640 × 200 points. The program then draws a grid appropriate to the resolution selected and an X cursor appears. The computer beeps when it is ready to draw.

Pressing the up arrow cursor key moves the cursor up one grid space. The other cursor keys control downward, left, and right cursor movements. The cursor cannot move past the edge of the grid. Pressing Function Key F9 changes the cursor step size so that the cursor now moves from point to point. This allows fine cursor movements for more exacting drawings. Pressing F9 again changes the step size back to the faster grid space steps.

Figure C-1 provides a listing of function key actions in medium-resolution mode. The author of the program explains that these function keys act like toggle switches. In other words, pressing a key once turns the function on. Pressing it a second time turns the function off. Key F1 switches between the two medium-resolution palettes available on the IBM Personal Computer. When the program is initially activated, palette 0 is in effect, producing green, red, and brown. By pressing F1, the colors change to palette 1, which produces cyan, magenta, and white. Depressing F1 for the second time causes the screen to revert to palette 0 colors.

The purpose of the F2 key is to tell the program that the cursor is at the end point of a line the user wants to draw a line to. The type of line drawn is determined by keys F3 and F4. In the default mode, the user moves the cursor to the beginning of the line to be drawn and then presses F2. He then moves the cursor to the point on the screen where the intended line is to end. F2 is pressed again and the line is drawn between the two points. The user then moves the cursor to the starting point of the next line and repeats this process. This mode may be used for drawing separate unconnected lines or for connecting lines. F2 is pressed immediately after the first line is drawn to establish the starting point for the second line. The cursor is moved by using the keys contained on the separate keypad to the right of the main keyboard. These include cursor left, cursor right, cursor up, and cursor down.

```
F1.....Change Palette
F2.....Start and End Line
F3.....Continous Lines
F4.....Star Pattern Lines
F5.....Line Color Red
F6.....Line Color Yellow
F8.....Display Drawing
F9.....Step Size
F10....Return to Main Menu
```

Fig. C-1. Medium-resolution function keys.

The F3 key is used to put the IBM Personal Computer into a continuous line mode. This means that all the user has to do is move the cursor to the point where a line is to be ended and then press F2. A line will then be drawn from the end of the last line on the screen to this new point. Pressing F3 again puts the machine back in the former mode.

Soft Key F4 is used to put the computer into what the program author refers to as star pattern mode. This means that all the user has to do is move the cursor to the point where he wishes to end the line and then press F2. A line is drawn from the starting point (original cursor position) to this new point. The cursor may then be moved to another screen location, and another line will be drawn between the original starting point and the new position when F2 is pressed again. This can be used to produce a star pattern, or more accurately, a pattern which resembles the spokes of a wheel with several radians emanating from a central point.

Soft Key F5 changes the foreground color. When the program is first run, the palette is 0 and the color is 1. When F5 is pressed, color 2, which is red in palette 0 and magenta in palette 1, is used. Pressing F5 for the second time returns the foreground to color 1.

Soft Key F6 changes the foreground color to color 3, which is brown in palette 0 and white in palette 1. It performs in exactly the same manner as F5, only a different foreground color is selected.

Soft Key F8 is used to display the drawing on the screen by itself. When the program is first run, a grid appears on the screen to help with line coordination. F8 causes the grid to disappear, leaving the drawing you produce against a plain background. When a drawing is finished, the user will normally press F8 once to remove the grid and then press it again. This latter move causes the shape to be committed to a file which has been previously opened.

Soft Key F9 controls cursor step. In the default mode, the cursor moves from one column to the next. However, when F9 is depressed, the cursor reverts to a medium-resolution point mode, traveling up and down, left and right, a signal point at a time.

Soft Key F10 exits the main body of the program and returns the user to the main menu.

Before entering the actual write mode, you are prompted to select one of two options. Choose the first when you wish to draw a new image. This allows you to set up a file on disk to contain the image you are about to draw. You are prompted to input a filename, along with the disk drive to which the write is to occur. Forever after, this will be the name of the shape you are going to draw. This is stored under the designation of "name.SHP".

The second choice allows you to recall a previous shape in order to edit or paint it. The edit mode may also be entered immediately after a drawing is completed by pressing F8 (to erase the grid) and then pressing F7. The edit mode lets the operator erase or change the color of the lines that were drawn previously. In the edit mode, only the up and down arrow cursor keys are active. When you press one of these keys, two cursors will appear, one at each end of a particular line. If this is not the line you wish to edit, you keep pressing these keys until the correct one is referenced on the screen. The soft keys now initiate different functions, which are listed in Fig. C-2. Keys F1 through F3 change the color of a particular line. Soft Key F4 erases a line completely, while pressing F9 erases the entire shape. Should you press F10, the drawing returns to the grid pattern to allow you to add more lines.

Once a shape is drawn and stored, this program allows the operator to quickly paint it by entering the paint mode. When you opt to enter the paint mode, the machine prompts you to give the filename of the image to be painted. This is the same name that was established for the image before writing ever began. For example, if you open the file "PLANT.SHP" to draw a flower on the screen and store the finished image in the file, you would input the same filename when instructed to do so after entering the paint mode. This tells the computer that you're going to paint the image contained in "PLANT.SHP". The program then creates another file that will be named "PLANT.PNT". This file will contain the paint

```
F1.....Change Color of Line to Color 1
F2.....Change Color of Line to Color 2
F3.....Change Color of Line to Color 3
F4.....Erase Line
F9.....Erase Shape
F10....Redraw Shape on Grid
```

Fig. C-2. Edit mode function keys.

information for the matching shape image.

As soon as the new PNT file has been established, the screen will be erased and the image will appear as it was originally written. A crosshair cursor then appears, and the operator moves it to a section within the area he wants to paint. Once this point has been reached, hitting the appropriate function key paints the area. Figure C-3 shows the functions of the various keys while in the paint mode. As is the case in the drawing mode, there are two cursor step sizes which are controlled by Soft Key F9.

Once the picture is painted, pressing F8 stores the coordinates and colors in the previously opened file and returns you to the main menu. F5 lets you set the background color to any of the sixteen possible on the IBM Personal Computer.

```
F1.....Paint Color 1
F2.....Paint Color 2
F3.....Paint Color 3
F4.....Paint Color 0
F5.....Change Background
       Color
F6.....Change Palette
F8.....Store File
F9.....Step Size
```

Fig. C-3. Painting routine function keys.

QuickDRAW is a very useful program for quickly producing simple to complex line drawings on the screen. The program does not allow you to do anything you couldn't do through straight graphics programming, but it saves a tremendous amount of time. Once the image is produced, the coordinates are committed to the shape file in a format that is retrieved by the main program itself. In other words, you can't simply load the shape file into current memory and run it without using the QuickDRAW program as well. What kind of drawings can you produce with this program? The answer is about anything imaginable, although you will be slowed up a bit when you have to produce curves or circles. There is no direct circle function contained in this program, and all arcs must be drawn a point or two at a time. However, for straight lines, the program is exceedingly fast, and I especially like the fact that you can plot lines a point at a time instead of in larger steps. While the program is protected and cannot be accessed, it appears that it is written entirely in BASIC without the need to resort to machine language subroutines. Admittedly, I found the instructions for the use of this program to be a bit difficult to decipher at first. Actually, the operation is quite simple, but describing it is another thing altogether. The author certainly must have realized this, because all instructions are produced on the IBM printer by loading "QUICK.DOC." This gives you a lengthy list of instructions in hard copy form which can be constantly referred to while learning to use the program.

To use QuickDRAW on your IBM Personal Computer, first load IBM DOS and then enter the Advanced BASIC (BASICA) mode. Insert the QuickDRAW disk. Type FILES and you will get the complete file listing of all that's contained on the QuickDRAW disk. Remember that you will also need the color/graphics adapter board and a suitable color monitor or color television/modulator combination.

This is a new program and it is certain that improvements will be made in future editions. However, you can take advantage of all of these future editions without paying extra money. Jack Strick & Associates urges users to write regarding their personal experiences and desires. If you will also enclose the original disk, they will send it back to you with any revisions included. The current version is designated 1.0. Free updating is available through version 1.5 if indeed the upgrading goes to this many steps.

I have found QuickDRAW to be quite interesting and very helpful in drawing many different types of pictures on the screen. It is available from Jack Strick & Associates, 949 S. South Lake Drive, Hollywood, Florida 33019 for $49.95.

Video Modulator Repair

The M & R Enterprises Sup'R Mod modulator is often used in connecting the output of the color/graphics board to a color television receiver, allowing the latter to serve as a color monitor. This is an excellent modulator, which derives its operating power from the IBM Personal Computer. Access to this power supply is handled through a four-pin Berg strip on the color/graphics adapter card.

Unfortunately, it is possible to connect the modulator to this Berg strip in two possible ways. In other words, the plug is not polarized. When connecting this modulator to the color/graphics board, it is mandatory that the yellow lead from the modulator be located at the top of the card when the plug is inserted. If you should reverse this pattern (white lead up), a reverse polarity situation will exist and will damage the modulator. To prevent accidental reverse connections, it's a good idea to place a drop of fingernail polish on the end of the modulator connector where the yellow lead is located. If you remember that this red dot is always up when connected to the color/graphics board, you won't have any problems.

I had the misfortune of damaging one of my modulators by a reverse connection and at a time when I could not afford to wait until it could be processed through a repair facility. I bought a new one and, you guessed it, three months later, I damaged it while hastily connecting it to a new machine. There I was, with two damaged modulators at a time when I absolutely had to have a color monitor.

I quickly removed the front and back covers from the recently damaged modulator and examined the circuitry. As is usually the case, there were no obviously damaged components, as might be evidenced by a ruptured IC or transistor case. Using a multimeter, I quickly checked voltages throughout the circuit. Naturally, the modulator was connected to the active computer during this check. After fifteen minutes or so, I traced the problem down to a component which appears to be a small plastic-encased transistor. However, this is not a transistor at all, but a miniature voltage regulator. It contains three leads just like a transistor and is approximately the same size. On the modulator board, this component has label IC2, shown in Fig. D-1. Not having a schematic to work from was quite a hindrance, but I could read the 12 volts from the computer at one terminal of this device and no voltage at the output. I laboriously located the connection pins on the back of the circuit board, removed the solder, and then pulled the component free.

The component used in my particular modulator bore the designation CSM78L05. I could not cross reference it with any of my manuals, so I checked at a local Radio Shack store. The personnel there were not able to match it either, but I deduced (due to the 05 designation) that this was a 5-volt regulator. Such devices accept a higher input voltage and output a regulated 5 Vdc, regardless of minor fluctuations in supply voltage. A polarity check at the modulator indicated the need for a positive voltage regulator, so I began looking for a component that might take its place.

Unfortunately, Radio Shack only stocks 5-volt positive regulators rated at 1 ampere and above. These are several times the size of the component I needed to replace, but I purchased one anyway. I was unable to mount it in the original position and simply hung it on the back of the modulator board. When I reconnected the modulator to the television receiver, the device worked perfectly. I was back in business again.

I hope my unfortunate experiences may serve to help others who find themselves suddenly without a modulator due to a polarity reversal. In almost every case, such a reversal will immediately destroy this IC regulator. This is not a highly exotic component and can be directly replaced by a National Semiconductor LM78L05ACZ. The device has three pins and is inserted on the circuit board in exactly the same position as the original component. This means that the flat face of the component should be facing toward the end of the modulator, where the 300-ohm cable exits for connection to the television receiver. The portion of the circuitry you are concerned with when making this replacement is found at the point where the cable from the computer enters the case. This portion of the board is separated from other parts by metal shields. You will see a number of resistors, capacitors, and what appear to be three transistors. The two units on the left (facing toward the 300-ohm cable end) are transistors. The component on the right (nearest the shield) is the IC voltage regulator. You will see a designation there of IC2.

Many things could happen to modulators and other electronic circuits, but the Sup'R Mod contains an automatic overvoltage protection circuit. The device is also protected from excessive video drive. About the only thing you could damage is the IC regulator under discussion.

Many persons are quite hesitant about going into a tightly packed electronic device such as a modulator, but if you have a bit of

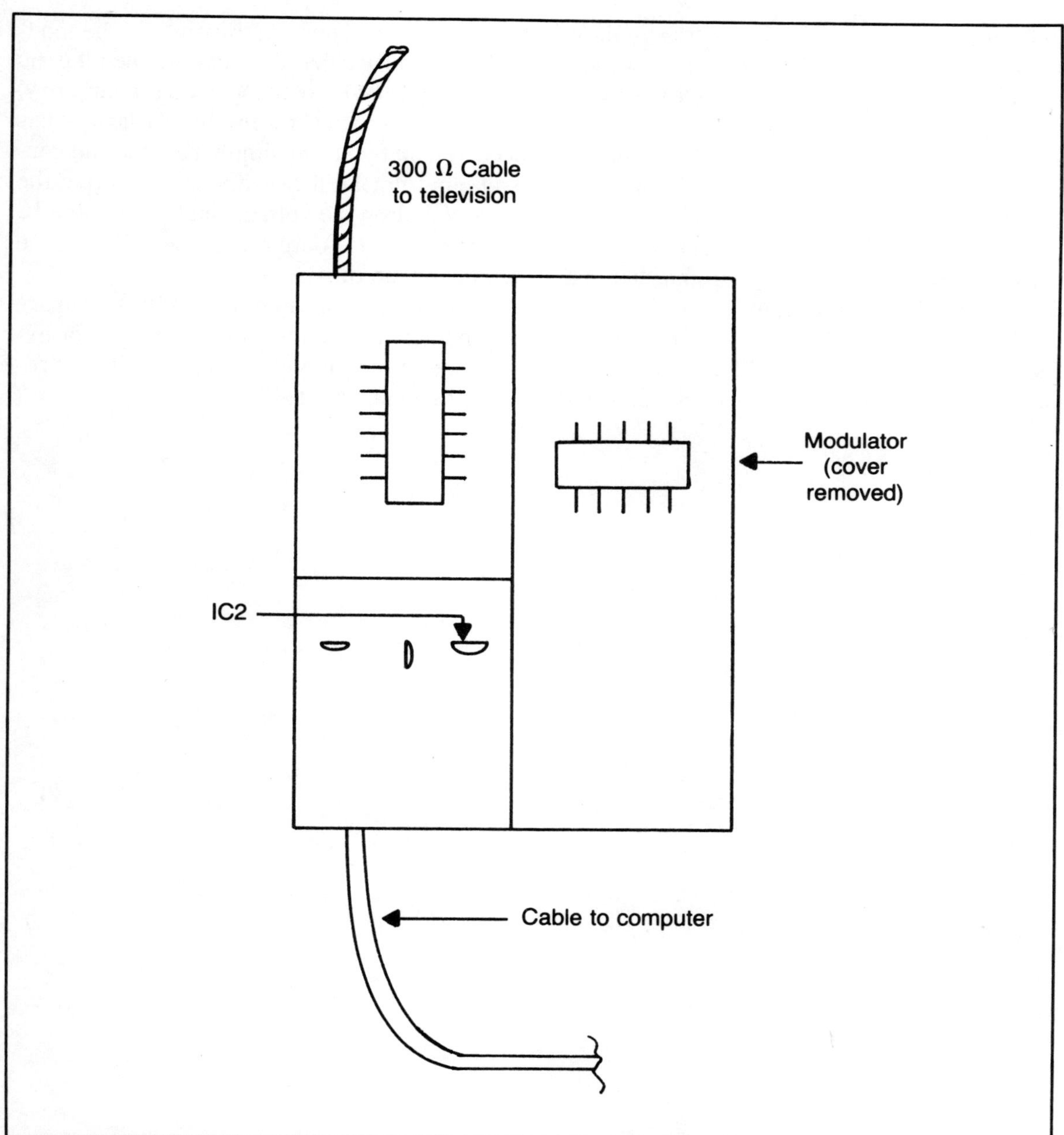

Fig. D-1. The location of the IC2 component.

soldering and repair experience, the replacement of this IC can be handled quite quickly. Remember, you probably will void your warranty by cracking the case, so you may not wish to perform repairs unless the warranty period has expired or if you've got to have a functioning modulator right away.

You can take steps to prevent the possibility of polarity reversal. You can snip the yellow lead shortly after it exits the Berg plug and install a 50-PIV diode in series with this line. The anode of the diode should connect to the lead from the Berg plug. The cathode connects to the lead portion traveling to the modulator. If you accidentally reverse the plug, no current will flow to the modulator circuitry. The modulator won'"t work, but no damage has occurred and you can simply reverse the connections to make it operational. Inserting the diode will drop the voltage slightly, but the IC regultor will still output a stable 5 Vdc to the modulator circuitry.

Again, don't attempt any of these repairs or modifications unless you have a bit of experience in building electronic circuits or repairing similar devices.

Glossary

Access Time—The interval between the application of an input pulse and the availability of data signals at the output is known as access time. In the IBM Personal Computer, access time is 250 nanoseconds.

Advanced Disk BASIC—Advanced Disk BASIC is the most extensive form of BASIC available on the IBM Personal Computer. Like Disk BASIC, it is a program on the DOS disk that must be loaded into memory for use. Advanced BASIC (BASICA) requires a disk-based machine with at least 48K of random access memory.

Algorithm—An algorithm is a precisely defined set of rules or a structured procedure that provides the solution to a problem in a finite number of steps.

Alphanumeric—Alphanumeric describes characters that includes the letters of the alphabet, numerals, and symbols used for punctuation and mathematical operations.

Array—An array is a group or table of values referenced by a single name in BASIC. Each individual value in the array is called an element. Array elements are variables and can be used in expressions and in any BASIC statement or function that uses variables.

ASCII—ASCII is an abbreviation for American Standard Code for Information Interchange, an eight-bit code (seven bits plus parity check). It is widely used for information interchange in data processing systems, communication systems, and associated equipment.

ASCII Printer Control Codes—ASCII control codes are various types of computer inputs handled via the keyboard that are recognized by the printer and perform specified functions when they are received. For example, when the carriage return button is pressed on the keyboard, a CR code is transmitted to the print buffer. The IBM Personal Computer utilizes 16 different ASCII control codes, which include line feed (LF), vertical tab (VT), form feed (FF), etc.

Asynchronous—Asynchronous describes a mode of computer operation in which performance of the next command is started by a signal indicating that the previous command has been completed.

Asynchronous Communications Adapter—The asynchronous communications adapter is a circuit board that plugs into the system expansion slots. It allows the computer to communicate with other terminals via phone lines, shortwave radio, and other telecommunications modes, provided that the proper modem has been installed between the output of the computer and the input of the communications line. This adapter is fully programmable and supports asynchronous communications only. A programmable data rate generator allows operation over a range of 50 to 9600 baud.

Backup Bisk—A backup disk contains information that was copied from another disk. It is kept in case the original information is unintentionally altered or destroyed.

BASIC—BASIC is a programming language that is used to write programs or sets of instructions to tell a computer what to do. A BASIC program consists of one or more BASIC statements that are preceded by line numbers. These numbers are used by BASIC to control the sequence in which the statements are run.

Batch Processing—Batch processing is a method of processing data in which a number of items are grouped for processing during the same machine run. Batch processing systems usually do not require immediate updating of files, as data is gathered up to a specific cutoff time and then processed.

Baud—A baud is a unit of signalling speed used to indicate the number of binary units of information transmitted per second. The IBM Personal Computer is capable of communicating at a rate of 50 baud on the low side to 9600 baud maximum.

Bidirectional Data Bus—In the IBM Personal Computer, a bus which accepts both input and output data signals on a single line.

Bit—An abbreviation for binary digit. This is an information unit which is equal to one binary decision or the designation of one out of two possible values. These values may be referred to as high/low, 1/0, yes/no, etc., when dealing with digital processing.

Boolean Algebra—Boolean algebra is a deductive system of reasoning named after George Boole, an English mathematician. It is a system of theorems which uses symbolic logic to denote classes of elements, true or false propositions, and on-off logic circuit elements. Symbols are used to represent operators such as AND, OR, NOT, EXCEPT, IF-THEN, etc. This system is now recognized as an effective method of handling single-valued functions with two possible output states. When Boolean Algebra is applied to binary arithmetic, the two states becomes 0 and 1. When applied to switching theory, the two states become open and closed.

Booting—Booting is the process of loading those segments of the IBM Disk Operating System (DOS) which will allow the system to operate.

Buffer—A buffer is a device or unit that serves as an isolator or interface between two dissimilar elements. It is used to match impedances, speeds, or other characteristics while maintaining isolation between matched elements. As a register, the storage buffer would serve as an intermediary storage point between two registers or data handling systems with different access times or data formats.

Bus—In its simplest form, a bus is a single conductor through which information is transmitted. In most digital computer applications, a bus will contain two or more conductors.

Byte—A byte is a sequence of bits, usually 8, that are operated on as a unit, and occupy a single memory location. The 5¼" disk used with the IBM Personal Computer can hold about 160,000 bytes, or 160,000 characters.

Card—In IBM Personal Computer terminology, a printed circuit board containing electronic components that form entire complex circuits. Each card is fitted with an edge connector to allow it to be simply plugged in place at a mating receptacle on the system board. The IBM machine uses printed circuit cards to expand machine capabilities. 32K and 64K memory cards are available, along with other cards that contain circuitry for an asynchronous communications adapter, color/graphics monitor adapter, disk drive adapter, monochrome monitor adapter, etc.

Cassette BASIC—Cassette BASIC is the nucleus of BASIC in the IBM Personal Computer. It is built into the machine in 32K of read-only storage. Programs in Cassette BASIC are saved on a cassette tape recorder.

Cathode-Ray Tube—A cathode-ray tube (CRT) is a device which contains electrodes surrounded by a glass sphere/cylinder and which will display information by creating a beam of electrons that strike the inside of the display surface. The electron/surface contact is only momentary, but the afterglow (or phosphorescence) of the phosphor coating on the inside of the screen causes the image to last (persist) until the electron beam scans it again. In the IBM Personal Computer, the monochrome adapter uses a cathode-ray tube with a P39 phosphor, which emits a yellow-green image.

Central Processor—The section of a computing machine that controls the interpretation and execution of instructions. It is divided into three main sections:

1. Arithmetic and Control: Performs the calculations, information routing, and control operations for the other sections.
2. Input and Output: Handles all information going into and coming out of the central processor, while controlling all peripheral equipment.

3. Memory: Provides the temporary storage for data and instructions. The memory cycle time usually determines the overall speed of the central processor.

Character—A character corresponds to a key on a keyboard, usually including the decimal digits 9 through 0, the letters A through Z, punctuation marks, operation symbols, and any other symbols that a computer may read, store, or write. A character may also be the electrical, magnetic, or mechanical profile used to represent a character in a computer and the computer's storage and peripheral devices. It may be made up of other elementary marks such as bits or pulses.

Character Set—A character set is an agreed-on set of representations, called characters, from which selections are made to denote and distinguish data. Each character differs from all others, and the total number of characters in a given set is fixed; e.g., a set may include the numerals 0 to 9, the letters A to Z, punctuation marks, and a blank or space.

Chip—In its most basic form, a chip is a thin slab of silicon material. Solid-state devices use a single chip to produce highly complex circuits, all contained on the chip surface. More common terminology lets this term be used to describe integrated circuits.

Code—A code is a system of symbols used to represent data or instructions in a computer or tabulating machine. Code also means to translate a program for the solution of a problem into a sequence of machine-language instructions or pseudo-instructions and addresses acceptable to the computer.

Color/Graphics Monitor—A color/graphics monitor is a television frequency monitor or television set capable of producing color images. CBM does not offer a color/graphics monitor for their computer, but has designed the color/graphics monitor adapter to interface with monitors made by other manufacturers and even color television receivers when a separate television modulator is used. (See Color/Graphics Monitor Adapter.)

Color/Graphics Monitor Adapter—In the IBM Personal Computer, monitor adapter is a plug-in circuit card which is designed to attach to a wide variety of television frequency monitors found in standard television sets (with a user-supplied RF modulator) or to direct-drive RGP monitors for graphics and color output. This card is capable of operating in black and white or color modes and provides three video interfaces: a composite video port, a direct-drive port, and a connection interface for driving a user-supplied RF modulator. A light pen interface is also provided.

Command—A command is an instruction that signals the machine to start, stop, or continue a specific operation. A command may be a portion of a statement that gives the specifics about the operation to be performed.

Composite Video—Composite video is television picture information and synchronization pulses combined. This is the equivalent of the output of a television camera. The

IBM Personal Computer may be outfitted with a color/graphics adapter that will output computer information in composite video form. This output may be connected directly to a television monitor or to an RF modulator that will then feed a standard television receiver. The composite video output from this adapter board is rated at 1.5 volts peak-to-peak.

Computer Game—A computer game is a program that allows one or more persons to compete with each other or the computer. The display screen often prints a graphic presentation of a game board, and game pieces are moved by keyboard input or linear controls called joysticks. Some computer games electronically mimic existing games, while others are unique and applicable only to computers.

Concatenate—Concatenation is the process of linking together in a series. A concatenated data set is one formed by combining the contents of several data sets in a specific sequence.

Cursor—The cursor is a small flashing hyphen or other symbol that appears on the monitor screen to indicate the point at which any characters or numerals input from the keyboard will be placed on the monitor.

Cycle Time—Cycle time is the period of time between the call for information and its delivery from storage. The IBM Personal Computer has a main storage cycle time of 410 nanoseconds with an access time of 250 nanoseconds.

Data Security—Any system which protects stored or hard copy data from being accidentally erased, damaged, or from falling into unauthorized hands is called data security. Since the IBM Personal Computer may be used to process sensitive or highly valuable information, simple security measures such as keeping backup copies of disks, removing disks when not in use, or installing a locked disk and hard copy filing system should assure proper security.

Debug—Debug is a term used to describe the detecting and removing of errors and malfunctions from a program, routine, or machine. Debugging usually involves the running and checkout of programs to detect the errors. Debugging aids are available to allow quick development of programs.

Debug Program—In IBM DOS, debug is a program which is used to provide a controlled testing environment to monitor and control the execution of the program to be debugged. It will load, alter, or display any part of any file and execute object files. The latter are executable programs in machine language format.

Default Drive—In an IBM Personal Computer with more than one disk drive, the default drive is the drive on which the disk operating system (DOS) will look to find any filenames entered without a specified drive. Most often, it is indicated by the letter A followed by the symbol >. The default drive can be changed by entering the designation letter (B) followed by a colon.

Diagnostics—Diagnostics are programs used to check the operation of a computer system. The IBM Personal Computer uses a specially formulated Diagnostics Program, which is contained on a prerecorded disk or cassette. When properly fed into the system, the Diagnostics Routine will allow the operator to check the entire system for any problems and indicate in what area the problem lies. The latter is accomplished by an appropriate monitor display.

Digital System—Digital systems handle information in digital form whereby quantities and other data are assigned numerical values. Most digital systems operate on a binary number configuration using "2" as a base and the digits zero (0) and one (1) as values that are referred to as bits. Combinations of these bit values provide the code by which data can be processed through electronic circuitry.

DIP—DIP stands for dual in-line package. This term describes an integrated circuit contained within a standard housing characterized by the symmetrical placement of leads along both long edges. The IBM Personal Computer contains hundreds of integrated circuits, most of which are mounted in DIP form. These include memory modules, the microprocessor itself, and many other circuit elements. The 16K memory option consists of nine memory modules, each of which is mounted in a dual in-line package.

DIP Switch—A small, rectangular device which actually contains many tiny switches in a single DIP package. DIP is an abbreviation for dual in-line package, which is a description of the physical makeup of switch construction. There are two rows of pins, one on each side of the switch, aligned opposite each other. The dual in-line package switches used in the IBM Personal Computer are found on the system board and on the 32K and 64K memory cards. Each of these devices contains eight discrete switches which may be placed in the on or off position. As new options are added to the computer system, the switch positions must be changed to allow the machine to have access to them. Switch changes are required for the addition (or deletion) of memory modules, memory cards, disk drives, etc.

Direct Memory Access—Abbreviated DMA, direct memory access is a technique for transferring data directly between memory and system peripherals. Direct memory access permits transfers to take place without the central processing unit (CPU) intervening on a cycle-stealing basis. In the IBM Personal Computer, the microprocessor is supported by a set of high-function support devices, providing four channels of 20-bit direct memory access. Three of the four DMA channels are available on the I/O bus and are provided to support high-speed data transfers between I/O devices and memory, again without processor intervention. The fourth DMA channel is programmed to refresh the system's dynamic memory. All DMA data transfers (with the exception of the refresh channel) take five processor clocks of 210 nanoseconds, or 1.05 nanoseconds if the processor ready line is not deactivated. Refresh DMA cycles take four clocks, or 840 nanoseconds.

Direct Mode—The direct mode is used when programming in BASIC when the user wants the computer to perform the request immediately after it is entered. This mode is operational when the instruction is not preceded by a line number. It is important to note that the instructions themselves are not saved after they are executed. This mode can be used to display results of arithmetic and logical operations immediately. It is useful for debugging and quick computations that do not require a complete program.

Directory—The directory is the list of the names of the files on a disk. Also included in a directory is pertinent information, such as the size of the file, its location on the disk, and the date it was created. The directory occupies four sectors at a specific location on each disk.

Disk—A disk is a device which is used to store information. It is a flexible device which is coated with a magnetic substance. When in use, the disk spins inside its permanent protective jacket. The read/write head comes in contact with the recording surface through the long hole in the protective jacket, called the head slot. Information is written to or read from the magnetic surface of the disk.

Disk BASIC—Disk BASIC is a version of BASIC used with the IBM Personal Computer. It comes as a program on the IBM disk operating system (DOS) disk and must be loaded into memory before it can be used. Disk BASIC requires a disk-based machine with at least 32K of random access memory.

Disk Drive Adapter—In the IBM Personal Computer, the disk drive adapter is a long circuit card that allows the computer to control two internal disk drives and to read from and write to 5¼″ disks. The adapter fits in one of the five system expansion slots on the system board and is attached to up to two internal drives by means of internal daisy-chained flat cable. The adapter has a second connector on its opposite end, which extends through the rear panel of the system unit. This allows two additional disk drives to be attached outside the system unit.

Disk Operating System—The disk operating system (DOS) is a collection of programs for the IBM Personal Computer stored on the DOS disk. These programs process commands to allow the user to manage information and the hardware resources of the computing system. DOS must be loaded into the computer before starting either Disk BASIC or Advanced BASIC programs.

Drive—In computer terminology, drive is a mechanical device which manipulates data storage media. In the IBM Personal Computer, the drive is usually a disk drive, which is capable of spinning the disk so that its electronic circuits may read the stored information.

Edit—Editing is the process of rearranging or revising data or program lines. Editing may involve the deletion of unwanted data, the application of format techniques, the insertion of symbols, the application of standard processes, and the testing of data for reasonableness.

EPROM—EPROM is an abbreviation for erasable programmable read-only memory.

It is a ROM in which the data pattern may be erased to allow a new pattern (and thus, new programming) to be used. In the IBM Personal Computer, the system board contains space for 48K × 8 of ROM or EPROM.

Error Message—An error message is a word or combination of words that appear on the monitor screen to indicate to the user that there is an error somewhere in the program. The IBM Personal Computer has a total of 73 different error messages that may occur. Most of these messages will inform the operator on which line the error has occurred and may even print out the line on the screen to enable the user to study it and determine the cause of the error.

Executable Statement—In BASIC, all statements are either executable or nonexecutable. Executable statements are program instructions that tell BASIC what to do next while executing a program. PRINT X, for example, is an executable statement. REM draw tree is nonexecutable.

File—A file is a logical block of information designated by a name and considered as a unit. A file can be stored on a disk or cassette. In order to use the information, it is necessary to tell BASIC where the information is and open the file. At this point, the file may be used for both input and output.

File Attribute—A file attribute is a term used to describe any of the characteristics of a file.

Filename—A filename is the name given to a disk file. It must be one to eight characters long and may be immediately followed by a filename extension, which can be one to three characters long. A filename can be made up of any combination of letters and numerals, but it should be descriptive of what is contained in the file. When a directory is requested, a list of filenames will appear on the monitor.

Floppy Disk Controller—In the IBM Personal Computer the floppy disk controller is a circuit card which contains a status register and a data register. The 8-bit main status register contains the status information of the floppy disk controller and may be accessed at any time. The data register stores data, commands, parameters and disk drive status information.

Flowchart—A flowchart is a graphical representation of the definition or solution of a problem, in which symbols are used to represent functions, operations, and flow. A flowchart might contain all of the logical steps in a routine or program in order to allow the designer to conceptualize and visualize each step. It defines the major phases of the processing, as well as the path to problem solution.

Font—A mechanical or electronic device which determines how printed characters will appear on paper. In the IBM Personal Computer, two character fonts are used on the character generator card and are selected by a card jumper, which is a small, interconnecting hookup wire.

Formatting—Formatting is the process of initializing or preparing a disk to receive information. It checks the disk for bad spots, builds a directory to hold information about the files that will eventually be written on it, and optionally, copies the DOS system files onto the disk. Formatting insures that bad areas are not used for files. It is important to know that formatting erases whatever was already on the disk. So it is to be used normally only once for each diskette.

Function Keys—On the IBM Personal Computer keyboard, there are ten function keys located on the far left hand side. These keys serve many different purposes, depending upon the language being used. When programming in IBM BASIC, the function keys are used to save keyboard input time. For example, to load a program from disk into Disk BASIC, it is necessary to input via the keyboard LOAD" (program name). However, typing time may be saved by pressing the third function key, F3, which will automatically input LOAD. All that is necessary then is to type the name of the program. In this case, depressing F3 saves operator time by enabling him to do in one keystroke what would normally take five keystrokes using the standard character keys.

Game Control Adapter—The game control adapter is a printed circuit board that may be installed in one of the five system expansion slots on the system board. This allows elements of the computer system to be controlled by game attachments such as paddles or joysticks. Up to two joysticks or four paddles may be attached, and four inputs for switches are also provided.

Graphics—Graphics refers to the methods and techniques for converting data to a graphic display using a computer. In the IBM Personal Computer, this is made possible by means of the color/graphics monitor adapter, which allows the user to display images in sixteen different colors. This graphics capability makes the system all-points addressable in medium and high resolution.

Handshaking—Handshaking is a term which implies an initial exchange between two units or items in a system connection. Handshaking usually requires matching at an interface, as when signals are exchanged between data set devices when a connection is made. A typical handshaking procedure takes place when a connection between a modem and an ACIA (asynchronous communications interface adapter) channel is established:

1. Local modem is enabled from the ACIA request-to-send signal.
2. Remote modem answers the call and sends back its carrier frequency.
3. Local modem detects this carrier and enables its clear-to-send output, which is detected by the computer.

Hardware—Hardware refers to the physical components that make up a microcomputer system. The hard components include microprocessors, semiconductors, integrated circuits, the mounting frame, etc. (Compare with Software.)

High Resolution—Using the IBM color/graphics monitor adapter, it is possible to use BASIC statements to draw in either medium or high resolution. In high resolution, there are 640 points horizontally and 200 points vertically. These points are numbered starting with 0 (zero) so that the lower right corner point is (639,199). High resolution consists of only two colors: 0 (zero) and 1 (one). Zero is always black, and one is always white. When text characters are displayed in high resolution, 80 characters per line can be displayed. One is the foreground color, and zero is the background color. Thus, characters will always be white on black.

Housecleaning—Housecleaning occurs when BASIC collects all of its useful data and frees up unused areas of memory that were once used for strings. The data is compressed so that the user can continue until there is no space left. BASIC will automatically do a housecleaning when it is running out of usable work space.

Indirect Mode—The indirect mode is the means of entering and running programs in BASIC. In this mode, each program line must begin with a line number. The line is then stored as part of the program in memory. The program can then be executed by entering the run command.

Input—Input is data transferred from an external storage medium into the internal storage of the computer.

Instruction—An instruction is a set of characters which define an operation and cause the computer to perform the operation on the indicated quantities.

Integrated Circuit—An integrated circuit (IC) is a circuit whose components are made by etching, doping and diffusing distinct areas on a single chip of semiconductor material such as silicon. Each IC is capable of performing at least one and sometimes many complete circuit functions. The majority of components found in the IBM Personal Computer are in integrated circuit form, as opposed to discrete solid-state units, such as transistors and diodes.

Intel 8088 Microprocessor—Mounted on the system board, the Intel 8088 Microprocessor is the heart of the IBM Personal Computer. This unusual microprocessor features an 8-bit I/O bus but has 16-bit internal architecture, thus combining the features of a 16-bit microprocessor with 8-bit communication capabilities. The processor supports 20 bits of addressing (1 megabyte of storage) and is implemented in maximum mode, so a coprocessor can be added as an optional feature. The processor is operated at 4.77 megahertz and is supported by a set of high-function support devices, providing four channels of 20-bit direct memory access, three 16-bit timer counter channels, and eight prioritized interrupt levels.

Input/Output Channel—An input/output (I/O) channel is a circuit path which allows independent communication between the processor and external devices. In general, I/O channels may transfer data between memory and external interfaces in blocks of any size without disturbing working registers in the processor. In the IBM Personal Computer, the I/O channel is an extension of the 8088 microprocessor bus.

Joystick—In computer graphics, a joystick is a lever that may be used to control operations such as movement of one or more display elements.

Keyboard—A keyboard contains keys for entering data or information into a system. Keyboards may be alphanumeric, as used for word processing, and data processing; or numeric, as used for touch-tone telephones, accounting machines, and calculators. The IBM Personal Computer keyboard falls into the alphanumeric category.

Light Pen—A lightpen is a photosensitive device that causes a computer to modify the display on a cathode-ray tube (CRT) screen. As the display information is selected by the operator, the light pen signals the computer using an electronically produced pulse. The light pen can be used to draw impressions on the computer monitor.

Logical Operator—Logical operators perform logical, or Boolean, operations on numeric values. A logical operator takes a combination of true-false values and returns a true or false result. An operand of a logical operator is considered to be true if it is not equal to zero, or false if it is equal to zero. The result of the logical operation is a number which is again true if it is not equal to zero, or false if it is equal to zero. The logical operators are NOT (logical complement), AND (conjunction), OR (disjunction), XOR (exclusive OR), IMP (implication), and EQV (equivalence). Each operator returns results.

Loop—A loop is a series of instructions in which the last instruction can cause the repetition of the series over and over again until the required number of cycles have been completed or a terminal condition has been reached.

LSB—LSB is an abbreviation for least significant bit, which is the rightmost bit in a word. The least significant bit contributes the least weight to the numerical value of the word in IBM coding.

Machine Language—Machine language can be used directly by a microprocessor. All other languages must be translated or compiled into binary code before entering the processor. Users generally write their programs in coded instructions that are more meaningful to them. Assembly programs are then used to translate the symbolic instructions into binary machine code.

Matrix Printer—A matrix printer is a device that uses an array of dots to form characters. The IBM Personal Computer printer is an 80-character per second matrix printer.

Medium-Resolution—Medium resolution is a term used to describe computer graphics. In medium resolution there are 320 points horizontally and 200 vertically on the display screen. These points are numbered from left to right and from top to bottom, starting with 0 (zero). That makes the upper left corner of the screen point (0,0), and the lower right corner point (-19,99). Medium-resolution is unusual because of its color features, which offer a choice of background colors and "palettes".

Memory—Memory is a basic component of a computer which stores information for future use. Memory and storage and interchangeable terms. A memory is used to accept and hold information in the form of binary numbers until required. To be effective, a computer must be able to store the data that will be operated on, as well as the program which directs what operations are to be performed.

Microprocessor—A microprocessor is a solid-state central processing unit which is very much like a computer on a chip.

Modem—A modem is an electronic device that performs the modulation and demodulation functions required for communications. A modem can be used to connect computers and terminals over telephone circuits.

Module—A module is an assembly which contains a complete circuit or subcircuit. Technically, integrated circuits fall under the module category. Printed circuit boards that are designed to be plugged into a computer or other electronic circuit may also be classified as modules.

Monochrome Display— A monochrome display is most often a cathode-ray tube (CRT) device which is capable of black and white output only.

MSB—An abbreviation for most significant bit, which is the leftmost bit in a word. The most significant bit contributes the most weight to the numerical value of the word in IBM coding.

Multiple Statement—A multiple statement is a program line which is made up of two or more separate statements. IBM BASIC uses a colon to separate statements on a program line.

Nanosecond—An amount of time equal to 10^{-9} second. It is abbreviated ns and is equivalent to 1/1,000,000 of a second. A time interval of 1,000,000 nanoseconds is equal to one second.

Negation—Negation is a Boolean operation, the result of which has the Boolean value opposite to that of the operand. It is synonymous with NOT.

Non-executable Statement—Non-executable statements, such as REM, do not cause any program action when BASIC encounters them.

Numeric Constant—Numeric constants are actual values used by BASIC during program execution. They are positive or negative numbers.

Numeric Expression—A numeric expression may be simply a numeric constant or variable, or it can be a combination of constants and variables using operators to produce a single numeric value.

Numeric Keypad—The numeric keypad is a keypad located at the far right of the IBM Personal Computer which is used for entering numeric data.

Operator—The operator is that portion of the program which tells the microprocessor what to do. An example of an operator in a program for the IBM Personal Computer would be: 10 PRINT "THIS IS THE CORRECT ANSWER". This program line tells the computer to display "THIS IS THE

CORRECT ANSWER" on the monitor screen.

Overscan—On the IBM Personal Computer color/graphics monitor adapter, overscan is that area which is outside the display area for characters. This area is known as the border screen. The color statement may be used to set the color of the border screen.

Parallel Printer Adapter—The parallel printer adapter in the IBM Personal Computer is designed to attach printers with a parallel port interface, but it may also be used as a general input/output port for any device which matches its input/output capabilities.

Program—A program is a set of instructions that direct a computer in performing a desired operation, such as the solution of a mathematical problem or the sorting of data.

Protected File—A protected file is one which is stored within memory and cannot be listed or edited. This prevents persons from being able to gain access to the various program lines and copying or changing the data.

Power-On Self Test—When power is initially applied, the computer will automatically scan many of its circuits and sound a beep from the internal speaker if this initial test indicates proper system performance. The power-on self test is really a check of the power supply to see if it is providing proper voltage to the unit.

Power Supply—A power supply is an electrical/electronic circuit which supplies all operating voltage and current to the computer system. Initial power is usually derived from the 115-volt household ac receptacle.

Printer Self Test—The printer self test is an automatic test of the IBM Personal Computer Printer during which it prints out a hard copy of all the characters it is capable of producing. The printer self test is activated by turning on the power switch while simultaneously pressing the Line Feed switch.

Random Access Memory—Random access memory is the main internal memory of a computer. The computer can store values in distinct locations in random access memory (RAM) and recall them, or alter, and restore them. The values which are in random access memory are lost when the power to the computer is turned off.

Random File—A random file is a type of disk data file in which data can be accessed randomly; i.e., anywhere on the disk. It is not necessary to read through all the information.

Read-Only Memory—Read-only memory is usually used to hold important programs or data that must be available to the computer when the power is first turned on. Information in read-only memory is placed there in the process of manufacturing and is unalterable. Information stored in ROM does not disappear when power is turned off.

Refresh Cycle—Refreshing is the constant restoring of information that fades from memory when left idle. The IBM Personal Computer uses a 20-bit direct memory access channel for its refresh cycle, which takes 840 nanoseconds to complete.

REM—REM, which is short for remark, is a statement used in IBM BASIC to indicate that the following text on the line provides an explanation of the program or a part of it. REM statements are not output to the monitor screen or printer during program execution. Rather, they serve as an explanation of the program when it is listed.

Rerun—A rerun is a repeat of a machine run from the beginning, usually made desirable or necessary by a false start, an interruption, or a change.

Reserved Word—Reserved words have special meanings in BASIC. They include all BASIC commands, statements, function names, and operator names. Reserved words may not be used as variable names. These reserved words should always be separated from data or other parts of a BASIC statement using spaces or other special characters.

RF Modulator—An RF modulator is a device that will accept an audio or video input and then place this information on a carrier, usually at radio frequencies. The IBM Personal Computer does not have an RF modulator, but one is required in order to send video information to a standard television receiver.

ROM BIOS—ROM BIOS is an abbreviation for read-only memory basic input/output system. In the IBM Personal Computer, this is a complex circuit which provides the device level control of the major I/O devices in the system unit. The BIOS routines allow the assembly language programmer to perform block level I/O operations without any concern for device address and operating characteristics.

Routine—A routine is an ordered set of instructions that perform a specific function. A routine may be considered as a subdivision of a program with two or more instructions that are functionally related.

Scratch Disk—A scratch disk contains no useful information and thus can be used as a backup disk.

Scrolling—Scrolling is a process in which, when the screen is filled, the display will move upward one line at a time to allow additional lines to be input at the bottom. When this occurs, the top line disappears.

Sequential File—A sequential file is one in which is stored one item after another in the order it is sent (sequentially) and is read back in the same manner. Sequential files may be stored on tapes or disks.

Software—In contrast to hardware, software is a term used to indicate the relative intangibles of computer operations. These include computer languages and programs.

Source Disk—The source a disk contains information that is to be copied onto another disk.

Storage—Storage is a term used to describe a device or medium in which data can be kept and from which it can be retrieved at a later time. Storage may use electrostatic, magnetic, acoustic, optical, electronic, or mechanical methods. This term is synonymous with memory.

String—A string is a linear sequence of items which are grouped in series according to certain rules.

String Comparison—A string comparison can be used to determine which of two strings comes first in alphabetical order. Lower case letters come after their upper case counterparts. Numbers come before letters. Two strings are actually compared by taking one character at a time from each string and comparing the ASCII codes. If all the ASCII codes are the same, the strings are equal. If the ASCII codes for a particular position differ, the character with the lower code number comes before the character with the higher code number. If during string comparison, all characters are the same but the end of one string is reached. First, the shorter string is said to come first. Leading and trailing blanks are significant.

String Constant—A string constant is a sequence of up to 255 characters enclosed in double quotation marks. In a BASIC program it is often used to display on the screen.

Subroutine—A subroutine is a segment of a program which can be executed by a single call. Subroutines are used to perform the same sequence of instructions at many different places in one program.

System Board—In the IBM Personal Computer, the system board is contained in the syytem unit and houses the microprocessor, ROM, RAM, and system expansion slots. This large circuit board fits horizontally in the base of the system unit and includes 40K ROM and a minimum of 16K memory. There are additional IC sockets which will allow for the expansion of 64K of memory. This board also includes an enhanced version of the Microsoft BASIC-80 Interpreter without disk functions.

System Expansion Slots—The system expansion slots in the IBM Personal Computer allow for the insertion of circuit cards that expand the capability of the computer. The slots are located on the rear left-hand side of the system board. Memory boards, the asynchronous communications adapter, the color/graphics adapter, etc., are all mounted in the system unit by means of the system Expansion slots. The IBM Personal Computer contains five such slots for the addition of up to five expansion modules.

System Unit—The system unit houses the microprocessor, read-only memory, read/write memory, power supply, and system expansion slots for the attachment of up to five options. One or two 5¼″ disk drives can also be mounted in the system unit, providing 160K of storage each.

Task—A task is a basic unit of work to be accomplished by a computer.

Telecommunication—Data transmission between a computing system and remotely located devices using a unit that performs the necessary format conversion and controls the rate of transmission.

Terminal Unit—A terminal unit is a part of a computer system that may be used for inputting or outputting information using a communications channel. Using the asynchronous communications adapter available for the IBM Personal Computer, the system unit and keyboard, as well as any other input devices, compose the terminal unit.

Timing Generator—A timing generator is a circuit which outputs evenly spaced signals to be used for timing control through machine operations. In the IBM Personal Computer, the timing generator sends timing signals to the 6845 cathode-ray tube controller. The signals are also used by the dynamic memory. Additionally, the timing generator resolves the CPU/graphic controller contentions for accessing the display buffer.

Track—A track is a concentric circle on a disk. There are 40 tracks on a single disk formatted by the IBM PC. Information that can be read by the read/write head of the disk drive is written onto the tracks. Each track is divided into eight sectors that are 512 bytes long.

Truncation—Truncation is the deletion or omission of a leading or trailing portion of a string in accordance with specified criteria. It may also be the termination of a computation process before its final conclusion or natural termination, if any, in accordance with specified rules.

Update—To update is to modify information already contained in a file or program with current information.

Variables—In a BASIC program variables are names used to represent quantities whose values can change. There are two types of variables: numeric and string. A numeric variable always has a value that is a number. A string variable may only have a character or string value.

Index

Graphics Programs for the IBM PC®

If you are intrigued with the possibilities of the programs included in *Graphics Programs for the IBM PC®* (TAB Book No. 1556), you should definitely consider having the ready-to-run disk containing the software applications. This software is guaranteed free of manufacturer's defects. (If you have any problems, return the disk within 30 days and we'll send you a new one.) Not only will you save the time and effort of typing the programs, the disk eliminates the possibility of errors that can prevent the programs from functioning. Interested?

Available on disk for the IBM PC 48K at $29.95 for each disk plus $1.00 each shipping and handling.

I'm interested. Send me:

_____ disk for Graphics Programs for the IBM PC ®, 48K (number 6606S)
_____ Check/Money Order enclosed for $_________ ($29.95 plus $1.00 for shipping and handling for each disk)
_____ VISA _____ MasterCard

Acct. No. ______________________________ Expires __________

Name ______________________________

Address ______________________________

City ____________________ State __________ Zip __________

Signature ______________________________

Mail To: TAB BOOKS Inc.
Blue Ridge Summit, PA 17214

(Pa. add 6% sales tax. Orders outside U.S. must be prepaid with international money orders in U.S. dollars.)

TAB 1556